BASIC ENGLISH REVISITED

A STUDENT HANDBOOK

5th Edition

Written and Compiled by

Patrick Sebranek, *Former English Chairman, Union High School, Union Grove, Wisconsin*

Verne Meyer, *Associate Professor, Dordt College, Sioux Center, Iowa*

Illustrated by Chris Krenzke

Basic English Revisited   **Burlington, Wisconsin**

Basic English Revisited may be used as a standard handbook or as a traditional textbook. The English teacher may present his lessons by citing instructions in the book and by assigning the exercises which coordinate with the materials in each chapter. (The exercises are arranged into workbooks which can be ordered from the publisher.)

However, *Basic English* is designed to do more. It is intended to be carried around in hip pockets and purses of students—to serve as a handy tool when they attempt to understand an essay question on a science test; to search for first aid instructions for a health class; or to assimilate guidelines regarding reading and writing—guidelines which the student must learn through exercise.

Exercise is the key to developing competence in reading and writing—two of the basic "3 R's." However, students never will gain the necessary exercise to master the skills if reading and writing are taught or accented only in English class—during one-sixth of the school day. Nor will students feel that reading and writing are worth learning in English class unless they are required to use the skills in other classes. In fact, if these two difficult skills basic to all disciplines are to be taught—and are worth teaching—then the teaching deserves the combined effort of all teachers.

Basic English Revisited is designed to encourage a school-wide effort to teach reading and writing. For that reason, it contains much information which is not included in standard textbooks or traditional handbooks. Information such as maps, traffic signs, and the table of weights and measures is included to encourage all students and teachers to use the book regularly as a common directive for clear communication in the entire school. If *Basic English* is a common tool which is commonly used throughout the school, the information it contains should be employed by students because it is efficient, handy, and familiar.

Acknowledgments

Basic English Revisited is a reality because of the help, advice, and understanding given by our families: Judy, Julie, and Janae; Gidge, Nathaniel and Benjamin. Also, several of our students allowed us to use their papers as samples in the handbook: Monica, John, Ann, Kris, Lisa, and Lynn.

The fifth edition contains many additions and alterations. We are grateful for the help and advice of a number of educators: Eunice Vanderlaan, Lois Krenzke, Phyllis Duda, and James Vanden Bosch. The section on journalism was written by Carl Vandermeulen, best known for his *Photography for Student Publications,* a book written especially for journalists who work with photography. The sections on poetry, the short story, and fallacies of thinking were written by Randall VanderMey.

5th Edition
4th Printing

ISBN 9605312-0-3 (Soft cover)
ISBN 9605312-1-1 (Hard cover)

Library of Congress Catalog Card No. 80-68894

CONTENTS

Using the Handbook

Your *Basic English Revisited* handbook is designed to be useful to you not only in your English class, but also as a handy reference book in other classes. It is a basic tool for any writing task from preparing a paper for a health course to taking notes in a geography class, from giving an oral report for a science class to taking an essay test in a history course.

Your *Basic English Revisited* handbook emphasizes writing, a challenge for students of all ages. But, the handbook does not stop with writing. It also provides information on memory techniques, vocabulary building, study skills, note-taking, using the library, and speech skills. In addition, the special section at the back of the book provides many extras like a map of the United States, a table of decimal equivalents of common fractions, the traffic signs, the periodic table of the elements, emergency first-aid instruction, and a copy of the Constitution of the United States.

The **Table of Contents** near the front of your handbook gives you a list of the major divisions and the units found under those divisions. It tells you the page number on which each unit begins.

The **Index** at the back of the handbook is one of its most useful parts. The index contains much more information than the table of contents. It is arranged in alphabetical order and includes every topic discussed in the handbook. The numbers after each word in the index refer to the **topic numbers,** not the page numbers. (The topic numbers are the numbers which appear to the left of each new topic in the handbook.) Since there are often many topics on one page, these topic numbers will help you to find information more quickly.

Let's say, for example, you were asked to find information on *collective nouns*. If the index of the handbook listed only page numbers, you would be directed to page 1. Go to page 1 and look for information on collective nouns. Did it take you a while to find this information?

Now look at the sample index to the left and locate *collective noun*. In addition to topic number 5 (which you found on page 1), you will also find a second topic number listed. Go to that number and locate this additional information. Was it easier and quicker this time? It should have been. That is the advantage of using topic numbers in an index rather than page numbers. It saves time.

Look through your handbook and notice the wide variety of material. Notice in particular the material which will be useful to you in your other classes. Then carry your handbook with you and use it. Like a dictionary, thesaurus, or any other reference book, your handbook won't do you much good sitting on a shelf or lining the bottom of your locker. You must take the time to become familiar with your handbook. If you do, you will find a number of explanations and guidelines which will help you improve your reading, writing, speaking, and study skills. Knowing how to use your handbook effectively will put you at a distinct advantage for years to come.

A 19-Year Calendar

GRAMMATICAL TERMS

Parts of Speech

1 **Parts of speech** refers to the ways in which words are used in sentences. Words can be used in eight different ways; therefore, there are eight parts of speech: *noun, pronoun, verb, adjective, adverb, preposition, conjunction, interjection.*

Noun

2 A **noun** is a word which is the name of something: a person, place, thing, or idea.

> Grandma Ulferts, uncle; Lake Michigan, river;
> John Deere tractor, carburetor; Labor Day, sympathy

3 Nouns fall into certain groups. Nouns are grouped according to their *form* (number, gender, and case), their *function* (subject, object, complement, appositive, and modifier), and their *class* (proper, common, concrete, abstract, and collective). The two main classes of nouns are **proper** and **common.**

A **proper noun** is the name of a particular person, place, thing, or idea. Proper nouns are always capitalized.

> Sandra Day O'Connor, Grand Ole Opry, Corvette,
> *Call of the Wild,* Negro, Friday, December

A **common noun** is any noun which does not name any particular person, place, thing, or idea. Common nouns are not capitalized.

> child, country, rainbow, nincompoop, winter, happiness, love

4 Nouns are also grouped according to the kind of thing (concrete or abstract) they name. A **concrete noun** names a thing that is tangible (can be touched or seen). Concrete nouns are either proper or common.

> Chevrolet, White House, car, guitar, drums, book, author

An **abstract noun** names an idea, a doctrine or thought, a theory, a concept, a condition, or a feeling; in other words, an object that cannot be touched or seen. Abstract nouns are either common or proper.

> New Deal, Judaism, satisfaction, poverty, illness,
> euphoria, excellence, relativity, creation, evolution

5 Another type of noun is the **collective noun.** A collective noun names a group or unit. Collective nouns are either common or proper. (See 318.)

> United States, New York State Assembly,
> faculty, audience, herd, flock, race

6 Nouns are also grouped according to their **number.** Number indicates whether the noun is singular or plural. A **singular noun** refers to one person, place, thing, or idea *(boy, stage, rock festival, fear)*. A **plural noun** refers to more than one person, place, thing, or idea *(boys, stages, rock festivals, fears)*.

7 A **compound noun** is a noun made up of two or more words. Some compound nouns are written as one word *(football)*, some as two words *(high school)*, and some as hyphenated words *(brother-in-law)*.

8 Nouns can be classified according to **gender.**

> masculine . . . . uncle, brother, men, bull, rooster *(male)*
> feminine . . . . mother, hostess, women, cow, hen *(female)*
> neuter . . . . tree, cobweb, fishing rod, spices, closet *(without sex)*
> indefinite . . . . president, teacher, doctor, child, lawyer, baby, duckling, clerk, assistant *(male or female)*

9 Nouns are also grouped into one of three cases. Their case tells how nouns are related to the other words used with them. There are three cases: **nominative, possessive,** and **objective.**

A noun is in the **nominative case** when it is used as the subject of the verb.

> The old *senator* pleaded with his colleagues to approve a freeze on nuclear weapons. "Even *survivors* are victims of a nuclear holocaust."

A noun is also in the nominative case when it is used as a predicate noun (or predicate nominative). A predicate noun follows a form of the *be* verb *(is, are, was, were, been)* and repeats or renames the subject. (In the examples below, *loser* renames *winner* and *death* renames *life.*)

> "Therefore," he asserted, "even the *winner is* a *loser* in a nuclear confrontation. *Life* for the survivors *would be* little more than a slow and painful *death.*"

A noun is in the **possessive case** when it shows possession or ownership.

> The younger *senator's* face pulled up into a smile as he spoke. "Nuclear weapons are *mankind's* salvation from war; fear of their use is our assurance that no one dares to use them."

A noun is in the **objective case** when it is used as the direct object, the indirect object, or the object of the preposition.

> A third senator spoke quietly, "In a nuclear age, winners and losers are obsolete. The human race needs *peacemakers.*" (*Peacemakers* is the direct object of *needs.*)
>
> "And even they can't promise *mankind* peace." (*Mankind* is the indirect object of the verb *can promise.*)
>
> "Our best hope for peace lies within the *hearts* of the common *people.*" (*Hearts* is the object of the preposition *within; people* is the object of the preposition *of.*)

Pronoun

10 A **pronoun** is a word used in place of a noun (him, it, which, they, whom, that, themselves, herself). Pronouns appear in different forms:

> Simple . . . . I, you, he, she, it, we, you, they
> Compound . . . . myself, yourself, himself, herself, ourselves
> Phrasal . . . . one another, each other

The following are five different types of pronouns: **personal, relative, indefinite, interrogative,** and **demonstrative.**

11 All pronouns have antecedents. An **antecedent** is the noun which the pronoun refers to or replaces.

> The *speaker* coughed and reached for the glass of water. The water touched his lips before he noticed the fly which lay bathing in the cool liquid. (*Speaker* is the antecedent of *his* and *he; fly* is the antecedent of *which.*)

12 The basic **personal pronouns** are these: I, you, he, she, it, we, they. These pronouns have other forms including the following: his, hers, her, its, me, myself, us, yours, etc.

13 There are three forms of personal pronouns. The form of a personal pronoun shows whether the pronoun is singular or plural in **number;** first, second, or third in **person;** nominative, possessive, or objective in **case.**

14 **Singular** personal pronouns are these: I, you, he, she, it. **Plural** personal pronouns are these:. we, you, they. Notice that the pronoun *you* can be singular or plural.

> You (plural) boys stop chasing her!
> Lisa, you (singular) stop teasing the boys!

15 **Person** indicates whether the pronoun is speaking, is spoken to, or is spoken about. A *first* person pronoun is used in place of the name of the speaker.

> *I* am speaking.
> *We* like snakes.

Second person is used to name the person or thing spoken to.

> Eliza, will *you* please stop bickering!
> *You* dogs stop growling right now!

Third person is used to name the person or thing spoken about.

> *She* said that garbage is good fertilizer.
> *He* always uses *it*.

16 Like nouns, pronouns have three cases. Their **case** tells how pronouns are related to the other words used with them. There are three cases: **nominative, possessive,** and **objective.**

17 A pronoun is in the **nominative case** when it is used as the subject of the verb. The following are nominative forms: I, you, he, she, it, we, they.

> *I* like myself when things go well.
> *You* must live life in order to love life.

18 A pronoun is also in the nominative case when it is used as a **predicate nominative.** A predicate nominative follows a form of the *be* verb (am, is, are, was, were, been), and it repeats the subject.

> "It is *I*," growled the big wolf from under Grandmother's bonnet.
> "It is *he*!" shrieked Little Red as she twisted his snout into a corkscrew.

19 A pronoun is in the **possessive case** when it shows possession or ownership. An apostrophe, however, is not used with a personal pronoun to show possession.

> my, mine, our, ours, his, her, hers, their, its, yours

20 A pronoun is in the **objective case** when it is used as the direct object, indirect object, or object of a preposition.

> Nathaniel hugged *me*. *(Me is the direct object of the verb, hugged.)*
> Benji told *me* a story. *(Me is the indirect object of the verb, told.)*
> Teddy Snappers listened because the story was about *him*. *(Him is the object of the preposition, about.)*

21 # Personal Pronouns

Singular			
	Nominative Case	**Possessive Case**	**Objective Case**
1st Person	I	my, mine	me
2nd Person	you	your, yours	you
3rd Person	he	his	him
	she	her, hers	her
	it	its	it
Plural			
	Nominative Case	**Possessive Case**	**Objective Case**
1st Person	we	our, ours	us
2nd Person	you	your, yours	you
3rd Person	they	their, theirs	them

22 A personal pronoun is called a **reflexive pronoun** when it reflects on the subject or refers to it. A reflexive pronoun can act as a direct object or indirect object of the verb, the object of a preposition, or a predicate nominative.

He hates *himself.*	(direct object of verb)
He gives *himself* no credit for anything.	(indirect object of verb)
He sees no good in *himself.*	(object of preposition)
He feels intense pressure; no wonder he cannot be *himself.*	(predicate nominative)

23 A reflexive pronoun is called an **intensive pronoun** when it intensifies or emphasizes the noun or pronoun it refers to.

> Leo *himself* taught his children to invest their lives in others.
> The lesson was sometimes painful—but they learned it *themselves.*

24 A **relative pronoun** relates one part of a sentence to a word in another part of the sentence. Specifically, a relative pronoun shows that a dependent clause describes a noun in the independent clause.

> The girl *who* had been hit by a drunken driver regained consciousness and cried because she did not feel pain.
> The accident *which* had happened ten days earlier had left her entire body paralyzed and numb.
> It was a drunk's decision to drive *that* destroyed the girl's opportunity to choose how to live.

25 An **indefinite pronoun** is indefinite because its antecedent (the word being referred to by the pronoun) is vague or unknown.

> The teacher stopped chewing, glanced at his sandwich, then glared at his snickering students and screamed, *"Whoever* put this caterpillar in here will be kicked out of school!"* (The antecedent of *whoever* is unknown.)

26 An **interrogative pronoun** asks a question.

> *Who* is knocking on the door, and *what* do you want?

27 A **demonstrative pronoun** points out or identifies a noun without naming the noun.

> *Those* are great!
> *That* was tremendous!

Kinds of Pronouns

Relative
who, whose, whom, which, what, that

Demonstrative
this, that, these, those

Interrogative
who, whose, whom, which, what

Intensive and Reflexive
myself, himself, herself, yourself, themselves, ourselves

Indefinite Pronouns

all	both	everything	nobody	several
another	each	few	none	some
any	each one	many	no one	somebody
anybody	either	most	nothing	someone
anyone	everybody	much	one	something
anything	everyone	neither	other	such

4

Verb

28　A **verb** is a word which expresses action or state of being. A verb has different forms depending on its **number** (singular or plural); **person** (first, second, third); **voice** (active, passive); **tense** (present, past, future, present perfect, past perfect, future perfect); and **mood** (indicative, imperative, subjunctive).

29　**Number** indicates whether a verb is singular or plural. The verb and its subject both must be singular, or they both must be plural.

> One *horse neighs.* (singular) Two *horses neigh.* (plural)

30　**Person** indicates whether the subject of the verb is **1st, 2nd,** or **3rd person** and whether the subject is **singular** or **plural.**

Verbs usually have a different form only in *third person singular* of the *present tense.*

	Singular	Plural
1st　Person	I sniff	we sniff
2nd　Person	you sniff	you sniff
3rd　Person	he/she/it *sniffs*	they sniff

31　**Active voice** indicates that the subject of the verb is acting.

> The *baseball hit* the batter.

32　**Passive voice** indicates that the subject of the verb is being acted upon. A passive verb is a combination of a *be* verb and a past participle.

> The *batter was hit* by the baseball.

Active voice: *Clyde rolled* the dice.
Passive voice: The *dice were rolled* by Clyde.

33　**Present tense** expresses action which is happening at the present time, or which happens continually, regularly.

> When you *call* him "Tubby," his jowls *quiver.* Tubby *hates* his name.

34　**Past tense** expresses action which is completed at a particular time in the past.

> The sow *grunted* at her tottering baby.

35　**Future tense** expresses action which will take place in the future.

> I *shall replace* the spark plugs tomorrow.

36 **Present perfect tense** expresses action which began in the past but continues in the present or is completed at the present.

> The boy *has hunted* many beautiful birds.

37 **Past perfect tense** expresses action which began in the past and was completed in the past.

> He *had shot* the pheasant that lay hiding under the corn stalks, bleeding through green and bronze feathers.

38 **Future perfect tense** expresses action which will begin in the future and be completed by a specific time in the future.

> The boy *will have returned* to his warm house long before the cold, frightened bird dies.

39

Tense	Active Voice		Passive Voice	
	Singular	**Plural**	**Singular**	**Plural**
Present Tense	I find you find he/she/it finds	we find you find they find	I am found you are found he/she/it is found	we are found you are found they are found
Past Tense	I found you found he found	we found you found they found	I was found you were found he was found	we were found you were found they were found
Future Tense	I shall find you will find he will find	we shall find you will find they will find	I shall be found you will be found he will be found	we shall be found you will be found they will be found
Present Perfect	I have found you have found he has found	we have found you have found they have found	I have been found you have been found he has been found	we have been found you have been found they have been found
Past Perfect	I had found you had found he had found	we had found you had found they had found	I had been found you had been found he had been found	we had been found you had been found they had been found
Future Perfect	I shall have found you will have found he will have found	we shall have found you will have found they will have found	I shall have been found you will have been found he will have been found	we shall have been found you will have been found they will have been found

Common Irregular Verbs and Their Principal Parts

Present Tense	Past Tense	Past Participle	Present Tense	Past Tense	Past Participle	Present Tense	Past Tense	Past Participle
am, be	was, were	been	fly	flew	flown	shine (light)	shone	shone
begin	began	begun	forsake	forsook	forsaken	shine (polish)	shined	shined
bid (offer)	bid	bid	freeze	froze	frozen	show	showed	shown
bid (order)	bade	bidden	give	gave	given	shrink	shrank	shrunk
bite	bit	bitten	go	went	gone	sing	sang, sung	sung
blow	blew	blown	grow	grew	grown	sink	sank, sunk	sunk
break	broke	broken	hang (execute)	hanged	hanged	sit	sat	sat
bring	brought	brought	hang			slay	slew	slain
burst	burst	burst	(suspend)	hung	hung	speak	spoke	spoken
catch	caught	caught	hide	hid	hidden,	spring	sprang,	sprung
choose	chose	chosen			hid		sprung	
come	came	come	know	knew	known	steal	stole	stolen
dive	dived	dived	lay	laid	laid	strive	strove	striven
do	did	done	lead	led	led	swear	swore	sworn
drag	dragged	dragged	lie (recline)	lay	lain	swim	swam	swum
draw	drew	drawn	lie (deceive)	lied	lied	swing	swung	swung
drink	drank	drunk	raise	raised	raised	take	took	taken
drown	drowned	drowned	ride	rode	ridden	tear	tore	torn
drive	drove	driven	ring	rang	rung	throw	threw	thrown
eat	ate	eaten	rise	rose	risen	wake	woke, waked	waked
fall	fell	fallen	run	ran	run	wear	wore	worn
fight	fought	fought	see	saw	seen	weave	wove	woven
flee	fled	fled	set	set	set	wring	wrung	wrung
flow	flowed	flowed	shake	shook	shaken	write	wrote	written

40 The **mood** of the verb indicates the tone in which the statement is made.

Indicative mood is used to state a fact or to ask a question.

> We *are buying* a fireplace.
> How *are* you *installing* it?

Imperative mood is used to give a command.

> *Pick* up that hammer! *Be* alert!

The **subjunctive mood** is no longer commonly used; however, it continues to be used by careful writers to express the exact manner in which their statements are made.

  1) Use the subjunctive *were* to express a condition which is contrary to fact. **Example:** If I *were* you, I wouldn't go.
  2) Use the subjunctive *were* after *as though* or *as if* to express doubt or uncertainty. **Example:** He looks as if he *were* about to faint.
  3) Use the subjunctive in "that clauses" which express necessity, parliamentary motions, or legal decisions.

> I move that twenty dollars *be allocated* for refreshments.
> In view of the fact that our balance on hand is $11.17, I move that the motion *be amended* to a ten-dollar allocation.
> That permanent custody of the child *be awarded* to her adoptive parents was the ruling of the court.

41 **Auxiliary verbs** or helping verbs *help* to form some of the **tenses** (33-38), the **mood** (40), and the **voice** (31, 32, 39) of the main verb. In the following examples, the main verbs are in boldface, and the auxiliary verbs are italicized.

> Two of Grandma Ulfert's fourteen children *had* **died** at birth.
> One child, Uncle Harry, *has been* severely **retarded** since birth.
> Grandma *will* **nurture** him until he dies because she loves all life.

Common auxiliary verbs are these: *shall, will, would, should, must, can, may, have, had, has, do, did;* and the various forms of the *be* verb: *is, are, was, were, am, been.*

42 Verbs are **transitive** or **intransitive.**

A **transitive verb** communicates action and is always followed by an object which receives the action. An object must receive the action of a transitive verb in order to complete the meaning of the verb.

> The python *ate* the fawn.

A verb in the active voice directs the action from the subject to the object.

> A small girl *held* a baby chick.
> The chick's tiny heart *pounded* her little fingers.

In the first example, the object, *chick,* receives the action of being held, from the girl. *Girl* is the subject. In the second example, the *fingers* receive the action of pounding, from the heart. *Heart* is the subject.

If a transitive verb is in the passive voice, the subject of the sentence receives the action. (In the following example, the *bell* receives the action of the verb.)

> The bell *was rung* by strong hands.

The name of the actor that creates the action in a passive verb is not always stated. (In the following example, the subject, *I,* receives the action of the verb *was hit.* However, the sentence does not say who did the hitting.)

> I *was hit!*

43 The object of a transitive verb is called the **direct object** if it receives the action directly from the subject.

> Jim bought a fishing *rod.*
> (*Rod* is the direct object.)

44 An **indirect object** receives the action of a transitive verb, indirectly. An indirect object names the person (or *thing*) to whom (or *to what*) or for whom (or *for what*) something is done.

> Jim bought *me* a fishing rod.
> (*Me* is the indirect object.)

Note: When the word naming the indirect receiver of the action is contained in a prepositional phrase, it is no longer considered an indirect object.

> Jim bought a fishing rod for *me*.
> (*Me* is the object of the preposition *for*.)

45 An **intransitive verb** does not have an object which receives action.

> The pitcher *fell* from my hands.
> Milk *spilled* over the floor.

46 Many verbs can be either **transitive** or **intransitive**.

> I *drove* my car. (transitive)
> I *drove* over a skunk. (intransitive)

47 A **linking verb** (copulative verb) is a special type of intransitive verb which links the subject to a noun or adjective in the predicate. Common linking verbs are the various forms of the *be* verb (*is, are, was, were, been, am*) and verbs such as *smell, look, taste, remain, feel, appear, sound, seem, become, grow, stand, turn.*

> She *is* an excellent physician.
> Applesauce *tastes* good.

48 In the first example above, the noun, *physician*, is linked to the subject, *she; physician* is called a **predicate noun** or **predicate nominative.** In the second example, the adjective, *good*, is linked to the subject, *applesauce; good* is called a **predicate adjective.**

49 A **verbal** is a word which is derived from a verb, has the power of a verb, but acts as another part of speech. Like a verb, a verbal may take an object, a modifier (adjective, adverb), and sometimes a subject; but unlike a verb, a verbal functions as a noun, an adjective, or an adverb. Three types of verbals are **gerunds, infinitives,** and **participles.**

50 A **gerund** is a verb form which ends in *ing* and is used as a noun.

> *Smoking* cigarettes rots your lungs.

Note: Smoking, functioning as a noun, is the subject of the verb *rots*. But in addition, *lungs* is the direct object of the verb *rots;* and *cigarettes* is the object of the gerund *smoking*.

51 An **infinitive** is a verb form which is usually introduced by *to;* the infinitive may be used as a *noun*, as an *adjective*, or as an *adverb*.

> *To love* children well sometimes hurts. *(To love*, as a noun, is the subject of *hurts. Well* modifies *to love. Children* is the object of the infinitive *to love.)*
> The girl *to ask* is that little one. (adjective)
> Ben's buddies came *to mess* around. (adverb)

52 A **participle** is a verb form ending in *ing* or *ed*. A participle functions as a verb because it can take an object; a participle functions as an adjective because it can modify a noun or pronoun.

> That man *exploding* the dynamite is Leo. *Exploded* dynamite smells. *(Exploding* functions as an adjective because it modifies man. *Exploding* functions as a verb because it has an object, *dynamite. Exploded* modifies the noun *dynamite;* this participle does not have an object.)

Adjective

53 An **adjective** describes or modifies a noun or pronoun. Articles *a, an,* and *the* are adjectives.

> *Little* people peek through *big* steering wheels.
> (*Little* modifies *people*; *big* modifies *steering wheels*.)

Adjectives can be common or proper. Proper adjectives are created from proper nouns and are capitalized.

> *Kalamazoo* (proper noun) is a city in western Michigan.
> The *Kalamazoo* (proper adjective) area is known for its parks and lakes.

54 A **predicate adjective** follows a form of the *be* verb (a linking verb), is part of the predicate, and describes the subject.

> Skinny legs are *beautiful*. (*Beautiful* modifies *legs*.)

55 Adjectives have three forms: **positive, comparative,** and **superlative.**

56 The **positive form** describes a noun or pronoun without comparing it to anyone or anything else.

> Superman is *tough*. Superman is *wonderful*.

57 The **comparative form** *(-er)* compares two persons, places, things, or ideas.

> Tarzan is *tougher* than Superman.
> Tarzan is *more wonderful* than Superman.

58 The **superlative form** *(-est)* compares three or more persons, places, things, or ideas.

> But I, Big Bird, am the *toughest* of all!
> But I, Big Bird, am the *most wonderful* of all!

Adverb

59 An **adverb** modifies a verb, an adjective, or another adverb. An adverb tells *how, when, where, why, how often,* and *how much.*

> She kissed him *loudly*. (*Loudly* modifies the verb, *kissed*.)
> Her kisses are *really* noisy. (*Really* modifies the adjective, *noisy*.)
> The kiss exploded *very* dramatically. (*Very* modifies the adverb, *dramatically*.)

Adverbs can be catalogued as follows:

A. Adverbs of **time**. (They tell *when, how often,* and *how long*.)

> weekly   yesterday   eternally

B. Adverbs of **place**. (They tell *where, to where,* and *from where*.)

> yonder   there   backward

C. Adverbs of **manner**. (They often end in *-ly* and tell *how* something is done.)

> precisely   regularly   regally   well

Note: Some adverbs can be written with or without the *-ly* ending. When in doubt, use the *-ly* form. (**Examples:** Slow, slowly; loud, loudly; fair, fairly; tight, tightly; deep, deeply; quick, quickly)

D. Adverbs of **degree**. (They tell *how much* or *how little*.)

> generally   too   entirely

Adverbs, like adjectives, have three forms: **positive, comparative,** and **superlative.** (See Handbook 55-58.)

Positive	Comparative	Superlative
well	better	best
badly	worse	worst
fast	faster	fastest
remorsefully	more remorsefully	most remorsefully
passively	less passively	least passively

Preposition

60 A **preposition** is a word (or group of words) that shows the relationship between its object (a noun or a pronoun that follows the preposition) and another word in the sentence.

> The caterpillar hung *under* Natasha's nose. (*Under* shows the relationship between the verb, *hung*, and the object of the preposition, *nose*.)

There are three kinds of prepositions: **simple** (*at, in, of, on, with*), **compound** (*within, outside, underneath*), and **phrasal** (*on account of, on top of*).

61 A **prepositional phrase** includes the preposition, the object of the preposition, and the modifiers of the object. A prepositional phrase may function as an adjective or as an adverb.

> Little girls run *away from caterpillars*.
> (The phrase modifies the verb, *run*.)
> But little girls *with inquisitive minds* enjoy their company.
> (The phrase modifies the noun, *girls*.)

62 A **preposition** which lacks an object may be used as an adverb.

> Natasha never played with caterpillars *before*.

(The object of the preposition is understood: before *this time* or before *today*. *Before* modifies *played*, a verb.)

63

List of Prepositions					
aboard	at	despite	in regard to	opposite	together with
about	away from	down	inside	out	through
above	back of	down from	inside of	out of	throughout
according to	because of	during	in spite of	outside	till
across	before	except	instead of	outside of	to
across from	behind	except for	into	over	toward
after	below	excepting	like	over to	under
against	beneath	for	near	owing to	underneath
along	beside	from	near to	past	until
alongside	besides	from among	notwithstanding	prior to	unto
alongside of	between	from between	of	regarding	up
along with	beyond	from under	off	round	up to
amid	but	in	on	round about	upon
among	by	in addition to	on account of	save	with
apart from	by means of	in behalf of	on behalf of	since	within
around	concerning	in front of	onto	subsequent to	without
aside from	considering	in place of	on top of		

Conjunction

64 A **conjunction** connects individual words or groups of words.

> A puffer fish is short *and* fat. (The conjunction *and* connects the word *short* to the word *fat*.)
> The puffer puts his lips on a snail *and* sucks out the flesh. (The conjunction *and* connects the phrase *puts his lips on a snail* to the phrase *sucks out the flesh*.)

65 A **coordinate conjunction** connects a word to a word, a phrase to a phrase, or a clause to a clause. The words, phrases, or clauses joined by a coordinate conjunction must be *equal* or of the *same type*.

> A brook trout *and* a lake trout can produce a splake. (connects equal nouns — both needed equally in sentence)
>
> A brown trout will wrap a line around weeds *and* between logs. (connects equal phrases)
>
> A little brook trout looks like a minnow, *but* it fights like a whale. (connects equal clauses)

10

66 **Correlative conjunctions** are coordinate conjunctions used in pairs. *(neither, nor)*

> *Neither* rainbow trout *nor* lake trout are as pugnacious as brown trout.

67 A **subordinate conjunction** is a word or group of words that connect, and show the relationship between, two clauses which are *not* equally important. A subordinate conjunction connects a dependent clause to an independent clause in order to complete the meaning of the dependent clause.

> A brown trout will study the bait *before* he eats it. (The clause *before he eats it* is dependent. It depends on the rest of the sentence to complete its meaning.)

Kinds of Conjunctions	
Coordinate:	and, but, or, nor, for, yet
Correlative:	either, or; neither, nor; not only, but also; both, and; whether, or; just, as; just, so; as, so
Subordinate:	after, although, as, as if, as long as, as though, because, before, if, in order that, provided that, since, so, so that, that, though, till, unless, until, when, where, whereas, while

Note: Relative pronouns (24) and conjunctive adverbs (150) can also connect clauses.

Interjection

68 An **interjection** is included in a sentence in order to communicate strong emotion or surprise. Punctuation is used to separate an interjection from the rest of the sentence.

> *Oh, no!* The boat's leaking. *Wow,* I can't swim.

Parts of a Sentence

69 A **sentence** is made up of one or more words which express a complete thought. *(Note: A sentence begins with a capital letter; it ends with a period, question mark, or exclamation point.)*

> This book should help you write. It explains many things. How do you plan to use it? I hope you find it helpful!

70 A **modifier** is a word or a group of words which alters or changes the meaning of another word.

> The *big* sow grunted. *(The* and *big* modify *sow.)*
> The *baby* pig *eagerly* sucked *the* milk. *(The* and *baby* modify *pig; eagerly* modifies *sucked;* and *the* modifies *milk.)*

71 A sentence must have a **subject** and **predicate** in order to express a complete thought. Either the subject or the predicate or both may not be expressed; but both must be clearly understood.

> (You) Pass the coffee over here. *(You* is the understood subject.)
> Who called? Uncle Duane. (called) *(Called* is the understood predicate.)
> What time is it? (It is) Ten minutes before midnight. *(It* is the understood subject, and *is* is the understood verb.)

72 A **subject** is the part of a sentence about which something is said.

> My *dog* licks my toes. *Freaking out* is a waste.

73 A **simple subject** is the subject without the words which describe or modify it.

> Many unhappy *people* hate their lives. *(People* is the simple subject.)

74 A **complete subject** is the simple subject and all the words which modify it.

> *Many unhappy people* hate their lives. *(Many* and *unhappy* modify *people.* Together, the three words compose the complete subject.)

75 A **compound subject** is made up of two or more simple subjects.

> *Students* and *teachers* need school.

11

76 A **predicate** is the part of the sentence which says something about the subject.

> Principals *remember.*

77 A **simple predicate** is the predicate without the words which describe or modify it.

> Little people *can talk* faster than big people. *(Can talk* is the simple predicate; *faster than big people* describes how little people *can talk.)*

78 A **complete predicate** is the simple predicate and all the words which modify or explain it.

> Little people *can talk faster than big people.*

79 A **compound predicate** is composed of two or more simple predicates.

> Big people *talk* slowly but *eat* fast.

80 A sentence may have a **compound subject** and a **compound predicate.**

> Sturdy *tongues,* long *lips,* and thick *teeth say* sentences slowly but *chew* food quickly.

81 Whatever receives the action indicated in the simple predicate is the **direct object.**

> Picasso painted *pictures.* His pictures express *feeling.*
> *(Pictures* receives the action of the verb *painted.* It answers the question *Picasso painted what?)*

The **direct object** may be **compound.** (See also 42-46.)

> Chickens eat *oyster shells* and *grit.*

82 A **phrase** is a group of related words which lacks either a subject or a predicate or both.

> *ran very fast* (The predicate lacks a subject.)
> *the young colt* (The subject lacks a predicate.)
> *down the steep slope* (The phrase lacks both a subject and a predicate.)
> *The young colt ran very fast down the steep slope.* (Together, the three phrases present a complete thought.)

Phrases take their names from the main words which introduce them or support them.

> The ancient oak *tree* .... noun phrase
> *with* crooked old limbs .... prepositional phrase
> *has stood* its guard, ... verb phrase
> *staunchly* resolute, ... adverb phrase
> *protecting* the little house and its big family. .... verbal phrase

83 A **clause** is a group of related words which has both a subject and a predicate.

84 An **independent clause** presents a complete thought and can stand as a sentence; a **dependent clause** does not present a complete thought and cannot stand as a sentence. (See 320.)

85 In the following sentences, the dependent clauses are underlined and the independent clauses are in *italics.*

> *A small pony can attack a large horse* <u>if it kicks its heels in the horse's belly.</u>
> *Sparrows make nests in cattle barns* <u>so they can stay warm during the winter.</u>

Types of Sentences

86 A **sentence** is classified according to the way it is constructed and according to the type of statement it makes. The structure of a sentence may be **simple, compound, complex,** or **compound-complex.** A sentence may communicate a message which is **declarative, interrogative, imperative,** or **exclamatory.**

12

87 A **simple sentence** may have a simple subject or a compound subject. It may have a simple predicate or a compound predicate. But a simple sentence has only one independent clause, and it has no dependent clauses. A simple sentence may contain one or more phrases.

> My *back aches.* (simple subject; simple predicate)
> My *teeth* and my *eyes hurt.* (compound subject; simple predicate)
> My *hair* and my *muscles are deteriorating* and *disappearing.* (compound subject; compound predicate)
> *I must be getting over the hill.* (simple subject: *I;* simple predicate: *must be getting;* phrase: *over the hill)*

88 A **compound sentence** consists of two independent clauses. The clauses must be joined by a coordinate conjunction, by punctuation, or by both.

> Energy is part of youth, *but* both are quickly spent.
> My middle-aged body is sore; my middle-aged face is wrinkled.

89 A **complex sentence** contains one independent clause (in italics) and one or more dependent clauses (underlined).

> *People often say wise things* like age is a state of mind. (independent clause; dependent clause)
> *Youth seems past,* however, when my back aches before the day is even half over. (independent clause; two dependent clauses)

90 A **compound-complex sentence** contains two or more independent clauses (in italics) and one or more dependent clauses (underlined).

> *My body is rather old; and age is not a state of mind* unless my bald head is an illusion. (independent clause; independent clause; dependent clause)

91 **Declarative sentences** make statements. They tell us something about a person, place, thing, or idea.

> The Statue of Liberty stands in New York harbor.
> For nearly a century, it has greeted immigrants and visitors to America.
> The statue was given to the American people by France in 1886 to commemorate America's first one hundred years of independence.

92 **Interrogative sentences** ask questions.

> Did you know that the Statue of Liberty is made of copper and stands over 150 feet tall?
> Would you know what it meant if someone said that the statue is the personification of Liberty?
> Do you know the official name of the statue?

93 **Imperative sentences** make commands. They often contain an understood subject *(you).*

> If you don't know the official title, go to the library and look it up.
> Then share your answer with the class the next time the topic comes up.

94 **Exclamatory sentences** communicate strong emotion or surprise.

> What! I can't believe you think I should simply tell you the official title!
> Whatever happened to that old pioneering spirit, that desire to be independent and self-sufficient, that never-say-die attitude that made America great!
> What do you mean you think I'm overdoing it!

THE MECHANICS
OF WRITING

Capitalization

95 Capitalize all proper nouns and all proper adjectives (adjectives derived from proper nouns). Capitalize the days of the week, months, holidays, holy days, periods and events in history, special events, political parties, official documents, trade names, geographical names, heavenly bodies, streets, formal epithets, official titles, and official state nicknames.

> Egypt, Egyptian, Phoenix, Laura Van Gorp, Thursday, January, Thanksgiving Day, Easter, Hanukkah, Middle Ages, the Renaissance, the Roaring Twenties, Jupiter, Mississippi River, Democratic Party, Declaration of Independence, the Battle of Bunker Hill, Twenty-first Street, Highway 36, the Milky Way, Colgate toothpaste, Alexander the Great, Corvette, Mayor Washington, the Badger State

96 Words like *father, uncle,* and *senator* are proper nouns when they are parts of titles or when they are substituted for proper nouns. (*Note:* Words referring to the office of the President of the United States—or to those offices in the order of the Presidential succession—are usually capitalized.)

> My *uncle,* Duane, likes me. (*Uncle* is not part of the name.)
> Hi, *Uncle* Duane! (*Uncle* is part of the name.)
> The *senator,* Bill Proxmire, is a cool guy.
> Did you know that *Senator* Proxmire kissed my mother?
> *Mom* has been appointed *Postmaster General.*

Note: To test whether a word is being substituted for a proper noun, simply read the sentence with a proper noun in place of the word. If the proper noun fits in the sentence, the word being tested should be capitalized; if the proper noun does not work in this sentence, the word should not be capitalized. (*Further note:* Usually the word is not capitalized if it follows a possessive.)

> Did *Mom* (*Sue*) say we could go? (*Sue* works in this sentence.)
> Did your *mom* (*Sue*) say you could go? (*Sue* does not work here.)
> The word *mom* also follows the possessive *your.*)

97 Words such as *home economics, history,* and *science* are proper nouns when they are the titles of specific courses, but are common nouns when they name a field of study.

> That guy failed his *home economics* assignment because he tried to cook eggs in the microwave oven.
> "Who teaches *History 202?*"
> "The same guy who teaches that *sociology* course."

Note: The words *freshman, sophomore, junior,* and *senior* are not capitalized unless they refer to an entire class or they are part of an official title: the *Sophomore Class* of Elkhorn High School, *Junior Prom, Senior Banquet.*

98 Words which indicate particular sections of the country are proper nouns; words which simply indicate direction are not proper nouns.

> Skiing is popular in the *North.*
> Sparrows don't fly *south* because they are lazy.
> We visited some friends in *western* Wisconsin.

14

99 Nouns or pronouns which refer to the Supreme Being are capitalized.

> Jehovah, the Lord, the Savior
> Capitalize God or any other word which refers to Him.

100 The word *Bible* and the books of the Bible are capitalized; likewise, the names for other holy books and sacred writings are capitalized.

> Bible, Book of Psalms, Ecclesiastes, the Koran

101 Capitalize the first word in every sentence and the first word in a direct quotation.

> *He* never saw a snake he didn't like.
> *The* old lady shouted up the stairs, "*You* kids stop fightin' this minute or I'll spank the both of ya!"

Capitalize the first word in each sentence which is enclosed in parentheses if that sentence comes before or after another complete sentence.

> Converted Democrat Ronald Reagan won the '84 election by a comfortable margin. (*He* won 49 of the 50 states.)

Do not capitalize a sentence which is enclosed in parentheses and is located in the middle of another sentence.

> Converted Democrat Ronald Reagan (*he* was an active member of the Democratic Party early in his career) won the '84 election by a comfortable margin.

Capitalize a complete sentence which follows a colon only if that sentence is not closely related to the sentence before the colon. Also, capitalize the sentence following a colon if you want to emphasize that sentence.

102 Capitalize the first word in a line of poetry when the author does the same.

> "The colors of their tails
> Were like the leaves themselves"
> — Wallace Stevens

> "wholly to be a fool
> while Spring is in the world"
> — e.e. cummings

103 Capitalize races, nationalities, languages, and religions. *Note:* Today some authors capitalize *Black* and *White* when the words are used as proper nouns in place of *Negro* and *Caucasian.*

Negro	Navajo	Canadian	Caucasian
Black	Hebrew	Catholic	White

104 Capitalize the first word of a title, the last word, and every word in between except articles (*a, an, the*), short prepositions, and short conjunctions. Follow this rule for titles of books, newspapers, magazines, poems, plays, songs, articles, films, works of art, pictures, and stories.

> *Bible; Milwaukee Journal; A Midsummer Night's Dream; Sports Illustrated; The Red Badge of Courage; Building Self-Respect*

105 Capitalize the name of an organization, association, or team and its members.

> New York State Historical Society; Elk Rapids High School Drama Club; Burlington Memorial Hospital Auxiliary; Fond du Lac Jaycees; the Boy Scouts; the Red Cross; Green Bay Packers; Republican, Democratic Party

106 Capitalize abbreviations of titles and organizations. (Some other abbreviations are also capitalized. See 116-119.)

> U.S.A.; NAACP; M.D.; Ph.D.; A.D.; B.C.; R.R.; No.

Also capitalize the letters used to indicate form or shape.

> U-turn, I-beam, S-curve; A-bomb

107 Do not capitalize any of the following: a prefix attached to a proper noun, seasons of the year, a common noun shared by (and coming after) two or more proper nouns, words used to indicate direction or position, the word *gods* or *goddesses* when they are referring to mythology, or common nouns which appear to be part of a proper noun.

Capitalize	Do Not Capitalize
American . . . . *un*-American	
January, February . . . . *winter, spring*	
Lakes Erie and Michigan . . . . Missouri and Ohio *rivers*	
The South is quite conservative. . . . . Turn *south* at the stop sign.	
Is Dad coming with us? . . . . Is your *dad* coming with us?	
Duluth Central High School . . . . a Duluth *high school*	
Governor Tony Earl . . . . Tony Earl, our *governor*	
President Ronald Reagan . . . . Ronald Reagan, our *president*	
The planet Earth is egg shaped. . . . . The *earth* we live on is good.	
I'm taking History 101. . . . . I'm taking *history*.	

Plurals

108   The plurals of most nouns are formed by adding *s* to the singular.

cheerleader — cheerleader*s*; wheel — wheel*s*

The plural form of nouns ending in *sh, ch, x, s,* and *z* are made by adding *es* to the singular.

lunch — lunch*es*; dish — dish*es*; mess — mess*es*;
fox — fox*es*; buzz — buzz*es*

109   The plurals of common nouns which end in *y* preceded by a consonant are formed by changing the *y* to *i* and adding *es*.

fly — fl*ies*; jalopy — jalop*ies*

The plurals of nouns which end in *y* preceded by a vowel are formed by adding only *s*.

donkey — donkey*s*; monkey — monkey*s*

Note: The plurals of proper nouns ending in *y* are formed by adding *s*.

110   The plurals of words ending in *o* preceded by a vowel are formed by adding *s*.

radio — radio*s*; rodeo — rodeo*s*; studio — studio*s*

Most nouns ending in *o* preceded by a consonant form plurals by adding *es*.

echo — echo*es*; hero — hero*es*; tomato — tomato*es*

Exception: Musical terms always form plurals by adding *s*; consult a dictionary for other words of this type.

alto — alto*s*; banjo — banjo*s*; solo — solo*s*; piano — piano*s*

111   The plurals of nouns that end in *f* or *fe* are formed in one of two ways: if the final *f* sound is still heard in the plural form of the word, simply add *s*; if the final sound is a *ve* sound, change the *f* to *ve* and add *s*. (*Note:* Several words are correct with either ending.)

Plural ends with *f* sound: roof — roof*s*; chief — chief*s*
Plural ends with *ve* sound: wife — wi*ves*; loaf — loa*ves*

112   Foreign words (as well as some of English origin) form a plural by taking on an *irregular* spelling; others are now acceptable with the commonly used *s* or *es* ending.

Foreign Words		English Words	
crisis	crises	child	children
criterion	criteria	goose	geese
appendix	appendices/appendixes	ox	oxen

113   The plurals of symbols, letters, figures, and words considered as words are formed by adding an *apostrophe* and an *s*.

He wrote three *x's* in place of his name.
"Hello's" and *"Hi there's"* were screamed at my dad.

Note: Some writers omit the apostrophe when the omission does not make the sentence confusing. The examples above must have apostrophes; the example below need not.

Give me four *5's (5s)* for a twenty.

114 The plurals of nouns which end with *ful* are formed by adding an *s* at the end of the word.

three pailful*s*; two tankful*s*

The plurals of compound nouns are usually formed by adding *s* or *es* to the important word in the compound.

brothers-in-law; maids of honor; Secretaries of State

115 Pronouns referring to a collective noun may be singular or plural. A pronoun is singular when the group (noun) is considered a unit. A pronoun is plural when the group (noun) is considered in terms of its individual components.

The faculty forgot its promise. (group as a unit)
The faculty forgot their detention pads. (group as individuals)

Abbreviations

116 **An abbreviation** is the shortened form of a word or phrase. (See list, 702.)
The following abbreviations are always acceptable in both formal and informal writing:

Mr., Mrs., Miss, Ms., Messrs., Dr., a.m., p.m. (A.M., P.M.), A.D., B.C.

Note: Do not abbreviate the names of states, countries, months, days, units of measure, or courses of study in formal writing. Do not abbreviate the words *Street, Road, Avenue, Company,* and similar words when they are part of a proper name. Also, do not use signs or symbols (%, &, ¢, #, @) in place of words. The dollar sign is, however, acceptable when writing a number containing both dollars and cents.

State Abbreviations

	Standard	Postal
Alabama	Ala.	AL
Alaska	Alaska	AK
Arizona	Ariz.	AZ
Arkansas	Ark.	AR
California	Calif.	CA
Colorado	Colo.	CO
Connecticut	Conn.	CT
Delaware	Del.	DE
District of Columbia	D.C.	DC
Florida	Fla.	FL
Georgia	Ga.	GA
Guam	Guam	GU
Hawaii	Hawaii	HI
Idaho	Idaho	ID
Illinois	Ill.	IL
Indiana	Ind.	IN
Iowa	Iowa	IA
Kansas	Kan.	KS
Kentucky	Ky.	KY
Louisiana	La.	LA
Maine	Maine	ME
Maryland	Md.	MD
Massachusetts	Mass.	MA
Michigan	Mich.	MI
Minnesota	Minn.	MN
Mississippi	Miss.	MS
Missouri	Mo.	MO
Montana	Mont.	MT
Nebraska	Neb.	NE
Nevada	Nev.	NV
New Hampshire	N.H.	NH
New Jersey	N.J.	NJ
New Mexico	N.M.	NM
New York	N.Y.	NY
North Carolina	N.C.	NC
North Dakota	N.D.	ND
Ohio	Ohio	OH
Oklahoma	Okla.	OK
Oregon	Ore.	OR
Pennsylvania	Pa.	PA
Puerto Rico	P.R.	PR
Rhode Island	R.I.	RI
South Carolina	S.C.	SC
South Dakota	S.D.	SD
Tennessee	Tenn.	TN
Texas	Texas	TX
Utah	Utah	UT
Vermont	Vt.	VT
Virginia	Va.	VA
Virgin Islands	V.I.	VI
Washington	Wash.	WA
West Virginia	W.Va.	WV
Wisconsin	Wis.	WI
Wyoming	Wyo.	WY

Address Abbreviations

	Standard	Postal
Avenue	Ave.	AVE
Boulevard	Blvd.	BLVD
Court	Ct.	CT
Drive	Dr.	DR
East	E.	E
Expressway	Expy.	EXPY
Heights	Hts.	HTS
Highway	Hwy.	HWY
Hospital	Hosp.	HOSP
Junction	Junc.	JCT
Lake	L.	LK
Lakes	Ls.	LKS
Lane	Ln.	LN
Meadows	Mdws.	MDWS
North	N.	N
Palms	Palms	PLMS
Park	Pk.	PK
Parkway	Pky.	PKY
Place	Pl.	PL
Plaza	Plaza	PLZ
Ridge	Rdg.	RDG
River	R.	RV
Road	Rd.	RD
Rural	R.	R
Shore	Sh.	SH
South	S.	S
Square	Sq.	SQ
Station	Sta.	STA
Terrace	Ter.	TER
Turnpike	Tpke.	TPKE
Union	Un.	UN
View	View	VW
Village	Vil.	VLG
West	W.	W

117 Most abbreviations are followed by a period. **Acronyms** are exceptions. An acronym is a word formed from the first (or first few) letters of words in a set phrase.

radar (radio detecting and ranging), CARE (Cooperative for American Relief Everywhere), VISTA (Volunteers in Service to America), UNICEF (United Nations International Children's Emergency Fund)

118

Acronyms and Initialisms for Government Organizations			
CIA	Central Intelligence Agency	NATO	North Atlantic Treaty Organization
FAA	Federal Aviation Administration	NYC	Neighborhood Youth Corps
FBI	Federal Bureau of Investigation	OEO	Office of Economic Opportunity
FCC	Federal Communications Commission	OEP	Office of Emergency Preparedness
FDA	Food and Drug Administration	REA	Rural Electrification Administration
FDIC	Federal Deposit Insurance Corporation	SSA	Social Security Administration
FHA	Federal Housing Administration	TVA	Tennessee Valley Authority
FmHA	Farmers Home Administration	VA	Veterans Administration
FTC	Federal Trade Commission	VISTA	Volunteers in Service to America
IRS	Internal Revenue Service	WAC	Women's Army Corps
NASA	National Aeronautics and Space Administration	WAVES	Women Accepted for Volunteer Emergency Service (Women's Reserve, USNR)

119 An **initialism** is similar to an acronym except that the initials used to form this abbreviation cannot be pronounced as a word.

> Initialism: CIA—Central Intelligence Agency
> Acronym: NASA—National Aeronautics and Space Administration

Numbers

120 **Numbers** from one to nine are usually written as words; all numbers 10 and over are usually written as numerals.

> two; seven; nine; 10; 25; 106; 1,079

Note: Numbers being compared or contrasted should be kept in the same style.

> 7 to 11 years old *or* seven to eleven years old

121 Use numerals to express numbers in the following forms: money, decimal, percentage, chapter, page, address, telephone, zip code, dates, time, identification numbers, and statistics.

> $2.39; 26.2; 8 percent; chapter 7; pages 287-89; 2125 Cairn Road; July 6, 1945; 44 B.C.; A.D. 79; 4:30 P.M.; Highway 36; a vote of 23 to 4

122 Use words to express numbers in these constructions:

A) Numbers which begin a sentence.

> *Fourteen* students "forgot" their assignments.

(Adapt the sentence structure if this rule creates a clumsy construction.)

Clumsy: *Six hundred and thirty-nine teachers were victims of the layoff this year.*

Better: This year, 639 teachers were victims of the layoff.

B) Numbers which precede a compound modifier that includes a figure.

> The girl walked on *two* 8-foot wooden stilts.
> The basket was woven from *sixty-two* 11½ inch ropes.

Spelling

Spelling Rules

Rule 1: Write *i* before *e* except after *c*, or when sounded like *a* as in *neighbor* and *weigh*.

Eight of the **exceptions** are included in this sentence:
Neither sheik dared leisurely seize either weird species of financiers.

When the *ie/ei* combination is not pronounced *ee*, it is usually spelled *ei*.

Examples: reign, foreign, weigh, neighbor
Exceptions: fiery, friend, mischief, view

Rule 2: When a one-syllable word *(bat)* ends in a consonant *(t)* preceded by one vowel *(a)*, double the final consonant before adding a suffix which begins with a vowel *(batting)*.

When a multi-syllable word *(control)* ends in a consonant *(l)* preceded by one vowel *(o)*, the accent is on the last syllable *(con trol')*, and the suffix begins with a vowel *(ing)*—the same rule holds true: double the final consonant *(controlling)*.

sum—summary; god—goddess; prefer—preferred
begin—beginning; forget—forgettable; admit—admittance

Rule 3: If a word ends with a silent *e*, drop the *e* before adding a suffix which begins with a vowel.

state—stating—statement; like—liking—likeness
use—using—useful; nine—ninety—nineteen

(Notice that you do *not* drop the *e* when the suffix begins with a consonant. Exceptions include judgment, truly, argument, and ninth.)

Rule 4: When *y* is the last letter in a word and the *y* is preceded by a consonant, change the *y* to *i* before adding any suffix except those beginning with *i*. (See 108-115.)

fry—fries; hurry—hurried; lady—ladies
ply—pliable; happy—happiness; beauty—beautiful

When forming the plural of a word which ends with a *y* that is preceded by a vowel, add *s*.

toy—toys; play—plays; monkey—monkeys

| ## Steps to Becoming a Good Speller

1. Be patient. Learning to become a good speller takes time.
2. Check the correct pronunciation of each word you are attempting to spell. Knowing the correct pronunciation of each word is essential to remembering its spelling.
3. As you are checking the dictionary for pronunciation, also check on the meaning and history of each word. Knowing the meaning and history of a word can provide you with a better notion of how and when the word will probably be used. This fuller understanding will provide additional incentive to remember the spelling of that particular word.
4. Before you close the dictionary, practice spelling the word. You can do this by looking away from the page and trying to "see" the word in your "mind's eye." Write the word on a piece of paper. Check the spelling in the dictionary and repeat the process until you are able to spell the word correctly.
5. Learn some spelling rules. The four rules in this handbook are four of the most useful, although there are others.
6. Make a list of the words which cause you the most difficulty. Select the first ten and practice spelling them. (You may use the list on the next three pages.)

   Step A: Read each word carefully, then write it on a piece of paper. Look at the written word to see that it's spelled correctly. Repeat the process for those words which you misspelled.

   Step B: When you have finished your first ten words, ask someone to read the words to you so you can write them again. Again check for misspellings. If you find none, congratulations! Repeat both steps with your next ten words.

Apparently?
... *a-p-p-a-i-r-a-n-t-l-y* ...
no, that's not right ...
a-p-a-i-r ... ummm, where's
my eraser? ...
a-p-p-a-r-i-n-t-l-y ...
THAT'S ... not right either
... where's
my handbook?

A List of Commonly Misspelled Words

A

ab-bre-vi-ate	ad-vis-able	anx-ious	at-tend-ance	bliz-zard
a-brupt	ad-vise (v.)	any-thing	at-ten-tion	book-keep-er
ab-scess	ae-ri-al	a-part-ment	at-ti-tude	bough
ab-sence	af-fect	a-pol-o-gize	at-tor-ney	bought
ab-so-lute (-ly)	af-fi-da-vit	ap-pa-ra-tus	at-trac-tive	bouil-lon
ab-sorb-ent	a-gain	ap-par-ent (-ly)	au-di-ble	bound-a-ry
ab-surd	a-gainst	ap-peal	au-di-ence	break-fast
a-bun-dance	ag-gra-vate	ap-pear-ance	au-thor-i-ty	breath (n.)
ac-cede	ag-gres-sion	ap-pe-tite	au-to-mo-bile	breathe (v.)
ac-cel-er-ate	a-gree-able	ap-pli-ance	au-tumn	brief
ac-cept (-ance)	a-gree-ment	ap-pli-ca-ble	aux-il-ia-ry	bril-liant
ac-ces-si-ble	aisle	ap-pli-ca-tion	a-vail-a-ble	Brit-ain
ac-ces-so-ry	al-co-hol	ap-point-ment	av-er-age	brought
ac-ci-den-tal-ly	a-lign-ment	ap-prais-al	aw-ful	bro-chure
ac-com-mo-date	al-ley	ap-pre-ci-ate	aw-ful-ly	bruise
ac-com-pa-ny	al-lot-ted	ap-proach	awk-ward	budg-et
ac-com-plice	al-low-ance	ap-pro-pri-ate	**B** bach-e-lor	bul-le-tin
ac-com-plish	all right	ap-prov-al	bag-gage	buoy-ant
ac-cor-dance	al-most	ap-prox-i-mate-ly	bal-ance	bu-reau
ac-cord-ing	al-ready	ar-chi-tect	bal-loon	bur-glar
ac-count	al-though	arc-tic	bal-lot	bury
ac-crued	al-to-geth-er	ar-gu-ment	ba-nan-a	busi-ness
ac-cu-mu-late	a-lu-mi-num	a-rith-me-tic	band-age	busy
ac-cu-rate	al-ways	a-rouse	bank-rupt	**C** caf-e-te-ria
ac-cus-tom (ed)	am-a-teur	ar-range-ment	bar-gain	caf-feine
ache	a-mend-ment	ar-riv-al	bar-rel	cal-en-dar
a-chieve (-ment)	a-mong	ar-ti-cle	base-ment	cam-paign
ac-knowl-edge	a-mount	ar-ti-fi-cial	ba-sis	can-celed
ac-quaint-ance	a-nal-y-sis	as-cend	bat-tery	can-di-date
ac-qui-esce	an-a-lyze	as-cer-tain	beau-ti-ful	can-is-ter
ac-quired	an-cient	as-i-nine	beau-ty	ca-noe
ac-tu-al	an-ec-dote	as-sas-sin	be-come	can't
a-dapt	an-es-thet-ic	as-sess (-ment)	be-com-ing	ca-pac-i-ty
ad-di-tion (-al)	an-gle	as-sign-ment	be-fore	cap-i-tal
ad-dress	an-ni-hi-late	as-sist-ance	beg-gar	cap-i-tol
ad-e-quate	an-ni-ver-sa-ry	as-so-ci-ate	be-gin-ning	cap-tain
ad-journed	an-nounce	as-so-ci-a-tion	be-hav-ior	car-bu-ret-or
ad-just-ment	an-noy-ance	as-sume	be-ing	ca-reer
ad-mi-ra-ble	an-nu-al	as-sur-ance	be-lief	car-i-ca-ture
ad-mis-si-ble	a-noint	as-ter-isk	be-lieve	car-riage
ad-mit-tance	a-non-y-mous	ath-lete	ben-e-fi-cial	cash-ier
ad-van-ta-geous	an-swer	ath-let-ic	ben-e-fit (-ed)	cas-se-role
ad-ver-tise (-ment)	ant-arc-tic	at-tach	be-tween	cas-u-al-ty
ad-ver-tis-ing	an-tic-i-pate	at-tack (ed)	bi-cy-cle	cat-a-log
ad-vice (n.)	anx-i-ety	at-tempt	bis-cuit	ca-tas-tro-phe

caught
cav-al-ry
cel-e-bra-tion
cem-e-ter-y
cen-sus
cen-tu-ry
cer-tain
cer-tif-i-cate
ces-sa-tion
chal-lenge
change-a-ble
char-ac-ter (-is-tic)
chauf-feur
chief
chim-ney
choc-o-late
choice
choose
Chris-tian
cir-cuit
cir-cu-lar
cir-cum-stance
civ-i-li-za-tion
cli-en-tele
cli-mate
climb
clothes
coach
co-coa
co-er-cion
col-lar
col-lat-er-al
col-lege
col-lo-qui-al
colo-nel
col-or
co-los-sal
col-umn
com-e-dy
com-ing
com-mence
com-mer-cial
com-mis-sion
com-mit
com-mit-ment
com-mit-ted
com-mit-tee
com-mu-ni-cate
com-mu-ni-ty
com-par-a-tive
com-par-i-son
com-pel
com-pe-tent
com-pe-ti-tion
com-pet-i-tive-ly
com-plain
com-ple-ment
com-plete-ly
com-plex-ion
com-pli-ment
com-pro-mise
con-cede
con-ceive
con-cern-ing
con-cert

con-ces-sion
con-clude
con-crete
con-curred
con-cur-rence
con-demn
con-de-scend
con-di-tion
con-fer-ence
con-ferred
con-fi-dence
con-fi-den-tial
con-grat-u-late
con-science
con-sci-en-tious
con-scious
con-sen-sus
con-se-quence
con-ser-va-tive
con-sid-er-ably
con-sign-ment
con-sis-tent
con-sti-tu-tion
con-tempt-ible
con-tin-u-al-ly
con-tin-ue
con-tin-u-ous
con-trol
con-tro-ver-sy
con-ven-ience
con-vince
cool-ly
co-op-er-ate
cor-dial
cor-po-ra-tion
cor-re-late
cor-re-spond
cor-re-spond-ence
cor-rob-o-rate
cough
couldn't
coun-cil
coun-sel
coun-ter-feit
coun-try
cour-age
cou-ra-geous
cour-te-ous
cour-te-sy
cous-in
cov-er-age
cred-i-tor
cri-sis
crit-i-cism
crit-i-cize
cru-el
cu-ri-os-i-ty
cu-ri-ous
cur-rent
cur-ric-u-lum
cus-tom
cus-tom-ary
cus-tom-er
cyl-in-der
dai-ly

dair-y
dealt
debt-or
de-ceased
de-ceit-ful
de-ceive
de-cid-ed
de-ci-sion
dec-la-ra-tion
dec-o-rate
de-duct-i-ble
de-fend-ant
de-fense
de-ferred
def-i-cit
def-i-nite (-ly)
def-i-ni-tion
del-e-gate
de-li-cious
de-pend-ent
de-pos-i-tors
de-pot
de-scend
de-scribe
de-scrip-tion
de-sert
de-serve
de-sign
de-sir-able
de-sir-ous
de-spair
des-per-ate
de-spise
des-sert
de-te-ri-o-rate
de-ter-mine
de-vel-op
de-vel-op-ment
de-vice
de-vise
di-a-mond
di-a-phragm
di-ar-rhe-a
di-a-ry
dic-tio-nary
dif-fer-ence
dif-fer-ent
dif-fi-cul-ty
di-lap-i-dat-ed
di-lem-ma
din-ing
di-plo-ma
di-rec-tor
dis-agree-able
dis-ap-pear
dis-ap-point
dis-ap-prove
dis-as-trous
dis-ci-pline
dis-cov-er
dis-crep-an-cy
dis-cuss
dis-cus-sion
dis-ease
dis-sat-is-fied

dis-si-pate
dis-tin-guish
dis-trib-ute
di-vide
di-vine
di-vis-i-ble
di-vi-sion
doc-tor
does-n't
dom-i-nant
dor-mi-to-ry
doubt
drudg-ery
du-al
du-pli-cate
dye-ing
dy-ing
ea-ger-ly
ear-nest
eco-nom-i-cal
econ-o-my
ec-sta-sy
e-di-tion
ef-fer-ves-cent
ef-fi-ca-cy
ef-fi-cien-cy
eighth
ei-ther
e-lab-o-rate
e-lec-tric-i-ty
el-e-phant
el-i-gi-ble
e-lim-i-nate
el-lipse
em-bar-rass
e-mer-gen-cy
em-i-nent
em-pha-size
em-ploy-ee
em-ploy-ment
e-mul-sion
en-close
en-cour-age
en-deav-or
en-dorse-ment
en-gi-neer
En-glish
e-nor-mous
e-nough
en-ter-prise
en-ter-tain
en-thu-si-as-tic
en-tire-ly
en-trance
en-vel-op (v.)
en-ve-lope (n.)
en-vi-ron-ment
equip-ment
equipped
e-quiv-a-lent
es-pe-cial-ly
es-sen-tial
es-tab-lish
es-teemed
et-i-quette

ev-i-dence
ex-ag-ger-ate
ex-ceed
ex-cel-lent
ex-cept
ex-cep-tion-al-ly
ex-ces-sive
ex-cite
ex-ec-u-tive
ex-er-cise
ex-haust (-ed)
ex-hi-bi-tion
ex-hil-a-ra-tion
ex-is-tence
ex-or-bi-tant
ex-pect
ex-pe-di-tion
ex-pend-i-ture
ex-pen-sive
ex-pe-ri-ence
ex-plain
ex-pla-na-tion
ex-pres-sion
ex-qui-site
ex-ten-sion
ex-tinct
ex-traor-di-nar-y
ex-treme-ly
fa-cil-i-ties
fal-la-cy
fa-mil-iar
fa-mous
fas-ci-nate
fash-ion
fa-tigue (d)
fau-cet
fa-vor-ite
fea-si-ble
fea-ture
Feb-ru-ar-y
fed-er-al
fem-i-nine
fer-tile
fic-ti-tious
field
fierce
fi-ery
fi-nal-ly
fi-nan-cial-ly
fo-li-age
for-ci-ble
fore-go
for-eign
for-feit
for-mal-ly
for-mer-ly
for-tu-nate
for-ty
for-ward
foun-tain
fourth
frag-ile
fran-ti-cal-ly
freight
friend

ful-fill
fun-da-men-tal
fur-ther-more
fu-tile
gad-get
gan-grene
ga-rage
gas-o-line
gauge
ge-ne-al-o-gy
gen-er-al-ly
gen-er-ous
ge-nius
gen-u-ine
ge-og-ra-phy
ghet-to
ghost
glo-ri-ous
gnaw
gov-ern-ment
gov-er-nor
gra-cious
grad-u-a-tion
gram-mar
grate-ful
grat-i-tude
grease
grief
griev-ous
gro-cery
grudge
grue-some
guar-an-tee
guard
guard-i-an
guer-ril-la
guess
guide
guid-ance
guilty
gym-na-si-um
gyp-sy
gy-ro-scope
hab-i-tat
ham-mer
han-dle (d)
hand-ker-chief
hand-some
hap-haz-ard
hap-pen
hap-pi-ness
ha-rass
har-bor
hast-i-ly
hav-ing
haz-ard-ous
height
hem-or-rhage
hes-i-tate
hin-drance
his-to-ry
hoarse
hol-i-day
hon-or
hop-ing

hop-ping
horde
hor-ri-ble
hos-pi-tal
hu-mor-ous
hur-ried-ly
hy-drau-lic
hy-giene
hymn
hy-poc-ri-sy
i-am-bic
i-ci-cle
i-den-ti-cal
id-io-syn-cra-sy
il-leg-i-ble
il-lit-er-ate
il-lus-trate
im-ag-i-nary
im-ag-i-na-tive
im-ag-ine
im-i-ta-tion
im-me-di-ate-ly
im-mense
im-mi-grant
im-mor-tal
im-pa-tient
im-per-a-tive
im-por-tance
im-pos-si-ble
im-promp-tu
im-prove-ment
in-al-ien-able
in-ci-den-tal-ly
in-con-ve-nience
in-cred-i-ble
in-curred
in-def-i-nite-ly
in-del-i-ble
in-de-pend-ence
in-de-pend-ent
in-dict-ment
in-dis-pens-able
in-di-vid-u-al
in-duce-ment
in-dus-tri-al
in-dus-tri-ous
in-ev-i-ta-ble
in-fe-ri-or
in-ferred
in-fi-nite
in-flam-ma-ble
in-flu-en-tial
in-ge-nious
in-gen-u-ous
in-im-i-ta-ble
in-i-tial
ini-ti-a-tion
in-no-cence
in-no-cent
in-oc-u-la-tion
in-quir-y
in-stal-la-tion
in-stance
in-stead
in-sti-tute

in-sur-ance
in-tel-lec-tu-al
in-tel-li-gence
in-ten-tion
in-ter-cede
in-ter-est-ing
in-ter-fere
in-ter-mit-tent
in-ter-pret (-ed)
in-ter-rupt
in-ter-view
in-ti-mate
in-va-lid
in-ves-ti-gate
in-ves-tor
in-vi-ta-tion
ir-i-des-cent
ir-rel-e-vant
ir-re-sis-ti-ble
ir-rev-er-ent
ir-ri-gate
is-land
is-sue
i-tem-ized
i-tin-er-ar-y
it's
jan-i-tor
jeal-ous (-y)
jeop-ard-ize
jew-el-ry
jour-nal
jour-ney
judg-ment
jus-tice
jus-ti-fi-able
kitch-en
knowl-edge
knuck-les
la-bel
lab-o-ra-to-ry
lac-quer
lan-guage
laugh
laun-dry
law-yer
league
lec-ture
le-gal
leg-i-ble
leg-is-la-ture
le-git-i-mate
lei-sure
length
let-ter-head
li-a-bil-i-ty
li-a-ble
li-ai-son
li-brar-y
li-cense
lieu-ten-ant
light-ning
lik-able
like-ly
lin-eage
liq-ue-fy

liq-uid
lis-ten
lit-er-ary
lit-er-a-ture
live-li-hood
liv-ing
log-a-rithm
lone-li-ness
loose
lose
los-ing
lov-able
love-ly
lun-cheon
lux-u-ry
ma-chine
mag-a-zine
mag-nif-i-cent
main-tain
main-te-nance
ma-jor-i-ty
mak-ing
man-age-ment
ma-neu-ver
man-u-al
man-u-fac-ture
man-u-script
mar-riage
mar-shal
ma-te-ri-al
math-e-mat-ics
max-i-mum
may-or
mean-ness
meant
mea-sure
med-i-cine
me-di-eval
me-di-o-cre
me-di-um
mem-o-ran-dum
men-us
mer-chan-dise
mer-it
mes-sage
mile-age
mil-lion-aire
min-i-a-ture
min-i-mum
min-ute
mir-ror
mis-cel-la-neous
mis-chief
mis-chie-vous
mis-er-a-ble
mis-ery
mis-sile
mis-sion-ary
mis-spell
mois-ture
mol-e-cule
mo-men-tous
mo-not-o-nous
mon-u-ment
mort-gage

mu-nic-i-pal
mus-cle
mu-si-cian
mus-tache
mys-te-ri-ous
na-ive
nat-u-ral-ly
nec-es-sary
ne-ces-si-ty
neg-li-gi-ble
ne-go-ti-ate
neigh-bor (-hood)
nev-er-the-less
nick-el
niece
nine-teenth
nine-ty
no-tice-able
no-to-ri-ety
nu-cle-ar
nui-sance
o-be-di-ence
o-bey
o-blige
ob-sta-cle
oc-ca-sion
oc-ca-sion-al-ly
oc-cu-pant
oc-cur
oc-curred
oc-cur-rence
of-fense
of-fi-cial
of-ten
o-mis-sion
o-mit-ted
o-pin-ion
op-er-ate
op-por-tu-ni-ty
op-po-nent
op-po-site
op-ti-mism
or-di-nance
or-di-nar-i-ly
orig-i-nal
out-ra-geous
pag-eant
paid
pam-phlet
par-a-dise
para-graph
par-al-lel
par-a-lyze
pa-ren-the-ses
pa-ren-the-sis
par-lia-ment
par-tial
par-tic-i-pant
par-tic-i-pate
par-tic-u-lar-ly
pas-time
pa-tience
pa-tron-age
pe-cu-liar
per-ceive

per-haps	pur-chase	sec-re-tary	sus-pi-cious	u-ten-sil
per-il	pur-sue	seize	sus-te-nance	u-til-ize
per-ma-nent	pur-su-ing	sen-si-ble	syl-la-ble	va-can-cies
per-mis-si-ble	pur-suit	sen-tence	sym-met-ri-cal	va-ca-tion
per-pen-dic-u-lar	qual-i-fied	sen-ti-nel	sym-pa-thy	vac-u-um
per-se-ver-ance	quan-ti-ty	sep-a-rate	sym-pho-ny	vague
per-sis-tent	quar-ter	ser-geant	symp-tom	valu-able
per-son-al (-ly)	ques-tion-naire	sev-er-al	syn-chro-nous	va-ri-ety
per-son-nel	qui-et	se-vere-ly	tar-iff	var-i-ous
per-spi-ra-tion	quite	shep-herd	tech-nique	veg-e-ta-ble
per-suade	quo-tient	sher-iff	tele-gram	ve-hi-cle
phase	raise	shin-ing	tem-per-a-ment	veil
phe-nom-e-non	rap-port	seige	tem-per-a-ture	ve-loc-i-ty
phi-los-o-phy	re-al-ize	sig-nif-i-cance	tem-po-rary	ven-geance
phy-si-cian	re-al-ly	sim-i-lar	ten-den-cy	very
piece	re-cede	si-mul-ta-ne-ous	ten-ta-tive	vi-cin-i-ty
planned	re-ceipt	since	ter-res-tri-al	view
pla-teau	re-ceive	sin-cere-ly	ter-ri-ble	vig-i-lance
plau-si-ble	re-ceived	ski-ing	ter-ri-to-ry	vil-lain
play-wright	rec-i-pe	sol-dier	the-ater	vi-o-lence
pleas-ant	re-cip-i-ent	sol-emn	their	vis-i-bil-i-ty
pleas-ure	rec-og-ni-tion	so-phis-ti-cat-ed	there	vis-i-ble
pneu-mo-nia	rec-og-nize	soph-o-more	there-fore	vis-i-tor
pol-i-ti-cian	rec-om-mend	so-ror-i-ty	thief	voice
pos-sess	re-cur-rence	source	thor-ough (-ly)	vol-ume
pos-ses-sion	ref-er-ence	sou-ve-nir	though	vol-un-tary
pos-si-ble	re-ferred	spa-ghet-ti	through-out	vol-un-teer
prac-ti-cal-ly	re-hearse	spe-cif-ic	tired	wan-der
prai-rie	reign	spec-i-men	to-bac-co	war-rant
pre-cede	re-im-burse	speech	to-geth-er	weath-er
pre-ce-dence	rel-e-vant	sphere	to-mor-row	Wednes-day
pre-ced-ing	re-lieve	spon-sor	tongue	weird
pre-cise-ly	re-li-gious	spon-ta-ne-ous	to-night	wel-come
pre-ci-sion	re-mem-ber	sta-tion-ary	touch	wel-fare
pre-cious	re-mem-brance	sta-tion-ery	tour-na-ment	where
pred-e-ces-sor	rem-i-nisce	sta-tis-tic	tour-ni-quet	wheth-er
pref-er-a-ble	ren-dez-vous	stat-ue	to-ward	which
pref-er-ence	re-new-al	stat-ure	trag-e-dy	whole
pre-ferred	rep-e-ti-tion	stat-ute	trai-tor	whol-ly
prej-u-dice	rep-re-sen-ta-tive	stom-ach	tran-quil-iz-er	whose
pre-lim-i-nar-y	req-ui-si-tion	stopped	trans-ferred	width
pre-mi-um	res-er-voir	straight	trea-sur-er	wom-en
prep-a-ra-tion	re-sis-tance	strat-e-gy	tried	worth-while
pres-ence	re-spect-a-bly	strength	tries	wor-thy
prev-a-lent	re-spect-ful-ly	stretched	tru-ly	wreck-age
pre-vi-ous	re-spec-tive-ly	study-ing	Tues-day	wres-tler
prim-i-tive	re-spon-si-bil-i-ty	sub-si-dize	tu-ition	writ-ing
prin-ci-pal	res-tau-rant	sub-stan-tial	typ-i-cal	writ-ten
prin-ci-ple	rheu-ma-tism	sub-sti-tute	typ-ing	wrought
pri-or-i-ty	rhyme	sub-tle	unan-i-mous	yel-low
pris-on-er	rhythm	suc-ceed	un-con-scious	yes-ter-day
priv-i-lege	ri-dic-u-lous	suc-cess	un-doubt-ed-ly	yield
prob-a-bly	route	suf-fi-cient	un-for-tu-nate-ly	
pro-ce-dure	sac-ri-le-gious	sum-ma-rize	unique	
pro-ceed	safe-ty	su-per-fi-cial	u-ni-son	
pro-fes-sor	sal-a-ry	su-per-in-tend-ent	uni-ver-si-ty	
prom-i-nent	sand-wich	su-pe-ri-or-i-ty	un-nec-es-sary	
pro-nounce	sat-is-fac-to-ry	su-per-sede	un-prec-e-dent-ed	
pro-nun-ci-a-tion	Sat-ur-day	sup-ple-ment	un-til	
pro-pa-gan-da	scarce-ly	sup-pose	up-per	
pros-e-cute	scene	sure-ly	ur-gent	
pro-tein	scen-er-y	sur-prise	us-able	
psy-chol-o-gy	sched-ule	sur-veil-lance	use-ful	
pub-lic-ly	sci-ence	sur-vey	using	
pump-kin	scis-sors	sus-cep-ti-ble	usu-al-ly	

Punctuation

Period

126 A **period** is used to end a sentence which makes a statement, or which gives a command which is not used as an exclamation.

> "That guy is coming over here."
> "Don't forget to smile when you talk."
> "Hello, Big Boy."
> "Hi."

127 It is not necessary to place a period after a statement which has parentheses around it and is part of another sentence.

> Euny gave Jim an earwich (an earwich is one piece of buttered bread slapped on each ear) and then ran away giggling.

128 An ellipsis (three periods) is used to show that one or more words have been omitted in a quotation. (Leave one space before and after each period when typing.)

> "Give me your tired . . . yearning to breathe free."

129 If an omission occurs at the end of a sentence, the ellipsis is placed after the period which marks the conclusion of the sentence.

> "Ernest Hemingway was fond of fishing. . . . His understanding of that sport is demonstrated in many of his writings."

Note: If the quoted material is a complete sentence (even if it was not in the original) use a period, then an ellipsis.

130 An ellipsis also may be used to indicate a pause.

> "Well, Dad, I . . . ah . . . ran out of gas . . . had two flat tires . . . and ah . . . there was a terrible snowstorm on the other side of town."

"Well, Dad, I ... ah ... ran out of gas ... had two flat tires ... and ah ... there was a terrible snowstorm on the other side of town."

131 A period should be placed after an initial.

> Dena W. Kloosterman; Thelma J. Slenk

132 A period is placed after each part of an **abbreviation** — unless the abbreviation is an acronym. An **acronym** is a word formed from the first (or first few) letters of words in a set phrase. (See 116-119.)

> **Abbreviations:** Mr., Mrs., Ms., A.M., P.M., Dr., A.D., B.C.
>
> **Acronyms:** WAC (Women's Army Corps); Radar (Radio Detecting and Ranging); NATO (North Atlantic Treaty Organization)

133 When an abbreviation is the last word in a sentence, only one period should be used at the end of the sentence.

> When she's nervous, she bites her nails, wrings her hands, picks at her clothes, etc.

134 Use a period as a decimal and to separate dollars and cents.

> 6.1 percent   28.9 percent $3,120.21

Comma

135 A **comma** may be used between two independent clauses which are joined by coordinate conjunctions such as these: *but, or, nor, for, yet, and, so.*

> My friend smokes constantly, *but* he still condemns industry for its pollution.

Note: Do not confuse a sentence with a compound verb for a compound sentence.

> My friend *smokes* but still *condemns* industry for its pollution. (This is a simple sentence with a compound verb; use no comma.)

136 Commas are used to separate individual words, phrases, or clauses in a series. (A series contains at least three items.)

> I used a rapalla, a silver spoon, a nightcrawler harness, and a Swedish pimple.
> The bait I used included kernels of corn, minnows, bacon rind, larva, and spawn sacks.

Note: Do not use commas when the words in a series are connected with *or, nor,* or *and.*

> I plan to catch bass *or* trout *or* sunfish.

137 Commas are used to separate an explanatory phrase from the rest of the sentence.

> Spawn, *or fish eggs,* is tremendous bait.

An **appositive**, a specific kind of explanatory word or phrase, identifies or renames a preceding noun or pronoun. (Do not use commas with *restrictive appositives.* See the third example below and 141.)

> My father, *an expert angler,* uses spawn to catch brook trout.
> The objective, *to hook fish,* is easier to accomplish with spawn.
> The word *angleworm* applies to an earthworm used for fishing.

138 Commas are used to separate coordinate adjectives, adjectives which *equally* modify the same noun.

> Trout gobble up the *small, soft, round* eggs.

Notice in the example above that no comma separates the last adjective from the noun.

> *Most pan* fish also eat spawn.

In the example above, *most* and *pan* are not separated by a comma because the two adjectives do *not* equally modify *fish.* To determine whether adjectives modify equally, use these two tests: 1) Shift the order of the adjectives; if the sentence is clear, the adjectives modify equally. (If *most* and *pan* were shifted in the example above, the sentence would be unclear.) 2) Insert *and* between the adjectives; if the sentence reads well, use a comma when *and* is omitted.

Note: If the first adjective modifies the second adjective *and* the noun, use a comma.

> He sat down on the *soft, velvet* couch.

139 Commas are used to separate contrasted elements from the rest of the sentence and are often used to show word omission in certain grammatical constructions.

> We need strong minds, not strong emotions, to solve our problems.
> The wise man learns from the mistakes of others; the fool, from his

own. (The comma is used to show that the word *learns* has been omitted from the second half of the sentence.)

140 A comma should separate an adverb clause or a long modifying phrase from the independent clause which follows it.

> After a few hours of exposure, the orange-colored fish eggs turn white and hard.
> To fully appreciate the joys of fishing, you must be patient.

Note: A comma is usually omitted if the phrase or adverb clause follows the independent clause.

> The orange-colored fish eggs turn white and hard after a few hours of exposure.

141 Commas are used to punctuate **nonrestrictive** phrases and clauses. Nonrestrictive phrases or clauses are those which are not essential or necessary to the basic meaning of the sentence. **Restrictive** phrases or clauses — those which are needed in the sentence because they restrict or limit the meaning of the sentence — are not set off with commas. Compare the following examples with their nonrestrictive and restrictive phrases.

> Rozi, *who liked to play with black cats,* is my sister.
> (*Note:* The clause, *who liked to play with black cats,* is merely additional information; it is nonrestrictive [not required]. If the clause were left out of the sentence, the meaning of the sentence would remain clear since the name of the girl is given.)

> The girl *who liked to play with black cats* is my sister.
> (*Note:* This clause is restrictive. The clause, *who liked to play with black cats,* is needed to identify the girl.)

Compare the following examples:

> The novelist *Sinclair Lewis* was the first American writer to win a Nobel Prize for literature. (restrictive)

> Sinclair Lewis, a *novelist,* was the first American writer to win a Nobel Prize for literature. (nonrestrictive)

142 Commas are used to distinguish items in an address and items in a date.

> They live at 2341 Pine Street, Willmar, Minnesota 56342, during the summer. (*Note:* Do not use a comma to separate the state from the ZIP code.)

> Democracy will be dead by Wednesday, July 4, 1984, according to George Orwell. Orwell wrote that in July 1949 with pen in cheek. (*Note:* If only the month and year are given, it is not necessary to separate them with a comma.)

143 Commas are used to set off the exact words of the speaker from the rest of the sentence.

> "Didn't you know," she exclaimed, "that dirty socks cause ingrown toenails?"

A comma is used to separate an interjection or weak exclamation from the rest of the sentence.

> *Hey,* will you do me a favor?
> *Yes,* I'd be happy to help.
> *Wow,* that was quite a test.

144 Commas are used to set off a word, phrase, or clause that interrupts the movement of a sentence. Such expressions usually can be identified through the following tests: 1) They may be omitted without changing the substance or meaning of a sentence. 2) They may be placed nearly anywhere in the sentence without changing the meaning of the sentence.

> I'm convinced, *however,* that tight hats are a spawning paradise for lice.
> *On the other hand,* maybe they wouldn't be able to breathe easily.

26

145 Commas are used to separate a series of numbers in order to distinguish hundreds, thousands, millions, etc.

> The Democrats wasted $720,806 on a foolish domestic program.
> The Republicans invested $1,320,252 to prove that the Democrats wasted money.

146 Commas are used to enclose a title or initials and names which follow a surname.

> J. L. Vanderlaan, Ph.D., and G. S. Bruins, M.D., sat in their pajamas playing Old Maid.
> Asche, H., Hickok, J. B., and Cody, William F., are three popular Western heroes.
> Casey Jones, Jr., was a good friend of John Henry, Sr.

147 Commas are used to separate a **vocative** from the rest of the sentence. (A *vocative* is the noun which names the person/s spoken to.)

> Don't you realize, George, that you're the very first president who thinks we need independence?
> Benedict, honey, stop giggling. Don't you know it's dangerous to let the little Franklin boy play with your kite in such awful weather?

148 A comma may be used for clarity or for emphasis. There will be times when none of the traditional comma rules call for a comma, but one will be needed to prevent confusion or to emphasize an important idea. Use a comma in either case.

> Several days before, he had complained of headaches. (clarity)
> What she does, does matter to us. (clarity)
> Those who can, tell us what happened. (clarity)
> Jim was very impressed with his new neighbor, and with his new neighbor's car. (emphasizes what Jim was most impressed with)

Note: Do not use a comma which could cause confusion. There should be no comma between the subject and its verb or the verb and its object. Also, use no comma before an indirect quotation. (The circled commas should not be used.)

> The man who helped us unload the truck ⊙ is my uncle.
> Uncle Hank said ⊙ he would never again move my player piano.

Semicolon

149 A semicolon is used to join two independent clauses which are not connected with a coordinate conjunction. (This means that each of the two clauses could stand alone as separate sentences.)

> I once had a '55 Chevy with a 283; that was the first V-8 I ever owned.

Note: The exception to this rule occurs when the two clauses are similar, short, or conversational in tone.

> To rule is easy, to govern difficult.

150 A semicolon is used to join two independent clauses within a compound sentence — when the clauses are connected only by a conjunctive adverb. (Common conjunctive adverbs are these: *also, as a result, besides, for example, furthermore, however, in addition, instead, meanwhile, moreover, nevertheless, similarly, then, therefore, thus.*)

> My neighbor proudly says that he is free from racism; *however,* he also feels compelled to say that one of his childhood friends was Black.

151 A semicolon is used to separate independent clauses which are long or contain commas.

> Someone righteously cleansed the library of all "dirty literature"; so the library now contains only "clean" classics such as *Hamlet, Gulliver's Travels,* and *The Canterbury Tales.*

152 A semicolon is used to separate groups of words or phrases which already contain commas.

> I packed a razor, toothbrush, and deodorant; blue jeans, bathing suit, and jacket; tennis balls, fish hooks, and golf clubs.

Colon

153 A colon may be used after the salutation of a business letter.

Dear Ms. Asche:

154 A colon is used between the parts of a number which indicate time.

8:32   11:03

155 A colon may be used to emphasize a word, phrase, clause, or sentence which explains or adds impact to the main clause.

> Television entertains America's children with the most popular pastime of the day: violence. In two hours my sons can witness rapes, robberies, fist fights, riots, and murders: all in the quiet confines of our living room.

156 A colon is used to introduce a list.

> Debbie dropped the purse and out spilled the contents: fingernail clipper, calculator, car keys, wallet, and a ragged old nylon.

A colon should not separate a verb from its object or complement, and it should not separate a preposition from its object.

Incorrect: Hubert hated: spelling, geography, history, and reading (separates verb from objects).
Correct: Hubert hated his subjects: spelling, geography, history, and reading.
Correct: Hubert hated these: spelling, geography, history, and reading.

Incorrect: He just looked at: his fingernails, the ceiling, the teacher, and girls (separates preposition from objects).
Correct: He just looked at other subjects: his fingernails, the ceiling, the teacher, and girls.

157 The colon is used to distinguish between title and subtitle, volume and page, and chapter and verse in literature.

> *Basic English Revisited: A Student Handbook*
> *Encyclopedia Americana* IV: 211
> Psalm 23:1-6

158 A colon may be used to formally introduce a sentence, a question, or a quotation.

> It was John F. Kennedy who said these words: ''Ask not what your country can do for you, but what you can do for your country.''

Dash

159 The **dash** is used to indicate a sudden break or change in the sentence.

> Indians were often called *savages*—yet Caucasians taught them to scalp.
> Comedy and tragedy—in literature and in life—can be distinguished only in terms of one's point of view.
> I always felt that she—But maybe I better not tell you this now.
> (*Note:* The period is not needed after a dash which indicates that the sentence was not concluded.)

160 A dash may be used to emphasize a word, series, phrase, or clause.

> He ran downstage, glared at the audience, screamed his terrible epithet—and his pants fell down.
>
> He wanted a car that matched his personality—flashy, powerful, and sporty.

161 A dash is used to set off an introductory series from the clause that explains the series.

> Health, friends, and family—we are not sufficiently thankful for these.

162 A dash is used to show interrupted or faltering speech in dialogue. (*Note:* A dash is indicated by two hyphens--without spacing before or after--in all handwritten and typed material.)

> Why, hello, Dear--yes, I understand--no, I remember--oh, I want to-- of course I won't--why, no, I--why, yes, I--it was so nice to talk with you again, Dear.

Note: A dash may also be used to show that words or letters are missing.

> Listen, you d— Yankee!

Hyphen

163 The **hyphen** is used to make a compound word.

> great-great-grandfather, run-of-the-mill, mother-in-law, three-year-old, twenty-six-year-old songwriter; teacher-poet (coequal nouns) The Ford-Carter debates helped make peanut butter as patriotic as apple pie.

164 A hyphen is used between the elements of a fraction, but not between the numerator and denominator when one or both are already hyphenated.

> four-tenths   five-sixteenths   (7/32) seven thirty-seconds

Note: Use hyphens when two or more words have a common element which is omitted in all but the last term.

> We have cedar posts in four-, six-, and eight-inch widths.

165 A hyphen is used to join a capital letter to a noun or participle.

> U-turn   A-center   V-shaped

166 A hyphen is used to form new words beginning with the prefixes *self, ex, all, great,* and *quasi.* It is also used to join any prefix to a proper noun, a proper adjective, or the official name of an office. A hyphen is used with the suffix *elect.*

> ex-mayor, self-esteem, all-knowing, pro-American, post-Depression, mid-May, president-elect, governor-elect, great-grandson, quasi-serious

Note: Use a hyphen with other prefixes or suffixes to avoid confusion or awkward spelling.

> re-cover (not *recover*) the sofa   shell-like (not *shelllike*)

It would take Herb a while to *recover* after seeing what it cost to *re-cover* the sofa.

167 The hyphen is used to join the words in compound numbers from *twenty-one* to *ninety-nine*; figures are usually used for numbers greater than ninety-nine. (See 120-122.)

168 The hyphen is used to separate a word at the end of a line of print. A word may be divided only between syllables, and the hyphen is always placed after the syllable at the end of the line—never before a syllable at the beginning of the following line.

Additional Guidelines for Using the Hyphen

1. Always leave enough of the word at the end of the sentence so that the word can be identified.
2. Never divide a one-syllable word: *rained, skills, through.*
3. Avoid dividing a word of five or fewer letters: *paper, study, July.*
4. Never divide a one-letter syllable from the rest of the word: *omit-ted,* not *o-mitted.*
5. Always divide a compound word between its basic units: *sister-in-law,* not *sis-ter-in-law.*
6. Never divide abbreviations or contractions: *shouldn't,* not *should-n't.*
7. Avoid dividing the last word in a paragraph.
8. Never divide the last word in more than two lines in a row.
9. When a vowel is a syllable by itself, divide the word after the vowel: *epi-sode,* not *ep-isode.*
10. Avoid dividing a number written as a figure: *1,000,000,* not *1,000,-000.* (If a figure must be broken, divide it after one of the commas.)
11. Always check a dictionary if you are uncertain where a word should be divided.

169 Use the hyphen to join two or more words which serve as a single adjective (a *single-thought* adjective) before a noun.

> ten-speed bike   mind-boggling problem   up-to-date forecast

Note: When words forming the adjective come after the noun, do not hyphenate them.

> My new bike is a *ten speed.*   The problem was *mind boggling.*

When the first of the words is an adverb ending in *ly,* do not use a hyphen; also, do not use a hyphen when a number or letter is the final element in a one-thought adjective.

> fresh*ly* painted barn   Grade *A* milk   number *360* sandpaper

170 The hyphen is used to join numbers which indicate the life span of an individual, the scores of a game, the term of an event, etc.

> The child lived a short life: 1971-1973.
> The score, 78-27, suggests the nature of the Elk Rapids-Traverse City basketball game.

Question Mark

171 A **question mark** is used at the end of a direct question.

> Are your relatives mushy when you visit them?
> Are your grandparents heavy on the kissy-huggy stuff?

172 No question mark is used after an indirect quotation.

> My aunt always asks how I am doing in school.
> I always wonder what "doing in school" means.

173 When two clauses within a sentence both ask questions, one question mark is used.

> Does your uncle greet you as mine greets me — with a "cootchy-coo" under the chin and a "How old are you now, little lady?" Do you think he would feel insulted if I gave him a "cootchy-coo" in the beard and said, "I'm thirteen, Uncle, and how old are you getting to be?"

174 The question mark is placed within parentheses to show uncertainty.

> Although my cousin is only 18 (?), he looks down his nose when he says "Hello" to his younger cousins.

175 A short question within parentheses is punctuated with a question mark.

> You may visit me next week (is that possible?) as long as your hand-shake is firm and you don't pat my head.

176 Only one question mark should punctuate a question. The following punctuation is both silly and incorrect.

> Do you mean that kid with a tall head???
> Really! Why did you ever date him???

Exclamation Point

177 The **exclamation point** is used to express strong feeling. It may be placed after a word, a phrase, or a sentence. (The exclamation point should be used sparingly.)

> Help! Mom! Help!
> Wow, man, what a way to go!
> The principal actually likes me!

178 Never write more than one exclamation point; such punctuation is incorrect and looks foolish.

> Isn't kissing fun!!!
> Who even thinks about the germs!!!

Quotation Marks

179 **Quotation marks** are placed before and after direct quotations. Only the exact words quoted are placed within quotation marks.

> "I really don't know," he said, "whether orchids are her favorite flowers or not." *(Note:* The words *he said* are not in quotation marks because the person did not say them. Also, the word *whether* is not capitalized because it does not begin a new sentence.)

180 Quotation marks do not come before and after each *consecutive* sentence in a quotation. Rather, quotation marks are placed before and after the entire quotation.

> "My brother built a horse which could walk, buck, trot, and gallop. The torso of this 'creation' was a telephone pole. One end of the pole was bolted to the hitch of a tractor. The other end of the pole was bolted to a fifty-gallon barrel (a saddle was tied on the barrel). The center of the pole was straddled by a metal *U-frame*. One end of a large spring was connected to the top of the *U*. The other end of the spring was connected to the pole and suspended in the center of the *U*. The legs of this *U* were carried by spoked metal wheels—the centers of which were welded off center. The mechanical horse could perform an interesting variety of tricks—depending on the direction and the speed of the tractor."

181 If more than one paragraph is quoted, quotation marks are placed before each paragraph and at the end of the last paragraph (Example A). Quotations which are more than four lines on a page are usually set off from the text by indenting ten spaces from the left margin. Quotation marks are placed neither before nor after the quoted material unless they appear in the original (Example B).

Example A	Example B

Note: Although it is no longer the preferred method, lengthy quotations are sometimes indented five spaces from both the left and right side and typed using single-spacing.

182 Quotation marks also may be used (1) to distinguish a word which is being discussed, (2) to indicate that a word is slang, or (3) to point out that a word is being used in a special way. (*Note:* Italics may be used in place of quotation marks for each of these three functions. Also remember, in handwritten material or in typed material, each word which should be in italics is underlined. See 188-192.)

> Mom replaced "angry" with "obnoxious."
> He really thinks he's "with it."
> In order to be popular, she works very hard at being "cute."

183 Quotation marks are used to punctuate titles of songs, poems, short stories, lectures, courses, episodes of radio or television programs, chapters of books, unpublished works, and articles found in magazines, newspapers, or encyclopedias. (For punctuation of other titles, see 191-192.)

> "I Believe in Music" (song)
> "Uncle Wiggly Loses His Pants" (short story)
> "The Raven" (poem)
> "Fundamentals of Oil Painting" (course title)

(*Note:* When you punctuate a title, capitalize the first word, the last word, and every word in between *except* articles, short prepositions, and short conjunctions. See 104.)

184 Single quotation marks are used to punctuate a quotation within a quotation. Double and single quotation marks are alternated in order to distinguish a quotation within a quotation within a quotation.

> "I never read 'The Raven'!"
> "Did you hear him say, 'I never read "The Raven" '?"

185 Periods and commas are always placed inside quotation marks.

> "I don't know," said Albert. Albert said, "I don't know."

186 An exclamation point or a question mark is placed inside quotation marks when it punctuates the quotation; it is placed outside when it punctuates the main sentence.

> I almost croaked when he asked, "That won't be a problem for you, will it?"
> Did the teacher really say, "Finish this by tomorrow"?

187 Semicolons or colons are placed outside quotation marks.

> I read "The Pasture"; "Chicago" is in another book.

Underlining (Italics)

188 **Italics** is a printer's term for a style of type which is slightly slanted. In this sentence the word *happiness* is typed in italics. In handwritten or typed material, each word or letter which should be in italics is underlined.

> The novel To Kill a Mockingbird tells an important story. (typed)
> The novel *To Kill a Mockingbird* tells an important story. (printed)

189 Underlining (*italics* in print) is used to indicate a foreign word which has not been adopted in the English language; it also designates scientific names.

> Angst is a painful state of mind. (foreign word)
> Would you actually allow your one and only daughter to marry a Homo sapiens? (scientific name)

190 Underlining (*italics* in print) is used to designate a word, number, or letter which is being discussed or emphasized. (See 182.)

> I got an A on my test because I understood the word classify.

191 Underlining (*italics*) is used to indicate the titles of magazines, newspapers, pamphlets, books, plays, films, radio and television programs, book-length poems, ballets, operas, lengthy musical compositions, record albums, legal cases, and the names of ships and aircraft. (See 183.)

> When the Legends Die (novel)
> The Cross and the Switchblade (film)

MASH (television program)
Motorists Handbook (pamphlet)
U.S.S. Arizona (ship)
New York Times or New York Times

(Note: When the name of a city is used as part of the name of a newspaper, the name of the city need not be underlined.)

Exceptions: Do not underline or put in quotation marks sacred writings (including the Bible and its many books) or the names of any series, edition, or society which might appear alongside (or in place of) the actual title. Also, do not underline or put in quotation marks your own title at the top of your page.

Bible, Genesis, Talmud (sacred writings)
NCTE Research Report No. 9 (series)
The Baltimore Edition of the Complete Works of Poe (edition)

192 When one title appears within another title, punctuate as follows:

"Upstairs, Downstairs Is Back" (television program in an article)
"An Interpretation of 'The Raven' " (poem in an article)
A Tale of Two Cities as History (book in the title of another book)

Parentheses

193 **Parentheses** are used to enclose explanatory or supplementary material which interrupts the normal sentence structure.

Abraham Lincoln began his political career in Springfield (Ill.) where he served four terms as a state legislator. Following his fourth term, Lincoln tried unsuccessfully to capture the Whig Party's nomination. (Lincoln later joined the Republican Party.) After failing a second time to secure the nomination, Lincoln decided to make one last effort; if he failed, he would retire from politics. His third attempt was a major triumph, for Lincoln won not only the nomination but the election as well (1846). He was soon off to Washington D.C. where he was to become one of the most controversial of all U.S. Presidents (Sandburg, p. 42).

Note: Punctuation is placed within parentheses when it is intended to mark the material within the parentheses. Punctuation is placed outside parentheses when it is intended to mark the entire sentence, of which the parenthetical material is only a part. Also note that words enclosed by parentheses do not have to begin with a capital letter or end with a period—even though the words may compose a complete sentence.

194 For unavoidable parentheses within parentheses, use brackets (. . . [. . .] . . .) .

Brackets

195 **Brackets** are used before and after material which a writer adds when quoting another writer.

"There is no question that his biography *[Hammerin' Hank]* is one of the poorest ever written."
(Note: The brackets indicate that the title, *Hammerin' Hank,* was not part of the quotation but was added for clarification.)

196 Place brackets around material which has been added by someone other than the author or speaker.

"And now, my friends, I say to you, aren't we having a delightful time?" [groans]

197 Place brackets around an editorial correction.

The French [Germans] relish sauerkraut.

198 Brackets should be placed around the letters *sic*; the letters indicate that an error, appearing in quoted material, was created by the original speaker or writer.

"No parent can dessert [sic] his child without damaging a human life."

Apostrophe

199 An **apostrophe** is used to show that one or more letters have been left out of a word to form a contraction.

> don't—*o* is left out; she'd—*woul* is left out; it's—*i* is left out

An apostrophe is also used to show that one or more letters or numbers have been left out of numerals or words which are spelled as they were actually spoken.

> class of '85—*19* is left out; good *mornin'*—*g* is left out

Note: When two apostrophes are called for in the same word, simply omit the second one.

> Be sure you follow closely the *do's* and *don'ts* (not *don't's*) on the checklist.

200 An apostrophe and *s* are used to form the plural of a letter, a number, a sign, or a word discussed as a word.

> A—*A's*; 8—*8's*; +—*+'s*
> You use too many *and's* in your writing.

201 The possessive form of singular nouns is usually made by adding an apostrophe and *s*.

> Carter's daughter; John Denver's song

Note: When a singular noun ends with an *s* or *z* sound, the possessive may be formed by adding just an apostrophe. When the singular noun is a one-syllable word, however, the possessive is usually formed by adding both an apostrophe and *s*.

> Thomas' cabin (or) Thomas's cabin
> boss's; lass's (one-syllable nouns ending in *s*)

202 The possessive form of plural nouns ending in *s* is usually made by adding just an apostrophe. For plural nouns not ending in *s*, an apostrophe and *s* must be added.

> Joneses' great-grandfather; bosses' office; children's book

Remember! The word immediately before the apostrophe is the owner.

kid's guitar	*kid* is the owner
kids' guitar	*kids* are the owners
boss's office	*boss* is the owner
bosses' office	*bosses* are the owners

(Please don't write, "My sisters' hip is out of joint.")

203 When possession is shared by more than one noun, use the possessive form for the last noun in the series.

> VanClumpin, VanDiken, and VanTulip's fish (All three own the same fish.)
> VanClumpin's, VanDiken's, and VanTulip's fish (Each guy owns his own fish.)

VanClumpin, VanDiken, and VanTulip's fish

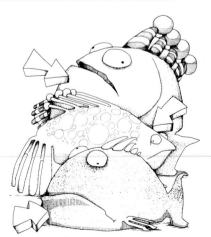

VanClumpin's, VanDiken's, and VanTulip's fish

34

204 The possessive of a compound noun is formed by placing the possessive ending after the last word. (See 114.)

> his mother-in-law's (singular) mouth; the Secretary of State's (singular) wife
>
> their mothers-in-law's (plural) husbands; the Secretaries of State's (plural) wives

205 The possessive of an indefinite pronoun is formed by placing an apostrophe and *s* on the last word. (See 25.)

> everyone's; anyone's; somebody else's

206 An apostrophe is used with an adjective which is part of an expression indicating time or amount.

> yesterday's news; a day's wage; a month's pay

Brace

207 The **brace** is used to join related matter. The brace is not a standard punctuation mark, but it is used often in notes, forms, or letters.

> pizzas { 10 in. / 12 in. / 14 in. } $2.98-4.76

Asterisk

208 The omission of one or more paragraphs from a quotation is indicated by centering three **asterisks** on one line. No other material should be printed on that line.

> * * *

209 An asterisk may be used in a short paper to indicate to the reader that additional information is included in a footnote at the bottom of the page.

> His first year* was very difficult.
> *1968

Diagonal

210 Place a **diagonal** between *and* and *or* to indicate that either is acceptable. A diagonal may also be used to form a fraction.

> I don't remember whether the dog belongs to Miriam and/or Naomi.
> My hat size is 6-7/8.

When quoting more than one line of poetry, use a diagonal at the end of each line.

> The following three lines from Frost's "The Road Not Taken" express clearly his thoughts on individuality: "Two roads diverged in a wood, and I — /I took the one less traveled by/ and that has made all the difference."

211

	Punctuation Marks		
´	Accent, acute	¨ (ö)	Dieresis
`	Accent, grave	. . .	Ellipsis (128)
'	Apostrophe (199)	!	Exclamation point (177)
*	Asterisk (208)	-	Hyphen (163)
{ or }	Brace (207)	. . .	Leaders
[ ]	Brackets (195)	¶	Paragraph
ʌ	Caret	( )	Parentheses (193)
╸ (ç)	Cedilla	.	Period (126)
^	Circumflex	?	Question mark (171)
:	Colon (153)	" "	Quotation marks (179)
,	Comma (135)	§	Section
†	Dagger	;	Semicolon (149)
—	Dash (159)	~	Tilde
/	Diagonal/Slash (210)	_____	Underscore (188)

Usage and Commonly Mixed Pairs

212   **a, an:** *A* is used before words which begin with a consonant sound; *an* is used before words which begin with a vowel sound.
>**Examples:** *a* heap; *a* uniform; *an* idol; *an* urban area; *an* honor; *a* historian.

213   **accept, except:** The verb *accept* means to receive; the verb *except* means to leave out or take out. The preposition *except* means other than.
>**Examples:** Melissa graciously *accepted* defeat. Mike *excepted* the wasp from his collection (verb). All the boys *except* Zach were here (preposition).

214   **adverse, averse:** *Adverse* means to be against or to oppose; *averse* means to have a dislike for something.
>**Example:** The father's *aversion* to rock music prompted an *adverse* reaction—jumping up and down on his son's radio.

215   **affect, effect:** *Affect* means to influence; the verb *effect* means to produce.
>**Examples:** Mark's giggle *affected* the speaker. Mark's giggle *effected* a pinch from his mother.

The noun *effect* means the result.
>**Example:** The *effect* of the pinch was a sore leg.

216   **allusion, illusion:** *Allusion* is an indirect reference to something; *illusion* is a false picture or idea.
>**Example:** The person who makes many *allusions* to his strength tries to reinforce the *illusion* that he's strong.

217   **alot:** *Alot* is not one word; *a lot* (two words) is a vague descriptive phrase which should not be used in formal writing.

A *lot* **should be written as two words, not one. Luckily, Buzz** *saw* **through the problem.**

218   **already, all ready:** *Already* is always an adverb.
>**Examples:** My little girl reads *already*. The class was *all ready* "to try out" the substitute.

219   **alright:** *Alright* is the incorrect form of *all right*. (Please note, the following are spelled correctly: *always, altogether, already, almost.*)

220   **altogether, all together:** *Altogether* is always an adverb.
>**Examples:** This is *altogether* too much noise. My cousins were *all together* in the hay barn.

221   **among, between:** *Among* is used when speaking of more than two persons or things. *Between* is used when speaking of only two.
>**Examples:** Putrid socks were scattered *among* sweaty uniforms. "Ya want a fist *between* your eyes?"

222 amount, number: *Amount* is used for bulk measurement. *Number* is used to count separate units. (See also 253.)
> **Examples:** The liquid produced a large *number* of burps. The burps were the result of a large *amount* of gas.

223 annual, biannual, semiannual, biennial, perennial: An *annual* event happens once every year. A *biannual* event happens twice a year *(semiannual* means the same as *biannual).* A *biennial* event happens every two years. A *perennial* event is active throughout the year and continues to happen every year.

224 ant, aunt: *Aunt* is a relative. *Ant* is an insect.
> **Example:** Do not say, "I carefully inspected my tiny *aunt's* crazy legs."

225 ascent, assent: *Ascent* is rising; *assent* is agreement.
> **Example:** The pilot *assented* that the plane's *ascent* was unusually bumpy.

226 base, bass: *Base* is the foundation or the lower part of something. *Bass* is a deep sound or tone. *Bass (a* pronounced as in *fast)* is a fish.

227 be, bee: *Be* is the verb. *Bee* is the insect.

228 berth, birth: *Berth* is a space or compartment. *Birth* is the process of being born.
> **Example:** We give up our most comfortable *berths* through *birth.*

229 beside, besides: *Beside* means by the side of. *Besides* means in addition to.
> **Examples:** Jeff laid his gum *beside* his plate. *Besides* some burned toast, Bernice fed him some warm lemonade.

230 blew, blue: *Blew* is the verb. *Blue* is the color.

231 board, bored: *Board* is a piece of wood. *Board* also means an administrative group or council.
> **Example:** The School *Board* approved the purchase of fifty 1" x 6" pine *boards.*
> *Bored* may mean to make a hole by drilling or to become weary out of dullness.
> **Example:** Dissecting fish *bored* Joe, so he took his tweezers and *bored* a hole in the tail of the perch.

232 brake, break: *Brake* is a device used to stop a vehicle. *Break* means to separate or to destroy.
> **Example:** I hope the *brakes* on my car never *break.*

233 bring, take: *Bring* means the action is directed toward the speaker; *take* means the action is directed away from the speaker.
> **Examples:** *Bring* me another empty box. *Take* that full one out of here.

234 by, buy: *By* is the preposition. *Buy* is the verb meaning to purchase.
> **Example:** Laurie stopped *by* the house to ask if I would *buy* some eggs.

235 can, may: *Can* suggests ability while *may* suggests permission.
> **Example:** *"Can* I go to the library?" literally means, "Do I have the skill to handle the business?"

236 cannon, canon: A *cannon* is a big gun; a *canon* is a rule or law made by an authority in a church or organization.

237 canvas, canvass: *Canvas* is a heavy cloth; *canvass* means to go among the people asking them for votes or opinions.

238 capital, capitol: The noun *capital* refers to a city or to money. The adjective *capital* means major or important. *Capitol* refers to a building.
> **Examples:** The *capitol* building is in the *capital* city for a *capital* reason. The city government contributed *capital* for the building expense.

239 cent, sent, scent: *Cent* is a coin; *sent* is the past tense of *to send; scent* is an odor or smell.
> **Examples:** For twenty-two *cents,* I *sent* my girlfriend a mushy love poem in a perfumed envelope. She adored the *scent* but hated the poem.

240 chord, cord: *Chord* may mean an emotion or feeling, but it also may mean the combination of two or more tones sounded at the same time, as with a guitar *chord.* A *cord* is a string or rope.

241 **chose, choose:** *Chose* (choz) is the past tense of the verb *choose* (chooz).
Example: This afternoon Mom *chose* tacos and hot sauce; this evening she will *choose* Alka-Seltzer.

242 **coarse, course:** *Coarse* means rough or crude; *course* means a path or direction taken. *Course* also means a class or series of studies.
Examples: Heidi took a *course* up the mountain which was very *coarse*.

243 **complement, compliment:** *Complement* refers to that which completes or fulfills. *Compliment* is an expression of admiration or praise.
Examples: I *complimented* Aunt Betty by saying that her hat *complemented* her coat and dress.

244 **continual, continuous:** *Continual* refers to something which happens again and again; *continuous* refers to something which doesn't stop happening.
Example: Sunlight hits Peoria, Iowa, on a *continual* basis; but sunlight hits the world *continuously*.

245 **counsel, council:** When used as a noun, *counsel* means advice; when used as a verb, *counsel* means to advise. *Council* refers to a group which advises.
Examples: The jackrabbit *council counseled* all bunnies to keep their tails out of the old man's garden. That's good *counsel*.

246 **dear, deer:** *Dear* means loved or valued; *deer* are animals. *(Note:* People will think you're strange if you write that you kissed your *deer* in the moonlight.)

247 **desert, dessert:** *Desert* is barren wilderness. *Dessert* is food served at the end of a meal.
Example: The scorpion tiptoed through the moonlit *desert*, searching for *dessert*.
The verb *desert* means to abandon; the noun *desert* also may mean deserving reward or punishment.
Example: The frightened, mutilated rabbit *deserted* the boy; the loss of his pet was the cruel boy's just *desert*.

248 **die, dye:** *Die (dying)* means to stop living. *Dye (dyeing)* is used to change the color of something.

249 **disinterested, uninterested:** *Disinterested* means indifferent, unbiased by personal opinion; *uninterested* means having no interest or concern.
Examples: A *disinterested* referee will judge a basketball game fairly. An *uninterested* referee will sit down on the center line and smoke his pipe.

250 **eminent, imminent:** *Eminent* means strong, distinguished, prominent. *Imminent* means close or near.
Examples: Embarrassment was *imminent* when the *eminent* politician quickly puckered his lips under the bonnet which lay nestled in the lady's left arm; he had not noticed the thick hairy tail which protruded from under her right arm.

251 **faint, feign, feint:** *Faint* means to be feeble, without strength; *feign* is a verb which means to present something in a pretended or false manner; *feint* is a noun which means a move or activity which is pretended or false.
Examples: The little boy *feigned* a bruised, blood-spattered face and fell to the floor in a *feint;* his teacher, who didn't notice that the blood smelled like catsup, *fainted* beside him.

252 **farther, further:** *Farther* refers to a physical distance; *further* refers to additional time, quantity, or degree.
Examples: Alaska is *farther* north than Iceland. *Further* information can be obtained at your local library.

253 **fewer, less:** *Fewer* refers to the number of separate units; *less* refers to bulk quantity.
Examples: Although there are *fewer* ugly guys this year, there is *less* dating. There is *less* sand to play with, so we have *fewer* sandboxes to make. (See 222.)

254 **flair, flare:** *Flair* means a distinctive and natural talent; *flare* means to light up quickly or burst out.
Example: Hotheads have a *flair* for tempers which *flare*.

255 **good, well:** *Good* is an adjective; *well* is nearly always an adverb.

> **Examples:** The strange flying machines flew *well*. (The adverb *well* modifies *flew*.) They looked *good* as they flew overhead. (The adjective *good* modifies *they*.)
> **Exception:** When used to indicate state of health, *well* is an adjective.
> **Examples:** The pilots looked *good* at the start of the race. Not all of them looked so *well* at the finish.

The race made a *good* story for the young reporter. He wrote *well* and made the event come alive for his readers.

256 **heal, heel:** *Heal* means to mend or restore to health. A *heel* is the back part of a human foot.

257 **hear, here:** You *hear* with your ears. *Here* means the area close by.
heard, herd: *Heard* is the past tense of the verb *hear; herd* is a large group of animals.
> **Example:** The *herd* of grazing mares raised their heads when they *heard* the neigh of the stallion.

258 **heir, air:** *Heir* is a person who inherits something; *air* is a gas.

259 **hole, whole:** A *hole* is a cavity or hollow place. *Whole* means entire or complete.

260 **immigrate, emigrate:** *Immigrate* means to come into a new country or environment. *Emigrate* means to go out of one country to live in another.
> **Example:** Martin Ulferts *immigrated* to this country in 1882. He was only three years old when he *emigrated* from Germany.

261 **it's, its:** *Its* is the possessive form of *it. It's* is the contraction of *it is*.
> **Examples:** *It's* obviously a watchdog; it prefers to watch thieves rather than bark for *its* master.

262 **kind of, sort of:** These expressions are clumsy in formal writing. However, when either one is used, no article *(a, an,* or *the)* should follow.
> **Example:** This *kind of* movie is raunchy. (Not: This *kind of a* movie is raunchy.)

263 **knew, new:** *Knew* is the past tense of the verb *know. New* means recent or novel.
> **Example:** She *knew* that a *new* life began with graduation.
know, no: *Know* means to understand or to realize. *No* means the opposite of *yes*.

264 **later, latter:** *Later* means after a period of time. *Latter* refers to the second of two things mentioned.
> **Example:** *Later* in the year 1965, Galen married Sam; the *latter,* Sam, is a lady.

265 **lay, lie:** *Lay* means to place. *Lay* is a transitive verb. (See 42-47.)
> **Examples:** I *lay* the cigar down today. I *laid* it down yesterday. I had *laid* it down before.
Lie means to recline. *Lie* is an intransitive verb. (See 42-47.)
> **Examples:** The mutt *lies* down. It *lay* down yesterday. It has *lain* down before.

266 **lead, led:** *Lead* is the present tense of the verb meaning to guide. The past tense of the verb is *led*. When the words are pronounced the same, then *lead* is the metal.
> **Examples:** "Hey, Nat, get the *lead* out!" "Hey, cool it, man! Who gave you a ticket to *lead* me around?"

267   **learn, teach:** *Learn* means to get information; *teach* means to give information.
Example: If you want to test yourself on something you've just *learned,* try *teaching* it to others.

268   **leave, let:** *Leave* means to allow something to remain behind. *Let* means to permit.
Example: Rozi wanted to *leave* her boots at home, but George wouldn't *let* her.

269   **like, as:** *Like* is a preposition meaning similar to; *as* is a conjunction meaning such as. *Like* usually introduces a phrase; *as* usually introduces a clause.
Examples: The glider floated *like* a bird. The glider floated *as* he had hoped.

270   **loose, lose, loss:** *Loose* (loōs) means free, untied, unrestricted; *lose* (loōz) means to misplace or fail to find or control; *loss* (lôs) means a losing or being lost.

271   **mail, male:** *Mail* refers to letters or packages handled by the postal service. *Male* refers to the masculine sex.

272   **meat, meet:** *Meat* is food or flesh; *meet* means to come upon or to encounter.

273   **metal, meddle, medal, mettle:** *Metal* is an element like iron or gold. *Meddle* means to interfere. *Medal* is an award. *Mettle,* a noun, refers to quality of character.
Example: The golden snoop cup is a *metal medal* which is awarded to the greatest *meddler.* Snooping is a habit of people of low *mettle.*

274   **miner, minor:** A *miner* digs in the ground for valuable ore. A *minor* is a person who is not legally an adult. A *minor* problem is one of no great importance.

The use of *minors* as *miners* is no *minor* problem.

275   **moral, morale:** *Moral* relates to what is right or wrong. *Morale* refers to a person's mental condition.
Example: "I don't care whether the act is *moral,*" she said. "I care about my *morale.*"

276   **pain, pane:** *Pain* is the feeling of being hurt. *Pane* is a flat side or a single section of a window.

277   **past, passed:** *Passed* is a verb. *Past* can be used as a noun, as an adjective, or as a preposition.
Examples: That Gremlin *passed* my 'Vette (verb). The old lady won't forget the *past* (noun). I'm sorry, Sweetheart, but my *past* life is not your business (adjective). Old Rosebud walked *past* us and never smelled it (preposition).

278   **peace, piece:** *Peace* means tranquility or freedom from war. *Piece* is a part or fragment.
Examples: Someone once observed that *peace* is not a condition, but a process — a process of building goodwill one *piece* or one person at a time.

279   **personal, personnel:** *Personal* means private. *Personnel* are people working at a particular job.

280   **plain, plane:** *Plain* means an area of land which is flat or level; it also means clearly seen or clearly understood.
Example: My teacher told me to "check the map" after I said it was *plain* to me why the early settlers had trouble crossing the Rockies on their way to the Great *Plains.*

Plane means flat, level, and even; it is also a tool used to smooth the surface of wood.
   Example: I used a *plane* to make the board *plane* and smooth.

281 **pore, pour, poor:** A *pore* is an opening in the skin. *Pour* means a constant flow or stream. *Poor* means needy or pitiable.
   Example: Tough exams on spring days make my *poor pores pour.*

282 **principal, principle:** As an adjective, *principal* means primary. As a noun, it can mean a school administrator or a sum of money. *Principle* means idea or doctrine.
   Examples: His *principal* gripe is lack of freedom. "Hey, Charlie, I hear the *principal* chewed you out!" After twenty years, the amount of interest was higher than the *principal.* The *principle* of freedom is based on the *principle* of self-discipline.

283 **quiet, quit, quite:** *Quiet* is the opposite of noisy. *Quit* means to stop. *Quite* means completely or entirely.

284 **real, very, really:** Do not use *real* in place of the adverbs *very* or *really.*
   Examples: Pimples are *very* (not *real*) embarrassing. Her nose is *really* (not *real*) long.

285 **right, write, wright, rite:** *Right* means correct or proper; it also refers to that which a person has a legal claim to, as in copyright. *Write* means to inscribe or record. *Wright* is a person who makes or builds something. *Rite* is a ritual or ceremonial act.
   Example: Did you *write* that it is the *right* of the ship*wright* to perform the *rite* of christening—breaking a bottle of champagne on the stern of the ship?

286 **scene, seen:** *Scene* refers to the setting or location where something happens; it also may mean sight or spectacle. *Seen* is part of the verb *see.*
   Example: An exhibitionist likes to be *seen* making a *scene.*

287 **seam, seem:** *Seam* is a line formed by connecting two pieces. *Seem* means to appear to exist.
   Example: The ragged *seams* in his old coat *seem* to match the creases in his face.

288 **sight, cite, site:** *Sight* means the act of seeing. *Cite* means to quote, name, or refer to. *Site* means location or position.
   Examples: Mark's *sight* was destroyed when a guy's cigarette exploded a gas can on the building *site.* The judge *cited* the man for careless use of smoking materials.

289 **sit, set:** *Sit* means to put the body in a seated position. *Set* means to place. *Set* is transitive; *sit* is intransitive. (See 42-47.)

"How can you just *sit* there and watch as I *set* all these chairs in place?"

290 **sole, soul:** *Sole* means single, only one; *sole* also refers to the bottom surface of the foot. *Soul* refers to the spiritual part of a person.
   Example: A person's *soles* develop blisters on a two-mile hike while his *soul* walks on eternally.

291 **some, sum:** *Some* refers to a certain unknown number or part. *Sum* means an amount.
   Example: The total *sum* was stolen by *some* thieves.

292 **stationary, stationery:** *Stationary* means not movable; *stationery* refers to the paper and envelopes used to write letters.

293 **steal, steel:** *Steal* means to take something without permission; *steel* is a metal.

294 **than, then:** *Than* is used in a comparison; *then* tells when.
Examples: *Then* he cried and said that his big brother was bigger *than* my big brother. *Then* I cried.

295 **their, there, they're:** *Their* is the possessive personal pronoun. *There* is a demonstrative pronoun used to point out location. *They're* is the contraction for *they are*.
Examples: *They're* upset because *their* neighbor drowned in the creek over *there*.

296 **threw, through:** *Threw* is the past tense of throw. *Through* means passing from one side of something to the other.
Example: She *threw* the spitball *through* the room.

297 **to, too, two:** *To* is the preposition which can mean in the direction of. *To* also is used to form an infinitive. *Too* is an adverb indicating degree. *Two* is the number.
Example: The *two* divers were careful not *to* swim *to* the sunken ship *too* quickly.
to, at: *To* should not be used in place of *at* in a sentence like this: He is *at* (not *to*) school.

298 **vain, vane, vein:** *Vain* means valueless or fruitless; it may also mean holding a high regard for one's self. *Vane* is a flat piece of material set up to show which way the wind blows. *Vein* refers to a blood vessel or a mineral deposit.
Example: The weather *vane* indicates the direction of the wind; the blood *vein* determines the direction of flowing blood; the *vain* mind moves in no particular direction or on any specific course and is content to think only about itself.

299 **waist, waste:** *Waist* is the part of the body just above the hips. The verb *waste* means to wear away, decay; the noun *waste* refers to material which is unused or useless.
Example: Large *waists* and much *waste* are sad symbols of our wealth.

300 **wait, weight:** *Wait* means to stay somewhere expecting something. *Weight* refers to a degree or unit of heaviness.

301 **ware, wear, where:** *Ware* refers to a product which is sold; *wear* means to have on or to carry on one's body; *where* asks the question, in what place? or in what situation?
Example: The little boy who sold pet fleas boasted, "Anybody can *wear* my *ware* any*where*, and he'll always know right *where* it is."

302 **way, weigh:** *Way* means path or route. *Weigh* means to measure weight.
Example: After being *weighed* at Weight Watchers club, the two sad friends walked the long *way* home . . . past the malt shop.

303 **weather, whether:** *Weather* refers to the condition of the atmosphere. *Whether* refers to a possibility.
Example: The *weather* will determine *whether* I go fishing.

304 **which, witch:** *Which* is the relative pronoun used to refer to something. *Witch* is an evil female who is believed to cast spells and keep company with black cats.
Example: The cool *witch* drives a broomstick *which* has a tachometer.

305 **who, which, that:** *Which* refers to nonliving objects or to animals; *which* should never refer to people. *Who* is used in reference to people. *That* may refer to animals, people, or nonliving objects.
who, whom: *Who* is used as the subject of a verb; *whom* is used as the object of a preposition or as a direct object.
Examples: *Who* ordered this pizza? The pizza was ordered by *whom?*
Note: To test for who/whom, arrange the parts of the clause in a subject, verb, object order (*who* works as the subject, *whom* as the object).

306 **who's, whose:** *Who's* is the contraction for *who is*. *Whose* is the possessive pronoun.
Examples: "*Who's* that kid with the red ears?" "*Whose* ears are you talking about, big mouth?"

307 **wood, would:** *Wood* is the stuff which trees are made of; *would* is part of the verb *will*.
Examples: The captain who had a *wooden* leg *would* always be shortening his trousers whenever termites were on board.

308 **your, you're:** *Your* is a possessive pronoun. *You're* is the contraction for *you are*.
Examples: "Tell me, Dear, are *your* kisses always this short?" "No, Sweetheart, only when *you're* standing on my feet."

THE WRITING PROCESS

309 Each paragraph, essay, or report you write is different from all the others you have ever written—and different from all those you have yet to write. Simply put, no two pieces of writing are alike. Each time you sit down to write, you are creating an original composition. For writing to be worth reading, however, it must be not only original, but also interesting. It must offer the reader an idea, a feeling, or a twist worth taking the time to read. It should say something fresh, unexpected, memorable, colorful. To do this, you must try to write freely and naturally, allowing your thoughts and feelings to work for you. You should try to discover something which neither you nor your reader has discovered before.

One of the best ways to make your writing personal and creative is to select a topic which has meaning to you, a topic which allows you to share something of yourself. Someone once said, "Writing comes easily if you have something to say." That's the whole point of selecting a personal topic—you will always have something to say.

310 Once you have selected a good topic, you must gather enough information to bring that topic to life. Begin by writing freely and openly on the topic, gathering details which are colorful, accurate, and specific. Without such details, your writing will not tell the real story. It will not give the reader a complete picture of the person, place, thing, or idea being written about. Consider the four pieces of writing below:

> 1. *Just outside of town, there is a cave where someone lives.*
> 2. *Just outside of town, there is a cave where a mysterious man lives with his dog.*
> 3. *Just outside of town is a cave which serves as the home of a solitary man and his dog. Not much is known about this man, but he has been seen enjoying some of the comforts of modern life.*
> 4. *Just outside of town, carved neatly out of the side of a mountain, is the unusual home of Frank Lee and his dog Spotless. Although Frank and his dog are seldom seen in town, they do enjoy many of the comforts of modern living, including television. The home is furnished well with comfortable furniture, a reading lamp, and even wall hangings. It appears Frank and Spotless have chosen to live in the place of their ancestors, but not necessarily in the style.*

Obviously, the closer the writer of these passages was able to observe the subject, the more specifically he was able to describe it. Still, even a fairly complete physical description of a person, his dog, and his living room isn't always enough. To create an effective, memorable description, you must bring the person, place, thing, or event to life.

After you have collected plenty of good details, you must arrange them into effective phrases, sentences, and paragraphs. This is where many people run into snags, snags which eventually wear them down and turn them off to writing. But it doesn't have to be a big problem, not if you gather the right tools for the job. In the case of writing, the right tools are a *dictionary,* a *thesaurus,* and an *English handbook.* Many people simply don't realize how often "good" writers use these tools when they write. No one is a perfect speller, no one knows every rule of punctuation, and no one always has "just the right word" at his pencil tip. In many cases the only real difference between someone who is considered a good writer and someone who isn't is that one uses these tools regularly and the other doesn't. Using these reference books will improve the clarity and form of your writing; it will not necessarily improve the content. The content is still only as good as the thinking that goes into it. To improve as a writer, you must make a sincere effort to improve both the form and content of your writing.

1. Follow the "Guidelines for Selecting a Topic" (313) and find a topic that suits both you and your assignment.

2. Follow the "Guidelines for Spontaneous Writing" (312) and write down all of your ideas on the topic you've chosen. Write as freely and naturally as you can, much the same as you would if you were simply telling someone about the topic. You are, after all, doing exactly that. (You can check the "natural" flow of what you have written by reading it out loud to yourself.)

3. Keep writing until you have exhausted all of your personal thoughts (*sensory, memory,* and *reflective*) on the topic or until you are fairly sure you have gathered enough good information to complete the writing task. Remember, for writing to be good, it must offer something to the reader—a fresh idea, an interesting experience, an unexpected twist, a memorable phrase.

4. If you have recorded all your thoughts on the topic, but still need more details, go to other sources for additional material. You can visit the library to scan books, magazines, pamphlets, etc. Take note of any information which might be useful. Talk to people (parents, teachers, workers) who might be able to provide information from personal experience. Observe people, places, things, and events which are somehow related to your topic. To help figure out exactly where you need more details, ask the journalistic questions *who, what, when, where, why,* and *how* about each of your ideas. Consider adding examples to illustrate a point, facts to prove a point, experiences to dramatize a point, or comparisons to clarify a point.

5. Select the specific details you plan to use in your paper and arrange them into a logical order. (See Handbook 350.) Make a list or an outline to help keep you on track as you write. Remember, though, that your list or outline is simply a guide. You may find a better way to arrange your details as you write.

6. Once you have gathered and arranged your ideas, you must next work on the overall flow and style of your writing. Your ideas must be turned into sentences, each of which expresses a complete thought. Some sentences will contain only one idea or detail; other sentences will contain several ideas or details which must work together to form a complete thought—a thought which is clear, concise, and colorful.

7. Your writing must be colorful. If your ideas are good, but they do not "sound" quite right on paper, your reader may lose interest. To add life to your writing, use active, vivid verbs and specific, concrete nouns. Use adjectives which add detail and emphasis to your important ideas. Use words and phrases which have rhythm, which bounce and glide rather than plod along. Use an occasional "stylistic device" (*parallel structure, simile, metaphor, alliteration,* etc.). Above all else, however, remember that the best writing sounds natural and sincere. Don't make any part of your writing so "colorful" that it calls undue attention to itself.

8. Your writing must be mature. If too many of your ideas are written in short, simple sentences, your writing will lose some of its impact. You must combine those sentences which are short and related into more mature sentences. To do this effectively, you will need to use a variety of sentence-combining techniques. (See the "Guidelines for Writing Sentences," 316.) Also, if your writing sounds like something you've heard before, check for cliches, slang, and other overused expressions. Finally, check the number of sentences which begin with *there, it, he, she, I,* or *they;* avoid an overdose of such sentences.

9. Your writing must be concise. If you find yourself saying basically the same thing over and over, go back and trim. As a writer, you should repeat words and ideas only if they strengthen or clarify what you have already said. Do not pad your writing simply to fill up space or to impress your reader. Also, do not go looking for a "big" word when a small one will do; and don't use adjectives or adverbs which add nothing new (*loud* blasts, jerked *quickly*).

10. Your writing must be clear. For writing to be good, it must be understandable—your handwriting must be legible, your word choice vivid, and your ideas logical. Anything less than that and your readers will not respond the way you want them to. Give your writing to others and get their reactions and advice. (Remind them they don't have to be experts to give you an honest opinion or some helpful hints.)

11. Lastly, your writing must be free of errors. Proofread your writing for errors in spelling, capitalization, punctuation, usage, agreement, and the like. Use a dictionary or handbook when in doubt. Write or type your final copy neatly so that it looks as good as it sounds.

Guidelines for Spontaneous Writing

Reminders . . .

1. Thoughts are constantly passing through your mind; you *never* have *nothing* on your mind.
2. Writing is simply getting these thoughts down on paper.
3. Your senses are always searching out details.
4. Many things seem awkward or difficult when you first try them; spontaneous writing is probably no different.
5. Some days will be better than others; don't be discouraged.
6. To succeed at anything, you must give it an honest effort.

The Process . . .

1. Start with plenty of paper and an extra pen.
2. Write whatever comes into your mind.
3. Don't stop to judge, edit, or correct your writing; that will come later.
4. Keep writing even when you think you have dried up; switch to another mode of thought (sensory, memory, reflective) if necessary, but keep writing.
5. Use all your senses and observe more closely than usual.
6. Continue to shift the focus of your thinking until ideas and details begin to flow.
7. When a particular topic seems to be working, stick with it and record as many specific details as possible.
8. Listen to and read the spontaneous writings of others; learn from them.
9. Practice writing notes and reminders to yourself as the need occurs.
10. Carry your journal with you and write freely in it whenever you have an idea you don't want to forget, or even when you simply have nothing else to do; believe it or not, these free writings will help you become a better writer.

The Result . . .

1. You will often use your spontaneous writings as the basis for a more formal writing assignment.
2. Make sure your spontaneous writing fits the topic and is also one you feel good about sharing.
3. Determine exactly what you plan (or are required) to write about and add specific details as necessary. (This may require a second, more selective free writing.)
4. If the topic seems to be working, keep writing; if you dry up, look for a new subject and begin with a new spontaneous writing.

Guidelines for Selecting a Topic

1. **Use brainstorming techniques.** Brainstorming is the process of gathering as many details, answers, or solutions as possible on a particular subject or problem. If the *problem* is what to write about, you should simply begin listing as many potential topics as possible without taking the time to judge whether each topic is suitable or not. You simply want to get a list of as many topics as you can in the time you have. (Brainstorming works best when it is done in groups.)

2. **Sentence completion** can work well with either groups or individuals. Simply complete any open-ended sentence in as many ways as you can. (*Note:* Try to word your sentence so that it leads you to a topic you can use for the particular writing assignment you are working on.) See the list below.

I wonder how...	I hope our school...	Our grading system...
Too many people...	I just learned...	Television is...
The good thing about...	One place I enjoy...	Cars can be...

3. **Be alert for "found" topics.** These are topics which are somewhat out of the ordinary, topics which you *find* unexpectedly as you are shopping, driving, playing, or walking home from school. You might come across an unusual event, person, or conversation which is unique in some way. Often the best topics are found when people are just being themselves — they are real people in real situations. What happens is interesting because two things have come together in the same time and place to create a result which is ironic or unexpected.

4. **Keep a journal.** Write in your journal on a regular basis the same way you would if you kept a diary. Enter your personal feelings, reactions, opinions, observations, etc., of what happens each day. This is good writing practice and a potential source of writing topics.

5. **Observe.** Watch and listen carefully to everything and everybody when you are searching for a topic. Think about possible topics as you read. Whenever possible, participate in something you are considering as a topic so that you have firsthand information and feelings about the subject. Interview someone who is knowledgeable or experienced in that field. Talking to this person could help you decide which topic in particular to write about.

6. **Use a checklist.** Oftentimes, you can find lists of topics and categories in the library. These may be lists of articles kept in the vertical file or nonfiction titles recently added to the library. An issue of the *Readers' Guide to Periodical Literature* can be useful as a checklist of current topics. Even a magazine or newspaper can serve to remind you of the numerous topics being written about today. Below you will find a checklist of the major categories into which most things in our lives are divided. The checklist provides a variety of subject possibilities. You must then decide which subject you would like to write about and which specific subtopic would work best for your writing assignment.

    Example: *clothing* . . . fashionable clothing . . . the changing fashion in school clothing . . . The type of clothing students wear today varies with each group of students.

Essentials of Life Checklist

clothing	natural resources	agriculture	plants/vegetation
housing	personality/identity	environment	freedom/rights
food	recreation/hobby	land/property	energy
communication	love	trade/money	rules/laws
exercise	measurement	literature/books	tools/utensils
education	senses	entertainment	heat/fuel
family	machines	work/occupation	health/medicine
friends	intelligence	community	art/music
purpose/goals	history/records	science	faith/religion

Sample Writing Topics

Quotations

"Knowledge is of two kinds. We know a subject ourselves, or we know where we can find information upon it." —Samuel Johnson

"A lie can travel half way around the world while the truth is putting on its shoes." —Mark Twain

"A problem well stated is a problem half solved." —C.F. Kettering

"I'm a great believer in luck, and I find the harder I work the more I have of it." —Thomas Jefferson

"The man who does not read good books has no advantage over the man who can't read them." —Mark Twain

"What appears to be the end may really be a new beginning."

"The impossible is often the untried." —Jim Goodwin

"Too often we give children answers to remember rather than problems to solve." —Roger Lewin

"Civilization is a race between education and catastrophe." —H.G. Wells

"The best argument is that which seems merely an explanation." —Dale Carnegie

"The man who makes no mistakes does not usually make anything." —W.C. Magee

"You can always tell a true friend; when you've made a fool of yourself, he doesn't feel you've done a permanent job." —Laurence J. Peter

"When people are free to do as they please, they usually imitate each other." —Eric Hoffer

"Happiness is not a state to arrive at, but a manner of traveling." —M.L. Runbeck

"We can't all be heroes because someone has to sit on the curb and clap as they go by." —Will Rogers

"In every child who is born, under no matter what circumstances, and of no matter what parents, the potentiality of the human race is born again." —James Agee

"Everybody is ignorant, only on different subjects." —Will Rogers

Descriptive

Person: friend, teacher, relative, classmate, minister (priest, rabbi), co-worker, teammate, coach, neighbor, entertainer, politician, sister, brother, bus driver, an older person, a younger person, a baby, someone who taught you well, someone who spends time with you, someone you wish you were more like, someone who always bugs you

Place: school, neighborhood, old neighborhood, the beach, the park, the hangout, home, your room, your garage, your basement, the attic, a roof top, the alley, the bowling alley, a classroom, the theatre, the lockerroom, the store, a restaurant, the library, a church, a stadium, the office, the zoo, the study hall, the cafeteria, the hallway, the barn

Thing: a billboard, a bulletin board, a poster, a photograph, a camera, a machine, a computer, a video game, a music video, a musical instrument, a tool, a monkey wrench, a monkey, a pet, a pet peeve, a bus, a boat, a book . . . a car, a cat, a camp . . . a dog, a drawing, a diary . . . a model, a miniature, a muppet . . .

Narrative

stage fright, just last week, on the bus, learning a lesson, learning to drive, the trip, a kind act, homesick, Christmas, mysteries, a big mistake, field trips, studying, a reunion, a special party, getting lost, being late, asking for help, after school, Friday night, getting hurt, success, flirting, an embarrassing moment, staying overnight, moving, the big game, building a _____, the first day of _____, the last day of _____, a miserable time, all wet, running away, being alone, getting caught, a practical joke, cleaning it up, being punished, staying after, a special conference, the school play, being a friend

Expository

How to . . . wash a car, make a taco, improve your memory, get a job, make a legal petition, prevent accidents, care for a pet, entertain a child, impress your teacher, earn extra money, get in shape, study for a test, conserve energy, program a computer, take a good picture

How to operate . . . control . . . run . . .
How to choose . . . select . . . pick . . .
How to scrape . . . finish . . . paint . . .

How to store . . . stack . . . load . . .
How to build . . . grow . . . create . . .
How to fix . . . clean . . . wash . . .
How to protect . . . warn . . . save . . .

The causes of . . . acid rain, acne, hiccups, snoring, tornados, inflation, northern lights, shinsplints, dropouts, rust, birth defects, cheating, child abuse

Kinds of . . . music, crowds, friends, teachers, love, intelligence, rules, compliments, commercials, punishment, censorship, dreams, happiness, pain, neighbors, pollution, poetry, taxes, clouds, stereos, heroes, chores, homework, fads, adoption, vacations, calendars, clocks, communication, mothers

Definition of . . . rock 'n' roll, best friend, "class," poverty, generation gap, free agent, a good time, a disabled person, hassle, government, a radical, a conservative, SALT, Arab, metric system, dialect, bankruptcy, "soul," grandmother, school, brain, nerd, arthritis, antibiotic, loyalty, credit union, astrology, CPR, Kosher

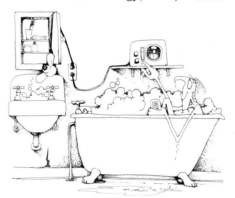

Persuasive

safety in the home, dieting, girls in all sports, organ transplants, sex education, homework, study halls, capital punishment, the speed limit, smoking in public places, shoplifting, seat belts, air bags, gun control, courtroom television, required courses, graduation requirements, final exams, tuition-free colleges, students on school boards, the drinking age, four-day work week, public housing, a career in the armed forces, teen centers, something that needs improving, something that deserves support, something that's unfair, something that everyone should have to see or do, something . . .

The Sentence: Writing Effectively

316 The sentence is a word or group of words which express a complete thought. Most sentences contain a subject and a verb. (The *tornado struck.*) By adding modifiers—descriptive words and phrases—to the subject and verb, the basic sentence can be expanded into a more mature sentence. When these modifiers are well chosen—colorful, vivid, specific—the result is a mature, colorful sentence. Creating effective sentences of this kind and combining them into paragraphs is a basic goal of writing. It is also important to use a variety of sentence types and lengths. This means an occasional question, exclamation, quotation, inverted sentence, or one-word sentence may be just what your writing needs.

Guidelines for Writing Sentences

Each sentence you write (if it is a complete sentence) contains at least one idea. Most sentences contain several basic ideas which work together to form a complete thought. For example, if you wanted to write a sentence about a tornado which struck a small town without warning, causing damage, injury, and death; you would actually be working with six different ideas in that sentence. Each of those ideas could be written as a separate sentence:

1. There was a tornado.
2. The tornado struck a small town.
3. The tornado struck without warning.
4. The tornado caused a great deal of damage.
5. The tornado caused a number of serious injuries.
6. The tornado caused several deaths.

317 As a writer, you must now decide how to arrange these six ideas into one or more effective sentences. There are many possibilities:

1. Use a **series** to combine three or more similar ideas.

   The unexpected tornado struck the small town causing *much damage, numerous injuries,* and *several deaths.*

2. Use a **relative pronoun** (*who, whose, that, which*) to introduce the subordinate (less important) ideas.

   The tornado, *which was completely unexpected,* swept through the small town causing much damage, numerous injuries, and several deaths.

3. Use an **introductory phrase or clause** for the less important ideas.

   Because the tornado was completely unexpected, it caused a great deal of damage, numerous injuries, and several deaths.

4. Use a **participial phrase** (-ing, -ed) at the beginning or end of a sentence.

   The tornado swept through the small town without warning, *leaving behind a trail of death and destruction.*

5. Use a **semicolon.** (Use a conjunctive adverb with the semicolon when appropriate.)

   The tornado swept through the small town without warning; *as a result,* it caused a great deal of damage, numerous injuries, and several deaths.

6. Repeat a **key word** or phrase.

   The tornado left a permanent *scar* on the small town, a *scar* of destruction, injury, and death.

7. Use a **dash** to set off a key word(s) or phrase at the beginning or the end of the sentence.

   The tornado which unexpectedly struck the small town left behind a grim calling card—*death and destruction.*

8. Use a **correlative conjunction** (either, or; not only, but also) to compare or contrast two ideas in a sentence.

49

The tornado *not only* inflicted much property damage, *but also* much human suffering.

9. Use a **colon** to emphasize an important idea.

The destruction caused by the tornado was unusually high for one reason: *it came without warning.*

10. Use an **appositive** (a word or phrase which renames) to emphasize an idea.

A single incident—*a tornado which came without warning*—changed the face of the small town forever.

The Sentence: Avoiding Weaknesses

318 **Agreement of subject and verb:** The subject and verb of any clause must agree in both person and number. There are **three persons:** the **first person** *(I)* is the speaker, the **second person** *(you)* is the person spoken to, and the **third person** *(he, she, it)* is the person or thing spoken about. There are **two numbers: singular** refers to one person or thing; **plural** refers to more than one person or thing.

a. A verb must agree in number (singular or plural) with its subject.

The *student was* proud of his quarter grades. (Both the subject *student* and the verb *was* are singular; they are said to agree in number.)

The student's *parents were* also proud of him. (Both the subject *parents* and the verb *were* are plural; they agree in number.)

Note: Do not be confused by other words coming between the subject and verb.

The *manager* as well as the players *is* required to display good sportsmanship. *(Manager,* not *players,* is the subject.)

Note: Do not neglect agreement in sentences in which the verb comes before the subject. In these inverted sentences, the true *(delayed)* subject must be made to agree with the verb.

There *is* (not *are*) present among many students today a *feeling* of self-worth. *(Feeling* is the true subject of this sentence, not *there. Feeling* is singular; therefore, the singular verb *is* must be used to agree with it.)

There *are* many hard-working *students* in our schools.

b. Compound subjects connected with *and* usually require a plural verb.

Strength and *balance are* necessary for gymnastics.

Note: When the nouns joined by *and* are considered as one unit, the verb is singular.

Macaroni and *cheese is* an inexpensive meal.

c. Singular subjects joined by *or* or *nor* take a singular verb.

Neither *Bev* nor *Connie is* going to the convention.

Note: When one of the subjects joined by *or* or *nor* is singular and one is plural, the verb is made to agree with the subject nearer the verb.

Neither *Mr. Kemper* nor his *students are* able to find the photographs. (The plural subject *students* is nearer the verb; therefore, the plural verb *are* is used to agree with *students.)*

d. The indefinite pronouns *each, either, neither, one, everybody, another, anybody, everyone, nobody, everything, somebody,* and *someone* are singular; they require a singular verb.

Everybody is invited to the cafeteria for refreshments.

Note: Do not be confused by words or phrases which come between the indefinite pronoun and the verb.

Each of the boys *is* (not *are*) required to bring a bar of soap on the first day of class.

50

e. The indefinite pronouns *all, any, half, most, none,* and *some* may be either singular or plural when they are used as subjects. These pronouns are singular if the number of the noun in the prepositional phrase is singular; they are plural if the noun is plural.

> *Half* of the bottles *were* missing. (*Bottles,* the noun in the prepositional phrase, is plural; therefore, the pronoun *half* is considered plural, and the plural verb *were* is used to agree with it.)
>
> *Half* of the movie *was* over by the time we arrived. (Because *movie* is singular, *half* is also singular.)

f. Collective nouns *(faculty, committee, team, congress, species, crowd, army, pair, assembly, squad)* take a singular verb when they refer to a group as a unit; collective nouns take a plural verb when they refer to the individuals within the group.

> The *faculty is* united in its effort to make this school a better place to be. *(Faculty* refers to a group as a unit; therefore, it requires a singular verb: *is.)*
>
> The *faculty are* required to turn in their keys before leaving for the summer. (In this example, *faculty* refers to the individuals within the group. If the word *individuals* were substituted for *faculty*, it would become clear that the plural verb *are* is needed in this sentence.)

g. Some nouns which are plural in form but singular in meaning take a singular verb: *mumps, measles, news, mathematics, economics, gallows, shambles.*

> *Measles is* still considered a serious disease in many parts of the world.

Note: Other nouns plural in form take plural verbs: *scissors, trousers, tidings.*

> The *scissors are* on the table.

Note: Some nouns ending in *ics (athletics, acoustics, gymnastics, politics, statistics)* are singular when referring to an organized body of knowledge; they are plural when they refer to activities, qualities, or opinions.

> *Politics is* an interesting field of study. *(Politics* here means *an organized body of knowledge.)*
>
> The *politics* of a Presidential campaign *are* intense. *(Politics* refers to the *activities* of an election campaign.)

Note: Phrases containing mathematical calculations usually take a singular verb.

> Three and three *is* six. Five times six *is* thirty.

h. When a relative pronoun *(who, which, that)* is used as the subject of a clause, the number of the verb is determined by the *antecedent* of the pronoun. (The *antecedent* is the word to which the pronoun refers.)

> This is one of the *books which are* required for geography class. (The relative pronoun *which* requires the plural verb *are* because its antecedent *books* is plural. To test this type of sentence for agreement, read the *of* phrase first: *Of the books which are . . .*)

i. When a sentence contains a form of the *to be* verb — and a noun comes before and after that verb — the verb must agree with the subject even if the *complement* (the noun coming after the verb) is different in number.

> The *cause* of his problem *was* his bad brakes.
> His bad *brakes were* the cause of his problem.

319 Agreement of pronoun and its antecedent: A pronoun must agree in number, person, and gender (sex) with its *antecedent.* (The *antecedent* is the word to which the pronoun refers.)

> *Bill* brought *his* gerbil to school. (The antecedent in this sentence is *Bill;* it is to *Bill* that the pronoun *his* refers. Both the pronoun and its antecedent are singular, third person, and masculine; therefore, the pronoun is said to agree with its antecedent.)

51

The *teachers* brought *their* gerbils to school. (Both the pronoun *their* and the antecedent *teachers* agree in number, person, and gender.)

a. Use a singular pronoun to refer to such antecedents as *each, either, neither, one, anyone, anybody, everyone, everybody, somebody, another, nobody,* and *a person.*

> *One* of the rowboats is missing *its* (not *their*) oars.

Note: When *a person* or *everyone* is used to refer to both sexes or either sex, the masculine pronouns (used in a universal sense to mean *mankind)* are preferred over the optional *his* or *her.*

> *A person* must learn to wait *his* turn. (preferred)
> *A person* must learn to wait *his* or *her* turn. (awkward)
> Those writers who find neither of the above choices acceptable may choose to avoid the problem by rewriting the sentence: *People* must learn to wait *their* turn. (rewritten)

b. Two or more antecedents joined by *and* are considered plural; two or more antecedents joined by *or* or *nor* are referred to by a singular pronoun.

> *Tom* and *Bob* are finishing *their* writing assignments.
> Either *Connie* or *Sue* left *her* coat in the library.

Note: If one of the antecedents is masculine and one feminine, the pronouns should likewise be masculine and feminine.

> Is either *Dave* or *Phyllis* bringing *his* or *her* frisbee?

Note: If one of the antecedents joined by *or* or *nor* is singular and one is plural, the pronoun is made to agree with the nearer antecedent.

> Neither the *manager* nor the *players* were willing to wear *their* new polka-dot uniforms.

320 A **fragment** is a group of words used as a sentence. It is not a sentence, though, since it lacks a subject, a verb, or some other essential part which causes it to be an incomplete thought. (See 82-90.)

Fragment: The Wonewoc-Center basketball team. (This phrase lacks a verb.)
Sentence: The Wonewoc-Center basketball team won.
Fragment: Every time I get ready to go hiking. (This clause lacks a subject and a verb which are needed to complete the thought of what happens "every time I get ready to go hiking.")
Sentence: Every time I get ready to go hiking, it rains.
Fragment: Running to catch the train. He tripped on his suitcase. (This is a fragment followed by a sentence. This error can be corrected by combining the fragment with the sentence.)
Sentence: Running to catch the train, he tripped on his suitcase.

321 A **comma splice** is a mistake made when two independent clauses are *spliced* together with only a comma.

Incorrect: The concert crowd had been waiting in the hot sun for two hours, many of the people were beginning to show their impatience by chanting and clapping (comma splice).
Corrected: The concert crowd had been waiting in the hot sun for two hours. Many of the people were beginning to show their impatience by chanting and clapping. (The comma splice here is corrected by changing the comma to a period.)
Corrected: The concert crowd had been waiting in the hot sun for two hours, and many of the people were beginning to show their impatience by chanting and clapping. (The comma splice here is corrected by adding the coordinating conjunction *and.* See 135.)
Corrected: The concert crowd had been waiting in the hot sun for two hours; many of the people were beginning to show their impatience by chanting and clapping. (The comma splice here is corrected by changing the comma to a semicolon. See 149.)

A comma splice can be corrected by rearranging the ideas in a sentence.

Incorrect: One of the players stands in front of the net and tries to keep the puck out, he is called the goalie.

Corrected: One of the players, called the goalie, stands in front of the net and tries to keep the puck out.

The problem can also be solved by adding a needed word(s).

Incorrect: Everyone must leave the building when the fire alarm rings, you never know when the alarm is for a real fire.

Corrected: Everyone must leave the building when the fire alarm rings, *since* you never know when the alarm is for a real fire.

322 Shift in construction is a change in the structure or style midway through a sentence.

Shift in number: When *a person* goes shopping for a used car, *he* or *she* (not *they*) must be careful not to get a lemon.

Shift in tense: The trunk should be checked to see that it *contains* a jack and a spare tire which *are* (not *were*) in good shape.

Shift in person: *One* must be careful to watch for heavy, white exhaust or *one* (not *you*) can end up with real engine problems.

Shift in voice: As you continue to look for the right car (active voice), many freshly painted ones will be seen (passive voice).

Corrected: You will see many freshly painted cars as you look for the right used car. (Both verbs are in the active voice. *Note:* Use the active rather than the passive voice in most writing.)

323 Redundancy is the unnecessary repeating of a word or a synonym.

Redundant: He had *a way* of keeping my attention by *the way* he raised and lowered his *voice* for *every single* word he *spoke*. (Needless repetition includes: *a way/the way; voice/spoke; every/single*.)

Double subject: Some *people they* don't use their voices as well as they could. (Drop *they*, since *people* is the only subject needed.)

Tautology: *widow woman, descend down, audible to the ear* (Each phrase says the same thing twice.)

324 Misplaced modifiers are modifiers which have been placed incorrectly; therefore, the meaning of the sentence is not clear.

Misplaced: We have an assortment of combs for active people with unbreakable teeth. *(People with unbreakable teeth?)*

Corrected: For active people, we have an assortment of combs with unbreakable teeth.

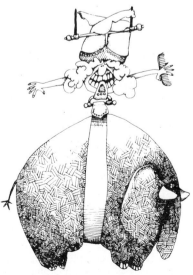

We have an assortment of combs for active people with unbreakable teeth.

325 **Dangling modifiers** are modifiers which appear to modify a word which isn't in the sentence. (Sometimes, they also appear to modify the wrong word *in* the sentence.)

Dangling: Swimming in the lake, Bill's mother called him. (There is nothing for the phrase *Swimming in the lake* to modify.)

Corrected: Swimming in the lake, Bill heard his mother call him. (Here the phrase modifies *Bill.)*

Dangling: After standing in line for five hours, the manager announced that all the tickets had been sold. (In this sentence, it appears as if the manager had been *standing in line for five hours.)*

Corrected: After standing in line for five hours, he heard the manager announce that all the tickets had been sold. (Now the phrase clearly modifies the person who has been standing in line: *he.)*

326 **Inconsistent (Unparallel) construction** is a change in the structure of the words being used.

Inconsistent: In my hometown, the people pass the time shooting bow, pitching horseshoes, and at softball games. (The change in word structure is from the *ing* words, *shooting* and *pitching,* to *at softball games.)*

Corrected: In my hometown, the people pass the time shooting bow, pitching horseshoes, and playing softball. (Now all three things being discussed are *ing* words—they are now **consistent** or **parallel**.)

327 **Ambiguous wording** is confusing because there are two possible meanings.

Ambiguous: Mike took Vince to the show, which proved to be a big success. (What proved to be a big success, Mike's taking Vince to the show or the show?)

Corrected: Mike's taking Vince to the show proved to be a big success.

Ambiguous: As he pulled his car up to the service window, it made a strange rattling sound. (Which *rattled,* the car or the window?)

Corrected: His car made a strange rattling sound as he pulled up to the service window.

328 **Awkward interruptions** or **split constructions** result when a word or phrase is placed in the middle of the main thought rather than before or after the main thought.

Awkward: You can pick up *this Friday* the film you left for developing.

Corrected: This Friday you can pick up the film you left for developing.

Awkward: Ken paid *even though he didn't have to* for our dinner.

Corrected: Ken paid for our dinner even though he didn't have to.

Corrected: Even though he didn't have to, Ken paid for our dinner.

329 **Period faults (Dick and Jane sentences)** are characterized by an overuse of periods; this results in many short, choppy sentences.

Ineffective: Bowling is a good winter sport. It is good exercise. It doesn't cost that much and it is a game of skill. I bowl a lot in the winter, but not so much in the summer.

Corrected: I like bowling because it is an inexpensive game of skill which provides a good deal of exercise even in the winter.

330 **Vague** or **split reference** occurs when the word being referred to is unclear.

Vague: I pulled a thin branch from a willow tree to which I tied my fishing line.

Corrected: I tied my fishing line to a thin branch which I pulled from a willow tree.

331 **Run-on sentences (fused sentences)** are the result of inadequate punctuation.

Run-on: Mrs. Johnson does not hire the typists she supervises them.

Corrected: Mrs. Johnson does not hire the typists; she supervises them.

Comma splice: Mrs. Johnson does not hire the typists, she supervises them.

Corrected: Mrs. Johnson does not hire the typists, *although* she supervises them.

332 **Word omission** is the result of leaving out necessary words in a sentence.

Telegraphic:	Writing is important. Should try to improve. Many people don't.
Corrected:	Writing is an important skill which everyone should try to improve, though many people don't.
Incomplete comparison:	I get along better with Jim than my sister. (Are you saying that you get along better with Jim than you do your sister? Or that you get along better with Jim than your sister does?)
Corrected:	I get along better with Jim than I do my sister.
Omitted preposition:	Peggy arrived January 1 at Billy Mitchell Field.
Corrected:	Peggy arrived *on* January 1 at Billy Mitchell Field.

333 **Mixed construction** results when a writer begins a sentence with one plan of construction but switches to another approach midway through the sentence.

Mixed:	A folk guitar is when you have a hollow body and no electrical pickup built in. (An object should not be described as a condition: *when.*)
Corrected:	A folk guitar has a hollow body and no electrical pickup.
Mixed:	The reason he forgot his assignment was because he cut class.
Corrected:	He forgot his assignment because he cut class.

334 **Split infinitive** results when the words which make up an infinitive are separated by one or more other words. *(Note:* It is sometimes necessary to split an infinitive to preserve the rhythm and balance of a sentence.)

Split:	I try to *not* think about it.
Corrected:	I try not to think about it.

335 **Anticlimax** is the term for a sentence which begins with the most important item (climax) and moves to the least important.

Anticlimax:	The flood left a path of death, disease, and destruction.
Corrected:	The flood left a path of destruction, disease, and death.

336 **Deadwood** is unnecessary wording. (Qualifiers such as *rather, little,* and *very* are usually unnecessary.)

Wordy:	At this point in time, I feel the study needs further investigation before it will be in readiness for resubmittal for consideration.
Corrected:	The study needs more work.

337 **Flowery language** is the result of using more or bigger words than needed. It is writing which often contains too many adjectives or adverbs.

Flowery:	The cool, fresh breeze, which came like a storm in the night, lifted me to the exhilarating heights from which I had been previously suppressed by the incandescent cloud in the learning center.
Corrected:	The cool breeze was a surprising and refreshing change from the muggy classroom air.

338 **Flat expression** is language which is either overused or not very descriptive; it is dull and ineffective. (Use vivid, specific words in your descriptive writing.)

Trite:	On this memorable occasion, it gives me a great deal of pleasure to look out on this sea of faces and promise to fight to the bitter end, which goes without saying.
Dead metaphor:	He was a pillar in the community.
Euphemism:	I am so exasperated that I could expectorate.
Corrected:	I am so mad, I could spit.
Jargon:	It might well appear to the man on the street that the diplomatic ties between the White House and the Kremlin are, for the present, stable. Only time will tell. (This is an example of broadcast jargon. There are many other types.)
Corrected:	Russia and the United States are still on fairly good terms.

339 Substandard (nonstandard) language is language which is often acceptable in everyday conversation, but never in formal writing.

> **Colloquial:** Avoid the use of colloquial language such as *go with.*
> Can I *go with?* (Substandard) Can I *go with you?* (Standard)
>
> **Double preposition:** Avoid the use of certain double prepositions: *off of, off to, in on.*
> I am going to start *in on* my homework. (Substandard)
> I am going to start *on* my homework. (Standard)
>
> **Substitution:** Avoid substituting *and* for *to* in formal writing.
> Try *to* (not *and*) get here on time. (Standard)
> Avoid substituting *of* for *have* when combining with *could, would, should,* or *might.*
> I should *have* (not *of*) studied for that test. (Standard)
>
> **Slang:** Avoid the use of slang or any *in* words.

340 Paraphrasing a speaker is usually not as clear as quoting a speaker. (A **paraphrase** is the writer's summary of the speaker's words.)

> **Paraphrased:** Jane explained to Jean that her new fireplace was a beautiful addition to the house. (Whose new fireplace? Jane's or Jean's?)
>
> **Quoted:** "Your new fireplace is a beautiful addition to the house," Jane explained to Jean.

341 Indefinite reference results from careless use of pronouns.

> **Indefinite:** *It* is an interesting story and *she* does a good job of telling about all of *their* problems.
>
> **Corrected:** *To Kill a Mockingbird* is an interesting story in which Harper Lee tells of the problems faced by Atticus Finch and his family.

342 And-and construction is brought about by the overuse of the word *and.*

> **And-and:** Judy spends her time sewing, and she likes to give parties, and she likes to travel.
>
> **Corrected:** Judy spends her time sewing, giving parties, and traveling.

343 Upside-down subordination occurs when the main idea of a sentence is expressed in the dependent clause or phrase rather than in the independent clause.

> **Upside-down:** As the lightning struck, Joe was putting his bike in the garage.
>
> **Corrected:** As Joe was putting his bike in the garage, the lightning struck.

344 Double negative is a sentence which contains two negative words. Because two negatives make a positive, this type of sentence usually takes on a meaning opposite of what is intended.

> **Confusing:** I haven't got no money. (This actually says—after taking out the two negatives which are now a positive—*I have got money.*)
>
> **Corrected:** I haven't got any money *or* I have no money.

Note: Do not use *hardly, barely,* or *scarcely* with a negative; the result is a double negative.

The centipede could *not hardly* keep his toenails clean.

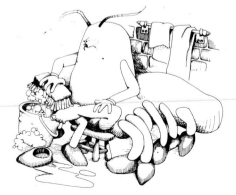

56

The Paragraph

345 A **paragraph** is a series of sentences developing one topic. Each paragraph contains a sentence which states the topic of the paragraph; that is, it tells you what that particular paragraph is about. This sentence is called the **topic sentence** and is usually found at or near the beginning of a paragraph.

346 Every sentence in a paragraph should be closely related to this topic sentence. This brings a sense of **unity** to the paragraph. Note how the bold-faced sentence in the paragraph below does not relate to the topic sentence and should *not*, therefore, be included in this paragraph. The topic sentence is italicized and does represent an acceptable topic sentence for that paragraph.

The announcement of the cancellation was all the rockfest crowd needed to turn into a frenzied mob. The entire audience of sun-baked fans rose out of disbelief and moved in the direction of the speaker. Those nearest the stage pushed forward and as if by instinct began tearing the canvas drapes from the side of the makeshift platform. The stage suddenly came alive as people poured on it from all directions. **The group scheduled to appear was the hottest name in the business.** It was soon a stage no longer, but a swarming mass of destruction. The curtains came ripping to the ground and the speaker stands fell like goalposts after a championship game. Those who had been sitting and watching were now drawn irresistibly into the chaos. No semblance of order remained.

Writing the Basic Paragraph

347 The key to writing good paragraphs is writing good topic sentences. It is the topic sentence which limits your subject and makes clear your feelings or impressions about it. In other words, a good topic sentence reveals what your subject is and what it is you plan to say about that subject. Below is a sample topic sentence and a simple formula to remember when writing topic sentences:

Music helps people relax.

Formula: A limited topic (*Music*) + a specific impression (*helps people relax*) = a good topic sentence.

Once you have a good topic sentence, you must gather a number of interesting details and arrange them into the best possible order (by location, time, importance, etc.). Next, work your details into well-worded sentences, writing as naturally as you can. Try to write in such a way that you feel comfortable with the words. Bring your personality and feelings to your writing. Give it a style and a flavor that is your own.

If the sentences which follow your topic sentence flow naturally and work together well, they will create a paragraph which is easy to read. Often sentences will simply fall into place as you write, and you will need to do nothing more than record them on paper. Other times, the sentences will not go together as well. When this happens, you should consult the list of "Useful Transitions and Linking Expressions" (351.5). These expressions will help tie words, phrases, and sentences together when they cannot make this connection on their own. The specific word or expression you choose will depend upon the paragraph you are writing and the kinds of details you are using to develop that paragraph.

Once you have arranged all of your sentences into a natural, logical order, it is time to add a concluding sentence to your paragraph. The concluding or clincher sentence serves two basic functions: it ties together all the details in the paragraph and draws attention to the message or impression you are trying to communicate. It gives you one last chance to help your reader see the overall picture.

348 There are four basic **types** of paragraphs: **narrative, descriptive, expository,** and **persuasive.**

A **narrative** paragraph is one which contains events in the order in which they happen, as with a story. (See "Guidelines for Describing an Event," 366e.)

> In first grade I learned some of the harsh realities of life. I found out that circuses aren't all they're supposed to be. We were going to the circus for our class trip, and I was really excited about it because I had never been to one before. Our class worked for weeks on a circus train made of shoe boxes, and Carrie Kaske told me her mom had fainted once when she saw the lion trainer. The day of the trip finally came, and my wonderful circus turned out to be nothing but one disappointment after another. I couldn't see why Carrie's mom fainted when she saw the lion trainer; I couldn't even see the lion trainer. I couldn't see much of anything for that matter. I could just barely make out some tiny figures scurrying around in the three rings that seemed to be a hundred miles away from my seat. After the first half hour, all I wanted to do was buy a Pepsi and a monkey-on-a-stick and get out of there. Of course, nothing in life is that easy. We weren't allowed to buy anything; so I couldn't have my souvenir, and instead of a cold Pepsi to quench my thirst, I had warm, curdled milk that the room mothers had so thoughtfully brought along. I returned to school tired and a little wiser. I remembered looking at our little circus train on the window ledge and thinking that I'd rather sit and watch it do nothing than go to another circus.

A **descriptive** paragraph is one in which the sentences work together to present a single, clear picture of a person, place, thing, or idea. (See "Guidelines for Describing a Person, . . . Place, . . . Object," 366a, b,. and c.)

> My Uncle John is normally a likable and friendly man, but when there is a group of people and one of those instant cameras around, he becomes a real pest. No matter what the occasion, even something as uneventful as a few of our relatives getting together for a visit after work, Uncle John appoints himself official photographer. He spends the whole time with one eye looking through the lens and the other scoping out the potential subjects for his pictures. In most situations, taking pictures is a great way to spend some time and have a little fun, but when Uncle John is pushing the button, it's quite another story. He doesn't believe in candids. Instead, Uncle John insists upon interrupting all activity to persuade his prey to pose for his pictures. In return, he gets photographs of people arranged in neat rows smiling through clenched teeth. Although we have tried again and again to convince Uncle John that his old, traditional methods of photography aren't necessarily the best, he continues to insist that we, "Come over here, so I can take your picture." About the only solution is to convince Uncle John that he should be in some of these pictures and that you'd be happy to snap a few. Then once you get the camera in your hands don't stop shooting until all the film is gone.

An **expository** paragraph is one which presents facts, gives directions, interprets facts, defines terms, and so on. This type of writing is factual and statistical; it is used when you wish to present or explain facts or ideas.

> Braille is a system of communication used by the blind. It was developed by Louis Braille, a blind French student, in 1824. The code consists of an alphabet using combinations of small raised dots. The dots are imprinted on paper and can be felt, and thus read, by running the fingers across the page. The basic unit of the code is called a "cell" which is two dots wide and three dots high. Each letter is formed by different combinations of these dots. Numbers, punctuation marks, and even a system for writing music are also expressed by using different arrangements. The small dots, which may seem insignificant to the sighted, have opened up the entire world of books and reading for the blind.

A **persuasive** paragraph is one which presents information to support or prove a point. It expresses an opinion and tries to convince the reader that that opinion is correct or valid. (See "Guidelines for Persuasive Writing," 366h, and "Using Evidence and Logic," 669.)

> Capital punishment should be abolished for three major reasons. First, common sense tells me that two wrongs don't make a right. To kill someone convicted of murder contradicts the reasoning behind the law that taking another's life is wrong. The state is committing the same violent act that it is condemning. Second, the death penalty is not an effective deterrent. Numerous studies show that murder is usually the result of a complex psychological and sociological problem and that most killers do not contemplate the consequences of their act; or if they do, any penalty is seen as a far-off possibility. The gain from the offense, on the other hand, brings immediate gratification. The third and most serious objection is that death is final and cannot be altered. Errors in deciding guilt or innocence will always be present in our system of trial by jury. There is too great a risk that innocent people will be put to death. For those three reasons, capital punishment should be replaced with a system that puts all doubt on the side of life—not death.

349 You can supply details for your paragraphs through three ways of thinking about something: **sensory, memory,** and **reflective.**

Sensory refers to details which come to you through the senses (smell, touch, taste, hearing, and sight):

> I could feel the warmth of the kerosene stove and smell its penetrating odor even before I opened the squeaky door leading to his third-floor apartment.

Memory refers to details which you recall:

> I can remember as a kid walking the noisy, wooden stairway to his attic room and how he was always waiting at the half-opened door to take the newspaper from my shaking hand.

Reflective refers to details which you wonder about (wish, hope, dream, wonder, if only, etc.):

> I wonder if he ever knew how frightened I was then and how I imagined there to be all varieties of evil on the other side of that half-opened door—beyond the kerosene stove.

350 Paragraphs can be developed with one of several different methods of **arrangement**:

Chronological (time) **order** is an arrangement of details in the order in which they happen, as in the paragraph which follows:

General Sherman and his men devised ingenious methods for the wrecking of the Southern railroads. They first used a portable rail-lifter which consisted of a chain with a hook on one end and a large iron ring on the other. The hook would be placed under the rail and a small pole put through the ring. By bracing the pole on the ground, a group of soldiers could lift the rail from the ties. The rails, which were made of a flimsy type of steel, could be heated and easily twisted into almost any shape. Initially, Sherman and his men took the heated rails and twisted them around nearby trees into what they called "Sherman's hairpins." After it was pointed out that the Confederates might be able to straighten these rails and use them again, Sherman's men devised a new system. They again heated the rails, but this time they used huge wrenches on either end and twisted in opposite directions. This left a useless, licorice-shaped rail.

Order of location is an arrangement of details according to where those details are located *(above, below, alongside, beneath, left, right,* etc.).

Order of importance is an arrangement in which the most important details are emphasized by being listed first (or last), and the other details are arranged around them.

A **cause and effect arrangement** contains a general statement giving a cause of a problem or situation and a number of statements expressing the specific effects. (The general statement can also be an effect supported by a number of specific causes.)

A **comparison** is an arrangement of details in which the subject is explained to the reader by showing how the subject is similar to another, more familiar subject. **Contrast** uses details which show how the subject is different from another, more familiar subject.

Definition or **classification** is an arrangement which is useful when explaining a term or concept (machine, theory, game, etc.). The writer begins by placing the subject in the appropriate species or class and then providing details which show how that term or concept is different from others in the same class. (See "Guidelines for Writing a Definition," 366d.)

Illustration *(general to specific)* is an arrangement of details in which the general idea being written about is stated first in the paragraph (topic sentence). Specific reasons, examples, facts, and other details are then added which illustrate or support the general statement.

Climax *(specific to general)* is an arrangement of specific details followed by the general statement or conclusion which can be drawn from the specific information provided.

351   **Paragraph coherence** (sticking together) is achieved through several basic techniques:
1) **Use a logical method of sentence arrangement.** (350)
2) **Use pronouns to refer back to previous sentences.** (346: *those, it*)
3) **Use repetition of words, synonyms, or ideas.** (350: repetition of *rail;* 353: repetition of *cold* synonyms)
4) **Use parallel structure.** (364: paragraph three)
5) **Use transitional words.** (See "Useful Transitions and Linking Expressions.")

352   **Sentence variety** is essential to a well-developed, creative paragraph. There are several ways in which variety can be achieved. (See also the "Guidelines for Writing Sentences," 316.)
1) **Vary the length** of your sentences so that you have a combination of all sizes. Short, concise sentences, for example, are appropriate for adding feeling or dramatic effect. They are effective, though, only when contrasted with longer, more complex sentences.

Useful Transitions and Linking Expressions

Transitions which can be used to **show location:**

above	among	beneath	in front of	on top of
across	around	beside	inside	outside
against	away from	between	into	over
along	back of	beyond	near	throughout
alongside	behind	by	off	to the right
amid	below	down	onto	under

Transitions which can be used to **show time:**

about	first	until	soon	then
after	second	meanwhile	later	next
at	third	today	afterward	in the meantime
before	prior to	tomorrow	immediately	as soon as
during	till	yesterday	finally	when
		next week		

Transitions which can be used to **compare two things:**

in the same way	likewise	as
also	like	similarly

Transitions which can be used to **contrast things** (show differences):

but	yet	on the other hand	although	otherwise
however	in the meantime	still	even though	counter to
even so	nevertheless	on the contrary	conversely	as opposed

Transitions which can be used to **emphasize a point:**

again	indeed	for this reason	truly
to repeat	with this in mind	in fact	to emphasize

Transitions which can be used to **conclude or summarize:**

as a result	consequently	accordingly	in short
finally	thus	due to	to sum up
in conclusion	therefore	in summary	all in all

Transitions which can be used to **add information:**

again	and	furthermore	next
also	besides	likewise	finally
additionally	equally important	moreover	as well
in addition	for example	further	together with
another	for instance	furthermore	along with

Transitions which can be used to **clarify:**

that is	put another way	to clarify
in other words	stated differently	for instance

2) **Vary your sentence beginnings.** Rather than beginning each sentence with the subject, use modifiers, phrases, and clauses in that position.

> *Tired* and *weary,* Jeff collapsed onto the couch. (**modifiers**)
> *Too tired to stand,* Jeff collapsed onto the couch. (**phrase**)
> *Because he was totally exhausted,* Jeff collapsed onto the couch. (**clause**)

3) **Vary the arrangement** of the material within the sentence. There are three basic classifications of sentence arrangement: **periodic, balanced,** and **loose.**

A **periodic sentence** is a sentence in which the main thought is not complete until the end of the sentence. (This delaying of the main idea can give a sentence added force or impact.)

> Following his mother's repeated threats of his being grounded for life, Jeff decided to clean his room.

A **balanced sentence** contains two parts which are similar in construction. Usually each part expresses an idea which compares or contrasts to the other.

> Jeff was not especially excited about cleaning his room, but neither was he excited about being grounded for life.

A **loose sentence** is one in which the main thought is expressed before the end of the sentence. (Caution: Overuse of loose sentences can lead to a rambling, weakened style.)

> Jeff decided to clean his room after listening to repeated threats from his mother about being grounded for life.

4) **Vary the kinds** of sentences you use. (See 87-90.)

> Of all the things a student needs to make it through a typical day, probably the most important, yet least recognized, is paper. (*Complex*) Paper is used for academic, social, and personal purposes by nearly all students. (*Simple*) The most obvious use is for the academic or classroom assignment, whether it comes in the form of a test, an essay, or a summary of plant life on Easter Island. (*Complex*) The social uses of paper center around "the note," which any student can tell you is as important a part of a student's social life as the Junior Prom. (*Complex*) As for the personal applications, there is *doodling* for the nervous mind, and there is *scrunching* for the nervous hand. (*Compound*) The more traditional paper airplanes and spitwads are still around, but they seem to be less popular than in days gone by—probably because it is easier for a student to move freely about the classroom today than it used to be. (*Compound-Complex*) In any case, there can be no doubt that paper is just as important—Bryan, may I borrow a piece of paper to finish my paragraph?—as ever to the high school student whose day would be a waste without it. (*Compound-Complex*)

353 Use **synonyms** to avoid redundancy (boring repetition). One of the best ways to break the habit of using the same words over and over is through the use of a **thesaurus.** (See 492 and 442.) This reference book, which is a dictionary of synonyms and antonyms, can provide the help needed to avoid monotonous repetition. Note the change in tone of the paragraph below after the redundant words (in italics) have been replaced or eliminated:

> January in Wisconsin can be bitter cold. The *coldness* (temperature) often drops to 20 and 30 degrees below zero. *That's cold!* (eliminate altogether) It is so *cold* (frigid) at times that you can't go outside for fear of *having some real problems with the cold hurting your hands or face* (frostbite). On these *really cold* (benumbing) days, people are warned against traveling except for an emergency. If the *cold* (arctic-like condition) continues for more than a couple days, almost all traffic stops since you cannot trust your car to run—even if it does start. Too often a car will stall in the middle of nowhere, leaving a traveler stranded in the *extreme cold* (frozen air). About the only way to beat the incredible *cold* (keep as is to draw the paragraph together) of a Wisconsin winter is to huddle around the fireplace and dream of the warm, sunny days of summer.

Whole Composition: The Essay

354   Once you are able to build good paragraphs, you are well on your way to being able to build good essays or other longer compositions. The essay has the same basic characteristics as a paragraph: it has a single controlling idea or theme, it uses a variety of details to develop that idea, and all of the individual details are tied or linked together into an effective, unified whole.

355   However, the essay is not the same as a paragraph. It is longer, more complex, and it covers a larger portion of the subject than does a paragraph. It requires that a good deal of special attention be given to transitions and linking devices. This must be done to assure the sense of wholeness or oneness which is characteristic of all good composition. Because the essay is more complicated than the paragraph, it is usually a good idea to organize your thoughts into an outline. In other words, the essay must be planned and written carefully. Below is a list of eleven steps which can be followed when doing this planning and writing. It might be helpful for you to follow these steps or to adapt them so they better suit your individual needs.

356 Planning and Writing the Composition

1. Select a general subject area, preferably one which interests you.
2. List all of your initial thoughts or ideas about the subject.
3. Use your list to help you focus in on a specific topic within the subject area.
4. Determine what it is you would like to say about this topic and write a tentative statement which reflects this purpose. (This statement is sometimes called a *thesis statement.*)
5. Work up a list of details which can be used to support your thesis statement.
6. Arrange this list of details into a well-ordered outline. (See 357-359.)
7. Do any reading, researching, or thinking necessary to provide additional support for specific areas of your outline.
8. Write the first draft of your paper.
9. Revise the first draft, paying special attention to your introductory and concluding paragraphs, as well as to transitions between all of your paragraphs. (Check "The Sentence" sections, 316-344, for help with additional sentences.)
10. Proofread your revised paper *twice:* once for spelling, punctuation, usage, and other mechanical errors and a second time for meaning and overall effectiveness. (Use the "Checklist for Revising and Proofreading," p.66, for a complete list of things to look for when proofreading.)
11. Type or write (in ink) your final copy

The Outline

357   An **outline** is an orderly arrangement of related ideas. It is a *sketch* of what the final composition will look like; it is a *guide* which keeps the writer on the right path; it is a *blueprint* which makes clear where each piece of information belongs. An outline must be flexible in the planning stage so as to allow for needed changes; yet, it must also be rigid enough to keep the writer from wandering off the topic. In the planning stages, your outline should be a changing, **working outline**; in its final form, your outline should be a permanent guide to your completed composition.

  The details in an outline should be listed from general to specific. (The following details are listed from general to more specific: transportation, motor vehicle, car, Ford, Mustang.) This means that the general topic of your writing (*thesis statement*) is listed first, followed by the major subtopics and the supporting details and examples. If, for instance, you were assigned to write a paper about the subject of "Trees," you might choose to write about "Trees used in landscaping" (*topic*). In the planning of your paper, you might decide to divide your topic into "Trees used for landscaping in cold climates" and "Trees used for landscaping in warm climates" (*subtopics*). You might then further divide your subtopics into the different kinds of trees suitable in each climate (*supporting details*). To complete your outline, you could list specific examples of each kind of tree (*specific examples*). It is important to remember that each additional division in an outline must contain information which is more specific than the division before it. (See the sample outline below.)

Outlining Details — General to Specific

Subject: Trees

I. **Topic**	I. Many trees can be used for landscaping.
A. **Subtopic**	A. Some trees are best suited for cold climates.
1. **Supporting detail**	1. Evergreens are hardy and provide year-round color.
a. **Specific example**	a. Norway pine...
b. **Specific example**	b. Scotch pine...
2. **Supporting detail**	2. Maples hold up well and provide brilliant seasonal color.
a. **Specific example**	a. Red maple...
b. **Specific example**	b. Silver maple...
B. **Subtopic**	B. Some trees are better suited for warm climates.

358 A **topic outline** is a listing of the *topics* to be covered in a piece of writing; it contains no specific details. Topics are stated in words and phrases rather than complete sentences. This makes the topic outline useful for short compositions, especially those for which little time is available as on an essay test. It is always a good idea to begin your outlining task by placing your *thesis statement* or controlling idea at the top of your paper. This will serve as a reminder of the specific topic you are going to be outlining and later writing about. Use the standard format shown below for labeling the lines of your outline. Do not attempt to outline your introduction or conclusion unless specifically told to do so.

Thesis statement: America's supply of resources is vast, but not unlimited, as shown in the energy crisis of 1973. (See essay: 364.)

Outline Format	I. A. B. 1. 2. a. b. (1) (2) (a) (b) II.	Topic Outline

		Introduction
		 I. Gasoline shortage
		   A. Long lines
		   B. Gas "rationing"
		   C. Station closings
		 II. Voluntary energy conservation
		   A. Gasoline
		   B. Electricity
		   C. Home heating fuel
		 III. Forced energy conservation
		   A. Fuel allocation
		   B. Speed limit .
		   C. Airline flights
		   D. Christmas lighting
		 Conclusion

Note: No new subdivision should be started unless there are at least two points to be listed in that new division. This means that each *1* must have a *2;* each *a* must be followed by a *b.*

359 The **sentence outline** contains not only the major points to be covered, but also lists many of the important supporting details as well. It is used for longer, more formal writing assignments; each point must, therefore, be set forth as a complete sentence. The sentence outline is especially useful when you find yourself asking others for help with your composition. It is much easier to understand an outline written in complete sentences than one written using single words and phrases. (See essay: 364.)

Sentence Outline	I. In the summer of 1973, gasoline was in short supply.
	  A. Long lines of cars at the pumps became a familiar sight.
	  B. Some stations "rationed" their gasoline.
	  C. Other stations closed early.
	II. The Arab oil boycott forced additional cutbacks in energy use.
	  A. Many Americans turned down their home thermostats.
	  B. Some businesses shortened working hours to conserve.
	  C. Unnecessary lighting and driving were cut.
	III. Late in 1973, new laws were passed to assure energy savings.
	  A. The amount of fuel available for heating was reduced.
	  B. A fifty-mile-per-hour speed limit took effect for all states.
	  C. Airline flights were cut back.
	  D. Outdoor Christmas lighting was banned.

360 Once you are satisfied that your essay topic is well organized (outlined), you can begin writing your **introductory paragraph.** Your opening paragraph must state the topic of the essay (thesis statement), gain the attention of the reader, and allow for a smooth transition into the body of the essay. There are several techniques or devices which you can use to develop this introductory paragraph:
- a series of questions about the topic
- an interesting story or anecdote about the subject
- a startling or unusual fact or figure
- a reference to a famous person or place associated with the topic
- a quotation from a well-known figure or literary work
- a definition of an important, topic-related term

361 The **developmental paragraphs** are the heart of the essay. They must be developed and arranged in a logical, yet interesting, way. If, for instance, you are going to explain the process of carving a figure from a bar of soap, you will most likely use a step-by-step explanation. Your developmental paragraphs will naturally follow one another from the beginning of the explanation through the last step in the carving process. At the same time, you cannot let the explanation become so matter-of-fact that the reader loses interest in it. You might call upon some additional sensory thinking (349) to make the paragraphs vivid and colorful as well as accurate. (*Note:* The same methods of arrangement (350) which are used for the single paragraph can also be used to arrange details in developmental paragraphs.)

A new paragraph is started whenever there is a shift or change in the essay topic. This change is called a paragraph shift and can take place for any of six basic reasons:

1) a change in emphasis or ideas 4) a change in speakers
2) a change in time   5) a change in place or setting
3) a change in action   6) to break up an exceptionally long paragraph

Each new paragraph should begin with a sentence which either serves as a transition or states a new or additional step in the development of the essay topic.

362 The concluding or summary paragraph should tie all of the important points in the essay together and draw a final conclusion for the reader. It should leave the reader with a clear understanding of the meaning and the significance of the essay.

363 Proofread and revise your paper carefully. Check all of your paragraphs for effective links. Each paragraph should be linked or tied to the paragraph before and after it. You can use many of the same devices to link the paragraphs in an essay as you did to link the sentences in a paragraph. (See 351 and 364.) Write your final copy with black or blue ink. Use only one side of your paper; leave a margin of approximately one inch on all sides. Place all essential information (name, subject, date, teacher's name, etc.) in the order and location your teacher requests. (See the checklist which follows.)

Checklist for Revising and Proofreading

Revising Content and Style

1. Read your paper aloud to test for overall sense and sound.

2. Check your sentences for rhythm, balance, and correctness. Is each sentence clear, concise, and colorful? Does each express a complete thought (no fragments)? Is each punctuated as a complete sentence (no comma splices or run-ons)?

3. Have you used a combination of sentence lengths, types, and arrangements? Doing so will add variety and interest to your writing.

4. Check your sentence beginnings. Do not, for example, start sentence after sentence with the subject.

5. Check each *simple sentence* to ensure effective use of prepositional phrases, participial phrases, and appositives.

6. Check each *compound sentence* to make sure it shows the proper relationship between the two ideas expressed. Use the best coordinate conjunction (and, but, or, nor, for, yet, so) for each sentence.

7. Have you used subordination effectively in each of your *complex sentences?* Is the most important idea expressed in the independent clause and the less important ideas in dependent clauses?

8. Locate and replace any words or phrases which are too general or overused to be effective. Use nouns which are specific, adjectives and adverbs which are fresh and colorful, and verbs which are lively and vivid.

9. Make sure your writing is concise. Take out any words, phrases, or ideas which are repeated unnecessarily, which sound flowery, or which pad rather than add to an explanation or description.

10. Replace any words or phrases which may confuse the reader. (See misplaced and dangling modifiers, ambiguous wording, and double negatives.) Also, define any terms which your reader may not understand.

11. Improving the style and clarity of your writing by using a simile, metaphor, or analogy whenever comparing something unfamiliar to something familiar might help the reader. Use repetition or parallel structure to add emphasis to those ideas you feel need more attention.

12. Replace any supporting examples or reasons which do not clearly illustrate or prove the point you are trying to make. Add supporting details wherever they are needed. (Ask when, where, why, how, to what extent, etc. about each of your ideas.)

13. Study each paragraph for overall effectiveness and clarity. Does each paragraph have a clear purpose and focus (topic sentence)? Is each major idea fully developed and supported? Are the details arranged logically? Have you used appropriate transitions within and between paragraphs?

14. Is your writing consistent in tone and structure? Does it sound sincere and natural? Does it accomplish what you set out to accomplish?

Proofreading for Accuracy

1. Check your writing for any words or phrases which may have been left out.

2. Check your writing for spelling, capitalization, and punctuation errors.

3. Review Handbook 212-308. Search for these commonly mixed pairs in your paper and correct any usage errors.

4. Be sure each subject agrees with each verb and each pronoun agrees with its antecedent. (See 318-319.)

5. Follow all the rules and guidelines given to you regarding your final copy. Use the correct paper, margins, and spacing. Always use ink for (or type) your final copy. Keep your paper neat and hand it in on time.

364 Below is a **sample essay** labeled to illustrate introductory, developmental, and concluding paragraphs, as well as transitional and linking devices. (Note that the details in this essay are arranged in chronological order. This arrangement combines with "repetition" to form a series of strong transitions between paragraphs.)

Introductory Paragraph	America had long been a nation of plenty. Even during its bleakest hours, America had always found the resources to keep surging ahead. During the 1960s and early '70s, America was at perhaps an all-time peak—it prospered as never before. More and more Americans enjoyed "all the comforts of home," including their own home. Nearly anything could be purchased on credit, and nearly everyone had plenty of that. No one would have believed it could all change so quickly or so drastically as it did in the summer of 1973. *It was in the summer of that year*
Statement of Topic	*that America saw its* **dream** *of forever being the "land of plenty" slowly dim.*
Transition	It was **early in the summer of '73** that the **first sign of this fading dream appeared.** It appeared in the front windows of gasoline stations across the land: the sign simply read "Closed." Closed for good reason: the product these stations needed to operate was not available—at least not to them. This substance, which had long been cheap and plentiful, was suddenly anything but cheap and even less plentiful. This suddenly rare commodity was gasoline. The gasoline Americans had taken for granted for so long was nothing to take for granted in the summer and fall of 1973. It was often difficult to find and just as difficult to get once you found it. People often waited in block-long lines for an hour or more to get their "ration" of six, eight, or perhaps ten gallons.
Transition	**Later in the year,** it appeared as if even a **six-gallon ration** might be too much to expect. It was in November that the Arab oil-producing nations cut off all oil shipments to the United States because it continued to support Israel in the Middle East war. The supply of gas was immediately at a critical low. The American homeowners responded by voluntarily turning down their thermostats by an average of 2°.
Parallel structure links	American business and labor leaders responded by voluntarily shortening working hours and by cutting back on unnecessary energy use. Unneeded lighting was turned off. Slower driving was encouraged; Sunday driving, discouraged. Still, most Americans felt the gasoline shortage was contrived to drive up prices and that the cries of "**energy crisis**" **were greatly exaggerated.**
Transition	But **then, before the year had ended,** the **reality of the crisis** hit home. A mandatory fuel allocation program was announced to take effect within thirty days. It called for a ten percent cutback in heating fuel for industries, a fifteen percent cutback for homes, and a twenty-five percent cutback for stores and other commercial establishments. It also called for a fifty-mile-per-hour speed limit nationwide. Airline flights were reduced in number, and perhaps most shocking of all, outdoor Christmas lights were banned. In all, Americans were told to reduce their energy consumption by ten percent immediately or the crisis would become a catastrophe. Nearly everyone reduced—a catastrophe was avoided.
Transition	Even though **most Americans still felt** the crisis was only temporary, they came to realize—many of them for the first time—that America was not a land of "unlimited" plenty. There was indeed a limit to the supply of energy products which even America would be allowed
Concluding paragraph	to consume. It was this limit which America had both reached and exceeded in the summer and fall of 1973. In that short, significant time, America had awakened from its dream-like sleep long enough to catch a glimpse of its own future—a future filled with many of the same hopes and dreams it has always had, but one also tempered with the reality of its limitations.

Writing Terms

Argumentation: Writing or speaking in which reasons or arguments are presented in a logical way.

Arrangement: The order in which details are placed or arranged in a piece of writing. (See 350.)

Audience: Those people who read or hear what you have written.

Balance: The arranging of words or phrases so that two ideas are given equal emphasis in a sentence or paragraph; a pleasing rhythm created when a pattern is repeated in a sentence.

Body: The paragraphs between the introduction and conclusion which develop the main idea(s) of the writing.

Brainstorming: Collecting ideas by thinking freely and openly about all the possibilities; used most often with groups.

Central idea: The main point or purpose of a piece of writing, often stated in a thesis statement or topic sentence.

Clincher sentence: The sentence which summarizes the point being made in a paragraph, usually located last.

Coherence: The arrangement of ideas in such a way that the reader can easily follow from one point to the next.

Composition: A process in which several different ideas are combined into one, unified piece of writing.

Data: Information which is accepted as being true—facts, figures, examples—and from which conclusions can be drawn.

Deductive reasoning: The act of reasoning from a general idea to a specific point or conclusion.

Description: Writing which paints a colorful picture of a person, place, thing, or idea using concrete, vivid details. (See 348 and 525.)

Details: The words used to describe a person, convince an audience, explain a process, or in some way support the central idea; to be effective, details should be vivid, colorful, and appeal to the senses.

Emphasis: Placing greater stress on the most important idea in a piece of writing by giving it special treatment; emphasis can be achieved by placing the important idea in a special position, by repeating a key word or phrase, or by simply writing more about this idea than the others.

Essay: A piece of prose writing in which ideas on a single topic are presented, explained, argued, or described in an interesting way.

Exposition: Writing which explains. (See 348.)

Extended definition: Writing which goes beyond a simple definition of a term in order to stress a point; it can cover several paragraphs and include personal definitions and experiences, similes and metaphors, quotations, and even verse.

Figurative language: Language which goes beyond the normal meaning of the words used; writing in which a figure of speech is used to heighten or color the meaning.

Focus: Concentrating on a specific subject to give it emphasis or clarity.

Form: The arrangement of the details into a pattern or style; the way in which the content of writing is organized.

Freewriting: Writing openly and freely on any topic; *focused* freewriting is writing openly on a specific topic.

Generalization: An idea or statement which emphasizes the general characteristics rather than the specific details of a subject.

Grammar: Grammar is the study of the structure and features of a language; it usually consists of rules and standards which are to be followed to produce acceptable writing and speaking.

Idiom: A phrase or expression which means something different from what the words actually say. An idiom is usually understandable to a particular group of people. (Example: *over his head* for *didn't understand*.)

Inductive reasoning: Reasoning which leads one to a conclusion or generalization after examining specific examples or facts; drawing generalizations from specific evidence.

Inverted sentence: A sentence in which the normal word order is inverted or switched; usually the verb comes before the subject.

Issue: A point or question to be decided.

Journal: A daily record of thoughts, impressions, and autobiographical information; a journal is often a source of ideas for writing.

Juxtaposition: Placing two ideas (words or pictures) side by side so that their closeness creates a new, often ironic, meaning.

Limiting the subject: Narrowing the subject to a specific topic which is suitable for the writing or speaking task.

Literal: The actual or dictionary meaning of a word; language which means exactly what it appears to mean.

Loaded words: Words which are slanted for or against the subject.

Logic: The science of correct reasoning; correctly using facts, examples, and reasons to support your point. (See "Fallacies of Thinking," 670.)

Modifier: A word, phrase, or clause which limits or describes another word or group of words. (See *adjective* and *adverb*.)

Narration: Writing which tells a story or recounts an event.

Objective: Relating information in an impersonal manner; without feelings or opinions.

Observation: Paying close attention to people, places, things, and events to collect details for later use.

Overview: A general idea of what is to be covered in a piece of writing.

Personal narrative: Personal writing which covers an event in the writer's life; it often contains personal comments and observations as well as a description of the event.

Persuasion: Writing which is meant to change the way the reader thinks or acts.

Poetic license: The freedom a writer has to bend the rules of writing to achieve a certain effect.

Point of view: The position or angle from which a story is told. (See 616.)

Premise: A statement or point which serves as the basis of a discussion or debate.

Process: A method of doing something which involves several steps or stages; the writing process involves pre-writing, composing, revising, and proofreading.

Prose: Prose is writing or speaking in the usual or ordinary form; prose becomes poetry when it takes on rhyme and rhythm.

Purpose: The specific reason a person has for writing; the goal of writing.

Revision: Changing a piece of writing to improve it in style or content.

Spontaneous: Doing, thinking, or writing without planning. (See 309-312.)

Subjective: Thinking or writing which includes personal feelings, attitudes, and opinions.

Syntax: The order and relationship of words in a sentence.

Theme: The central idea in a piece of writing (lengthy writings may have several themes); a term used to describe a short essay.

Thesis statement: A statement of the purpose, intent, or main idea of an essay.

Topic: The specific subject of a piece of writing.

Topic sentence: The sentence which contains the main idea of a paragraph. (See 345-347.)

Transitions: Words or phrases which help tie ideas together.

Unity: A sense of oneness; writing in which each sentence helps to develop the main idea.

Universal: A topic or idea which applies to everyone.

Usage: The way in which people use language; language is generally considered to be standard (formal and informal) or nonstandard. Only standard usage is acceptable in writing.

Vivid details: Details which appeal to the senses and help the reader see, feel, smell, taste, and hear the subject.

1. Whenever possible, write about someone you know well.

2. Begin gathering details by observing the person you are describing; notice in particular details of personality and character which set your subject apart from other people. (Remember that descriptive writing is based on the writer's careful observation of people, places, things, and events. The better the observing, the better the writing.)

3. List the important physical characteristics, mannerisms, and personality traits, especially those which contribute to making your subject unique.

4. Next, notice the way other people react to your subject. This can tell you a great deal about the kind of person your subject truly is.

5. Ask others about your subject. Often you will be given information and insights you would otherwise never have known existed.

6. Add details about things your subject has said or done in the past. Try to recall at least one specific incident which reveals something interesting about your subject.

7. Finally, interview the subject. Get his or her reactions to the information you have collected and the observations you have made. Quote your subject directly whenever possible; summarize when quoting directly isn't possible or desirable. (Read about your subject if he or she is well known.)

8. After you have collected as many details as you feel you will need, decide what overall impression your subject has made on you. Work this impression into a *topic sentence* or *thesis statement* and list the points you plan to cover beneath it. This list can serve as a working outline for your description.

9. If you begin your description with your topic sentence, it should be well worded so that it creates interest in your subject and helps the reader to immediately "picture" the person you are describing. You may choose to begin your description with an incident or story about your subject and place your topic sentence after it.

10. Each of the sentences which follow must support this central impression. Each sentence should flow naturally from the others as it would if you were simply talking to another person about your subject. (See "Useful Transitions," 351.5.)

11. As you write, remember that effective description requires the use of specific, vivid details. This is the only way you will be able to convey a precise, memorable picture to the reader. Use similes and metaphors to compare your subject to someone or something well known.

12. Avoid the use of **cliches** or **overused expressions**:

autumn of his years	graceful as a swan	runs like a deer
bull in a china shop	heart of gold	sings like a bird
busy as a bee (beaver)	memory of an elephant	sly as a fox
chip off the old block	mind like a sponge	strong as an ox
doesn't pull any punches	quiet as a mouse	stubborn as a mule
fish out of water	red as a beet	stuck-up

13. End your description with an appropriate closing statement, one which reminds your reader what it is that makes your subject unique and worth knowing.

Topics: Describing a Person

I know an interesting person who . . .

is clever/funny	is a living legend	is a little weird	is the ultimate fan
is stubborn	is always happy	is always in trouble	is always upset
is helpful/kind	is everyone's friend	is afraid of nothing	is always talking
is very talented	is very patriotic	is a perfectionist	is always in a panic
is phony	is a complainer	is always around	is always collecting

1. Whenever possible, write about a place you know well or one which left an impression on you.

2. Begin gathering details by observing the place you are describing; notice those physical characteristics which set your subject apart from other places. (Remember that descriptive writing is based on the writer's careful observation of people, places, things, and events. The better the observing, the better the writing.)

3. List the important feelings, events, and people that contribute to making this place unique. (Do not, however, try to describe everything about your place.)

4. Next, notice the way other people react. This can tell you a great deal about their attitude and feelings toward the place you are describing.

5. Ask others about your subject. Often you will be given information and insights you would otherwise never know existed.

6. After you have collected as many details as you feel you will need, decide what overall impression your subject has made on you. Work this impression into a *topic sentence* or *thesis statement* and list the points you plan to cover beneath it. This list can serve as a working outline for your description.

7. If you begin your description with your topic sentence, it should be well worded so that it creates interest in your subject and helps the reader to immediately "picture" the place you are describing. You may choose to begin your description with an incident, story, or historical background about your subject and place your topic sentence after it.

8. Each of the sentences which follow must support this central impression and build your description one piece at a time. Each sentence should flow naturally from the others as it would if you were simply talking to another person about your subject.

9. As you write, remember that effective description requires the use of specific, vivid details. This is the only way you will be able to convey a precise, memorable picture to the reader. Use similes and metaphors to compare your subject to something well known.

10. Avoid the use of **cliches** or **overused expressions**:

black as coal	in all its glory	patter of rain
black as ink	little by little	pretty as a picture
black as pitch	loomed on the horizon	quaint
blanket of snow	mantle of snow	raining cats and dogs
blue as the sky	ocean's roar	sea of faces
covered like a blanket	ominous silence	silhouetted against the sky
cold as ice	flat as a pancake	smooth as glass
crack of dawn	fresh as a daisy	smooth as silk
dawn breaks	God's country	trees like sentinels
dry as dust	green as grass	white as snow

Topics: Describing a Place

a nursing home	a fishing or sailing boat
the school library	the park after a picnic
the principal's office	the stadium before a concert
the dentist's office	your favorite classroom
a music store	a deserted house
a church or chapel	an unusual hole on a golf course
your favorite hangout	a shoreline or beach
an auto salvage yard	a polluted river
a drive-in theater	a busy highway

Guidelines for Describing an Object

1. Select a topic you are familiar with or interested in knowing more about. (Look around your home, school, and neighborhood for objects which might make interesting subjects.)

2. Gather information by observing the object as closely as possible. Look especially for the details which make this object different from the others in the same category or class.

3. Note the color, size, shape, and texture of the object. Look at each part and note its relationship to the other parts. Determine what the object is used for, what it can do, and how it works. Does it have a practical or aesthetic (artistic) value? Try to gain a complete understanding and appreciation of the object you are describing.

4. Observe how other people use this object or how they feel about it.

5. Try to recall an interesting incident or story involving this object.

6. After you have gathered enough details, determine your dominant impression and begin writing.

7. Follow the usual process for writing description; *show* rather than *tell*, using details and interesting examples. You might begin by using a simile or analogy to give your reader an overall picture or impression of the object.

8. *Note:* Don't overdo your attention to detail. Include only as many specific details as are necessary to get your point or impression across to the reader.

9. Avoid the use of **cliches** and **overused expressions**:

big as a house	bright as a button	imposing structure
red as a rose	blunt instrument	sturdy as an oak
believe it or not	clean as a whistle	drop in the bucket
needle in a haystack	cold as ice	scarce as hen's teeth
words cannot describe	free as a bird	last but not least
from A to Z	straight as an arrow	old as the hills
soft as silk	flat as a pancake	things like that

10. Conclude your description with a summary of the impression this object has had on you.

Topics: Describing an Object

a souvenir	a rare antique	a wall hanging
a street lamp	an album cover	an unusual bridge
a guitar	a stereo	your favorite snack
a park bench	an animal	a fireplace
a paper cutter	your locker	your old bike

Guidelines for Writing a Definition

1. The first step in writing a **simple** or **limited definition** is to place the term you are attempting to define into the *next larger class* or category of similar objects. Then add the special *characteristics* which make this object different from the rest of the objects in that class. See the example below.

> **Term** - *A computer . . .*
> **Class** - *is an electronic machine . . .*
> **Characteristic** - *which stores and manipulates information.*

2. Avoid the temptation to use the term or a variation of it in your definition. (*Example:* "A computer is an electronic machine that computes.")

3. Also avoid defining a term using either "is when" or "is where." (*Example:* "A computer is where you have a machine to do the thinking for people.")

Guidelines for Describing an Event

1. Always write about an event you have actually been a part of or have witnessed firsthand.

2. Observe closely (or recall) all the essential details of the event you are describing. Notice things which happened even before the event began. These details can be especially useful in your introduction; they can help set the mood and prepare your reader to share the experience with you.

3. List the *who, what, when, where, why,* and *how* of the event — or at least as many of the six questions as are important to a complete understanding of the event.

4. Now go back to the six questions and write freely about each. As you write, try to imagine yourself telling someone else about this event, about what happened that made this event special.

5. After you have gathered all of your thoughts and recorded all of your details, decide what overall impression you would like to share with your readers.

6. Work this impression into a topic sentence or thesis statement and list the major points you plan to cover beneath it. This list can serve as a working outline for your description.

7. You can begin your description with your topic sentence or with an incident, story, or background about the event. In any case, try to create some interest in your description so that your reader will want to continue reading.

8. Each sentence which follows your opening should support the impression you are trying to communicate. Each sentence should flow naturally from the others and sound as if you were simply telling another person about the event. (See the list of "Useful Transitions," 351.5, if you need help tying your description together.)

9. Use specific, vivid details — details which help your reader see, smell, taste, feel, and hear the event just as you did.

10. Avoid the use of **cliches** or **overused expressions:**

assembled multitude	eyes of the world	cold sweat
slowly but surely	broad daylight	lock, stock, and barrel
few and far between	out of the blue	more easily said than done
clockwork precision	Mother Nature	raining cats and dogs
sadder but wiser	festive occasion	bury the hatchet
over a barrel	par for the course	drop like flies
gala event	sell like hot cakes	

11. End your description with a statement which summarizes the importance of the event and leaves your reader with a good feeling about having read your description.

Topics: Describing an Event

an early snowstorm	an air or water show
a protest march	a wedding
a prom or dance	a parade
my proudest moment	the first day of school
winning a prize	a near accident
a concert or show	a time to remember
a cherished moment	a surprise visit
a vacation stop	a fire/accident
something lost/found	a real mess
the big showdown	an act of charity
a brush with greatness/disaster	a family affair
a case of stage fright	a circus or carnival
an unwelcome guest	a sidewalk sale

Guidelines for Writing Explanations

1. Select a topic which you are either familiar with or one which you are sure will work well for this assignment.

2. Go through the steps in the process one at a time, noting any steps which may need extra explanation. (You should assume your reader or listener knows very little about your subject.)

3. Begin your explanation with a sentence(s) which states your topic and creates an interest in it. Define any terms which might not be known by your audience. (See the "Guidelines for Writing a Definition," 366d.)

4. Explain each step carefully and completely. Use short, clear sentences rather than long, complex ones. Make good use of transitions; they can help both you and your reader keep everything in the proper order. (See the list of "Useful Transitions and Linking Expressions," 351.5, especially those transitions listed as being useful to *show time* or *location.)*

5. Read what you are writing out loud to test the clarity of your explanation. Restate "in other words" any part which could be confusing to the reader.

6. Some explanations require illustrations or examples. Be ready to use whatever support is needed to clarify your writing.

7. You may find it helpful to tell how your topic is like or unlike something else. (In an explanation it is usually better to compare with an *analogy* rather than a simile or metaphor.)

8. End your writing with a summary of why this explanation is important or how knowing it could be helpful to the reader.

9. Test your explanation and revise as necessary. (*Remember:* Your purpose is to make what may at first seem very technical or complicated suddenly clear and understandable.)

Guidelines for Writing Directions

1. Do not attempt to write directions to a place until you are absolutely sure of how to get there yourself.

2. Make a list of the steps which must be followed to get to the destination. This list — similar to a working outline — is very important; double-check it.

3. Begin writing your directions with a clear statement of where you are now and where it is you want your reader to end up. (Assume you are writing for someone who does not know the area you are describing.)

4. Write your directions one step at a time. Include accurate distances (feet, yards, blocks, miles), compass headings (east, west, left, right), and landmarks (first stop sign, large white church, railroad bridge).

5. Make good use of transitions in your directions. (See the list of "Useful Transitions and Linking Expressions," 351.5, especially those listed as being useful to *show time* and *location.)*

6. Some explanations and directions require illustrations, so be prepared to include illustrations. (You need not be an artist — even simple line drawings can be very helpful.)

7. Avoid lengthy or complex sentences. Although this is good advice for nearly all writing tasks, it is especially important when writing directions.

8. Give your directions to someone and have him or her test them. If it isn't possible to actually follow the directions, have this person visualize or draw out each step and let you know which steps might be confusing to the reader. Change your directions accordingly.

1. Select a topic (issue) which is both current and controversial. This means the issue should be of concern to a sizable group of people — and that the people in that group have more than one reasonable opinion on the subject. This issue should also be one which you have strong, personal feelings about.

2. Begin collecting information by listing your personal feelings about the issue and the reasons you feel that way. This may be the most important stage in the persuasive writing process; you simply cannot be convincing unless you have "you" on your side.

3. Ask other people how they feel about this issue. Listen closely, especially to those with whom you disagree. They will give you a preview of the response you can expect from your audience. Ask them why they feel the way they do; test your opinion and reasons on them. You must understand well what you are up against before you begin to write.

4. Next, gather any additional facts and evidence which you now realize must be included in your writing to be convincing. Use the *Readers' Guide to Periodical Literature* in your library to help you find current magazine articles on the issue. Take careful notes on what you read and use these notes to build a strong case. Discuss your list of arguments and evidence with someone else to make sure you have covered all the important points related to this issue.

5. Once you have gathered enough information, work out a clear statement of the purpose of your persuasive writing. In persuasive writing this thesis statement is called the *proposition* — it is a statement of what you *propose* to prove in your writing. Always state your proposition in positive terms. ("Teachers should be prohibited from secretly searching student lockers," rather than "Teachers should not be allowed to secretly search student lockers.")

6. Place your proposition at the top of your paper and list your reasons underneath it in outline form. Beneath each reason list the facts, figures, examples, or quotations which help support it.

7. The writer of persuasion can use most of the same techniques of support and development used in expository writing; in addition, there are a number of stylistic devices (Handbook 653) which can also work well. Essentially, stylistic devices should be used to get the reader's attention when you want to emphasize an important point.

8. Use a calm, reasoning tone throughout your writing; rely on logic, not emotion. (See the unit on "Using Evidence and Logic," 669.) Likewise, be diplomatic. Give credit to the reasonable arguments on the other side of the issue; then point out clearly the weaknesses of each.

9. Appeal to the needs of your audience. Let each of them know what's in it for him or her. Prove to them that they do have something to gain by changing their opinions.

10. Use your two strongest arguments first and last. People are much more likely to remember arguments placed in these positions than the others.

11. Use examples to illustrate your main points. Use statistics sparingly. Instead, compare one thing to another using visual images. ("Each day we bury in our dumpsites enough garbage to completely cover the state of Rhode Island.") If you do use numbers, round them off. ("Each day we bury in our dumpsites nearly 50 million tons of garbage.")

12. Choose your words very carefully. Remember that words convey feeling (connotation) as well as meaning (denotation). Select words which your audience will react to positively. Define any terms directly related to the issue which your reader may not understand.

THE RESEARCH PAPER

367 A **research paper** is a highly organized, documented essay which, as its name implies, requires extensive research and analysis. Quite often the research paper is called a **term paper** because a term (a quarter or semester) is traditionally the length of time given for its completion. The paper is sometimes called a **library paper** because the writer relies on the library for his basic information. (An original research paper uses firsthand, original sources rather than books; this type of paper is seldom written by the high school student.)

368 A research paper can be broken down into four basic parts: **title page, outline, text** (essay) with footnotes, and **bibliography.** Each will be discussed in this section.

369
Steps for Preparing the Research Paper

1 **Choose a general subject.** A suitable subject is one which meets your instructor's requirements, one which you have some interest in reading and writing about, and one which you can handle in the time and space allowed.

2 **Do some preliminary reading.** Check area libraries for available material on the subject and select several articles to read. Begin your reading with a general reference book (an encyclopedia, perhaps). Check the list of *related articles* and *see* references located at the end of nearly all reference book articles. This information can be extremely helpful in your search for a specific research topic within the general subject area.

3 **Limit your topic.** After you have finished your preliminary reading, you must then focus on a particular topic. Write a temporary thesis statement which makes clear what you plan to cover in your research paper. You will probably consider several different topics before you settle upon the one you will finally use for your paper.

4 Prepare a **preliminary bibliography.** Using the card catalog, *Readers' Guide to Periodical Literature,* the vertical file, and other library resources, put together a list of all materials available on your topic. Place this information on 3- by 5-inch bibliography cards and arrange them in alphabetical order. Number each card in the upper right-hand corner; place the call number of each book in the upper left-hand corner.

Sample Bibliography Card

```
393   Mitford, Jessica.  The American Way          ②
      of Death.  New York:  Simon
      and Schuster, 1963.
```

Sample Note Card

```
Embalming -- necessity of                          ②

      Embalming is not required by law
in any state or religion.  Health and
sanitation do not enter into the picture.
"The sole purpose of embalming is to
make the corpse presentable for public
viewing in a costly container."
                                    (p. 66)
```

5 **Begin taking notes.** As you continue to read the material you have gathered, jot down all ideas and quotations which you feel may be useful in the writing of your paper. Place this information on note cards; follow the guidelines below:

- Use cards of the same size and style (4- by 6-inch cards recommended).
- Use black or blue ink.
- Place only one idea or quotation on each card.

- Use abbreviations and phrases (as your teacher allows).
- Place all *verbatim (word for word)* notes in quotation marks. Use the ellipsis when necessary (128). Place any information which you add to these direct quotes in brackets (195).
- Use a diagonal (/) to indicate where a quote has gone from one page to another in the original source. This will be very useful when you are citing the exact page of a quote in a footnote.
- Look up any unfamiliar words you come across in your reading. If you find that a particular word is important to your topic, copy the definition onto a note card.
- Leave space at the bottom of each card for notes on how and where you might use the information. Add your notes in pencil.
- Place a descriptive *slug* (heading) at the top of each card. The slug should be a word or phrase which clearly reflects the main idea of each note.

6 **Write your working outline.** Organize your note cards into their most logical order and use them to construct a preliminary or working outline. Your descriptive slugs may be used as main and sub points in your outline. (See 357.)

7 **Continue your research.** You should now begin searching for specific information which is needed to support your thesis.

8 **Revise your outline.** Your working outline must be changed as you continue to find new information. Your thesis statement may also have to undergo revision to bring it in line with the specific direction you plan to take in your final draft.

9 **Write your rough draft.** You can begin with an *introduction* which states clearly the purpose of your research paper (*thesis statement*). If there are any complex terms or concepts which are essential to a clear understanding of your paper, explain them in your first paragraph.

- The body of the paper will require a great deal of patience and hard work; set aside plenty of time, especially for the first several work sessions.

- Lay out one section of note cards (cards with the same headings) so that you can see all or most of the cards at the same time.

- Write a generalization which covers the main idea of that section of cards; then determine which cards contain the best information to support that generalization. If you find that your generalization is valid, but you do not have enough information to support it, gather more material or drop that point from consideration.

- Repeat this process for each section of note cards. Put your essay into your own words; use direct quotes only when the point being made is stated precisely as you want it to be in the original source. As you sort through your cards, examine each for possible use as a transition.

- Keep your paper formal: do not use fragments, abbreviations, or substandard language. However, do not attempt to impress your reader by using language which is too lofty or flowery. This will only distract the reader and cause him to wonder whether you truly understand what you are writing about. Work to achieve a writing style which is formal, yet interesting.

- Keep your writing objective. This means you must concentrate on the facts about the object of your paper rather than your feelings or attitude toward it. This does not mean, however, that the language of your paper must be so objective and factual that it is dull or boring. What follows is an example of objective writing that is both factual and colorful. Notice that the writer uses a simile, a metaphor, several vivid verbs, and a number of colorful adjectives. (The passage is taken from an article entitled "The Wonderfully Diverse Ways of the Ant" by Bert Holldobler. It appeared in the June 1984 issue of *National Geographic*.)

Sharp as a buzz saw, the serrated mandibles [jaws] of the leaf cutter slice up greenery and then hold the pieces high on the trek to the underground nest. The task, going on all night, is carried out by a caste of medium-size workers called medias, assisted by pint-size minors in one of the most unusual roles in the insect kingdom. The hitchhiking minors scurry along the traveling leaf. With flailing mandibles, they protect the carriers against phorid flies that try to lay eggs on living ants. The procession follows a chemical trail some 100 meters long blazed by scouts that lay down an odor reinforced by passersby. Colonies of a million leaf cutters can defoliate a citrus tree in a night; in Central and South America they are considered major pests.

The final paragraph in your paper should tie all of the important points together and draw a final *conclusion* about what has been written. It should leave the reader with a clear understanding of the meaning and significance of your research paper.

10 **Revise your rough draft twice:** once for meaning and overall effectiveness and a second time for punctuation, usage, and other mechanical errors. (Use the *Writing Checklist,* 363, as a proofreading guide.)

11 **Fill in the footnotes or endnotes** (or include author and page numbers in parentheses) (370-375) and **assemble your bibliography** (376-380).

12 **Prepare your final copy.** Type (or write in ink) on good quality typing paper. Leave a margin of 1 inch on all sides. (Leave a margin of 3 inches at the top of the first page.) Double-space your entire paper except as single-spacing is required for footnotes.

13 **Arrange and number your pages.** Begin numbering your pages with the first page of the essay; do not, however, type the numeral *1* on the first page. Begin by typing the numeral *2* on page two, *3* on page three, etc. Type each number in the upper right-hand corner (3-4 spaces to the right of the text and ½ inch from the top of the page). Number the bibliography as if it were a continuation of the text.

14 **Add your title.** No title page is usually required for the research paper. Simply type the author's name, instructor's name, course title, and date in the upper left corner of the first page of the paper. (Begin one inch from the top and double-space throughout.) Center the title (double-space before and after); then type the first line of the paper. *Note:* If a title page is required, center the title of the paper one-third of the way down from the top of the page; likewise, center the author's name, instructor's name, and any additional information required two-thirds of the way down.

(Title on First Page)　　　**(Sample Title Page)**　　　**(Sample Final Outline)**

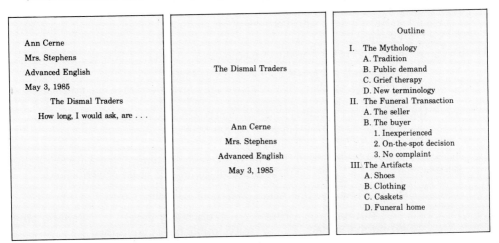

Ann Cerne
Mrs. Stephens
Advanced English
May 3, 1985
　　The Dismal Traders
　　How long, I would ask, are . . .

The Dismal Traders

Ann Cerne
Mrs. Stephens
Advanced English
May 3, 1985

Outline

I. The Mythology
　A. Tradition
　B. Public demand
　C. Grief therapy
　D. New terminology
II. The Funeral Transaction
　A. The seller
　B. The buyer
　　1. Inexperienced
　　2. On-the-spot decision
　　3. No complaint
III. The Artifacts
　A. Shoes
　B. Clothing
　C. Caskets
　D. Funeral home

15 **Type your final outline.** Add, delete, or rearrange material as is necessary to make your outline consistent with the final version of your paper. Use either a *topic outline* or a *sentence outline* (or as your teacher requires); do not mix the two into the same outline. (See 357-359.) If your outline is more than one page in length, number it with small Roman numerals (i, ii, iii, iv). Double-space throughout your outline.

16 **Check your paper for typing errors.** A final check of the entire paper from beginning to end will prove worthwhile. Even the most diligent workers make errors. Your research paper should not be handed in until it is "error free."

Documentation: Endnotes, Footnotes, and Parenthetical Reference

370 The writer of the research paper must always give credit for any information or ideas he gets from another source. Failure to give credit for material used, whether quoted or not, is called **plagiarism** and is not acceptable. Notice how the student who wrote the sample paper which follows this explanation avoided plagiarism by giving credit for the idea she used in the second paragraph of the first page (footnote 2). Credit can be given in the text of the paper itself or in a note; the note should appear either at the bottom of the page (**footnote**) or in a list at the end of the paper (**endnote**).

The 1984 edition of the *MLA Handbook for Writers of Research Papers* suggests giving credit in the text of the paper rather than in footnotes or endnotes. This can be done by inserting the appropriate information (in parentheses) after the words or ideas borrowed from another source. The references should be kept as brief as possible, listing only the information needed to identify the source. Usually, the reference will need to include the author's last name and the page number(s) or a shortened version of the title if that is how the source is entered in the bibliography. Place the parenthetical reference where a pause would naturally occur, usually at the end of the sentence.

> "The sales talk, while preferably dignified and restrained, must be designed to take maximum advantage of this arrangement" (Mitford 23-24).

> "A funeral is not an occasion for a display of cheapness. It is, in fact, . . . an occasion when feelings of guilt and remorse are satisfied to a large extent by the purchase of a fine funeral" ("Funeral Customs" 13).

If the author's name is already included in the text, you need not repeat it in the reference; simply list the page number(s):

> Thus as Jessica Mitford states in <u>The American Way of Death</u>, "The undertaker is the stage manager of the fabulous production that is the modern American funeral" (18).

If the quoted material is lengthy and set off from the rest of the text, place the period and quotation marks at the end of the final sentence. Then leave two spaces before adding your reference in parentheses. (See the sample entries on page 84.)

Note: No abbreviation (p. or pp.) is needed before the page number(s) in a note; however, if there is some doubt as to which of several numbers is the page number, use p. or pp. to avoid confusion.

371 If you are instructed to give credit in footnotes or endnotes, follow the **form** below:
- Single-space all footnotes; double-space endnotes.
- Raise the note number slightly above the typed line; leave one space after the number.
- Quadruple-space (double-space twice) between the last line of the text and the first footnote; double-space between notes.
- Indent the first line of each note five spaces.

372 The **order** of the information in the note varies with the type of literature being cited. (See the charts which follow.) Notes for a book follow the order shown below:

[1] Richard Wheelen, <u>Sherman's March</u> (New York: Crowell, 1978) 167.

Author	Title	(Publishing data)	Page(s) cited
(in normal order)		(city, publisher, copyright)	

Model Notes for Books: First References

One author	[1] Richard Wheelen, <u>Sherman's March</u> (New York: Crowell, 1978) 167.
No author's name listed	[2] <u>Sherman's March</u> (New York: Crowell, 1978) 167. *Note:* This same note arrangement can be used when the author's name is given in full in the text of the paper.
Two authors *(a book in a series)*	[3] Alan C. Purves and Victoria Rippere, <u>Elements of Writing about a Literary Work: A Study of Response to Literature,</u> NCTE Research Report No. 9 (Urbana: NCTE, 1968) 21-22. *Note:* The above entry can also be used as a model for a work which is **one in a series.**
More than three editors or authors *(volume)*	[4] Robert A. Pratt et al., eds., <u>Masters of British Literature</u> (Boston: Houghton, 1958) I, 15. *Note:* For a book with more than three authors, simply drop *eds.* from the entry. *Also note:* When both the volume and page number are given, the abbreviation for volume (Vol.) is dropped.
A single work from an anthology *(paperback edition)*	[5] William Morris, "The Haystack in the Floods," in <u>Nineteenth Century British Minor Poets,</u> ed. by Richard Wilbur and W.H. Auden (New York: Dell, Laurel Edition, 1965) 265-270. *Note:* The publisher of the **paperback edition** is listed rather than the original publisher because of possible differences in the text or pagination.
A corporate author	[6] The Rockefeller Panel Reports, <u>Prospect for America</u> (New York: Doubleday, 1961) 207.
One volume of a multi-volumed work	[7] William B. Benton, <u>Discovering a New World</u>, Vol. I of <u>The Annals of America</u> (New York: Encyclopedia Britannica, 1968) 18-24.
Government publication *(subtitles)*	[8] Congressional Quarterly Service, <u>Congress and the Nation: A Review of Government in the Postwar Years</u> (Washington, D.C.: GPO, 1965) 27. *Note:* The **subtitle** may be omitted in the note but not in the bibliography.
Encyclopedia or other reference work *(signed)*	[9] Wilson D. Wallis, "Superstition," <u>World Book Encyclopedia,</u> 1970. *Note:* Publication information may be omitted for all well-known reference books. Likewise, volume and page number may be omitted unless the article is not located in the usual alphabetical order.
Full-length play or long poem	[10] William Shakespeare, <u>King Lear</u>, II, iii, 17-21. *Note:* The numerals following the title are understood to be *Act* II, *scene* iii, and *lines* 17-21.
Material from one source quoted in another	[11] Ian Watt, <u>The Rise of the Novel</u>, quoted by Wayne C. Booth in <u>The Rhetoric of Fiction</u> (Chicago: Univ. of Chicago, 1961) 41.

Model Notes for Periodicals: First References

Signed article in a weekly	[12] Robert Hughes, "Futurism's Farthest Frontier," Time 9 July 1979: 58-59.
Unsigned article in a weekly	[13] "Changing Way of Death," Time 11 April 1969: 22.
Signed article in a monthly	[14] Kevin N. Lewis, "The Prompt and Delayed Effects of Nuclear War," Scientific American July 1979: 35-47.
Review of book in a magazine	[15] Timothy Foote, "The Eye of the Beholder," rev. of Testimony and Demeanor by John Casey, Time 9 July 1979: 66.
Signed newspaper article	[16] Jesse L. Jackson, " 'Must' is Key Word in Outlawing Bias," Milwaukee Sentinel 9 July 1979, sec. 2: 15.
Unsigned editorial or story	[17] "Some Better Ways to Curb Teen Drinking," Editorial, Milwaukee Journal 17 June 1979, sec. 1: 1.
Signed pamphlet	[18] Jean E. Laird, The Metrics Are Coming (Burlington, Iowa: National Research Bureau, 1976) 6.

Second and Later References to a Book or Periodical

Work with one author	[19] Wheelen 168. (or) [19] Ibid. 168. The above notes are for second or later reference to a work which has been cited in the immediately preceding note. *Note:* Although the use of *Ibid.* and *op. cit.* is no longer considered necessary by many authorities, some instructors still require their students to use them. Therefore, an explanation of each is included at the end of this section.
(Parenthetical reference) Drop the footnote number.	[20] Wheelen 168. (or) (Wheelen 168) If a work has been fully identified in a footnote or endnote, all later references to that work need only include the author's last name and the page(s) cited. (Drop author from parentheses if listed in text.)
Work with two authors	[21] Purves and Rippere 21-22.
Multivolumed work	[22] Benton 160. *Note:* If a volume other than the one listed in the first note is referred to, add the new volume number after the author's name.
Two works by the same author	[23] Frye, Anatomy 154. [24] Frye, Critical Path 62. *Note:* When citing two or more books by the same author, list the title (or abbreviated version) after the author's name.
Play or long poem	[25] King Lear II.iii.17-21. (or) [25] King Lear 2.3.17-21 *Note:* Use periods (no spacing) between the act, scene, and lines.
Periodical article	[26] "Changing Way of Death" 22.
Encyclopedia	[27] Wallis, "Superstition." *Note:* Both the author and title are listed for reference works.

374

375 As noted earlier, the use of *ibid.* and *op. cit.* is no longer considered necessary by most authorities. Should you need to use them, however, follow the instructions below:

- *Ibid.* is the Latin abbreviation of *ibidem,* which means "in the same place." *Ibid.* is used rather than writing out the same note twice in a row. Simply write the note number, *Ibid.,* and the page number of the material used. *Ibid.* should not be underlined. (*Note: Ibid.* appears in italics when it is printed or published.)
- *Op. cit.* is an abbreviation for *opere citato,* which means "in the work cited." When you use three consecutive notes—and the first and third refer to the same source—use *op. cit.* for the third entry instead of writing the first note another time. *Op. cit.* is simply repeated for each of the next consecutive notes which are the same as notes one and three. Underline op. cit.

Bibliography

376 A **bibliography** is a list of books, articles, etc., about a particular subject or by a particular author. The bibliography page is found at the end of a research paper or book.

377 There are three basic kinds of bibliography: **practical, working,** and **complete.**
- A **practical bibliography** is a list of the works actually used in the paper. The list will include all of those works noted throughout the paper. This type of bibliography is often labeled *Works Cited.*
- A **working bibliography** is a list of all the works consulted during the construction of the paper, and so is often titled *Works Consulted.* This type of bibliography indicates the amount of research which has actually taken place.
- A **complete bibliography** lists all available material on a particular subject. A list of this kind gives readers additional resources to consult should they desire to do so. The *Subject Bibliography,* as it is often called, makes clear the extent to which the subject has been researched by others.

378 The **form** of an entry in the bibliography is different from that of the note:
- Each entry is listed alphabetically by the author's last name. (If you use two or more works by the same author, arrange these entries by title. Type the author's name for the first entry; use ten hyphens followed by a period for each additional entry by that author. See "Works Cited" at 381.)
- If there is no author, the first word of the title (disregard *A, An, The*) is used.
- Leave two spaces between the author and title and title and publishing data.
- The second and subsequent lines are indented five spaces.
- Each entry is double-spaced; double-spacing is also used between entries.

379 A bibliography entry for a book is set down as shown here:

Mitford, Jessica. The American Way of Death. New York: Simon & Schuster, 1963.

Author (last name first)   Title   Publishing data (City, Publisher, Copyright)

380

Model Bibliographical Entries	
One author	Wheelen, Richard. Sherman's March. New York: Crowell, 1978.
Two authors *(book in series)*	Purves, Alan C. and Victoria Rippere. Elements of Writing about a Literary Work: A Study of Response to Literature. NCTE Research Report No. 9. Urbana: NCTE, 1968.
More than three authors or editors	Pratt, Robert A., et al., eds. Masters of British Literature. 2 vols. Boston: Houghton, 1956. *Note:* For a book with more than three authors, simply drop *eds.* from the entry.
A single work from an anthology *(pages listed)*	Morris, William. "The Haystack in the Floods." Nineteenth Century British Minor Poets. Ed. Richard Wilbur and W.H. Auden. New York: Dell, Laurel Edition, 1965. 265-279.

A corporate author	The Rockefeller Panel Reports. Prospect for America. New York: Doubleday, 1961.
One volume of a multivolume work	Benton, William B. Discovering a New World. Vol. I of The Annals of America. New York: Encyclopedia Britannica, 1968.
Government publication	Congressional Quarterly Service. Congress and the Nation: A Review of Government in the Postwar Years. Washington, D.C.: GPO, 1965.
Encyclopedia article *(signed)*	Wallis, Wilson D. "Superstition." World Book Encyclopedia, 1970. *Note:* It is not necessary to give full publication information for familiar reference works. If the article is initialed rather than signed, check in the index of authors (usually located in the opening section of each volume) for the author's full name.
Full-length play or long poem	Shakespeare, William. King Lear.
Material from one source quoted in another	Watt, Ian. The Rise of the Novel. Quoted by Wayne C. Booth in The Rhetoric of Fiction. Chicago: Univ. of Chicago Press, 1961.
Signed article in a weekly	Hughes, Robert. "Futurism's Farthest Frontier." Time 9 July 1979: 58-59.
Unsigned article in a weekly	"Changing Way of Death." Time 11 April 1969: 22.
Signed article in a monthly	Lewis, Kevin N. "The Prompt and Delayed Effects of Nuclear War." Scientific American July 1979: 35-47.
Review of a book in a magazine	Foote, Timothy. "The Eye of the Beholder." Rev. of Testimony and Demeanor by John Casey. Time July 1979: 66.
Signed newspaper article	Jackson, Jesse L. " 'Must' is Key Word in Outlawing Bias." Milwaukee Sentinel 9 July 1979, sec. 2: 15.
Unsigned editorial or story	"Some Better Ways to Curb Teen Drinking." Editorial. Milwaukee Journal 17 June 1979, sec. 1: 1. *Note:* For an unsigned story, simply omit *Editorial.*
Signed pamphlet	Laird, Jean E. The Metrics Are Coming. Burlington, Iowa: National Research Bureau, 1976.
Pamphlet with no author, publisher, or date	Pedestrian Safety. [United States]: n.p., n.d. *Note:* List the country of publication (in brackets) if known.
Recording	Guthrie, Woody. Woody Guthrie Sings Folk Songs. With Leadbelly, Cisco Houston, Sonny Terry, and Bess Hawes. Intro. by Pete Seeger. Folkways Records, FA 2483, 1962.
Radio or television program	"An Interview with Sadat." 60 Minutes. CBS, 11 Nov. 1979. *Note:* Other information (director, producer, narrator, writer) may be listed if appropriate.

First Page of the Research Paper

Indent lengthy quotes ten spaces; double-space throughout

3" margin on first page

How long, I would ask, are we to be subjected to the tyranny and custom of undertakers? Truly it is all vanity and vexation of spirit–a mere mockery of woe, costly to all, far, far beyond its value; and ruinous to many; it is an abomination to all, yet submitted to by all because none have the moral courage to speak against it and act in defiance of it.[1]

Triple-space

Though written hundreds of years ago, Lord Essex's criticism of the excessive expense of funerals is still relevant today. This paper will not advocate the extermination of the simple funeral ritual–a ceremony is necessary to publicly, and more importantly, to openly face the reality of death. However, society in general and the funeral establishment in particular have created pressures which often result in more elaborate and expensive funerals than are really necessary.[2] Therefore, the purpose of this paper is to examine the American way of death and to explore possible alternatives to the status quo.

Indent five spaces

Raise number; leave one space

1 Alfred Fellows, The Law of Burial (London: Hadden-Best, 1952), Introduction.
2 Elizabeth Kuebler-Ross, Questions and Answers on Death and Dying (New York: Macmillan, 1974) 102.

Second Page of Research Paper

2

The twentieth century American funeral industry has created a new "mythology" in order to perpetuate the peculiar customs involved in the disposal of the dead. The public has been sold a series of fallacies which has changed the way they look at funerals.[3]

First of all, the notion that existing funeral practices are a part of "American tradition" is a fictitious one, yet one that is often expounded upon by members of the funeral industry. A glimpse at American funerals of past times establishes a complete contradiction to the myth of "tradition." As Jessica Mitford, authority on the various aspects of the funeral trade, once stated, "Simplicity to the point of starkness, the plain pine box, the laying out of the dead by friends and family who also bore the coffin to the grave–these were the hallmarks of the traditional funeral until the end of the nineteenth century."[4]

Secondly, funeral directors maintain that the American public is being given only what it wants. Wilber Kriegler, managing director of the National Selected Morticians, stated, "A funeral should cost exactly what you desire, for the cost and selection is entirely in your hands."[5] The fact of the matter is, however, that the cost

Quadruple-space before notes

3 Jessica Mitford, The American Way of Death (New York: Simon & Schuster, 1963) 17.

Single-space within notes

4 Mitford 17.

Double-space between notes

5 Wilber M. Kriegler, Successful Funeral Service Management (New York: Prentice Hall, 1951) 73.

Endnotes

½"

9

1"

Notes

1 Alfred Fellows, The Law of Burial (London: Hadden-Best, 1952), Introduction.
2 Elizabeth Kuebler-Ross, Questions and Answers on Death and Dying (New York: Macmillan, 1974) 102.
3 Jessica Mitford, The American Way of Death (New York: Simon & Schuster, 1963) 17.
4 Mitford 17.
5 Wilber M. Kriegler, Successful Funeral Service Management (New York: Prentice Hall, 1951) 73.
6 Kuebler-Ross 102.
7 Mitford 18.
8 Mitford 23.
9 Mitford 23-24.
10 "Funeral Customs," National Funeral Service Journal, August 1961: 13.

Double-space throughout

Note: If you are instructed to use endnotes rather than footnotes, simply place the footnote information on a separate sheet. (See sample above.) Center the title "Notes" one inch from the top. Double-space, indent five spaces, and type your first note number. If you use endnotes, you may not need a separate bibliography. Follow the instructions of your teacher.

(Bibliography)

Works Cited

"Changing Way of Death." Time 11 April 1969: 22.

Fellows, Alfred. The Law of Burial. London: Hadden-Best, 1952.

"Funeral Customs." National Funeral Service Journal. August 1961.

Grollman, Earl A. Concerning Death: A Practical Guide to the Living. Boston: Beacon Press, 1974.

Kriegler, Wilber M. Successful Funeral Management. New York: Prentice-Hall, 1951.

Kuebler-Ross, Elizabeth. Questions and Answers on Death and Dying. New York: Macmillan, 1974.

Mitford, Jessica. The American Way of Death. New York: Simon & Schuster, 1963.

———. Kind and Unusual Punishment. New York: Knopf, 1973.

Volkart, Edmond H. Explorations in Social Psychology. New York: Basic Books, 1957.

(Double-space throughout)

Science, writes in Mortuary Management Idea Kit:

> Your selling plan should go into operation as soon as the telephone rings and you are requested to serve a bereaved family. . . . Never preconceive as to what any family will purchase. You cannot possibly measure the intensity of their emotions, undisclosed insurance, or funds that may have been set aside for funeral expenses. (124)

The "hard sell" is considered inappropriate and self-defeating by modern industry leaders; thus, the selling plan is subtle rather than high-pressured. Yet, no arrangements are left to chance, as exemplified by the Selection Room, where customers are taken to purchase a casket. The most important factor of funeral salesmanship, according to the trade, is the proper arrangement of caskets in the Room. "The sales talk," states Mitford, "while preferably dignified and restrained, must be designed to take maximum advantage of this arrangement" (23-24).

And what of the buyer's role in the funeral transaction? The bare truth is that the buyer in total ignorance of what to expect when he enters a funeral home–what to look for, what to avoid, how much to spend. By its very nature, it is unlikely that anybody will have discussed the funeral with anybody in advance. The buyer is in no mood to compare prices and examine quality–he is anxious to get the entire process over with.

---

of a funeral almost always varies, not according to a family's means, but according to the amount of pressure that family feels to provide a "nice" funeral.

Thirdly, a variety of myths have been created based on psychiatric theories. The "memory picture" and its importance is stressed–meaning the last glimpse of the deceased lying in an open casket and done up with the latest embalming techniques is essential. A newer and equally impressing term is the need the family and friends have for "grief therapy." The custom of viewing the dead is basically American–only in this country do persons seem incapable of managing loss and/or grief, which is why there is a reliance on specialists. This elaborate and unnecessary ritual, with all its commercial aspects, not only prolongs the agony of the family, but adds further expensive costs (Kuebler-Ross 102).

Lastly, an entirely new vocabulary has been created by the funeral industry to replace the terms of former times. The undertaker is now a "funeral director" or "mortician"; coffins are "caskets"; hearses are "coaches" or "professional cars"; corpses are referred to as "the loved ones"; cremated ashes are "cremains"; and even flowers become something else: "floral tributes" (Mitford 18).

Thus, as Jessica Mitford states in The American Way of Death, "The undertaker is the stage manager of the fabulous production that is the modern American funeral" (23). The funeral director, like any good salesman, is concerned with price, profit, and selling techniques. As Leon Utter, dean of the San Francisco College of Mortuary

---

Abbreviations for Research Paper

anon.	anonymous	i.e.	that is; id est	rpt.	reprinted (by), reprint
bk., bks.	book(s)	ill., illus.	illustration, illustrated by	sc.	scene
©	copyright	introd.	(author of) introduction, introduced by, introduction	sec., secs.	section(s)
c., ca.	about (used for approximate dates: c. 1492); circa	l., ll.	line(s)	sic	thus (used with brackets to indicate an error is that way in the original)
cf.	compare; confer	loc. cit.	in the place cited; loco citato	tr., trans.	translator, translation
chap.,ch.,chs.	chapter(s)	MS, MSS	manuscript(s)	v., vv. (or vs., vss.)	verse(s)
col., cols.	column(s)	narr., narrs.	narrated by, narrator(s)	viz.	namely; videlicet
comp.	compiler, compiled; compiled by	N.B.	note well; nota bene	vol., vols.	volume(s): capitalize when used with Roman numerals
ed., eds.	editor(s), edition(s), or edited by	n.d.	no date given		
e.g.	for example; exempli gratia	no., nos.	number(s)		
et al.	and others; et alii	n. pag.	no pagination		
et seq.	and the following; et sequens	n.p.	no place of publication and/or no publisher given		
ex.	example	op. cit.	in the work cited; opere citato		
f., ff.	and the following page(s)	p., pp.	page(s)		
fig., figs.	figure(s)	pl., pls.	plate(s)		
GPO	Government Printing Office, Washington, D.C.	pseud.	pseudonym		
ibid.	in the same place as quoted above; ibidem	pub. (or publ.), pubs.	published by, publication(s)		
		q.v.	which see; quod vide		
		rev.	revised		

THE ESSAY TEST

382 The key to writing a good essay test is being well prepared. You must begin by organizing and reviewing what you have studied. You must remember the important names, dates, and places and be prepared to work them into an essay which makes clear what these details add up to. Even though this is often easier said than done, there are a number of steps which can be taken to improve your ability to handle an essay test. Studying the guidelines below is a good first step.

Guidelines for Taking an Essay Test

1. Make sure you are ready for the test both mentally and physically. (See the "Guidelines for Taking Tests," 484.)
2. Check to see that you have all the materials you need for a particular test.
3. Report to the room as quickly as possible on the day of the exam.
4. Review especially difficult material right up to the time the test starts.
5. Listen carefully to the final instructions of the teacher. How much time do you have to complete the test? Do all the questions count equally? Can you use any aids such as a dictionary or handbook? Are there any corrections, changes, or additions to the test?
6. Begin the test immediately and watch the time carefully. Don't spend so much time answering one question that you run out of time before answering the others.
7. Read all the essay questions carefully, paying special attention to the key words.
8. Ask the teacher to clarify any question you may not understand.
9. Rephrase the question into a controlling idea for your essay answer.
10. Think before you write. Jot down all the important information and work it into a brief outline. Do this on the back of the test sheet or on a piece of scrap paper.
11. Use a logical pattern of organization and a strong topic sentence for each paragraph.
12. Write concisely without using abbreviations or nonstandard language.
13. Emphasize those areas of the subject you are most sure of.
14. Keep your test paper neat with reasonable margins. Neatness is always important; readability is a must, especially on an exam.
15. Revise and proofread as carefully and completely as time will permit.

Understanding the Wording of the Essay Test Question

Understanding what the teacher is asking for in an essay test question is very important. Too many students make the error of thinking the best way to answer an essay question is to write down everything and anything about the topic as fast as they can. This frenzied method of handling an essay test has the pen flying across the paper in a desperate attempt to fill as many pages as is physically possible. No time is taken to think about the essay test question or to organize an appropriate answer. The resulting grade is usually disappointing.

The poor result is not necessarily from the student's lack of knowledge about the subject, but from his lack of the basic skills needed to write a good essay test answer.

The first step in correctly handling an essay test question is to read the question several times until you are sure you know what the teacher is asking. As you read, you must pay special attention to the key words found in every essay question. Your ability to understand and respond to these key words is a basic skill necessary to handling the essay question. For example, if you are asked to *contrast* two things on a test and you *classify* them instead, you have not given the teacher the information requested. Your score will obviously suffer.

A list of key terms, along with a definition and an example of how each is used, can be found on the next three pages. Study these terms carefully. It is the first step to improving your essay test scores.

383 Classify To **classify** is to place persons or things (especially plants and animals) together in a group because they are alike or similar. In science there is an order which all groups follow when it comes to **classifying** or **categorizing**: *phylum* (or *division*), *class, order, family, genus, species,* and *variety.*

384 Compare To **compare** is to bring both points of *similarity* and *difference,* but generally with the greater emphasis on similarities.

> "Compare the British and American forms of government."

385 Contrast To **contrast** is to particularly stress *differences.* In a sense, *compare* covers this, but with less emphasis on *differences.*

> "Contrast the views of the North and the South on the issue of States' Rights."

386 Criticize To **criticize** is to point out the *good* points and the *bad* points of a situation or idea. To be a "critic" is *not* simply to be *negative;* a good critical analysis must deal with both sides of the issue.

> "Criticize Roosevelt's foreign policy during the middle 1930s."

387 Define To **define** is to give a clear, concise meaning for a term. Generally, to define consists of identifying the class to which a term belongs and how it differs from other things in that class. (See the section on "Writing a Definition," 366d.)

> "Define what is meant by the term *filibuster.*"

388 Describe To **describe** is to recount, sketch, or relate something in sequence or story form. What is called for here is to give a good *word picture* of the concept.

> "Describe Scout's appearance on the night of the Halloween party."

389 Diagram To **diagram** is to organize in some pictorial way — a flow chart, a map, or some other graphic device. Generally, a good diagram will include appropriate labeling of both the whole figure and each of its parts.

> "Diagram the levels of authority and responsibility of our town's government officials."

390 Discuss To **discuss** is to examine and talk about an issue *from all sides.* A **discussion** answer is usually fairly long and must be carefully organized.

> "Discuss the long-range effects of the atomic bomb on the people of Hiroshima."

391 Enumerate To **enumerate** (root: *numer* or *number*) is to write in list or outline form a set of related facts, ideas, objects, or issues. Though actual numbering isn't truly demanded by this term, it often helps.

> "Enumerate the causes of the Great Depression of 1929."

392 Evaluate To **evaluate** is to make a *value* judgment, a statement of negative and/or positive worth. Generally speaking, it is better to back up this type of answer with *evidence* (facts, figures, instances, etc.) rather than simply with appeals to authority (the opinions of particular *experts*).

> "Evaluate the contributions of the automobile to the average American's overall standard of living."

393 Explain To **explain** (*ex* = out; *plain* = open space) is to bring out into the open, to make clear, to analyze, and to clarify. This term is similar to *discuss* but implies more of an emphasis on cause-effect relationships or step-by-step sequences.

> "Explain the immediate effects of the atomic bomb on Hiroshima."

394 Illustrate To **illustrate** is, according to its definition, to show by means of a picture, a diagram, or some other graphic aid. At times, however, the term may be used to call forth specific examples or instances which *illustrate* a law, rule, or principle.

> "Illustrate the relationships between the Senate and the House of Representatives."

395 Interpret To **interpret** is to explain, translate, or show a specific application (how it works) of a given fact or principle. Generally, an *interpretation* should go beyond previously cited examples or instances.

> "Interpret the following statement: Power corrupts, and absolute power corrupts absolutely."

396 Justify To **justify** is to tell why a position or point of view is good, right, or proper. A *justification* should be mostly *positive*; stress the *advantages* of a position over its *disadvantages*.

> "Justify the U.S.A.'s intervention into Cuban-Russian relations during Kennedy's administration."

397 List To **list** is like enumerating but calls even more clearly for a formal *numbering* or *sequencing*.

> "List three examples of naturalism in Jack London's *Call of the Wild.*"

398 Outline To **outline** is to organize a set of facts or ideas in terms of main points and sub points. Though a formal system of identifying these points one from another is not necessarily *demanded* by this term, it is usually a good idea. (See 357.)

> "Outline the events in the Tom Robinson affair."

399 Prove To **prove** means to give evidence, to present facts, to use logic as a base for clear, forthright argumentation.

> "Attempt to prove that capital punishment is **not** an effective deterrent to crime."

400 Relate To **relate** is to show how two or more things are connected because of similar reasons for being, similar results, or similar characteristics. Don't confuse this use of the word with the verb *to relate* meaning simply *to tell,* as in "He related the story of his life."

> "Relate the invention of the cotton gin to the spread of slavery into the territories of the West during the early 1800s."

401 Review To **review** (to view again) is to reexamine or to summarize the key characteristics or major points of an overall body of facts, principles, or ideas. Generally speaking, a **review** should present material in *chronological* (in the order in which it happened) or in *decreasing order* of importance or concern.

> "Review the steps leading to the founding of the United States."

402 State To **state** means *to say.* However, to state also means to present a *brief,* concise statement of a position, fact, or point of view. Usually a **statement** requires a shorter response than discussion.

> "State your reasons for having taken the position you now hold on the issues of States' Rights versus Federal Power."

403 Summarize To **summarize** (root: *sum*) is to present the main points of an issue in *condensed, shortened* form. Details, illustrations, and examples are not given.

> "Summarize Lincoln's reasons for issuing the Emancipation Proclamation."

404 Trace To **trace** is to present — in step-by-step sequence — a series of facts which are somehow related either in terms of time, order of importance, or cause and effect. The approach used most frequently is *time-order.*

> "Trace the events leading up to the attempted secession of several Southern states from the Union."

Reprinted by permission. Adapted from Dr. Kenneth L. Dulin's "The Vocabulary of Essay Questions."

Planning and Writing the Essay Test Answer

405   In addition to a basic understanding of the key words mentioned above, you must also understand how to go about writing the essay answer. The steps below should help:

1. **Read** the question several times or until you clearly understand what is being asked for. (Pay specific attention to the "key word" being used in the question.)

2. **Rephrase** the question into a statement which can serve as the thesis statement for your essay answer or the topic sentence for a one-paragraph answer. *Note:* It often works well to drop the key word and not attempt to include it in your thesis statement.

> **Question:** <u>Explain</u> the immediate effects of the atomic bomb on Hiroshima. *Thesis statement:* The immediate effects of the atomic bomb on Hiroshima were devastating.

3. **Outline** the main points you plan to cover in your answer. Time will probably not allow you to include all supporting details in your outline. (Using a topic outline rather than a sentence outline will also save time.)

4. **Write** your essay. Your opening sentence will be your thesis statement (the rephrased question). Follow this with any background information which is necessary for a complete understanding of your answer.

One-paragraph Answer   If you feel that only one paragraph is needed to answer the question, use the main points of your outline as supporting details for your thesis statement. (Your thesis statement now serves as the topic sentence of your single-paragraph answer.)

Multi-paragraph Answer   If the question is too complex to be handled in one paragraph, your opening paragraph will include only your thesis statement and background information. (See step 4.) Begin your second paragraph by rephrasing one of the main points from your outline into a suitable topic sentence. Support this topic sentence with examples, reasons, or other appropriate details. (Additional paragraphs should be handled in the same manner as paragraph two.) If time permits, add a summary or concluding paragraph to bring all of your thoughts to a logical close. By adding or changing an appropriate word or two, your original thesis statement can be used as a closing sentence (*clincher sentence*) for your essay answer.

The Essay Test Answer

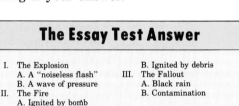

I.	The Explosion		B. Ignited by debris
	A. A "noiseless flash"	III.	The Fallout
	B. A wave of pressure		A. Black rain
II.	The Fire		B. Contamination
	A. Ignited by bomb		

The immediate effects of the atomic bomb on Hiroshima were devastating.

The initial explosion of the atomic bomb on Hiroshima has often been described by those who survived it as a "noiseless flash." The bomb which was dropped on this island city was equal in power to 13,000 tons of TNT; incredibly, no explosion was heard by the residents of Hiroshima. Instead, they recall an enormous flash of blinding light followed by a tremendous wave of pressure. The wave and the violent wind which followed did an unbelievable amount of damage. Train cars, stone walls, and bridges as far as two miles away from the impact area were toppled. Of the 90,000 buildings in Hiroshima, an estimated 62,000 were destroyed in an instant. In that same instant, the smoke and dust carried by the wind turned day into night.

The darkness quickly gave way to light as fires sprang up throughout the city. Buildings near the center of the explosion were ignited at once by the tremendous heat (estimated at 6,000 degrees C) which was generated by the splitting atoms. Away from the impact area, it was simply a matter of time before the splintered wreckage was ignited by exposed wiring and overturned cooking stoves. By late afternoon of the first day, very nearly every building in Hiroshima was ablaze.

As the fires raged, additional effects of the bomb became evident. Huge drops of "black rain" began to fall. The explosion had lifted tremendous amounts of smoke, dust, and fission fragments high into the atmosphere over Hiroshima. Soon a condensed moisture, blackened by the smoke and dust and contaminated with radiation, began to fall like rain on the city. The radioactive "fallout" polluted the air and water adding to the problems of those who had survived the blast and fires.

Before the day had ended, the devastation from the bomb was nearly complete. Very little of Hiroshima remained.

(Note: For information on taking objective tests, see 484-489.)

WRITING RELATED TO BUSINESS

The Business Letter

406 People communicate much differently today than they did even a few years ago. It is not uncommon for a message sent today to make use of memory chips, fiber optics, or even satellites as it travels from the sender to the receiver. The language used in the original message is transformed into electronic impulses, light rays, radio signals, and so on until it is finally transformed back into written or spoken form. Yet, regardless of how many times or ways the language is transformed or transmitted, the message which is received at the other end is still only as effective as the original sender made it.

What this means is that it doesn't really matter whether you use a computer, a telephone, a laser beam, or a letter to transfer your message; you are still the author of that message. But we all know that a telephone call is faster and more convenient than a letter, so why would anyone be concerned about knowing how to write a letter? Well, for one thing, faster and more convenient isn't always better. In the business world, for example, a letter has a number of very important advantages over a telephone conversation. Here are a few of those advantages:

The Advantages of a Letter

1. A letter provides the writer with plenty of time to think about what he or she wants to say.

2. A letter communicates a very specific message. Too often a phone conversation wanders from one topic to another and people can be left with several impressions of what was said.

3. A letter not only communicates a specific message, but it also provides the receiver with a copy of the message and the specific details of what action must be taken.

4. A letter is a written reminder to both parties of when and why the message was sent. This makes it more likely that the appropriate action will be taken and taken on time.

5. A letter can also serve as an official record of what was agreed upon by the two parties; for this reason, people in business often follow up a phone conversation with a letter so that they have a written record of what was discussed. Some businesses operate on the philosophy that if it isn't written down, it doesn't exist.

6. Written language usually has more impact than spoken language, especially in the business world.

7. A letter can be corrected and edited before it is sent; words said in haste or anger can never be completely erased.

As you might imagine, business letters are written for "business" reasons: to make a request, to order materials, to file a complaint, to apply for a job, and so on. A business letter is usually concise and to the point. Preferably, it should fit on one page. Business letters also have a very businesslike appearance and follow a specific pattern of form, style, and spacing.

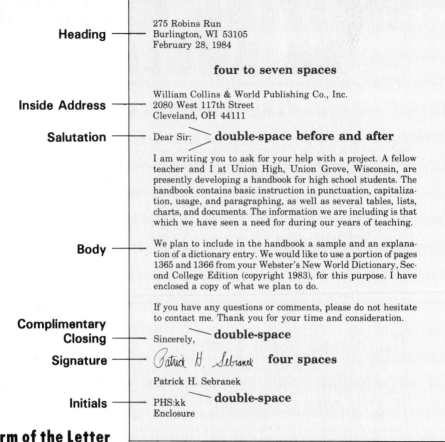

Heading

Inside Address

Salutation

Body

Complimentary Closing

Signature

Initials

275 Robins Run
Burlington, WI 53105
February 28, 1984

four to seven spaces

William Collins & World Publishing Co., Inc.
2080 West 117th Street
Cleveland, OH 44111

Dear Sir: **double-space before and after**

I am writing you to ask for your help with a project. A fellow teacher and I at Union High, Union Grove, Wisconsin, are presently developing a handbook for high school students. The handbook contains basic instruction in punctuation, capitalization, usage, and paragraphing, as well as several tables, lists, charts, and documents. The information we are including is that which we have seen a need for during our years of teaching.

We plan to include in the handbook a sample and an explanation of a dictionary entry. We would like to use a portion of pages 1365 and 1366 from your Webster's New World Dictionary, Second College Edition (copyright 1983), for this purpose. I have enclosed a copy of what we plan to do.

If you have any questions or comments, please do not hesitate to contact me. Thank you for your time and consideration.

Sincerely, **double-space**

Patrick H. Sebranek **four spaces**

Patrick H. Sebranek

PHS:kk **double-space**
Enclosure

407 Form of the Letter

The **heading** for the business letter includes the complete address and full date and is placed about an inch from the top of the page. (*Note:* If letterhead stationery is used, only the date need be placed in the heading position. The date should be placed several spaces below the letterhead.)

The **inside address** is placed on the left margin several (approximately four to seven) line spaces below the heading. It should include the name and address of the person and/or company the letter is being sent to. (*Note:* If the person you are writing to also has a title with the company he represents, place that title after his name. Separate the two with a comma. Place the title on the next line if it is two or more words long.)

The **salutation** is placed two spaces below and directly under the inside address. The most common salutations when addressing a company or firm are *Gentlemen:, Dear Sirs:,* or *Dear (Company Name).* If you are writing to an individual within that company, you should address him or her *Dear Mr. . . . , Dear Miss . . . , Dear Ms. . . . , Dear President. . . .*

The **body** of the business letter is the same in form as the body of any letter. It should be single-spaced (unless it is very short: seven lines or less) with a double-space between paragraphs. If the body carries over to a second page, the name of the addressee should be typed at the top left margin. Two line spaces should be placed after the name.

The **closing** comes between the body and the signature. The most commonly used closings for the business letter include *Very truly, Very truly yours, Yours truly, Sincerely yours,* etc. *Respectfully yours* is often used when writing to an employer or government official. In each case, the closing is followed by a comma.

The **signature** of a business letter should always include a handwritten signature of the writer, followed by the typed name and title of the writer. If someone other than the writer types the letter, it is customary to place the typist's initials after those of the writer against the left margin, two or three spaces below the typed signature. If an enclosure is sent with the letter, this fact should be made clear by placing the word *Enclosure(s)* or *Enc.* below the signature.

Styles of the Business Letter

Semi-Block   **Block**   **Full Block**

Guidelines for Writing a Business Letter

408

1. A good business letter is written for a definite purpose; know what your purpose is and make it clear early in the letter. (It can be helpful to actually write this purpose out on a piece of paper and keep it in front of you as you write.)

2. Collect all the information you will need for your letter and jot down the basic order in which you plan to cover this information. Organize your material in the most natural or most persuasive order.

3. Keep your reader in mind as you write, and select a tone for your letter which is appropriate for the reader and the "business" you are writing about. Your tone might be friendly, but firm; tactful, but insistent; etc. Whatever the tone, however, you must always be courteous. Use positive rather than negative words.

4. Use a writing style which is natural and easy to read; business letters need not be boring or complicated. Avoid the use of words and phrases which are stiff, technical, or overused. (See the "Expressions to Avoid in Business Writing," 411.)

5. Read your first draft out loud to test it for overall "sound" and effectiveness. Be sure your letter states clearly what it is you want your reader to do after he or she reads your letter. List only as many of the specific details as your reader needs to know. End your letter with a pleasant statement and a reminder of what action you hope your reader will take.

6. Follow the correct form for the kind of letter you are writing and use that form throughout your letter. For example, if you indent one paragraph, indent them all. If you place the heading along the left margin, place the closing there as well.

7. Make sure your final copy is typed or written (in ink) neatly and is attractive in appearance. Change typewriter ribbons if yours is light or inconsistent. Use a good quality paper whenever possible, and erase or cover your errors completely.

8. Revise and proofread your letter the same way you would any other piece of writing. Look for errors in sentence structure, usage, punctuation, spelling, capitalization, etc. (Use a proofreading checklist.)

9. Fold your letter following the method used with a standard-sized (4¼" x 9½") business envelope.

10. Address the envelope carefully, using either the traditional system of upper- and lower-case letters or the new postal system of all capital letters and no punctuation.

The Letter of Complaint

A letter of complaint should be written following the same guidelines as any other business letter. In addition, it is very important to include all the essential information surrounding the complaint so that the appropriate action can be taken by the reader.

1. Begin your letter with a brief description of the **product** (or service), including the brand name, model number, and where and when you bought the product.

2. Also include a description of just what the **problem** is, when you first noticed it, and what you think may be the **cause** of the problem.

3. If you have already tried to resolve the problem, explain what you did and what the result of that **action** was. Include the names of those people you talked to about the problem.

4. Finally, suggest what action you would like the reader to take to **solve** the problem.

Sample Letter of Complaint

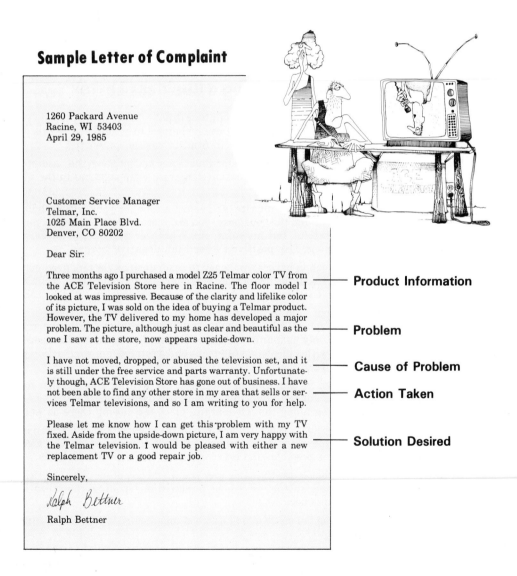

1260 Packard Avenue
Racine, WI 53403
April 29, 1985

Customer Service Manager
Telmar, Inc.
1025 Main Place Blvd.
Denver, CO 80202

Dear Sir:

Three months ago I purchased a model Z25 Telmar color TV from the ACE Television Store here in Racine. The floor model I looked at was impressive. Because of the clarity and lifelike color of its picture, I was sold on the idea of buying a Telmar product. However, the TV delivered to my home has developed a major problem. The picture, although just as clear and beautiful as the one I saw at the store, now appears upside-down. — **Problem**

I have not moved, dropped, or abused the television set, and it is still under the free service and parts warranty. Unfortunately though, ACE Television Store has gone out of business. I have not been able to find any other store in my area that sells or services Telmar televisions, and so I am writing to you for help. — **Cause of Problem** / **Action Taken**

Please let me know how I can get this problem with my TV fixed. Aside from the upside-down picture, I am very happy with the Telmar television. I would be pleased with either a new replacement TV or a good repair job. — **Solution Desired**

Sincerely,

Ralph Bettner

Ralph Bettner

Product Information

410 Addressing the Business Envelope

Addressing your letter correctly can be critical to the promptness of its delivery. The destination address on the envelope must be exactly the same as the inside address on the letter, and the return address must match the heading. The destination address begins in the center of the envelope, and the return address is placed in the upper left-hand corner.

There are two acceptable formats for business addresses. In the older, traditional system, both upper- and lower-case letters are used, as are punctuation and abbreviations. The newer system is preferred by the postal system. Their bulletins state: "You will get the best possible service if you remember these four important steps in addressing your letters:

1. Capitalize everything in the address.
2. Use the list of common abbreviations found in the National ZIP Code Directory. (See 116.)
3. Eliminate all punctuation.
4. Use the special state (two-letter) abbreviations found in the ZIP Directory." (See index.)

Old System	New System
Mr. James Evans	MR JAMES EVANS
512 North Adams Ave.	512 N ADAMS AVE
Winona, MN 55987	WINONA MN 55987

Alternate Forms of Addresses

There are various combinations for addresses. Here are some examples:

MISS TRISH DATON
BOX 77
HOUSTON TX 77008

NORTHERN CORP
ATTN D J HENKHAUR
XYZ CORP RM 4A
MAJOR INDUSTRIAL PARK
CLEVELAND OH 44135

MR TEDDY BARE
PRESIDENT
ACME TOY COMPANY
4421 RANDOLPH ST
CHEYENNE WY 82001

ACCOUNTING DEPT
STEVENSON LTD BLDG 18
2632 FOURTH ST
DULUTH MN 55803

MS JOAN JACKSON
261 MASON ST APT 44
TORONTO ONTARIO
CANADA

Folding the Letter

The *preferred* method for folding a letter is used with a standard-sized (4 1/4" x 9 1/2") business envelope.

1. Begin by folding the bottom edge of the letter so that the paper is divided into thirds.
2. Next, fold the top third of the letter down and crease the edges firmly.
3. Finally, insert the letter into the envelope with the open end at the top.

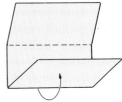

A second method of folding is used when your envelope is smaller than the traditional business envelope.

1. Begin by folding the letter in half.
2. Next, fold the letter into thirds.
3. Insert the letter into the envelope.

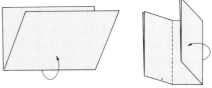

A
above-mentioned
accidents will happen
acid test
a factor in the problem
after all is said and done
all boils down to
all in all
all things being equal
all things considered
along this line
a matter of concern
and/or
are in receipt of
as a last resort
as a matter of fact
as per
at an early date
attached hereto
at the present writing
at this point in time
at your earliest convenience

B
bear in mind
belabor the point
benefit of the doubt
best foot forward
be that as it may
better late than never
beyond the shadow of a doubt
bit off more than I can chew
break the ice
bring the matter up
burning my candle at both ends
by and large
by leaps and bounds
by no means
by the same token

C
calm before the storm
cart before the horse
come through with flying colors
conspicuous by its absence
constructive criticism

D
days on end
don't rock the boat

E
earliest possible moment
easier said than done
enclosed herewith
enclosed please find
explore every avenue

F
face the fact

fall down on the job
far be it from me
far-reaching effects
few and far between
fill the bill
food for thought
for your information

G
get down to brass tacks
get down to business

H
have on good authority
heart of the matter
honesty is the best policy

I
I beg to remain
I beg to stay
I'd like to share
if and when
in conclusion
in reference to
in short supply
in the final analysis
in the foreseeable future
in the long run
in the matter of
in view of the fact that
it goes without saying
it is interesting to note
it stands to reason

L
last but not least
leave no stone unturned
leaves much to be desired

M
make a concerted effort
make a long story short
make contact with
map out a plan

N
needless to say
no action has been taken
no time like the present
now or never

O
once and for all
on the right track
out of the blue

P
par for the course
permit me
please advise me
please feel free to
pursuant to your request

Q
quick as a flash

R
rank and file
red letter day
regarding the matter of
rest assured

S
sadder but wiser
see eye-to-eye
sell like hot cakes
sharp as a tack
shift into high gear
shot in the arm
slowly but surely
so richly deserved
status quo
stitch in time saves nine
straight and narrow path
strike while the iron is hot

T
take a dim view
take into account
take the bull by the horns
take this opportunity to
tendered his resignation
this will acknowledge
thus I have shown
time is money
to all intents and purposes
token of our appreciation
to make a long story short
to no avail
to put it mildly
to the bitter end
tried and true

U
unaccustomed as I am

V
venture to predict

W
water under the bridge
we are pleased to advise
we wish to state
with reference to
words are inadequate
words cannot describe
words cannot express
words fail to express
word to the wise

Y
you are hereby advised

Form and Appearance

☐ 1. The letter is neatly written in ink or typed with no smudges or obvious corrections.

☐ 2. The letter contains all necessary parts of a business letter.

☐ 3. The letter is centered on the page, with spacing equal above and below and on left and right. Correct spacing is also necessary between parts of the letter. (See sample letter, 407.)

☐ 4. All left-hand margins are exactly even.

☐ 5. The right-hand margin of the body of the letter is fairly even.

☐ 6. The signature is legible and written in blue or black ink.

Punctuation

☐ 1. A comma always separates the city and state. There is no comma between the state and ZIP code.

☐ 2. A comma separates the day of the month from the year in the heading.

☐ 3. A colon is used after the salutation.

☐ 4. A comma is used after the closing.

Capitalization

☐ 1. The names of streets, cities, and people in the heading, inside address, or body are capitalized.

☐ 2. The month in the heading is capitalized.

☐ 3. The title of the person you are writing to and the name of the department and company listed in the inside address are capitalized.

☐ 4. The word *Dear* and all nouns in the salutation are capitalized.

☐ 5. Only the first word of the closing is capitalized.

Spelling

☐ 1. The numbered street names up to ten are spelled out. Figures are used for numbers above ten.

☐ 2. The names of cities, streets, and months in the heading and inside address are spelled out. The state may be abbreviated, but make sure it is abbreviated correctly.

Wording

☐ 1. Avoid using words and expressions which are phony, vague, or sexist.

Avoid these expressions	Use these instead
ceased functioning	quit working
excessive amount	too many
furthermore	then, also
likewise	and, also
numerous	many
subsequent	next
chairwoman	chair, moderator
foreman	supervisor
mailman	letter carrier
salesman	sales representative
manpower	work force

Writing In-House Messages

413 Memos, bulletins, and short reports which are well written make good impressions on co-workers and bosses. This fact alone is reason enough to learn how to write them well. Below are several basic guidelines to follow when writing in-house papers.

  *State the purpose in the first sentence.
  *Include the date and time.
  *Be specific.
  *Write neatly and clearly.
  *Use only those abbreviations that are clearly understood.
  *Arrange information in the order that will be most useful to the reader.

Writing Memorandums

A standard form is used within many organizations for writing longer messages, including memorandums, bulletins, and short reports. It is usually written to a number of people, not just one. It can be used to help organize a meeting, to report on the meeting, or to circulate useful information about the meeting. This form might be circulated to specific people (*memorandum*), or it could be posted for all interested parties to see (*bulletin*).

INTER-TECH, INC.

Memorandum   **Date:** October 21, 19___

To: Secretarial Staff

From: Jane Brand, Personnel Director

Subject: Career Advancement Program

     This month's meeting will be held next Thursday at 8:00 p.m. It will feature Dr. G.F. Gillis, a professor at City Technical College. He will speak on moving up the career ladder, a topic which I'm sure interests all of us. He is planning a winter term training program which will feature all facets of office administration and communication. Sign up with me if you plan to attend.

BULLETIN

To: All Sales People   **Subject:** Inventory

To keep our inventory information up to date, please indicate the type of record or tape sold on each sales slip. Choose one of the following categories:

Popular	--P	Folk	--F
Classical	--C	Rock	--R
Jazz	--J		

Use the first letter of each category and put it next to the price on the sales slip.

Signed: *Will U. Tally*

Writing Messages

On-the-job skills often include writing short but important messages to fellow employees. In many cases, standardized forms are used throughout an office or business. However, if no standardized form is available, you can use the 5 W's as a guideline of what to include.

Who - Who is the message for?
Who is the message from?
Who is writing the message?

What - What is the message? (Be brief but complete)

When - When was the message written? (Date and time)
When is the meeting, appointment, etc. mentioned in the message?

Where - Where is the receiver of the message to go?

Why - Why is there a need for a meeting, appointment, etc.?

Note: When writing down any message (telephone or personal), be sure to get all the facts correctly. Accuracy and clarity are essential. Telephone numbers must include area codes; names must be spelled correctly. Ask the caller to clarify any information which you are unsure of. Each good message you write will help establish your reputation as an efficient, dependable worker.

Using A Standard Message Form

MESSAGE

To: *Mr. Smith* Date: *Sept. 5, 1984*
Time: *10:00 a.m.*

From: *Elinor Stacey of the Daily Press*

Telephone:

- [ ] Telephoned:
- [ ] Called to see you
- [x] Returned your call
- [ ] Please call
- [ ] Will call again
- [ ] URGENT

Message: *There will be no problem in rescheduling your interview. She will meet you at the dump site on Thursday, Sept. 14, at 9:00 a.m.*

By: *Stan Killberg*

Message When No Form Is Used

Mr. Smith, you received a call from Elinor Stacey of the Daily Press at 10:00 a.m. today (Sept. 5, 1984). She said there would be no problem in rescheduling your interview. She will meet you at the dump site on Thursday, Sept. 14, at 9:00 a.m.

Stan Killberg

The Letter of Application and Résumé

In the very near future and several times throughout your lifetime, you will be applying for a job. Some authorities estimate that a worker entering the work force in the next several years will change jobs an average of six times in his or her lifetime. The competition for good jobs is bound to increase as the job market changes. Those workers who know how to go about applying for a job will be at a distinct advantage. One very important part of applying for and landing a job is the letter of application and personal résumé.

Your **letter of application** is your introduction, your calling card. It creates that all-important first impression and usually determines whether or not you will be considered and interviewed for the job. The effectiveness of your letter will depend in large part on how well you tell your own story — how well you communicate your qualifications for the job and what it is you can contribute to the employer. There are two types of job application letters: the cover letter, which is sent with a résumé, and the independent letter of application, which contains much of the information normally contained in a résumé.

A **résumé** is an organized summary of the job applicant's background and qualifications. It lists the applicant's education, work experience, talents, skills, etc. It should be a vivid word picture of the person applying for the job. It must be organized in such a way that the prospective employer can see at a glance whether the applicant has the necessary background for the job.

The content and format of résumés may vary slightly, but generally all résumés contain the following information:

Personal data	Employment objective
Educational background	Work experience
Special skills or knowledge	Other experience (military, clubs
Accomplishments	and organizations, volunteer
References (on a separate sheet)	work, etc.)

When you use a résumé to apply for a job, you also need a short **cover letter**. The cover letter should not simply repeat information given in the résumé; instead, it should begin by identifying the job for which you are applying and telling how you heard about it. You can then add any other information not included in the résumé which might be important for this particular job. Finally, request an interview; include your phone number and when you can be reached.

On the pages which follow you will find samples of a **cover letter**, a **résumé**, an **independent letter of application**, and a **follow-up letter**.

Guidelines for Writing a Cover Letter

Do ...

1. Address the letter to a specific individual whenever possible.
2. Develop a bridge between yourself and employer at the very beginning — tell how you learned of the vacancy.
3. Give a brief statement emphasizing your qualifications for this position.
4. Use words directly from the job ad to describe what you can do.
5. Emphasize what you can do for an employer rather than what he can do for you.
6. Highlight parts of the enclosed résumé which specifically pertain to the job offered.
7. Indicate the dates you are available for interviewing.
8. Show enthusiasm throughout your letter.
9. Sign each letter.
10. Follow up the mailing with a telephone call.

Don't . . .

1. Don't use awkward salutations as, "To Whom It May Concern" or "Dear Sir or Madam."

2. Don't begin each sentence or paragraph with "I."

3. Don't fill the page; stick to three or four short paragraphs.

4. Don't use cliches or overused expressions.

5. Don't change from one style to another in the same letter. Stick to either block or semi-block.

6. Don't send out duplicated letters.

Guidelines for Writing a Résumé

Do . . .

1. Put your name (in caps), address, and phone number (and when you are available at that number) at the top of your résumé.

2. List your career aims and objectives. This allows you an opportunity to express enthusiasm for the job as well as to list your general qualifications for the job.

3. Include information about your educational background.

4. Be specific when describing your achievements — use numbers and figures (. . . graduated in top five percent, . . . maintained a *B* average, . . . missed only one day of school, . . . supervised seven other workers).

5. List your work experience. Include positions held, names of employers, specific duties, and dates you held each position.

6. Include information about related experiences. List volunteer work, club duties, family responsibilities, and any other experience or activities which reflect positively on your ability to work in a responsible, dependable manner.

7. Keep the résumé as brief as possible. Cover all the essential information clearly and concisely; try to limit your résumé to one typed page (never more than two pages).

8. Arrange the information within the résumé in order of the most impressive or most important to the job for which you are applying.

9. Proofread carefully for spelling, punctuation, and typographical errors.

10. Experiment with the layout of the résumé for overall appearance and readability.

11. Get someone else's reaction before typing the final copy.

12. Use only typed originals (or high-quality photocopies or offset printed copies).

13. Be timely in responding to ads.

Don't . . .

1. Don't emphasize what you want in a job; stress how you fit into the employer's needs.

2. Don't use the same résumé for every job application — custom design each résumé to fit that particular job.

3. Don't list personal statistics such as your weight, height, and age.

4. Don't use "big" words or long, complicated sentences.

5. Don't use unfamiliar abbreviations or unnecessary jargon.

6. Don't include information about salaries or wages.

7. Don't include references on the same sheet as the résumé. (Have them available on a separate sheet in case the employer requests them.)

8. Don't include strictly personal references such as a neighbor or friend.

Sample Cover Letter

5340 Tower Avenue
Bolton, MA 01437
September 29, 1985

Mr. David Schroeder
Schroeder Chevrolet and Pontiac
1320 Highland Avenue
Bolton, MA 01437

Dear Mr. Schroeder:

Mrs. Burton, your office manager, mentioned that you are
in need of an auto mechanic in your shop. The enclosed
résumé will show you that automotive repairs has been my
occupation and my recreation.

A successful dealership like yours depends on reputation. I
have had good customer relations all the time I worked at
Frank's Texaco. My stock car experience has made me
familiar with a variety of parts and engines.

May I call you after 2:30 p.m. on Thursday, October 3, to set
up a time and date for an interview? If this is not a convenient time, please call me any day after 2:30 at 848-7653.
I look forward to meeting you.

Thank you for your consideration.

Sincerely,

Bob Keefe

Bob Keefe

BK:skj
Enclosures

Sample Résumé

ROBERT E. KEEFE

5340 Tower Avenue   (413) 848-7653
Bolton, MA 01437   (after 2:30 p.m.)

JOB OBJECTIVE: Automobile mechanic in car dealership

EDUCATION: Northwest Technical College
                       Large engine repair (night courses)
                     Bolton High School - Graduated June,
                     1983
                       Major course emphasis:
                       Auto Mechanics I, II, III
                       Small Engine Repair
                       Power Mechanics

EXPERIENCE: Frank's Texaco Service
1981 - present   Auto mechanic, gas station attendant
                       (part-time)
                         *Numerous customers
                          request me to do their work.
                         *88% customer satisfaction
                         *Own automotive tools
1980 - present   Restored several stock cars
                         *Was asked to display one car
                          at Bolton Mall.
                         *Sold two cars at 50% profit.

AWARDS AND
MEMBERSHIPS:
1981-1983   Member, Bolton High School
                     Automotive Club
1983   Stock car entry took 3rd place, Dade
                     County Fair.

REFERENCES: Available upon request.

MOLLY C. KEYES

Present	Permanent
310 North Ninth, Apt. B	409 West Spring Street
La Crosse, Wisconsin 54601	Burlington, Wisconsin 53105
(608) 784-4722	(414) 763-9705

EDUCATION

University of Wisconsin-La Crosse
La Crosse, Wisconsin 54601

* Certified to teach grades 1-8, certification number
  118 of the Wisconsin code.
* Bachelor of Science Degree received May 1984
* Major: Elementary Education
  Minor: Special Education
* Experienced a comprehensive view of the field of
  education
* Aware of current trends and issues in education
* Obtained direction in the methods and ideology of an
  effective teacher
* Financed total education

PROFESSIONAL EXPERIENCE

Student Teacher, Ludwig Middle School
La Crosse, Wisconsin 54601

* Taught in a variety of curriculum areas including
  math, science, reading, spelling, health, and the
  language arts
* Developed and implemented daily lesson plans
* Participated in unit and faculty meetings
* Acquainted with the daily
  duties of the teacher

Activity Assistant, Coulee Region Infant Development
Center, La Crosse, Wisconsin 54601

* Assisted with activities for the developmentally
  disabled on a weekly basis
* Aided in the daily living instruction in both the EMR
  and TMR rooms

WORK EXPERIENCE

Tour Guide/Tourist Coordinator,
La Crosse Area Convention and Visitors Bureau (Riverside
USA), La Crosse, Wisconsin 54601

* Greeted and welcomed tourists to La Crosse
* Helped tourists find hotel and restaurant
  accommodations
* Maintained the operation of Riverside USA
* Supervised the employees of Riverside USA

Waitress, Natale's
Burlington, Wisconsin 53105

* Maintained public relations with customers
* Established a working relationship with the staff

CREDENTIALS

Available upon request.

Career Services, Wilder Hall
University of Wisconsin-La Crosse
La Crosse, Wisconsin 54601
(608) 785-8514

**Sample Résumé
of College
Graduate Applying
for First Job**

Guidelines for the Letter of Application

1. Follow the "Guidelines for Writing a Business Letter," 408.

2. Include essentially the same information as that which is included in a résumé.

3. Keep the letter as short as possible while still including the essential information. (Three-quarters to one full sheet is an acceptable length.)

4. Use a separate letter for each job opening; include information about the specific job for which you are applying.

5. Tell why you are writing, identify the job you are applying for, and tell how you heard of the opening. Do this in the opening sentence(s).

6. Show an understanding of the requirements of the job and point out how you are able to fill those requirements.

7. List your qualifications, personal data, and your references. (Include the "optional" information if it is appropriate for the job for which you are applying.)

Qualifications	Personal Data	References (optional)
Job experience	Educational background	Teachers, coaches
Related experience	Grades, accomplishments	Clergymen
Special training	Age, health (optional)	Former employers
Career plans	Work habits, attitude	Professional acquaintances

8. Be positive and enthusiastic — sell yourself. Don't, however, claim to be qualified for something you are not.

9. Keep the tone of the letter honest and natural. Avoid cliches and overused phrases.

10. Request an interview; list your phone number and when you can be reached.

---

415 Empire Avenue
Glen Ellyn, IL 60137
January 17, 19__

Sample Letter of Application

Ethel Richards, Manager
Sea 'n' Sky Travel Agency
4444 Burright Building
Glen Ellyn, IL 60137

Dear Ms. Richards:

Mr. Lee Underhill, our work-study program advisor here at Central High, pointed out your advertisement for a part-time office assistant. I would like you to consider me for the position.

I know I might at first seem young for this job, but I assure you I have the necessary office skills. My grades are the highest in the business classes I take, and I have completed both basic and advanced computer courses. The second qualification I have for this job is my experience in traveling. I have visited all but four of our states and have toured in Europe, Africa, and Mexico in the last five years. I speak Spanish fluently and can communicate passably in French. I intend to continue my studies in languages next year at City College and work toward my goal of being an interpreter for the United Nations.

I am finished with classes every day at noon, so I am free to work afternoons, evenings, and weekends. Please contact me at home to arrange for an interview at your convenience. My number is 763-2532. Since I enjoy meeting people and am enthusiastic about the joys of traveling, I feel I could be a good addition to your staff.

Sincerely,

Richard Greggs

Richard Greggs

The Letter of Request

One of the most important parts of the job-hunting process is lining up good references. In many cases, it is the recommendation of a respected member of the community which can make the difference between getting or not getting a job. Before you can list a person as a reference on your résumé or letter of application, however, you must first get his or her permission. The letter below is one example of how a letter of request can be worded. Make your letter personal whenever possible; always make it clear exactly why you are writing.

The Follow-Up Letter

Another important step in the job-hunting process, one that is often ignored, is the follow-up letter sent after the interview. A follow-up letter will get your name before the interviewer one more time; it is your chance to further influence the decision. A good follow-up letter should contain the following:

1. A thank-you-for-the-interview comment.
2. A statement that reaffirms your interest in the position and your value as an employee in that position.
3. A statement that you will be available for further interviews at their convenience.

Letter of Request

4149 Osage Drive
Burlingame, IA 54321
December 2, 19—

Fr. Jerry Sawill
195 Smith Street
Farwell, ND 53467

Dear Fr. Sawill:

I am writing to request your permission to use your name as a reference. I am going to begin to apply for part-time jobs to save money for next year's college tuition.

You have known me as long and as well as anyone, except for my parents, of course. I would greatly appreciate it if you would serve as a personal reference. I will send this semester's grades when they arrive and any other recent information that you might be able to use.

We really miss seeing you and our other friends since we moved here to Iowa. I will stop in to see you when we come to visit over the Christmas holidays.

Sincerely,

Sue Fugate

Sue Fugate

Follow-Up Letter

6455 North Lincoln Street
Chicago, IL 60606
February 16, 19__

Mr. George Carter
Bart Wholesale Furniture Company
7194 Shermac Drive
Chicago, IL 60606

Dear Mr. Carter:

Thank you for your time and courtesy yesterday. I enjoyed meeting you and all your employees at the store. The tour you gave me answered all the questions I had. I was especially impressed with the efficiency exhibited throughout your store.

My enthusiasm for gaining the position of sales manager is even greater now that I have seen the possibilities. I believe that my managerial ability, coupled with the positive attitudes and talents of the present staff, could lead to an increase in overall sales.

I have already begun considering a number of ideas for improvements which I would try if hired. If you have any further questions, I will continue to be available for additional interviewing at your convenience.

Sincerely,

Jackie Penkotti

Jackie Penkotti

THE BOOK REVIEW

419 A book review is not simply a plot summary or an unsupported opinion of how well the reader did or did not like the book. A book review includes information about the book (plot, characters, setting, theme, etc.) and the reviewer's opinion of how well the author has succeeded in writing an effective story. A good book review presents evidence to support this opinion, and, in the process, helps the reader gain an insight into the story. In general, the writer of a book review gives enough information to help the reader decide whether he or she wants to read the book, but not so much as to spoil the joy of discovery which comes from reading a good book.

To do a good job of reviewing a book, the writer must know the book thoroughly. This requires a careful, attentive reading (and rereading of certain parts). The writer must also know what kind of book it is he or she is reading (romance novel, biography, historical novel, science fiction, etc.) and what characterizes good literature of this type. For example, it would be wrong to criticize a biography because it lacked a strong plot or to find fault with a science fiction novel because it had an unrealistic setting. As you read, consider the following points:

As You Read

1. Determine the author's purpose in writing this book. Read the preface and introduction—they often contain clues and occasionally a specific statement of the author's purpose or intention.

2. Look closely at the title and subtitle. Sometimes (but not always) the title or subtitle can provide an important clue as to the "meaning" of the book.

3. As you read, take notes on anything which you feel could be useful to you later when you attempt to piece everything together. (*Example:* "The author's description of the character's first day of school is very believable. The overly friendly attitude of the teacher is especially effective.")

4. Make a list of especially good or especially weak passages, as well as any passages which you might use as quotations in your review.

5. Summarize each chapter (or every 15-20 pages). React to your summaries: Are you enjoying the story to this point? Why or why not? Are you confused about anything in the story? What questions would you like to ask someone else about the book?

Before You Write

1. Read about the author in other sources, especially if you find yourself needing to know more about his or her background, qualifications, or philosophy. (Include this information in your actual review only if it will help the reader understand the book or your review more clearly.)

2. Read books or articles which discuss the kind of literature you are reviewing or which cover the historical time period in which the story was written or is set.

3. Decide what the theme or central point of your review is going to be. Be sure you have a significant and well-defined theme. Avoid themes which are too obvious, too general, or vague. Word your theme (*thesis statement*) carefully, making certain you understand all the key literary terms used.

4. Go over your notes and list the evidence (examples, quotations, summaries) which supports your theme. You might use a support sheet like the one which follows:

Sample Support Sheet

Thesis: Gatsby is a true crusader for the American Dream, but a crusader with a flaw.

1. We could all admire Gatsby if it weren't for the obscure hint of tarnish on his armor or those tiny, black rumors that float among his party guests like the "foul dust" Nick speaks of (147).

2. We know of Gatsby's shady dealings and his "connections," yet we cannot really accuse him of being wrong because we can see into his fanciful dreams and unrealized ambitions (98).

3. The trouble with Gatsby is that he gets some of the important things in his life a little mixed up--one of them is love. He thinks he is in love with a wealthy girl by the name of Daisy Fay; in fact, it is her wealth he has fallen in love with (47).

4. Perhaps Gatsby's greatest flaw is his inability to comprehend the difference between the rich and the wealthy--between his world and Daisy's. The rich have the money, but not the culture, tradition, or standing of the wealthy (49).

5. Gatsby continued to believe that one day he would achieve his goals and that one day Daisy would come back to him. "Gatsby believed in the green light, the orgiastic future that year by year recedes before us. It eluded us then, but that's no matter--tomorrow we will run faster, stretch our arms farther. . . . And one fine morning . . . " (187).

6. But Gatsby has little chance of realizing his goals: "So we beat on, boats against the current, borne back ceaselessly into the past" (201).

5. Arrange into an outline your "evidence" and all other points you plan to cover in your review. Make sure that all of the information in your outline relates to your theme and is important enough to include. Arrange your points in a logical way so that the reader will be able to follow your thinking and will understand how you came to the conclusion you did.

Beginning Your Review

1. Keep your thesis statement and outline in front of you as you write your first draft.

2. Leave room on your paper (skip lines, double-space, or leave wide margins) for revising and correcting.

3. Using your outline as a guide, write freely about the book. You might also write freely using other general questions about the book: What is your general impression of the book? Was it exciting or dull and predictable? Did you learn anything from it? What is most real or believable about it? Which parts are especially good or memorable? Which characters are most believable or lifelike? What truth about life is revealed? What seems to be the point, lesson, or theme of the story?

4. Next, work on an opening or introduction for your review. There are a number of possibilities you might try. You might, for example, use one (or combine several) of the suggestions below into an opening paragraph:

   a. Summarize the novel very briefly. Include in this summary the title, author, and type of book. This can be done with a statement of "what and how" about the book. (*Example:* In his allegorical novel, Lord of the Flies, William Golding writes about [*what?*] the evil side of man [*how?*] by describing what happens to a group of young boys who are marooned on a deserted island with no adults to control their actions.)

   b. Use a passage from the book and follow it with a comment on how this quotation is typical (or not typical) of what is contained in the book.

c.   You might begin with what you believe to be the author's purpose in writing the book and how well you think he or she achieves this purpose.

d.   You can discuss briefly the theme or major problem dealt with in the book.

e.   You can present information about the author and his or her background, qualifications, or philosophy.

f.   Finally, state your specific theme.

5.   In the body of your review, you must restate your theme and support it with significant details. The body should be developed with a clear focus and a specific sense of direction and purpose. It can be helpful to present your theme early in your review and follow with these three steps: 1. *State* each of your ideas about your theme clearly (*generalization*). 2. *Support* each of your generalizations with specific details from the story (*evidence*). 3. *Explain* how each of these specific details proves your point (*interpretation*). Continue to focus on your theme as you add and analyze your details; remember that it is very easy to get off the track.

6.   Make each new paragraph in your review a continuation of your central theme. Be careful not to leave any thought gaps as you switch from one paragraph to another. Tie your paragraphs together with ideas related to your theme; very often in a book review, a key word or phrase can be used as a linking device. Resist the temptation to rely heavily on plot for transitional material. Try to build your theme to a high point where all your ideas finally come together.

7.   End your review with a paragraph (or two) which brings your theme into final focus for the reader. You might, for instance, arrive at a specific conclusion about your theme, the author's purpose, or the overall effectiveness of the story.

Writing about Content

Once you have written your introduction, you should next experiment with the arrangement of the material in the body of the review. Go over your outline and freewritings and decide what information would logically follow your introduction. Below are a number of approaches you might follow when writing about the content of a book.

1.   If you are reviewing a novel, you will have to write something about each of the four main elements of fiction: *plot, character, setting,* and *theme.* You will give most of your attention to the element(s) which is most important to the overall effectiveness of the novel.

a.   **Plot** — Discuss only as much of the plot as is necessary to give your reader a general idea of the story. Never give away the ending or any unusual twist in the plot.

b.   **Character** — You should pay particular attention to the characters and the author's method of developing these characters throughout the story. If there is one character who is central to the entire novel, you should point this out to your reader. You might trace the changes this character goes through and comment on the reasons for these changes. You can consider what forces—internal and external—motivate a particular character or shape his personality. You can discuss a particular character and how he does or does not adjust to the new situations which arise in the story. Or you can write about the characters in general and to what extent they are believable, consistent, and interesting.

c.   **Setting** — The setting is very important in some novels, not nearly so important in others. Typically, setting is most important in historical and science fiction novels, and novels wherein atmosphere or mood are especially important. If it is important for your reader to know the specific time and place in which this story takes place, include a description of the setting. This description may be quite short; if so, you may want to combine it with other information.

d.   **Theme** — You should always pay some attention to the theme of the story and how well the author has developed this theme. Sometimes a theme can be stated as a moral or lesson: "If you give someone too much power, he is bound to abuse it." Other times a story is based on a more general theme: ambition, charity, duty, fame, freedom, greed, guilt, happiness, hypocrisy, jealousy, love, loyalty, patriotism, poverty, prejudice, pride, responsibility, sacrifice, survival, tradition, etc. A story might also deal with several themes. You must decide how important the theme is to the overall effectiveness of the story and how much attention you should give to the theme in your review.

    e.   **Other Elements** — If the author uses other elements (*symbolism, satire, irony,* etc.) to add impact to his story, you should mention this in your review. If these elements are present in the story, but do not contribute significantly to the overall effectiveness, you need not write about them.

2.   If the book you have read includes a good deal of symbolism or satire, you should consider the different levels of meaning which may be present. The plot will provide the first and most obvious level, but there may be a deeper meaning which is closer to the author's purpose. Look carefully at the author's use of symbolism, irony, satire, personification, and other figures of speech (549-559). If possible, discuss your interpretation with someone else who has read the book and compare thoughts. Then decide whether your interpretation is valid enough to share with your readers.

3.   If the author is attempting to convey a strong message of political or social importance, you should comment on how well this message comes across and whether it enhances or detracts from the story.

4.   Include your opinion or reaction to the book. Point out where the book succeeds or fails and support your opinion with specific references or examples from the book.

Writing about Style

In some books, the style of the author plays an especially important part in the overall success of the book. In those cases you may choose to include information about the author's style in your review. Style is the manner of writing (*how* something is said rather than *what* is said). Style is determined by the author's choice of words, his arrangement of those words into sentences, and the relationship of those sentences to each other. Below you will find a guideline to follow when analyzing and writing about style.

1.   **Diction** — The author's choice of words is generally referred to as *diction*. In a novel or short story, there are two distinct needs an author must consider when it comes to word choice. He will need to provide language for his characters to use (*dialogue*) and language for the narrator to use (*narration*). Both his dialogue and narration must be worded carefully. When considering dialogue, for instance, each character must be given a manner of speaking which is appropriate for a person of his background, education, attitude, and so on. This is the *level of language* and is generally described using one or more of the terms in the list below. Likewise, the narration must be consistent with the subject being described.

Dialogue		Narration	
Archaic	Slang	Common or technical	Conversational or stilted
Artificial	Standard	Connotative or denotative	Plain or poetic
Colloquial	Vulgar	Figurative or literal	Simple or bombastic

2.   **Sentence Patterns** — After an author has "chosen" his words, he must next arrange them into sentences (*sentence patterns*). When assessing sentence patterns, you must consider such things as their simplicity or complexity, their balance and emphasis, and their variety. You might use some of the words listed below in your description.

	Sentence Patterns	
Balance	Simple/complex	Emphasis/stress
Parallel	Short/long/varied	Juxtaposition
Repetition	Symmetrical	Climactic (anti) order
Inversion	Loose/periodic/balanced	Beginnings (varied)

3. **Sensory Details** — As the author chooses and arranges his words, he must attempt to build colorful, yet meaningful, thought groups. The use of sensory details is extremely important in building effective description.

Sensory Details (See, hear, taste, feel, touch)

Vivid verbs	Colorful details	Compelling	Subtle
Concrete nouns	Illusion of reality	Word pictures	Intimate
Precise modifiers	Evocative	Abstract	

4. **Figurative Language** — Figurative language can also be used by the author to add color and meaning. This figurative meaning is often deeper and more important than the literal meaning of the words which compose it. A *figure of speech* can help convey an idea or an emotion which is so complex and illusive that our language has no exact term for it. They are also used for economy or emphasis.

Figures of Speech

Metaphor	Hyperbole (exaggeration)	Apostrophe
Simile	Understatement	Antithesis
Personification	Synecdoche	Symbolism

5. **Fluency** — The next task is to coordinate the words, sentences, and passages so that they move smoothly and forcefully. This movement or "flowing of ideas" is often called *fluency*.

Fluency (Effective)

Flows well/smoothly	Good symmetry/order	Sense of rhythm
Strong coherence	Vigorous	Emphasis
Well linked	Suspenseful	Graceful
Continuity	Anticipation	Elegant
Unity	Immediacy/importance	Natural

Fluency (Ineffective)

Awkward	Loss of focus	Not balanced
Choppy/sluggish	Deadwood	Distractions (excessive
Rambling/drifting	Affected	punctuation, subplots)
Uncontrolled	No strong force or thrust	Poor emphasis

6. **Clarity** — All writing must be clear and logical. Writing which is clear and understandable is said to have *clarity*.

Clarity (Clear)

Clear	Concise	Concrete	Distinct
Exact	Vivid	Explicit	Graphic
Specific	Logical	Lucid	Hard-hitting

Clarity (Unclear)

Ambiguous	Unclear	Deadwood	Nebulous
Verbose	Muddy	Confusing	Overused pronouns
Rambling	Distracting	Obscure	Overly ornate
Vague	Redundant	Incomprehensible	Flowery
Wordy	Cliche	Inexplicable	Hazy

7. **Tone** — The author's attitude (*tone*) is an important consideration when attempting to evaluate style. If, for instance, an author is being sarcastic or satiric, his word choice will be greatly affected. An author's attitude can be discussed just as anyone else's. Some of the common terms used in this type of discussion are included below:

Tone

Ironic	Sarcastic	Mocking	Facetious	Impersonal
Bitter	Pessimistic	Objective	Witty	Light-hearted
Satiric	Moralistic	Vindictive	Derogatory	Sympathetic
Solemn	Tragic	Empathetic	Impartial	Compassionate
Cynical	Serious	Personal	Didactic	Opinionated
Comic	Benevolent	Malevolent	Altruistic	Contemptuous

8. **Sound** — Additional consideration should be given to the *sound* or *musical quality* of the writing. Although it may at first seem difficult to evaluate the "sound" of an author's writing, it really isn't. Let your ear do the work. If it sounds good to you, it probably is good. Below are a number of terms which may help you pinpoint what it is that makes this writing "sound" good:

Sound or musical quality

Alliteration	Parallel structure	Rhythm	Lyrical
Consonance	Repetition	Balance	Musical
Onomatopoeia	Antithesis	Impact	Poetic

9. **Additional Stylistic Devices** — There are a number of *stylistic devices* or techniques commonly used by authors to add variety and interest to their writing. These are among the most popular:

Flashback   Foreshadowing   Allusion

Revising and Proofreading Your Review

One of the most important stages in the process of writing a book review is to revise carefully. No reader is going to take seriously a review which is filled with incomplete thoughts or careless errors. Follow the suggestions below when preparing the final copy of your review.

1. Let your review sit for a day or two before you go back to revise it. This will allow you to be more objective about what you have written and judge the review much as your readers will. You will also bring to your review the renewed energy needed to make the necessary changes.

2. Read your review out loud as you revise. The ear will often pick out errors and awkward expressions your eye does not.

3. Read especially for clarity and unity. Poorly written book reviews tend to hop from one point to the next with little sense of continuity. Work carefully to tie all parts of your review into one, coherent piece of writing.

4. Check your quotations for accuracy and appropriateness. Also, do not overload your review with quotations which simply sound good. Double-check your use of quotation marks and punctuation (ellipses, period, and comma placement at the end of quoted material, etc.).

5. Follow the same guidelines you would for any formal writing assignment and write or type your final copy neatly on unlined paper.

Things Not to Do in Your Review

1. Do not attempt to write a review unless you have read the book carefully and competely.

2. Do not simply write a plot or character summary, or include so much summary that it buries your interpretation.

3. Do not make general statements about the book without supporting them with specific examples or quotations.

4. Do not turn your review into a mere string of quotations; the explanations which tie these quotations together should be the heart of your review.

5. Do not, however, make your review a "running commentary" on one quotation after another; comment on those quotations which need explanation and leave the others to speak for themselves.

6. Do not include so much factual information in your review that it becomes more of a "report" than a review. Use personal, colorful language and include your opinions, interpretations, and observations.

Student Book Review: Nonfiction

420 Below is a sample list of things which you might include in a book review. (This list was used by the student who wrote the review of *Black Like Me*.)

a. an excerpt from the book and a follow-up comment
b. the point of view and setting
c. the plot and how it contributes to the development of the theme
d. the topic or theme and its importance in our society today

e. the accuracy or truth of the theme
f. the believability of the characters
g. the author's background
h. the author's tone and style
i. the diction or language used
j. the overall ease/difficulty of reading
k. a personal reaction/opinion

Black Like Me: A Student Review

Rest at pale evening . . .
A tall slim . . .
Night coming tenderly
Black like me.

John Howard Griffen, the author of <u>Black Like Me</u>, used the verse above to describe himself in a strange world where friends were lacking and hate stares were everywhere.

Griffen tells his readers how he had undergone a series of treatments and medications to temporarily darken the color of his skin. He literally abandoned his white world and crossed the line into an atmosphere of hate, fear and hopelessness — the world of the American black man. To make his exit complete, he was compelled, for a time, to give up his family, friends, and the life that was familiar to him in Mansfield, Texas.

During his six weeks in the Southern states, Griffen learned about the struggles and hardships a

black man must go through day after day. Even though he was rejected and pushed around, Griffen never stopped trying to understand the white man's point of view. He describes the contrast between the two races: "The atmosphere of a place is entirely different for Negro and White. The Negro sees and reacts differently not because he is Negro, but because he is suppressed. Fear dims even the sunlight."

Every time he stepped onto a bus, sat down in a diner, or checked into a hotel, Griffen was reminded of the burden of being Black. It was as if having black skin meant you were afflicted with a contagious disease. But Griffen was an exception; his time for pain and suffering was only temporary. As soon as the dark color wore out of his skin, he would once again join the white race. But the thought of this did not appeal to Griffen. If it weren't for his wife and children, he probably would have rather continued living as a Negro and helping other Blacks in their struggle for Civil Rights, as opposed to existing in an atmosphere of bigotry. Griffen was often reminded of the cruelty of white men in his dreams.

It was the same nightmare I had been having recently. White men and women, their faces stern

and heartless, closed in on me. The hate stares burned through me. I pressed back against a wall. I could expect no pity, no mercy. They approached slowly and I could not escape them. Twice before, I had awakened myself screaming.

On December 14, Griffen was ready to return to his home in Mansfield. The dark pigment had worn out of his skin, allowing him to resume his white identity once again. Through newspaper and magazine articles, photographers, and television broadcasters, Griffen's project became known to people throughout the country. Although he was anxious to be reunited with his family and friends, he was not nearly so anxious to return to the bigoted part of society: "I felt the greatest love for this land and the deepest dread of the task that now lay before me — the task of telling truths that would make me and my family the target of all the hate groups."

Griffen's wife and children welcomed him with hugs and kisses, while many of his "friends" greeted him with abusive phone calls and hateful remarks.

In one instance, some racists went so far as to hang his effigy on Main Street. The dummy, half black — half white, with Griffen's name on it and a

yellow streak painted down its back, was hanging from the center red-light wire in downtown Mansfield. This aroused the town even more and caused riots between the Blacks and the Whites. Griffen was very aware of what was happening. He was also conscious of the bad consequences it could have on his family's life. So, in order to restore a normal existence for themselves, the Griffens moved from their home in Mansfield, Texas, to start a new life in Mexico.

It was at his new home that Griffen laid the foundations for his book, <u>Black Like Me.</u> The project was undertaken to discover how deeply America was involved in the practice of racism against Blacks. Most Whites denied any stain of bigotry and claimed to believe that in this land we judge every man by his qualities as an individual human being.

Reading this book really opened my eyes and helped me understand the Negro and his plight in this country. I think John Howard Griffen did an excellent job of conveying the feelings as well as the facts. By traveling through the Southern states and living as a Negro for six weeks, Griffen was able to experience, rather than just see, how a black man is mistreated and how different his world is from that of the white man. I, too, was able to experience that.

Student Book Review: Fiction

The following review of *The Great Gatsby* concentrates on the central character of the novel, Jay Gatsby. However, in the process of discussing this character, the reviewer ties in important information about plot, setting, and theme as well.

The Great Gatsby

The Roaring Twenties: A curious concoction of prosperity and immorality, the rise of the self-made man, and the birth of the American Dream--the Great Gatsby era.

Before reading the book by F. Scott Fitzgerald, I never understood just what the Great Gatsby was. I honestly thought it was a dance like the Charleston. Now, however, I am much wiser. I know that Gatsby is a person who stands for that time in America when young and boisterous crowds combed the cities at night, slept through the morning, and made their fortunes in the afternoon. Gatsby is a true crusader for the American Dream, but a crusader with a flaw.

Gatsby is, as the title implies, a great person. Knowing him, we feel he would be able to accomplish anything he set out to do. In the beginning of the novel, our narrator, Nick Carroway, gives us this description of Gatsby:

> If personality is an unbroken series of successful gestures, then there was something gorgeous about him, some heightened sensitivity to the promises of life. . . . It was an extraordinary gift for hope, a romantic readiness such as I have never found in any other person. . . . No, Gatsby turned out all right at the end; it is what preyed on Gatsby, what foul dust floated in the wake of his dreams that temporarily closed out my interest in the abortive sorrows and shortwinded elations of men. (147)

We know Gatsby has what it takes, from his winning smile to his boyhood "list of improvements." Yet, there is something wrong with Gatsby. We would all be justified in admiring him if it weren't for the obscure hint of tarnish on his armor or those tiny, black rumors that float among his party guests like the "foul dust" that Nick speaks of. We know of his shady dealings and his "connections," yet we cannot really accuse him of being wrong because we can see into his fanciful dreams and unrealized ambitions. We feel instead that some injustice has been done here. We feel a sorrow for Gatsby--an unreal man in a real world.

The trouble with Gatsby is that he gets some of the very important things in life a little mixed up. One of them is love. He finds himself, by some extraordinary circumstance, trespassing in a garden of wealth, and he dares to pick a flower; her name is Daisy Fay. Daisy Fay on the white, wicker porch of her grand, grand home, in her beautiful dresses, with a voice that jingles like a pocket full of gold--she feeds him all the sweetness of her wealth, and that is what Gatsby loves: not the girl, but the gold.

This infatuation is Gatsby's driving force for five years, and his conviction that what he feels really is love makes this force all the stronger. In reality, Daisy and Gatsby can never be together simply because Daisy is too weak to ever stand by his side. Out of necessity, she marries while he is away because it is time for her life to be "shaped." Gatsby, on the other hand, is the shaper of his own life and never simply gives up on his dreams.

But Gatsby's fondest dream never comes true, the reason being the difference between someone who is rich and someone who is wealthy. Perhaps the greatest tragedy of all is that Gatsby is unable to comprehend this difference, a difference best illustrated by the setting of the story. It is set on two small islands off the tip of Manhattan, New York: East Egg and West Egg. Daisy lives on East Egg among the stately mansions and the wealthy people. Gatsby lives on West Egg which is looked upon, by the East Eggers, as being somewhat tacky because it has about it an air of "eccentric impulsiveness." This is to be expected, however, as it is the home of the rich--those who have the money, but not the "culture" of the wealthy.

In several places throughout the novel, reference is made to the light on the end of Daisy's dock on East Egg, a light which Gatsby can see from his yard on West Egg. It is green like a crisp, new dollar bill, and it stands for everything Gatsby is striving for. The first time Nick sees Gatsby, he is standing with his arms outstretched toward the light as if he is trying to somehow touch it, somehow reach his goal; and he believes he can do it just as he believed that Daisy would actually show up at one of his extravagant parties.

Gatsby believed in the green light, the orgiastic future that year by year recedes before us. It eluded us then, but that's no matter--tomorrow we will run faster, stretch our arms farther. . . . And one fine morning. . . . (187)

Yes, one fine morning, in Gatsby's mind, Daisy will come back to him, and they will live happily ever after. But, in reality, Daisy and Gatsby are two different people in two different worlds, separated by one large body of water. Gatsby has as much a chance of getting Daisy back as he has of making it across that water on foot.

The last line of the book states it well: "So we beat on, boats against the current, borne back ceaselessly into the past." Similarly, I can see Gatsby as a man trying to go up a down escalator. He climbs and climbs and climbs, yet he gets nowhere. It is unfortunate that he has access only to down escalators, but on West Egg, that is the only kind. All of the up escalators are on East Egg where the people have only to stand still, and they rise to the top. That is the injustice of this story, the reason for the foul dust and the tarnish on the armor. That is why we put ourselves behind owl-eye glasses at the grave of the Great Gatsby; and that is why, when I read this story, I want no more escalators, those ugly machines that thoughtlessly deposit people here and there and trip them getting on and off. Instead, I want to take the hand of Gatsby and show him to the stairway.

SPECIAL FORMS OF WRITING

Summary Writing

The best test of how well you understand something you've read is whether you can write in your own words an accurate summary of the important ideas. Adding summary writing to your study routine can increase your ability to understand and remember what you have read. There are three popular forms of summary writing—the abstract, the paraphrase, and the précis.

421a The Abstract

The abstract is a shortened form of a written selection using the important words of the selection itself. An abstract should have the same style and essential content as the original. Words and phrases are taken from the original and used as part of the abstract. There should be no attempt at originality. You simply select the important words and connect them into a shortened, readable version of the original selection.

Original

The human brain, once surrounded by myth and misconception, is no longer such a mystery. It is now understood to be the supervisory center of the nervous system, and, as such, it controls all voluntary (eating and thinking) and most involuntary behavior (blinking and breathing). The brain functions by receiving information from nerve cells which are located throughout the body. Recent research has provided a clear picture of exactly what happens when information first reaches the brain. It has been discovered that the cells in the cortex of the brain which receive the information are arranged in a regular pattern in columns. The columns are, in turn, arranged into a series of "hypercolumns." Each cell within each column has a specific responsibility to perceive and analyze certain kinds of incoming information. Within the columns, the analysis of this information follows a formal sequence. Eventually, the information is relayed to the higher centers of the brain where a complete picture is assembled. The brain then evaluates the information and either sends a return message to the muscles and glands or stores the information for later use. The return message travels through the body in the form of electrical and chemical signals via the billions of nerve cells (neurons). When the message reaches its destination, the muscles or glands respond with the appropriate reaction. With each additional experience, the brain is better able to analyze, evaluate, and respond to the information it receives each day.

Abstract

The human brain controls all voluntary and most involuntary behavior. The brain functions by receiving information from nerve cells which are located throughout the body. The cells in the cortex of the brain which receive the information are arranged in columns; each cell within each column has a specific responsibility to perceive and analyze certain kinds of incoming information. After the information has been analyzed following a formal sequence, it is relayed to the higher centers of the brain where a complete picture is assembled. The brain then evaluates the information and either sends a return message to the muscles and glands or stores the information for later use.

421b The Paraphrase

A paraphrase is a restatement of someone else's ideas written in your own words. A paraphrase states fully and clearly the meaning of a complex piece of writing. Because a paraphrase often includes your interpretation of complicated phrases and ideas, it can actually be longer than the original. A paraphrase is used to clarify the meanings of poems, proverbs, legal documents, and any other writing which is obscure or symbolic.

Original

Nothing Gold Can Stay

Nature's first green is gold,	(1)
Her hardest hue to hold.	(2)
Her early leaf's a flower;	(3)
But only so an hour.	(4)
Then leaf subsides to leaf.	(5)
So Eden sank to grief,	(6)
So dawn goes down to day.	(7)
Nothing gold can stay.	(8)

—Robert Frost

Paraphrase

The first growth of spring is more gold in color than green.	(1)
But this golden shade of green doesn't last very long.	(2)
The first leaf is actually a blossom or flower,	(3)
but it remains for only a very short time.	(4)
Then the buds and blossoms give way to full, green leaves.	(5)
Just as the Garden of Eden was taken away,	(6)
so day is taken away by the night.	(7)
Nothing in nature—especially those things most beautiful— lasts forever.	(8)

421c The Précis

A précis is perhaps the most useful kind of summary writing for general studying. A précis is a summary in your own words of something you have just read. You select only the most important ideas and combine them into clear, concise sentences. A precis of a paragraph, for example, may be only one sentence long. In most cases your precis should be no more than one-third as long as the original. Follow the guidelines below the next time you need to write a summary of something you have read.

Guidelines for Writing a Précis

1. Skim the selection to get the overall meaning.

2. Reread the selection carefully, paying particular attention to key words and phrases. (Check the meaning of any words with which you are unfamiliar.)

3. List the major ideas on your own paper.

4. Quickly skim the selection a final time so that you have the overall meaning clearly in mind as you begin to write.

5. Write a summary of the major ideas, using your own words except for those "few" words in the original which cannot be changed. Keep the following points in mind as you write your précis:

    a. Your opening (topic) sentence should be a clear statement of the main idea of the original selection.

    b. Stick to the essential information — names, dates, times, places, and similar facts are usually essential; examples, detailed data, and adjectives are usually not.

c. Try to state each important idea in one clear sentence.

d. Arrange your ideas into the most logical order, and link your sentences with effective connecting words so that your précis becomes a complete paragraph in itself.

e. Use vivid, efficient words which help keep the précis to no more than one-third the length of the original.

f. Use a concluding sentence which ties all of your points together and brings your summary to an effective end.

6. Check your précis for accuracy and conciseness by rereading the original passage and comparing it thought for thought with your précis. Ask yourself the following questions:

a. Have I kept the original writer's point of view in my précis?

b. Have I cut or compressed the supporting details contained in the original?

c. Could another person get the main idea of the original selection by simply reading my précis?

7. Proofread your précis for mechanical errors and overall effectiveness. (Follow the same checklist or proofreading guidelines you use for your paragraph or essay writing.)

Original

"Acid rain" is precipitation with a high concentration of acids. The acids are produced by sulfur dioxide, nitrogen oxide, and other chemicals which are created by the burning of fossil fuels. Acid rain is known to have a gradual, destructive effect on plant and aquatic life. The greatest harm from acid rain is caused by sulfur dioxide, a gas produced by the burning of coal. As coal is burned in large industrial and power plant boilers, the sulfur it contains is turned into sulfur-dioxide gas. This invisible gas is funneled up tall smokestacks and released into the atmosphere some 350-600 feet above the ground. As a result, the effects of the gas are seldom felt immediately. Instead, the gas is carried by the wind for hundreds and sometimes thousands of miles before it floats back down to earth. For example, sulfur dioxide produced in Pennsylvania at noon on Monday may not show up again until early Tuesday when it settles into the lakes and soil of rural Wisconsin. Adding to the problem is the good possibility that the sulfur dioxide has undergone a chemical change while in flight. By simply taking on another molecule of oxygen, the sulfur dioxide could be changed to sulfur trioxide. Sulfur trioxide, when mixed with water, creates sulfuric acid—a highly toxic acid. If the sulfur trioxide enters a lake or stream, the resulting acid can kill fish, algae, and plankton. This, in turn, can interrupt the reproductive cycle of other life forms, causing a serious imbalance in nature. If the sulfur enters the soil, it can work on metals such as aluminum and mercury and set them free to poison both the soil and water. Damage from acid rain has been recorded throughout the world, from the Black Forest in Germany to the lakes in Sweden to the sugar maple groves in Ontario, Canada. The result is a growing concern among scientists and the general public about the increasing damage being done to the environment by acid rain.

Précis

"Acid rain," the term for precipitation which contains a high concentration of harmful chemicals, is gradually damaging our environment. The greatest harm from acid rain is caused by sulfur dioxide, a gas produced from the burning of coal. This gas, which is released into the atmosphere by industries using coal-fired boilers, is carried by the wind for hundreds of miles. By the time this gas has floated back to earth, it has often changed from sulfur dioxide to sulfur trioxide. Sulfur trioxide, when mixed with water, forms sulfuric acid—a highly toxic acid. This acid can kill both plant and aquatic life and upset the natural balance so important to the cycle of life.

The Short Story

Writing the Short Story

By the time you finish high school, you will have seen and felt enough of life to fill a Nobel prize-winning novel, not to mention a good short story or two. Putting that experience on paper in artistic form is, of course, the problem.

But you know the difference between interesting and boring, between deep and shallow, between fresh and worn out, between detailed and general, between *zip* and *thud*. The artist is one who can make that knowledge work. The artist, in other words, can be you.

What Is a Short Story?

Broadly speaking, a short story is a piece of prose fiction short enough to be read comfortably in one sitting. Because it is fiction, it shows us a world which is plausible in the imagination but not literally true; in that sense, it is different from prose forms such as the essay, the research paper, the report, the biography, the autobiography, or the sermon. And because it is short, it details best with only a handful of characters, a short stretch of time, and a concentrated action; a novel, by contrast, may introduce us to a rainbow of characters spanning several generations and caught up in a complicated web of events.

The Story Writer's Aim

When you write your short story, aim high. Aim at capturing truth about human experience, even if you have to *discover* that truth in the very writing of the story, even if that "truth" turns out to be a whole new set of questions. You'll first have to get rid of your favorite truisms, cliches, and stereotypes. Leave all your "safe" ideas behind: maybe might *doesn't* make right, maybe not *all* Dutchmen are penny-pinchers, maybe you *should* cry over spilt milk!

The whole truth of a short story, however, is never in a statement some character coughs up, never in a moral you as author tack on at the end. Instead, it is in the shape of the events you describe, in the depth of character, in the texture or "feel" of life you describe and the texture of language you use. The truth of a story can only come out of your secret store of knowledge about life. So let this be your aim: *to write the story that only you can write.*

Anatomy of a Short Story Writer

Writing a short story will involve your whole self, though some parts of you will play more important roles than others. Your success will depend, however, on how well you can blend the work of your brain, your five senses, your heart, and your hands. Let's study the anatomy of a writer more closely.

Brain

Brain physiologists claim that the left half of a human brain works best at grasping facts, thinking logically, processing speech, and the like; the right half, by contrast, deals best with feelings, intuitions, recognition of images, and so on. Let your whole brain, left and right halves both cooperating, go to work. In other words, "think feelingly."

Eye

Your eyes must be used to see these two things: 1) the world as it is, and 2) your writing as it is. To see the world with insight, merely opening your eyes is not enough. You must *look, see, notice,* and *comprehend.* Look at the sky, see the cloud, notice its anvil shape, and comprehend that hail may be pounding some farmer's wheat field. Look at your bloodhound, see his swollen nose, notice the three scarlet pricks at the tip, and comprehend that Old Blue turned up a porcupine again. This is the way an artist sees, and *anyone can do it*!

If this kind of seeing becomes a habit, you will soon begin to crave words that express the concrete *nuances* of your thought — words like "sallow," "inferno," and "dragoon" where once you might have settled for general terms like "sick-looking," "fire," and "soldier." Your trained eye should then be able to tell you whether your story places a living world before the eye of imagination; if not, back you must go to the drawing board.

Ear

Your ears — if used, like your eyes, to notice and comprehend — can discover for you not only the sounds of nature (the plops, razzes, and hiccups) but also the sounds of human nature, especially that of human speech. How does a grandmother complain about her arthritis so that you *know* she is really thinking about her husband who died three years ago on that date? How many different things could a kid mean by the words, "Stop it, you guys"? Your ears can tell you, if they are kept clean and ready. Written dialogue, which appears somewhere in almost every short story, can be a dead giveaway that a writer's imagination is in a coma, or it can be the spark and proof of life. Some writers like to record dialogues, real and imaginary, in a journal, just to keep their skill alive. You might give it a try.

Other Senses

Ear and eye easily dominate the other senses, but people are blessed with five senses, not two. Everyone knows what a rock concert sounds like, but what does it *smell* like? What sensations does your skin *feel* on a two-hour bus ride in 90-degree heat? What does a campout *taste* like? Throw open all five windows on the world: look, listen, smell, taste, and feel. The words in a vivid description should play all five senses like chords on a piano.

Voice: Your voice is more than your vocabulary; it is the unique combination of pace, pattern of repetition and contrast, use of detail, level of energy, pitch of excitement, and so on, that, like your fingerprint, distinguishes you from every other person alive. Those who waste all their effort trying to sound unique ultimately will sound uniquely boring. Better to be yourself, speaking an honest tongue. If your self needs *improving,* then work at that, but always be yourself. After all, a frog with the voice of a prince is still a frog.

Heart: To have "heart" can mean both to have courage and to have a capacity for love. The short story writer needs both. Why courage? Because if a short story is not the taking of a chance, it is not worth writing. Why love? Because only love of life and of language can make the hard work of writing, rewriting, and re-rewriting seem worthwhile.

Hands: Pen in hand, the writer manipulates the various elements of the short story, such things as characterization, plot, setting, point of view, tone, atmosphere, and language. The way you handle these elements is called your craft. Many techniques of craft in short story writing have become established by common practice and common sense over many years. The following is a list of basic instructions in the craft of short story writing. But a warning is in order: Abiding by rules may be a way to produce acceptable writing, but the best short stories are produced as often by the breaking as by the obeying of rules, if the breaking of rules makes a more powerful sense.

Elements of the Short Story

1. **Character/Characterization** Note the difference between these two terms: character is something a person in a story *has,* while characterization is something the author *does.* The character in a story supposedly (i.e., in the imagination) has a personality too complicated to describe in full, just as you do. But the writer must *select, order,* and *highlight* certain features of that personality (in other words, "characterize" the character) in order to focus and emphasize that character's role in the action.

It is not enough, however, to say that a character has this trait or that. The main character, especially, must be tested against circumstances outside or inside of himself. He must be forced to rethink his basic vision of life. Unfortunately, many a beginning writer fails at this point by falling so much in love with his main character that he tries to protect that character against suffering. That's silly. What would you say about a drummer who loved his drum so much that he refused to beat it? The lesson is this: don't coddle your characters. Make them sweat. Action is essential to character and vice versa.

2. **Plot**   If you start with a character and set him in *motion* (shaving, brushing his teeth, putting on a sport coat, etc.) you still do not have a story. Now if you add *conflict* (man against man, man against woman, man against nature, man against God, man against toothbrush, etc.) you have a story, but still no plot. Plot arises when you select, arrange, and present the parts of the story in such a way that they seize and hold a reader's interest. Plot, in other words, is the artificial but effective arrangement of action in a story.

The novelist Kurt Vonnegut has been heard to say that plot is simple: all you need is a character who wants something, plus something that stands in his way, plus his effort to get it anyway. The classic plot structure shows this same pattern; it calls for an introduction to a situation, a series of developments arranged in a pattern of rising tension, a climax in which the central character's fate is determined, a falling action in which the implications of the climactic moment are gradually discovered, and a wrap-up, or *denouement,* in which loose ends are tied up.

However, not all stories follow this classic pattern. Some use subplots to parallel or contrast with the main action. Some save a major surprise for the end, but such neatly ironic "O'Henry" stories, as they are called, are likely to seem gimmicky today and should ordinarily be avoided. Many modern stories hinge on a subtle, psychological change or realization in the protagonist. Others, in which the protagonist is a hapless, dumpy "anti-hero," may show a series of frustrations and deadends rather than a smoothly rising action. Experiment with plot, if you will, to serve your own purposes, but remember that conflict is useless unless something valuable or significant is at stake — not only a person's wealth, but perhaps his sense of self-worth, happiness, or ability to hope. A reader is more likely to enjoy your story if he feels that he might want the same thing if he were the protagonist.

Where should a plot begin? Preferably, in the middle of things, near to the heart of the matter, and in motion. You would then be wise to dramatize, close up, only those scenes that are crucial in the development and climax of the conflict, while using brief narrative bridges ("Three days later . . .") to pass over those scenes that are of lesser interest. Somehow the story writer has to find a proper blend between *telling* (to set up or interpret the conflict) and *showing* (to focus on the heart of the drama). The exact blend will be determined by the nature of the action and by your purpose in presenting it to your audience. If this sounds like show biz, you aren't far from the truth.

3. **Setting**   Since space is very limited in a short story, and since character and action are normally supreme, descriptions of setting should ordinarily play a supporting, not leading, role in the story. Yet description need not be crossed out; if it is blended into the description of action, it can make the action sparkle. Note, for example, how action is blended with physical description in the following paragraph:

> The secondhand store looked more like an attic than a shop on street-level; molding sea lockers, chipped white bassinets, and shadeless lamps elbowed one another like patients in a waiting room. But here, in a dark corner, a surprised Duane found the moose antlers he was searching for.

Not bad, you might say. But here is that same setting *blended* with the action:

> Tired of bumping his knees on old sea lockers and chipped white bassinets, and slightly irritated by the gaze of so many headless lamps, Duane resolved to leave; only then, knocking his ankle on something horizontal, did he reach down into a half century of dust and touch a raspy plate that turned out to belong, oh joy, to the moose antlers of his dream.

One plus one adds up to more than two.

4. **Point of view**   As a short story writer, you must create the illusion of a narrator who tells the story for you. You may use the first-person narrator ("*I* was hopping mad"), the objective or dramatic third-person narrator ("*Her* face suddenly flushed with anger"), or a compromise between the two extremes, the third-person *limited omniscient*

narrator (*She felt* herself grow suddenly angry"), who freely takes the reader into the mind of the main character (though not into the minds of others). Skillful writers may vary and combine these basic points of view when they can achieve a more appropriate effect by doing so.

Furthermore, the narrator must have a position in time. Does he report an action after it has happened ("I *was* mad," "She *appeared* angry," "She *felt* herself growing angry")? Or does the narrator report an action as it is happening now ("I *am* mad," "She *flushes* with anger," "She *feels* herself growing angry")?

Whatever limitation you place on your narrator to clarify his point of view, stick with it. Don't commit the narrative "sin," as so many beginning writers do, of jumping without warning from one point of view to another. The reader can't appreciate your story if he has to keep asking, "Who's talking now?"

5. **Mood**   By choosing certain words rather than others and by weaving their connotations together, you can give whole settings and scenes a kind of personality, or mood. Note the difference if you describe a tall, thin tree as "erect like a steeple," "spiked like a witch's hat," "a leafy spear," or "rather inclining toward the slim." However, no single image can work alone; mood can only arise from a steady pressure in your language toward one major atmospheric effect. That effect should support your main purpose for writing the story.

You might have fun by choosing a mood *first* — say, the throat-tightening anxiety of a piano recital — then let a story grow out of it.

6. **Tone**   Tone is your (not necessarily your narrator's) overall outlook or attitude toward your material. Ironic, matter-of-fact, bemused, outraged, curiously respectful, disdainful — how do you feel about the fragment of life you display in your story? The curious thing about tone is that it may *change*, but it must never *waver*.

7. **Style**   Your personal writing style is the outward boundary of your energy, the sum and pattern of all your choices. Styles do sort into general types; no one would confuse Ernest Hemingway's tight style with the ballooning, throbbing style of William Faulkner. But style is often identified as well by what in it is odd, daring, and never-before-heard.

Should you labor to improve your style? Maybe. But that's a fine way, alas, to develop a labored-sounding style. Much better that you labor to live more fully, more deeply, more honestly. Travel, read, learn a language, fight for a cause, discover what you value. Learn what makes your reader tick. But above all, labor to learn the capacity of the English language to do your bidding. After all that, style will happen. Count on it.

The Story Writer's Audience

"He who writes to please himself, caters to a fool." All right, you win — nobody ever really said this, until now. And yet it bears a grain of truth, namely this: We are all, generally speaking, too easily pleased with ourselves. We need to strike the iron of our minds against the flint of someone else's to produce fire in writing. That means that the short story writer must know as much as he or she can about human nature and write to engage that nature. About a good writer we might say, "He seems to speak from his heart." But about a <u>great</u> writer we are most likely to say, "He seems to speak from within <u>us</u>."

Unfortunately, the readers of your story are not likely to help you as much as you might like. Mom and Dad will, of course, think your story is wonderful. Your worst critics will use it to wrap fish, while your best critics, most of them, will keep agonizingly quiet. And your teacher, as always, may have some good things to say and some bad.

Where does that leave you? Ultimately, alone. For that reason you must become an uncompromising critic of your own work, if you can. Try to be more fair but also more demanding than any other reader will be. The poet and critic John Ciardi has written, "A writer can, in fact, develop only as rapidly as he learns to recognize what is bad in his writing." If you write to please that critic in you, and forgive yourself when you fall short, you will have a wise man or woman for a reader.

The Poem

The Poet in You

If you want better *mpg* ("miles per gallon") out of that old Chevy, why not try to get more *mpw* — "meaning per word" — out of your writing? Try writing a poem. To paraphrase an old saying, "a poem is worth a thousand words."

If, like millions of others, you would claim to hate poetry, let us notice where poetry already intersects with your life. When you were a baby, you probably smiled at the cradle-rhythms of "Róckabye báby, in the treetóp, / Whén the wind blóws," etc., etc. A few years later and you were twirling a rope, chanting, "Hank and Freda, sittin' in a tree / K-I-S-S-I-N-G; / First comes love, then comes marriage, / Then comes Hubert in a baby carriage!" Lots of fun. Poetry.

Today, you are more sophisticated, of course, but you may still have a favorite hymn in church, a favorite jingle on TV, or a favorite rock lyric. You turn up the radio when you hear your favorite band singing, "Lying on my bed of nails / I think / Oh-Oh I know / That I'm beginnin' to get the point." We all seem to appreciate poetry in some form. Even when you say, "This day started like a brass band and ended like a kazoo," you are expressing yourself poetically.

What Is a Poem?

Definitions

First, let us distinguish **poetry** from **verse**, noting the definition of poetry (Handbook 589) and list of poetry terms which follow. Verse, or a composition of metrical or rhythmic lines, earns the name poetry when it becomes distinctly a work of thoughtful, imaginative art in which sounds, figures of speech, expressive structures, and some degree of make-believe play an important role. A poem may be any length and may use the whole range of sound effects possible in a language, but it certainly need not be filled with jingly rhythms, mushy sentiment, and rhymes that chime (like the words *rhyme* and *chime*).

While here, let us try a poetic definition of poetry. Since a poem looks both *out* on a world of imagination (the *what* of the poem) and *in* on itself (the *how* of the poem), we might say that a poem is

> Words
> dreaming in a bed
> of language.

Where Short Story and Poem Overlap

Like a story, a poem always has a speaker. Sometimes that speaker is a clearly identifiable narrator with a specific point of view and an intriguing tale to tell. Like a story, a poem may focus on character. Like a story, a poem always *enacts* its ideas, sometimes dramatizing scenes. A poem always uses vivid language, appealing to the senses while conveying emotions and thoughts. Like a story, a poem typically has a sort of plot: entrance into an idea, deepening of its significance, development toward a question, crisis, or key insight, and final resolution (or deepening, or explosion) of meaning. Almost any poem is a seed from which a story could be grown.

Here the major similarities end. Poems differ from stories in many ways: 1) poems usually detach themselves from any specific, physical setting; 2) poems make more exclusive use of compact figures of speech like symbols, metaphors, similes, metonymy, synecdoche, and so on; thus they create the impression of achieving meaning through more indirect means; 3) through indirection, poems zero in on the emotional-logical heart of a matter without dwelling on outward circumstances; 4) poems are self-consciously artificial; thus the real plot of a poem is the unveiling of its own form.

The Form of Poetry

Our century has seen the rise of *free verse*, poetry whose lines are free of the requirements of regular length, meter, or rhyme. Before any poet claims the somewhat dangerous freedom of free verse, however, he or she must realize that poetry is practically as old as civilization and that as it has developed, many major achievements in poetic form have become conventions and taken on a life of their own.

By convention, lines in most English poetry are labeled according to basic meter (*iambic, anapestic*, etc.) and length (*trimeter, pentameter*, etc.). Groups of lines, comparable to paragraphs in prose, are called stanzas and designated according to number of lines (*couplet, tercet, quatrain, sestet, octave*, etc.). Furthermore, certain overall forms — like the haiku, ballad, limerick, sonnet, and so on — have, by convention, more or less exact specifications for line length, meter, rhyme scheme, and stanza length. Some forms are specified to the exact number of syllables in each line.

Whole books have been devoted to the formal conventions in poetry. Here we need add only two comments:

First, the form of a poem involves much more than simply rhyme, meter, line length, and shape of stanza; *any* recognizable elements in the poem — letters, grammatical structures, figures of speech, types of images, connotations, even empty spaces — can be repeated, contrasted, sequenced, juxtaposed, or in some other way set in meaningful relation. Relation is the basis of pattern, pattern is the basis of form, and poetic form *speaks*.

Second, formal conventions restrict the poet, that is true. But restricting is not the same as stifling. When you put a nozzle on a garden hose, you restrict the water. But why? So you can shoot farther and shape the spray! Formal restrictions in poetry, similarly, should be seen as enhancers of the spirit of sport in the poem. That, perhaps, is what the poet Robert Frost was implying when he commented that writing poetry without rhyme is like playing tennis without the net.

The Sound of Poetry

" 'Tis not enough no harshness gives offense," wrote the poet Alexander Pope, "The sound must seem an echo to the sense." Thus, the sense of a poem may be silly, and likewise the sound:

> I fished up in Saskatchewan—
> Alas, I did not catch a one!

The sound may seem to imitate other sounds in nature:

> Through hiss of spruce, a single drop

Or perhaps the very variety in a poet's use of vowels and consonants creates a sense of richness and life appropriate to the poem's theme:

> Nine bean-rows will I have there, a hive for the honey-bee
> And live alone in a bee-loud glade.
>
> W.B. Yeats

In each case the sound is self-consciously crafted to help evoke the thought. The poet has at his disposal all the devices of rhyme (end-rhyme, internal rhyme, perfect rhyme, slant-rhyme, etc.), alliteration, assonance, consonance, repetition, contrast, pause, and rhetorical emphasis with which to build formal patterns of sound.

Such patterns are valueless, of course, as soon as they draw undue attention to themselves. Many a beginning poet, writing an alliterated line like "The grapes, grey-green and golden, tasted great," thinks he has discovered something, when what he has discovered is simply a new brand of monotony.

The Meaning of Poetry

Here are three common false notions about the meanings of poems:

1. Poems have no meaning. (Only a person who, through careless reading, lack of

exposure to poetry, or deep skepticism, has never found personal meaning in a poem would dare to say this.)

2. Poems can mean anything you want them to. (This is really the same falsehood as the first, with the added belief that in the absence of obvious external meaning, one's private feelings are of ultimate importance. You can use your mother's fried chicken for a doorstopper, too, if you feel like it, but you won't get much nutrition that way.)

3. Every poem should have one basic meaning which can be stated in a sentence. (If the meaning of a poem could be stated in a sentence, all good poets would quit. Each good poem is the shortest way of saying *all* that it says.)

Uses of a Poem

We may use poems for placemats and greeting cards if we wish, but poetry can be suited for more dignified uses, too. Poems can celebrate an occasion or time of joy; praise a famous person; preserve an insight; mourn someone's death; probe a mystery; dramatize a problem; call the universe for help; crack a joke; tell the history of a nation; and on and on. Taken together, the poems from the given civilization are the keenest record available of the vision of its people.

How to Read a Poem

Here is a list of methods for reading poems for more understanding and enjoyment:

1. *Read slowly*, syllable by syllable. You wouldn't comb your hair with a garden rake; don't speed-read a poem.

2. *Read aloud* (except in the library). Ignore the smirks of strangers.

3. *Read a poem over and over again*, once to let the strangeness wear off, again to recognize the form, a third time to assimilate the themes and images, a fourth time to hear the music of the language, and as many more times as you wish to probe the questions raised by the earlier readings. The best poems will give back far more than you ask of them.

4. *Try to catch the "arc" of the whole poem* rather than stopping at individual lines as if they could stand by themselves. The "drift" of the whole poem may provide a clue to some of the difficult phrases.

Conventional forms like the sonnet or ballad often have conventional "arcs," but when you have recognized the familiar pattern, pay special attention to any notable variations from that pattern. Remember, too, that blank spaces may also be informative parts of the structure.

5. *Listen for voices.* A poet will sometimes purposely mimic the speech of other types of people. If you miss the false voice, you'll miss the irony of the poet's technique, and you may get the meaning of the poem just backwards.

6. When you encounter imagery appealing to the senses ("bee-loud glade"), *call up your own past sensations*; do not treat images as slot-filling pieces of data. Feel the smallness of the bees, hear the electric energy of their buzzing; sense the sheltered coolness of a glade, and finally sense the poet's seeming pleasure (or other emotion) in the whole scene.

7. *Take pleasure in the artfulness of poetic language*, even if the poem is about suicide, lost love, or some hopeless state of affairs. Poetry always has two faces; one face may look on life's ugliness and despair, but the other always looks hopefully on the power of language to express the theme in fitting form.

8. *Use your memory.* First, use memory to hold the early lines of a poem in mind as you pass on to the succeeding ones; doing so is necessary if you want to catch patterns as they develop. Second, use your memory to recall any feelings you have had similar to those presented in the poem; doing so will place you in a dialogue with the poem, a technique guaranteed to improve comprehension of whatever you read.

9. *Trust the poet*, even if you do not immediately grasp the poem's meaning. If there

is any doubt that the poet is in control of his words and ideas, give the poet the benefit. If after the 352nd reading, however, the poem still makes no sense, you may begin to suspect that the poet doesn't understand it either.

10. *Anticipate, in two ways.* First, as you read the poem, try to play the role of poet and guess where the poem will go next. You will then be reading creatively, even if the poem completely reverses your expectations. Second, approach the poem with the expectation that as a result of reading it, you may learn to view some aspect of life in a whole new way. Not to read with that sort of openness is not to appreciate fully the power of poetry.

Writing a Poem

Here we step a few feet into a land of mystery. No one knows exactly how good poems are written, not even poets. Without a doubt, however, the best preparation for writing poetry is reading good poetry. A few hours of deep communion with a short poem by Shakespeare, Emily Dickinson, or W.B. Yeats, for example, will teach you more than twenty-seven sweaty afternoons with a poetry manual. Nevertheless, a few hints may help.

Choosing a Subject

Anything looked at closely is worth seeing, as one poet has said. The corollary is this: That anything looked at closely — from a drop under a microscope to a galaxy in deep space — is worth writing a poem about.

1. Try making "found poetry" by searching pamphlets, newspapers, magazine ads, etc. for snatches of prose which, when yanked out of context and cut into poetic lines, make a new kind of sense.

2. Think of an animal that impresses you and try to write about it in such a way that your language mirrors the animal's manners.

3. Think of an important event in your life but try writing a poem about the moments just prior to it or just after.

4. Think of a subject that "eats away at you" but write a poem about it in the form of a newspaper account that gets more and more out of hand.

5. Write a poem celebrating a time, place, or thing that no one else seems ever to have noticed (the oil spot under your car, or the moment after the dishwater has drained from the sink but the suds remain, talking to you).

6. Write a poem about something you love but in the voice of someone who hates it.

7. Write a poem in the form of a dialogue between two inanimate objects.

8. Write a poem in which each line has exactly nine syllables.

9. Look up, in your mind, at something much bigger than you and write a poem addressing it.

10. Write a poem about a time when you felt slightly crazy, using language that is slightly crazy.

If in the course of writing these or any other poems you discover that something larger is at stake, let the poem expand to take it in. Many poems are truly discovered in the process of writing another one. It may be worth starting a horrendously bad poem just so you can shake the good one out of your grey matter.

Tips on Technique

The following suggestions may save you from some of the errors most common among beginning writers of poetry:

1. If your poem is about overly sentimental subjects like puppies, kittens, little birdies, or pretty flowers, avoid writing it if you can.

2. If you spot a cliche anywhere in your poem — a tired phrase like "raining cats

and dogs," "green with (of course) envy," or "happy as a (yawn) lark" — cross it out and approach the idea from a new angle.

3. Avoid overused, cute forms such as last lines that step
> down
> > like
> > > this.

4. Use *enjambment* occasionally to break up a pattern of too many end-stopped lines in a row. *Enjambment* is the spilling over of one line into the next:

> The end-stopped line is strong and bold.
> But in the spilling of a line one
> Now and then may strike poetic gold.

5. Certain metric schemes may give the verse a comical flavor when you least intend it. Anapests, for example, when used without interruption, tend to sound as if the poet is riding a toy horse:

> I would like to be serious but, lo I cannot.
> Anapestic tetrameter makes the verse trot.

Similarly, any rhythmic scheme, used without variation, tends to sound like a caricature of poetry.

6. Use rhyme if you wish to pair two words meaningfully; use rhyme, that is, but don't let it use you. Certain chiming old rhyming pairs will seem almost to have written themselves. If "Moon" appears, for example, can "June" be far behind?

7. Like certain meters, certain rhymes are likely to sound comical despite your most serious intentions, especially when three-syllable words are made to rhyme perfectly.

> Despite my somber intention,
> This rhyme follows comic convention.

8. The universal response to a pun is a groan. Be sure a groan is the response you want before you use a pun prominently in your poem. Used well, of course, a pun can be subtle, suggestive, and meaningfully ambiguous.

9. Alliteration is one of the easiest sound devices to use in English verse, but its very availability makes it prone to overuse. It works best when woven with other sound devices like assonance and contrast. Try to keep the technical machinery of your language hidden, or clearly subordinate to your themes, unless you are trying specifically to write a sound poem.

10. Many a fine image or figure of speech in poetry has been ruined when the poet went on to state the same basic idea in different words. Repetition is a useful element of design in a poem, but redundancy (unintentional looping back over ground already covered) is a logical flaw which often seems to stem from the poet's anxiety that the first expression of the idea was not effective. More broadly speaking, whenever a poet uses more words than necessary, the poetry in the poem dies at that point. Poetry is motion.

Writing about Poetry

Before you can possibly begin writing about a poem, you must first understand what the poem is saying. You must consider the poem as a whole and as the sum of its parts. This requires careful attention to the details, rhymes, rhythms, and symbolism which together create poetry. Follow the suggestions given earlier in this unit on how to read a poem and get as close to the meaning and significance of the poem as you possibly can. Then follow the suggestions below:

1. **Paraphrase** (put in your own words) the poem. Your paraphrase will be the *prose meaning,* or denotative meaning, of the poem. It may be a simple story, a brief description, or a statement of an emotion or feeling. Putting the poem in your own words will give you only the surface-level meaning of the poem, not

the *total meaning*. However, this is an essential first step whenever you write about poetry.

2. **Interpret** the poem. In other words, put into writing what the poem means to you. (It is important to remember that each word in a poem has three parts: sound, denotation, and connotation.) Because the total meaning of a poem is based on sound and feeling as well as print, you must read the poem out loud before you attempt to interpret it. Your interpretation will then be based on the sounds, feelings, and images, as well as the "words," of the poem. Be prepared to support your interpretation with references to the poem.

3. **Examine** the poem. Look carefully at the individual elements which make up the poem and how each element contributes to the overall effectiveness of the poem. In other words, try to figure out what makes this poem work (or not work). Among the elements to examine are the theme, the tone, the structure, the central purpose, the speaker and the occasion, the use of figurative language, and the use of rhyme, rhythm, and repetition. (See 590-615.)

4. **Evaluate** the poem. Based on your examination of the poem, decide where and how the poem succeeds or fails. (Remember, the value of a poem is determined by the impact it has on the reader; if the poem had an effect on you, it has value.) Support your feelings by referring to specific passages in the poem.

   a. Does the poem say anything interesting? Does it sound good? Does the poem use rhyme, rhythm, and repetition effectively? Or does the poem follow a pattern which becomes predictable or monotonous?

   b. Did the poem have any impact on you as a reader? Is it likely the poem will have a similar effect on other readers?

   c. Does the poem bring the reader a new outlook or a better understanding of the subject? Does it recreate a worthwhile experience and allow the reader to participate in it?

   d. Is the poem powerful enough to involve not only the reader's senses, but also his intelligence, emotions, and imagination?

   e. Does the poem contain language which appeals to the reader's senses? Does the language help create an effective image of what is being described?

   f. Does the poet use figurative language effectively (simile, metaphor, allusion, personification, symbol, etc.)?

   g. Does the poet use language which is unusual or language which is difficult to understand (archaic, colloquial, ornate, rhetorical)?

   h. Is the poet's tone (attitude) exactly what it appears to be, or does he use language which is intentionally ambiguous, mocking, or contradictory (irony, paradox, pun, understatement, overstatement)?

   i. What is your overall feeling about the poem?

5. **Compare** your poem. You can compare the poem you are writing about to another poem, a short story, a novel, a film, or some other literary work. You will most likely compare only one element of the poem to the other work although it is possible several points may be comparable.

6. **Read** other poems. This might include other poems written by the same author, poems written in the same form or style, or poems written on the same theme. Reading of this kind should give you additional insight into the poem you are writing about.

7. **Read** related material. Among the materials which would prove beneficial would be biographical sketches or articles about the poet, books on how poetry is written or analyzed, and books written about the particular time period referred to in the poem.

The News Story

Journalism is information in a hurry. It is written and produced on a tight schedule for a wide variety of readers, most of them planning to read only parts here and there and wanting to find them quickly. To meet this demand for instant information, newspapers and news magazines have not only made each kind of story or feature easy to find but also have evolved a style of writing the news which promotes fast writing and fast reading. *Note:* For a complete list of journalism terms, see 681.

Writing the News Story

It isn't difficult to write a good news story once you see how it fits together and learn what steps to follow:

1. To cut down the risk of missing a deadline, start work as soon as you get an assignment. A good story may take two or three times as long to complete as you expect.

2. Do thorough research. Otherwise, your story will just repeat facts already familiar to most of your readers. Begin your preparation by listing possible sources of information — people, books and magazines, direct investigations, and so on — and add to this list as you go along. Get complete, accurate information as well as interesting details and quotations, and then select the best of these for your story. Make sure that all the basic questions — *who, what, when, where, why, how* — are answered in your research.

3. Identify the fact or discovery of greatest news value to your readers and state it in your **lead** — the first sentence or first paragraph in your story. You should be seeking this lead idea as soon as you start research. Avoid the too-common practice of starting with time and place unless those are very important. A good lead serves two purposes:

    a. It helps you unify your story by forcing you to choose a dominant idea to which you then subordinate the other ideas the same way that a flower arrangement has lesser blooms clustered around and beneath a dominant one.

    b. A good lead helps readers, too, by enabling them to see immediately whether the content of the story will be interesting or valuable to them. Thus, a good story won't get many readers if it has a weak lead.

4. If the story is a very routine one, try to put the facts in a perspective that will offer something new to your readers. For example, most situations can be compared with similar ones in other places or in previous years. Without such comparisons, your readers cannot grasp the full significance of the facts you give them.

Another way to avoid routine-appearing stories is to include the basic facts within a **feature**, a story that looks at the subject in a particular way, from some human interest angle. In the case of an annual contest, for instance, you could focus on reasons for entering, time and methods of preparing, some of the outstanding competitors, or some other aspect.

5. Once your lead is effectively stated, proceed to write the story by imagining the questions that would logically occur to your reader in response to your lead sentence. Save your least important content for last. That way, readers can quit halfway through, knowing they've gotten the "meat" of the story; and page layout people can just cut off the last paragraphs if space is lacking. Speeches and essays usually work up to a strong conclusion, but news stories usually just run out of details and stop.

6. Now go back and write a headline, if you haven't done so already. For simple stories, the headline may be just a compressed version of the lead; for more complex stories, the head should suggest the significance of the entire story.

A headline should be a statement with subject and verb included or implied. Make it attention-getting, but not too "cute" and not in conflict with the tone of the story. Make it specific; write "Three rate superior at music festival" rather than "Musicians do well in competition." (Besides being too general, this example also commits the fault of editorializing.)

7. Rewrite the story to strengthen the lead, to make the sentences clearer, and to

make the parts of the story flow together better. Double-check correctness of details — spellings of names, times, dates, places, and so on. Newspapers are relied on to get facts straight, and reporters have to take that responsibility seriously.

Interviewing

One of the main news-gathering techniques is the interview. Here are some guidelines for successful interviewing:

1. Unless you have only one or two brief questions, arrange an appointment and tell the interviewee what kinds of questions you plan to ask.

2. Do background research so you can make up a complete set of questions that must be answered in the interview.

3. During the actual interview use your prepared questions to get things going and to avoid missing important areas, but never limit yourself to just these questions. Your best material will come from good follow-up questions that you can't know enough to ask until you get answers to the prepared questions.

4. If the interview focuses on personality, include some details about setting, action, gesture, and tone. These help make the person more real to the reader.

5. Take good notes. If you use a tape recorder, get the person's permission — and take some notes anyway.

6. Write up the interview as soon as possible, while facts and phrasing are still fresh in your mind. When you get done, check back with the interviewee about any facts or quotations about which you are uncertain.

Following Standard Journalistic Style

Beginning reporters usually make several mistakes. By following these guidelines, you can avoid the most common ones:

1. Always present the *subject*, while keeping yourself as reporter out of the story. Besides leaving out references to your feelings ("My knees shook as I knocked on the principal's door"), you should also avoid referring to the fact-finding process:

> When asked how he chooses his starting five, Coach Bouma said that he makes the choice during the last practice before each game. (wrong)
> Coach Bouma chooses his starting five during the last practice before each game. (right)

2. Don't add comments or opinions to news or sports stories. Such comments ("So come on out and cheer for the team tonight") leave the reader wondering whether the reporter is objective enough to report the whole truth, good or bad. Confine cheers and jeers to editorials and comment columns.

3. Generally, use short sentences and paragraphs.

4. The first time a person is mentioned in a story, use the full name along with some additional identification that suits the story. Later references to the same person should be by last name only (or sometimes, as in personality profiles, by first name only):

> Biology instructor Beth Brand has announced that the Ecology Club she advises will celebrate Arbor Day by starting a seedling nursery. Brand seeks additional student volunteers for the project.

5. Support your statements by alternating direct and indirect quotations from your sources. Use direct quotes only when the subject's choice of words provides more than just factual information — some insight into character, mood, tone, and so on.

6. Any time you report a statement which is more than a fact — an opinion, prediction, interpretation, etc. — you must *attribute* it to its source:

> This year the student newspaper will be better than ever, according to Dennis DeGroot, adviser.

7. Except in extensive interviews with a single subject, break up long quotes with statements of attribution. Otherwise, the readers forget that they are reading a quote.

> "At first the tendency was to run all over after the ball," said Van Driel, "but we've been working on playing positions and slowing down the game."

LIBRARY SKILLS

425 A student writer has two sources of material. The first source is his own experiences, ideas, and knowledge. The second source is other people's experiences, ideas, and knowledge. This second kind of material can be collected firsthand by observing, listening, and talking to other people. Unfortunately, you are very restricted in both the amount and kind of information you can gather in this manner. There is one place, however, which offers very few restrictions. It is a place where you can freely gather information from all times, places, and people. You can share in the experiences, ideas, and knowledge of thousands of other people. The place, of course, is your library.

Before you can take full advantage of this remarkable resource, you must first understand a little bit about the library and how to use it. Libraries come in all shapes and sizes, but most contain the following sections:

1. Card Catalog	6. Vertical file
2. Fiction books	7. New/special books
3. Nonfiction books	8. *Readers' Guide*
4. Reference books	9. Magazines/newspapers
5. Reserved books	10. Audio visual materials

The Card Catalog

426 Of all these sections, the **card catalog** is among the most important. The card catalog is an index (listing) of nearly all the materials in the library. All books, for example, are listed in the card catalog by *subject, author,* and *title.* This means you can find a book you are interested in even if you don't know the author or the exact title. The **catalog cards** give the following information: call number, author, title, subject, publisher, illustrator, copyright date, number of pages, and information (sometimes called an *annotation)* about the content of the book. (See the sample cards on the following page.)

Sample Catalog Cards

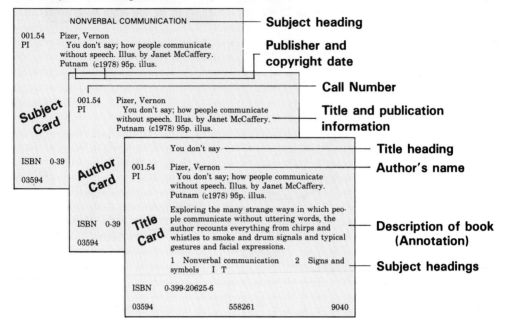

Subject Card

NONVERBAL COMMUNICATION —————— **Subject heading**

001.54 Pizer, Vernon
PI   You don't say; how people communicate
          without speech. Illus. by Janet McCaffery.
          Putnam (c1978) 95p. illus.

ISBN 0-39
03594

Author Card

————— **Publisher and copyright date**

001.54 Pizer, Vernon
PI   You don't say; how people communicate
          without speech. Illus. by Janet McCaffery. —— **Call Number**
          Putnam (c1978) 95p. illus.   **Title and publication information**

ISBN 0-39
03594

Title Card

              You don't say ——————————— **Title heading**
001.54 Pizer, Vernon ————————————— **Author's name**
PI   You don't say; how people communicate
          without speech. Illus. by Janet McCaffery.
          Putnam (c1978) 95p. illus.

          Exploring the many strange ways in which peo-
          ple communicate without uttering words, the
          author recounts everything from chirps and —— **Description of book (Annotation)**
          whistles to smoke and drum signals and typical
          gestures and facial expressions.

          1 Nonverbal communication   2 Signs and —— **Subject headings**
          symbols   I T

ISBN   0-399-20625-6

03594   558261   9040

The cards in the card catalog are arranged alphabetically and filed in drawers similar to those shown below. Each drawer is labeled clearly so that you can see at a glance which cards are contained in that drawer.

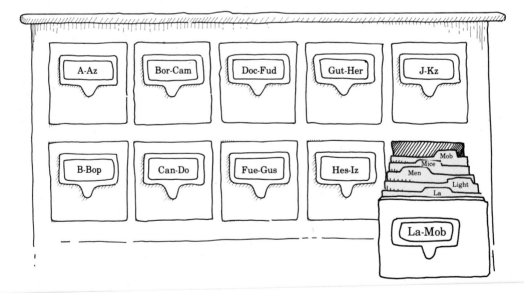

By checking in the appropriate drawer for the title, you can determine quickly whether the library has the book you are interested in finding. If you aren't able to locate that particular book, you can check elsewhere in the card catalog for other books on the same subject. By reading the annotations on the subject cards, you can determine which books best suit your needs.

To use the card catalog efficiently, it is important to know that certain words, numbers, and abbreviations are handled in a special way when they are first in a title. Look carefully at the samples and guidelines below:

> McCarthy, Mary
> Magnificent Seven (The)
> MEDICINE—HISTORY
> Medicine Before Physicians
> 1,000,000's of Everything
> Mr. Chips Takes a Vacation

Titles

- If a title begins with an article (*a, an, the*) the article is ignored and the title is filed alphabetically by the second word. **Example:** The title card for *The Magnificent Seven* is placed in the *M* drawer under *Magnificent*.

- If a title begins with a number, the card is placed in alphabetical order as if the number were spelled out. **Example:** The title card for *1,000,000's of Everything* is placed in the *M* drawer under *millions*.

- If the title begins with an abbreviation, the title is filed as if the abbreviation were spelled out. **Example:** The title card for *Mr. Chips Takes a Vacation* is placed in the *M* drawer under *Mister*.

Authors

- Authors are listed by last name first. **Example:** McCarthy, Mary
- Last names beginning with *Mc* are filed as if they were written *Mac*.

Subjects

- Subject cards are listed alphabetically and are generally placed before titles which begin with the same word. **Example:** The subject card for MEDICINE — HISTORY comes before the title card for *Medicine Before Physicians*.

Finding a Book: The Call Number

Once you have located your card in the card catalog, you must next locate the book in the library. To do this, you will need to copy down the **call number** of the book and locate that number on the library shelves. Nonfiction books, the type used most often for school reports and research papers, are arranged by subject according to one of two systems of classifications, the *Dewey Decimal* or *Library of Congress* system. This means that books with similar contents are placed together on the shelves, making your job of locating a variety of material on a particular topic much easier.

The Dewey Decimal System

427 In the **Dewey Decimal System,** all knowledge is divided into ten main *classes*, each of which is assigned a set of numbers. Each of these classes is further divided into *divisions*. (See the chart on the following page.)

Each division is then divided into ten *sections*, each with its own number. These sections are divided into as many *subsections* as are needed for that particular topic. Together these numbers make up the **class number** of a book.

Divisions of the Dewey Decimal Class Number		
900	History	Class
970	History of North America	Division
973	History of the United States	Section
973.7	History of the U.S. Civil War	Subsection
973.74	History of Civil War Songs	Subsection

The Dewey Decimal System

000	**Generalities**	**340**	Law	**670**	Manufactures processible
010	Bibliographies and catalogs	350	Public administration	680	Assembled and final products
020	Library science	360	Welfare and association	690	Buildings
030	General encyclopedic works	370	Education		
040	General collected essays	380	Commerce	**700**	**The Arts**
050	General periodicals	390	Customs and folklore	710	Civic and landscape art
060	General organizations			720	Architecture
070	Newspapers and journalism	**400**	**Language**	730	Sculpture and the plastic arts
080	General collections	410	Linguistics and nonverbal lang.	740	Drawing and decorative arts
090	Manuscripts and book rarities	420	English and Anglo-Saxon	750	Painting and paintings
		430	Germanic languages	760	Graphic arts
100	**Philosophy and related**	440	French, Provencal, Catalan	770	Photography and photographs
110	Ontology and methodology	450	Italian, Romanian, etc.	780	Music
120	Knowledge, cause, purpose, man	460	Spanish and Portuguese	790	Recreation (Recreational arts)
130	Pseudo- and parapsychology	470	Italic languages		
140	Specific philosophic viewpoints	480	Classical and Greek	**800**	**Literature and Rhetoric**
150	Psychology	490	Other languages	810	American Literature in English
160	Logic			820	Engl. and Anglo-Saxon literature
170	Ethics (Moral philosophy)	**500**	**Pure sciences**	830	Germanic languages literature
180	Ancient, med., Oriental philos.	510	Mathematics	840	French, Provencal, Catalan lit.
190	Modern Western philosophy	520	Astronomy and allied sciences	850	Italian, Romanian, etc. literature
		530	Physics	860	Spanish and Portuguese literature
200	**Religion**	540	Chemistry and allied sciences	870	Italic languages literature
210	Natural religion	550	Earth sciences	880	Classical and Greek literature
220	Bible	560	Paleontology	890	Lits. of other languages
230	Christian doctrinal theology	570	Anthropolog. and biol. sciences		
240	Christ. moral and devotional theol.	580	Botanical sciences	**900**	**General geog./history**
250	Christ. pastoral, parochial, etc.	590	Zoological sciences	910	General geography
260	Christ. social and eccles. theol.			920	General biog., geneal., etc.
270	Hist. and geo. of Christ. church	**600**	**Technology (Applied science)**	930	Gen. history of ancient world
280	Christ. denominations and sects	610	Medical sciences	940	Gen. history of modern Europe
290	Other religions and compar. rel.	620	Engineering and allied operations	950	Gen. history of modern Asia
		630	Agriculture and agric. industries	960	Gen. history of modern Africa
300	**The social sciences**	640	Domestic arts and sciences	970	Gen. history of North America
310	Statistical method and statistics	650	Business and related enterprises	980	Gen. history of South America
320	Political science	660	Chemical technology, etc.	990	Gen. history of rest of world
330	Economics				

In addition to its class number, a **call number** contains the first letter of the author's last name. It may also contain a cutter number assigned by the librarian to help in shelving the book and the first letter of the title's first significant word. The call number determines where a book is located in the library.

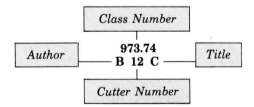

Note: The exceptions to this classification system are fiction books and the individual biography. Fiction is usually kept in a separate section of the library where the books are arranged by the author's last name. (Classic literature is, however, listed and shelved in the literature class.) Individual biographies and autobiographies are arranged on separate shelves by the last name of the person written about.

The Library of Congress System

428 In the **Library of Congress** system of classifying books, the call number begins with a letter rather than a number. The letter(s) used in this system represent the twenty-one subject classes; each is listed on the next page alongside the corresponding Dewey Decimal number.

The Library of Congress and Dewey Decimal Systems

LC Category		Dewey Decimal	LC Category		Dewey Decimal
A	General Works	000-099	K	Law	340-349
B	Philosophy	100-199	L	Education	370-379
	Psychology	150-159	M	Music	780-789
	Religion	200-299	N	Fine Arts	700-799
C	History:	910-929	P	Language and	400-499
	auxiliary sciences			Literature	800-899
D	History:	930-999	Q	Science	500-599
	general and Old World		R	Medicine	610-619
E-F	History:	970-979	S	Agriculture	630-639
	American		T	Technology	600-699
G	Geography	910-919	U	Military Science	355-359,
	Anthropology	571-573			623
	Recreation	390-399	V	Naval Science	359, 623
		790-799	Z	Bibliography and	010-019
H	Social Sciences	300-399		Library Science	020-029
J	Political Science	320-329			

Note: Under the Library of Congress system, the books are placed on the shelves first by letter(s), then by the numbers which follow.

Locating Books by Call Number

429   When you go to the shelves to get your book, you must remember to look carefully at the call numbers. Because some numbers contain several decimal points and are longer than others, they can easily distract you into looking in the wrong place for your book. For instance, the call number 973.2 is located on the shelf after a book with the call number 973.198. (See the illustration below.) Also, you will most likely find several books with the same Dewey Decimal number. Whenever this happens, the books are arranged alphabetically by author abbreviation.

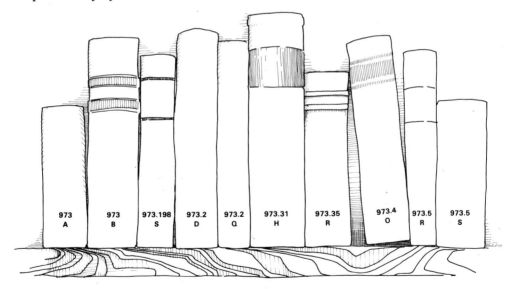

| 973 | 973 | 973.198 | 973.2 | 973.2 | 973.31 | 973.35 | 973.4 | 973.5 | 973.5 |
| A | B | S | D | Q | H | R | O | R | S |

Readers' Guide to Periodical Literature

430   *The Readers' Guide to Periodical Literature* is another useful index to library information. It indexes magazine articles by subject and author. If you are looking for information on a current topic, the *Readers' Guide* will direct you to specific magazine articles which contain more recent information than most books. It will also help you find magazine articles from years ago. To use the *Readers' Guide,* simply select a volume which covers the appropriate year(s) and search alphabetically for the author or subject in which you are interested. When you find a listing for an article you would like to

Sample Readers' Guide Page

ENGLER, PAUL
Oil Shortage today. Beef tomorrow? por Farm J 99:B16 Mr '75

ENGLISH

ENVIRONMENTAL engineering (buildings)
Architecture, energy, economy, and efficiency. G. Soucie. Audubon 77:122 S '75

Autonomous living in the Ouroboros house. S.J. Marcovich. il Pop Sci 207:80-2+ D '75

Conditioned air gets used three times in an energy-conscious design. il Archit Rec 158:133-4 N '75

Energy house from England aims at self-sufficiency. D. Scott. il Pop Sci 207:78-80 Ag '75

Houses designed with nature: their future is at hand; Ouroboros and integral projects. S. Love. bibl il Smithsonian 6:46-53 D '75

OCF presents awards for energy conservation. il Archit Rec 158:34 D '75

PM visits a house full of energy-saving ideas. J.F. Pearson. il Pop Mech 144:59+ Ag '75

Profession and industry focus on solar energy. il Archit Rec 158:35 Ag '75

Round table: toward a rational policy for energy use in buildings; with introd by W. F. Wagner, Jr. il Archit Rec 158:8, 92-9 mid-Ag '75

Solar energy systems: the practical side. il Archit Rec 158:128-34 mid-Ag '75

ENVIRONMENTAL health
Environmental hazards and corporate profits. Chr Cent 92: 404 Ap 23 '75

See also
Environmental diseases

ENVIRONMENTAL impact statements. See Environmental policy

ENVIRONMENTAL indexes. See Environment—Statistics

ENVIRONMENTAL law
Capitol watch. G. Alderson Liv Wildn 38:60 Wint '74; 39:33 Spr; 42 Jl; 41 O '75

How to save a river; Bellport, N.Y. high students, sponsoring Carmans River bill.
A. Rubin, Sr Schol 105:4-7 Ja 16 '75

Overview: law. A.W. Reitze Jr and G.L. Reitze. See issues of Environment

See also
Air pollution — Laws and legislation
Land utilization — Laws and regulations

ENVIRONMENTAL movement
After setbacks — new tactics in environmental crusade. J. McWethy. il U.S. News 78:62-3 Je 9 '75

Be a part of Food day every day. Org Gard & Farm 22:32+ Ap '75

Dialogue: C. Amory versus environmental groups on hunting issue. R.E. Hall. Conservationist 29:1 Ap '75

Ecological view. J. Marshall. Liv Wildn 39: 5-10 Spr '75

Environment, a mature cause in need of a lift. L.J. Carter. Science 187:45-6+ Ja 10 '75

Junior leagues focus on community education; environmental projects. M.D. Poole, por Parks & Rec 10:21+ D '75

Obligation and opportunity. R.F. Hall. Conservationist 29:1 Je '75

Organic living almanac. See issues of Organic gardening and farming

Prophets of shortage; address, July 11, 1975. D. Hodel. Vital Speeches 41:621-5 Ag 1 '75

What conservationists think about conservation; results of questionnaire. H. Clepper. il Am For 81:28-9+ Ag '75

See also
Canada-United States environmental council
Industry and the environmental movement

Exhibitions

See also
International exposition on the environment. 1974

AUTHOR ENTRY
NAME OF AUTHOR
DATE
NAME OF MAGAZINE
VOLUME
"SEE ALSO" CROSS REFERENCE
PAGE NUMBER
SUBJECT ENTRY
TITLE OF ARTICLE
"SEE" CROSS REFERENCE
SUBTOPIC

read, fill out a request form (*call slip*) or put the title, date, and volume of the magazine on a piece of paper and take it to the librarian. The librarian will get the magazine for you.

Look closely at the sample page from the *Readers' Guide*. Notice the following:

- The *Readers' Guide* is cross referenced, giving you other subject headings where you may find additional articles on related topics.

- Articles are arranged alphabetically by subject and author; the title is listed under both of these entries.

- Each subject entry is divided into subtopics whenever there are a large number of articles on the same subject listed together.

The Reference Section

431 Another special section of the library is the **reference section.** Students are usually familiar with the reference section because this is the area where the encyclopedias are kept. But there are a number of other helpful reference books with which all students should be familiar. The most popular titles are listed below:

Information Please Almanac is an atlas and yearbook which is published annually. The book contains facts, statistics, and short articles. Information is not arranged according to a specific pattern, but a detailed index makes information easy to find.

Statesman's Yearbook is a statistical and historical annual of the nations of the world. The information about each country includes facts concerning its government, geographical area, population, religions, education, judicial system, social welfare, and so on. A bibliography follows each entry.

The World Almanac and Book of Facts is an annual publication which contains facts and statistics concerning the following subjects: industry, politics, history, finances, religion, education, and social institutions or programs. In addition to this information, the book also includes a chronological review of major events in the past year. The book has a very detailed index.

The McGraw-Hill Encyclopedia of World Biography is a twelve-volume set which contains 5,000 biographies of world figures. The last volume contains a detailed index.

Webster's Dictionary of Proper Names has more than 10,000 entries. Entries include real people, fictional characters, literary works, events, sports figures, political personalities, specific terms, and acronyms.

Current Biography is published monthly and annually. Each article includes a photo of the individual, a biographical sketch, and information concerning the person's birth date, address, occupation, etc. Each yearbook contains an index of names, an index of professions, and a cumulative index.

Dictionary of American Biography is prepared under the direction of the American Council of Learned Societies. It includes biographies of noteworthy persons who lived in the United States. It does not include biographies of people living today.

American Writers: A Collection of Literary Biographies is a four-volume set which includes a series of reports on American authors. Each report contains a brief biographical sketch, a selected bibliography, and a rather lengthy evaluation of the writer's work.

Contemporary Authors is a biographical dictionary of authors who have written fiction, juvenile books, general nonfiction, and books on social sciences. Most entries are American writers. Each entry gives basic biographical information including titles written, honors given, etc. This publication is printed semiannually.

Something About the Author: Facts and Pictures About Contemporary Authors and Illustrators of Books for Young People contains about 200 biographical sketches. Each edition is a two-volume set and each volume contains an index. Entries are similar in content to those found in *Contemporary Authors*.

Bartlett's Familiar Quotations contains 20,000 quotations arranged in chronological order from ancient times to the present.

Peter's Quotations; Ideas for Our Time by Laurence J. Peter is a collection of useful and often witty quotations arranged by subject.

Brewer's Dictionary of Phrase and Fable contains real, fictitious, and mythical names from history, romance, the arts, science, fables, phrases, superstitions, and customs. Entries are grouped under key words and names.

Granger's Index to Poetry indexes 514 volumes of poetry anthologies containing works of 12,000 poets and translators. Poems are arranged according to subject, author, title, and first line.

Other Special Sections

432 Books, magazines, and reference materials are important sources of information, but they are not the only resources available in the library. Many libraries have *newspapers* with today's news and *vertical files* of older newspaper clippings and current pamphlets. Vertical files are arranged in alphabetical order by subject. Valuable current information can be found there. Records, tapes, slides, picture and photograph files, and numerous other *audio visual materials* may be features of your library. If they are, they are probably color coded in the card catalog. This means each type of audio visual material is on a card with a different color.

Note: Ask your librarian to explain the various resources of your library. *Remember:* The librarian is the best resource you have in the library. Don't be afraid to ask him or her for help in locating material and finding answers to any questions you may have.

Parts of a Book

If the book you have searched for and located in the library is a nonfiction book which you need for a research paper or assignment, it is necessary to understand how to use that book efficiently. Below you will find a brief description of each part of a book. It is especially important, for instance, to make full use of the index when using nonfiction books. (Additional information on using books is included in the *Reading, Study Skills,* and *Research Paper* sections of the Handbook.)

433 The **title page** is usually the first printed page in a book. It gives you (1) the full title of the book, (2) the author's name, (3) the publisher's name, and (4) the place of publication.

434 The **copyright page** is the page right after the title page. It is here you will find the year in which the copyright was issued which is usually the same year the book was published.

435 The **preface** (also called **foreword, introduction,** or **acknowledgment**) comes before the table of contents and is there to give you an idea of what the book is about and why it was written.

436 The **table of contents** is one section most of you are familiar with since it shows you the major divisions of the book (*units, chapters,* and *topics*). It comes right before the body of the book and is used to help locate major topics or areas to be studied.

437 The **body** of the book, which comes right after the table of contents, is the main section or *text* of the book.

438 Following the body is the **appendix.** This supplementary section gives extra information, usually in the form of maps, charts, tables, diagrams, letters, or copies of official documents.

439 The **glossary** follows the appendix and is the *dictionary* portion of the book. It is an alphabetical listing of technical terms, foreign words, or special words, with an explanation or definition for each.

440 The **bibliography** is a list of books or articles used by the author when preparing to write the book; the list also serves as a suggestion for further reading.

441 The **index** is probably the most useful of all the parts of a book. It is an alphabetical listing of all important topics appearing in the book. It is similar to the table of contents, except that the index is a much more detailed list. It will tell you on what page you can find practically anything you would need to locate in that book.

Using the Thesaurus

The **thesaurus** has been a welcome companion to generations of students and writers. A thesaurus is, in a sense, the opposite of a dictionary. You go to a dictionary when you know the word but need the definition. You go to a thesaurus when you know the definition but need the word. For example, you might want a word that means *fear*, but specifically the kind of fear that causes more worry than pain. You need the word to fill in the blank of the following sentence:

> Joan experienced a certain amount of
> _____ over the upcoming exam.

If you have a thesaurus which is in dictionary form, simply look up the word *fear* as you would in a dictionary. If, however, you have a more traditional thesaurus, you must first look up your word in the INDEX at the back of the thesaurus. The index is arranged alphabetically. You will find this entry for *fear* in the index:

> **FEAR 860**
> **fearful** *painful* 830
> *timid* 862

The numbers after *fear* are GUIDE NUMBERS, not page numbers. (Guide numbers are similar to the topic numbers of your Handbook index.) The bold-faced guide numbers indicate that the word in the index is the heading or key word for that particular group of synonyms. For instance, if you look up number 860 in the body of the thesaurus, you will find (on page 259) a long list of synonyms for the word *fear*. These include *timidity, diffidence, apprehensiveness, fearfulness, solicitude, anxiety, care, misgiving, mistrust, suspicion,* and *qualm.* You select the word *anxiety* and your sentence becomes

> Joan experienced a certain amount of
> *anxiety* over the upcoming exam.

Another feature of the traditional thesaurus is the useful placement of synonyms and antonyms directly before or after the other. Suppose you wanted a word that meant the opposite of *fear*. You could look up *fear* as you did above (guide number 860) and find that guide word 861 is *courage*. The guide word is then followed by a list of antonyms of fear such as *boldness, daring, gallantry, heroism,* and *confidence*.

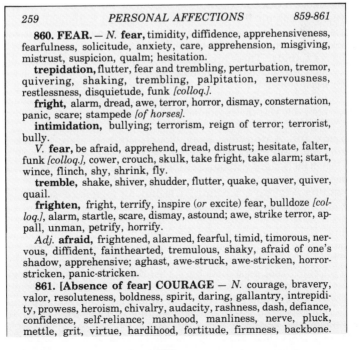

259   *PERSONAL AFFECTIONS*   *859-861*

860. FEAR. — *N.* **fear,** timidity, diffidence, apprehensiveness, fearfulness, solicitude, anxiety, care, apprehension, misgiving, mistrust, suspicion, qualm; hesitation.

trepidation, flutter, fear and trembling, perturbation, tremor, quivering, shaking, trembling, palpitation, nervousness, restlessness, disquietude, funk *[colloq.]*.

fright, alarm, dread, awe, terror, horror, dismay, consternation, panic, scare; stampede *[of horses]*.

intimidation, bullying; terrorism, reign of terror; terrorist, bully.

V. **fear,** be afraid, apprehend, dread, distrust; hesitate, falter, funk *[colloq.]*, cower, crouch, skulk, take fright, take alarm; start, wince, flinch, shy, shrink, fly.

tremble, shake, shiver, shudder, flutter, quake, quaver, quiver, quail.

frighten, fright, terrify, inspire (*or* excite) fear, bulldoze *[colloq.]*, alarm, startle, scare, dismay, astound; awe, strike terror, appall, unman, petrify, horrify.

Adj. **afraid,** frightened, alarmed, fearful, timid, timorous, nervous, diffident, fainthearted, tremulous, shaky, afraid of one's shadow, apprehensive; aghast, awe-struck, awe-stricken, horror-stricken, panic-stricken.

861. [Absence of fear] COURAGE — *N.* courage, bravery, valor, resoluteness, boldness, spirit, daring, gallantry, intrepidity, prowess, heroism, chivalry, audacity, rashness, dash, defiance, confidence, self-reliance; manhood, manliness, nerve, pluck, mettle, grit, virtue, hardihood, fortitude, firmness, backbone.

Using the Dictionary

Too often a dictionary is used only when someone needs to know the meaning of a word. Even though this is the main reason for the existence of the dictionary, it is only one of several reasons. A dictionary can serve many of your needs, including several you have probably never associated with the dictionary before. Below are some of the most important ways a dictionary can help you. *(All are illustrated following this section.)*

443 **Spelling** Not knowing how to spell a word can make it difficult to find in the dictionary but not impossible. You will be surprised at how quickly you can find a word by following its *sounded-out* spelling.

444 **Capital Letters** If you need to know whether a certain word is capitalized, it is probably going to be faster (certainly more accurate) to look it up in the dictionary than to ask a friend who thinks he knows.

445 **Syllabication** Other than for meaning and pronunciation, the dictionary is most often used to determine where you can divide a word. This is especially important when you are typing a paper or when you are working with strict margin requirements.

446 **Pronunciation** Many times people become lost or confused when they look at a word because they don't *hear* the word properly. They may even know the meaning of the word, but without the correct pronunciation they cannot recognize it. To remember a word and its meaning, you must know the correct pronunciation of it. (The dictionary gives you a **Pronunciation Key** at the bottom of all right-side pages.)

447 **The Parts of Speech** The dictionary uses nine abbreviations for the parts of speech:

n.	noun	**v.t.**	transitive verb	**adj.**	adjective
pron.	pronoun	**interj.**	interjection	**adv.**	adverb
v.i.	intransitive verb	**conj.**	conjunction	**prep.**	preposition

448 **Etymology** (History) Just after the pronunciation and part of speech, you will find [in brackets] the history of that particular word. The value of this section will be clear later when you must recall the meaning of a word; if you know a little about the history of each word you look up, it is going to be much easier to remember a meaning when the need arises. This is especially true of many Greek and Latin words where entire stories or myths are told to dramatize the origin of a particular word. (See 496.)

449 **Restrictive Labels** There are three main types of labels used in a dictionary: **subject labels,** which tell you that a word has a special meaning when used in a particular field *(mus.* for *music, med.* for *medicine, zool.* for *zoology,* etc.); **usage labels,** which tell you how a word is used *(slang, colloq.* for *colloquial, dial.* for *dialect,* etc.); and **geographic labels,** which tell you the region of the country where that word is mainly used *(N.E.* for *New England, West, South,* etc.).

450 **Synonyms and Antonyms** Even though the best place to look for a selection of synonyms and antonyms is a thesaurus (353, 442)—a dictionary of synonyms and antonyms—a dictionary will quite often list and label synonyms and antonyms after the meaning.

451 **Illustrations** Whenever a definition is difficult to make clear with words alone, a picture or drawing is used. These sketches can be extremely helpful since the mind can grasp more easily (also remember longer) definitions which are well illustrated.

452 **Meaning** Even though you probably know how to look up the meaning of a word, it is not quite as easy to figure out what to do with *all those meanings* once you have found them. The first thing to do is to read (or at least skim) all the meanings given. It is important to realize that most dictionaries list their meanings chronologically. This means the oldest meaning of the word is given first, then the newer or technical versions. You can see why it is extremely dangerous to simply take the first meaning listed—it is quite possible that this first one is not the meaning you are after at all. Remember to read all the meanings, and then select the one which is most appropriate for your use.

spark² (spärk) *n.* [ON. *sparkr*, lively: for IE. base see prec.]
1. a gay, dashing, gallant young man **2.** a beau or lover
—*vt.*, *vi.* ☆[Colloq.] to court, woo, pet, etc.   An old-fashioned term —**spark'er** *n.*

USAGE LABELS

spar·kle (spär'k'l) *vi.* **-kled, -kling** [ME. *sparklen*, freq. of *sparken*, to SPARK¹] **1.** to throw off sparks **2.** to gleam or shine in flashes; glitter or glisten, as jewels, sunlit water, etc. **3.** to be brilliant and lively [*sparkling* wit] **4.** to effervesce or bubble, as soda water and some wines —*vt.* to cause to sparkle —*n.* **1.** a spark, or glowing particle **2.** a sparkling, or glittering **3.** brilliance; liveliness; vivacity
SYN. see FLASH

SPELLING OF VERB FORMS

SYNONYM

spar·kler (-klər) *n.* a person or thing that sparkles; specif., *a*) a thin, light stick of pyrotechnic material that burns with bright sparks *b*) [*pl.*] [Colloq.] clear, brilliant eyes *c*) [Colloq.] a diamond or similar gem
☆**spark plug**   **1.** a piece fitted into the cylinder of an internal-combustion engine to ignite the fuel-mixture within: it carries an electric current into the cylinder, which sparks between two terminals in the presence of the mixture **2.** [Colloq.] a person or thing that inspires, activates, or advances something —**spark'plug'** *vt.* **-plugged', -plug'ging**

MEANINGS

— TERMINAL

— INSULATOR

— ELECTRODES

GAP

ILLUSTRATION

spark transmitter an early type of radio transmitter that uses the oscillatory discharge of a capacitor through an inductor in series with a spark gap to generate its high-frequency power

spar·ling (spär'lin) *n., pl.* **-ling, -lings:**   SPARK PLUG
see PLURAL, II, D, 2 [ME. *sperlynge* <   (in cross section)
MFr. *esperlinge* < MDu. *spirlinc*, orig.
dim. of *spīr*, a small point, grass shoot: see SPIRE²] a
European smelt (*Osmerus eperlanus*)

SPELLING OF PLURAL FORMS

spar·oid (sper'oid, spar'-) *adj.* [< ModL. *sparoides* < *sparus*, gilthead < L. < Gr. *sparos*: for IE. base see SPEAR] of or pertaining to the sparids —*n. same as* SPARID
sparring partner any person with whom a, prizefighter boxes for practice

PRONUNCIATION

spar·row (spar'ō) *n.* [ME. *sparwe* < OE. *spearwa*, akin to MHG. *sparwe* < IE. base *sper-*, bird name, esp. for sparrow, whence Gr. *sporgilos*, sparrow, *psar*, starling] **1.** any of several old-world weaverbirds; esp., any of a genus (*Passer*) including the ENGLISH SPARROW **2.** any of numerous finches native to both the Old and New Worlds; ☆esp., any of various American species, as the SONG SPARROW **3.** any of several other sparrowlike birds

SYLLABICATION AND PARTS OF SPEECH

spar·row·grass (spar'ō gras', -gräs') *n.* [altered by folk etym. < ASPARAGUS] dial. var. of ASPARAGUS
sparrow hawk [ME. *sparowhawke*: so named from preying on sparrows] **1.** a small European hawk (*Accipiter nisus*) with short, rounded wings ☆**2.** a small American falcon (*Falco sparverius*) with a reddish-brown back and tail

PRIMARY AND SECONDARY ACCENTS

ETYMOLOGY

spar·ry (spär'ē) *adj.* **-ri·er, -ri·est** of, like, or rich in mineral spar
sparse (spärs) *adj.* [L. *sparsus*, pp. of *spargere*, to scatter: see SPARK¹] thinly spread or distributed; not dense or crowded —*SYN.* see MEAGER —**sparse'ly** *adv.* —**sparse'ness, spar'si·ty** (-sə tē) *n.*

SPELLING OF ADJECTIVE FORMS

Spar·ta (spär'tə) city in the S Peloponnesus, Greece, a powerful military city in ancient Laconia
Spar·ta·cus (spär'tə kəs) ?-71 B.C.; Thracian slave & gladiator in Rome: leader of a slave revolt
spar·te·ine (spär'ti ēn', -tē in) *n.* [< ModL. *Spartium*, name of the broom genus (< L. *spartum*, broom (see ESPARTO) + -INE⁴] a clear, oily, poisonous, liquid alkaloid, C₁₅H₂₆N₂, obtained from a broom (*Spartium scoparium*)

SPELLING AND CAPITAL LETTERS

PRONUNCIATION KEY

READING AND STUDY SKILLS

The Mechanics of Reading

Reading is such an automatic activity for most people that they seldom stop to think about what takes place when they read. These same people are quite surprised when they discover what actually does take place during the act of reading. Below is a summary of the reading process, explained in the terminology normally used to describe it.

454 **Left-to-right eye movement** is the route the eyes take when they move across a line of print. As the eyes follow this left-to-right path, they do not move in a smooth, even flow as many people imagine. Instead, the eyes move in a jerky, stop-and-start fashion. Each of these stops is called a **fixation.** A reader can have anywhere from two to twenty fixations per line, depending upon the difficulty of the material and the skill of the reader.

455 To better understand the idea of fixations during the left-to-right movement of the eyes, you can perform the following test: First, get another student to help you. Move your desks together so that they are facing and actually touching one another. Give your friend something to read and ask him to hold it well off the desk so that his eyes are even with yours. Now, tell him to begin reading. Watch his eyes as they move across the page. Do you notice how they stop and start? See if you can count the number of stops or fixations he makes per line. You will have to count very quickly since each fixation takes only a split second. Now switch around. Let him see what you saw.

456 What is probably the most important thing to remember from this exercise is that the eyes read *only* when they are stopped—and they do not stop for very long. As your eyes move from one fixation point to the next, you are not able to read because the words are blurred. Another way of thinking about this is to recall what happens when you take a picture at the same time your camera is bumped or moved. Unless the camera you are using is an especially good one, the picture will come back blurred and out of focus. It is the same way with your eyes. Unless they are stopped, even though it is only for a fraction of a second, the picture (words) will appear blurred. You do not see this blur, fortunately, because the brain blots it out. If the brain did not have this built-in blotter, reading would be an impossible task.

457 Once the eyes pick up a word, they transfer it to the brain by way of one of three routes:

458 1) The *direct route* (**sight reading**) is the most efficient and desirable of the three. The eyes pick the words off the page and send them directly to the brain for interpretation. There is no delay or detour and, therefore, less chance for an important idea to become lost or confused along the way.

459 2) The *indirect route* (**auditory reading**) includes an unnecessary and time-consuming step: **sub-vocalization.** When you sub-vocalize, you say each word to yourself. This extra step slows your reading rate considerably. This slower rate in turn affects your comprehension because words are read one at a time, rather than two or three at a time as they should be. (*Exception:* If the material you are reading is especially difficult or complex, sub-vocalizing can help you concentrate on one idea at a time.)

460 3) The *interrupted route* (**motor reading**) includes two unnecessary steps. The second of these can cause a complete interruption of the reading process. In this situation, you actually say (**vocalize, mumble**) each word and then listen to yourself read. Rather than being a simple *see-thought* process as it should be, reading becomes a *see-say-hear-thought* process. This is the least efficient of the three kinds of reading.

Poor Reading Habits

> In addition to auditory and motor reading (discussed on the previous page), there are several other bad reading habits you should come to recognize.

461   **Head movement** is a very common roadblock to efficient reading. It causes your reading speed to be limited by the speed with which you can move your head from left to right. Even though that may seem fast enough, it is considerably slower than the rate used by good readers. Excessive head movement can also be the cause of headaches or reading fatigue. You should work to control or eliminate head movement.

462   **Pointing** is a second bad reading habit. As the pointer (usually a finger or pencil) moves from left to right, the eyes follow it very closely. This forces you, the reader, to focus on each word (in some cases each syllable) one at a time. Because it is necessary to read groups of words during each fixation to become an efficient reader, pointing becomes a roadblock to reading improvement.

463   **Regressions** have always been a common barrier to overall reading efficiency and comfort. A regression is going back over what you have already read because you failed to read it properly the first time. This can be caused by any of several factors: physical or mental distractions, poor vocabulary, poor vision, etc. If there are no serious physical problems connected with the regression habit, it can often be corrected with a simple exercise. Select a book or magazine which is fairly easy and interesting. Use a card or book marker as a pacer. Move the pacer at a steady (slightly faster than usual) pace down the page just *above* the line you are reading. Since the card quickly covers what you have just read, there is no chance for you to go back for a second reading. Continue to practice regularly so that this reading problem can be eliminated. *(Note:* Going back to reread a passage you didn't understand is not the same as a regression.)

464   **Margin reading** is reading the margins as well as the printed material. If you are a margin reader, you will continue looking for words beyond the line of print. You will also return to the far left edge of the page and begin *reading* there rather than at the beginning of the line. This poor habit can be corrected by placing a colored straightedge over the margin which seems to cause the most trouble. This colored edge alerts you to your overshooting and forces you to concentrate on correcting this bad reading habit.

Good Reading Habits

465   To make yourself a more efficient reader, you must work to reduce the number of fixations or stops in each line. To do this, you can use any of a number of *eye-stretching exercises* including those below. These exercises will help you learn to read words in groups rather than one at a time, just as you once learned to read letters in groups (words) rather than one letter at a time. In this way you become a thought reader, instead of a word reader. *Eight cylinder engine,* for example, is a logical thought group because the three words work together to form one thought.

Increasing Recognition Span

466   In the following exercise, you are to follow the line down the middle of the columns of thought groups. Do not move your head or your eyes either to the left or the right. The objective is to stretch your eye or recognition span by forcing your eyes to use more of their peripheral vision. *(Note:* You will not "see" every word in this exercise.)

467

Increasing Recognition Span	
A poll published in a recent issue of *Time* magazine indicates that in nearly all of our modern families childbearing has become exclusively a female task.	bathrooms.
An article in the July issue of *Atlantic Monthly* states that a clear majority of American elementary and secondary schools still require that male and female students use separate	As recently as June, 1977, renowned newsman Walter Harvey reported that 99 percent of American religious institutions continue to refuse fair recognition of both sexes.
	Ministers, rabbis, and priests all stubbornly continue the tradition of concluding prayers with "Amen" rather than "Awomen."

(Note: This first exercise, 467, can be continued by using old newspapers and magazine articles. Simply draw a colored line down the middle of the columns. Remember to focus on the line and eliminate all left and right movement.)

Space Reading Exercises

468 The exercises above are aimed at increasing your *recognition span:* the number of words a reader can see or *recognize* in one fixation. To further encourage thought grouping, you can use a *space reading* exercise. This exercise is designed to draw your attention to a horizontal line (or series of dots) just above the line of print. By focusing your eyes on this line (and moving quickly from left to right), you should be able to sense your eye span spreading outward and downward. You should then be able to read the thought groups without first focusing on each of the words. (Again, use old newspapers for practice.)

469

Space Reading Exercise
I have considered it to be my heartfelt duty to engage in three years of investigative
study into the problem of sex discrimination. It is with meek pride and resounding
humility that I now share with you the results of my examination. I entrust my findings
into your care, knowing that your love of our dear country will compel you to share
the results of the study with your friends. First, I should say that my study revealed
ten basic sources of the evil that presently pervades our system. Those ten sources
are, at the same time, both distinct and related. The sources are distinct in the sense
that they are separated; they are related in the sense that all have something to do
with literature—primarily children's literature. (Certainly the forces behind this move-
ment most wanted to infiltrate the minds of our young.)

Anticipating Thought Groups

470 You can also train your eyes to *anticipate* thought groups by recognizing clues in the sentence. Prepositions, for example, are almost always followed by two or more related words. These words combine with the preposition to form a thought group: *on the floor, by the door, in the house, around the corner,* etc. Nouns are also found quite often as key words in thought groups. Usually they are combined with an article (a, an, the) and one or more modifiers: *the wrong turn, the left halfback, the crosstown bus, the northtown shopping center, the two English teachers,* etc. A very simple exercise for increasing awareness of thought groups is to go through an article in an old magazine or newspaper and divide the entire article into thought groups as shown below. Then read each of the marked articles several times. You should start to feel yourself reading with a rhythmic or bouncy pace. This is exactly the pace you need to develop for reading thought groups.

471

Anticipating Thought Groups
Our culture / has conquered / all frontiers / of the biological sciences. / Yet today / few husbands are willing / to learn the skills / necessary for childbirth. / Sanitary conditions / are universally high / in all the bathrooms / of our schools / but manipulating educators / continue to post / the signs "Boys" and "Girls." / Nearly all church leaders / encourage large donations / to fall into / their collection plates / from the hands / of males and females; / but only a handful / of these leaders / conclude their prayers / in such a fashion / as to credit / members of both sexes.

(Note: This exercise, too, can be continued. Mark several pages in a paperback or magazine for thought groups and read each several times. When you are tired of reading the same pages over and over, mark out several new ones.)

Reading Techniques and Study Aids

There are several additional reading techniques which can strengthen your reading and studying skills.

472 **Previewing** is taking a brief, but planned, look at the material before you begin to read. The following procedure can be followed when previewing:

1) Read the title, author, date, and any other information important to your purpose.
2) Read the headnote (the paragraph between the title and the body of the reading) and the first two or three paragraphs.
3) Read all subheadings, chapter titles, and bold-faced and italicized words.
4) Read the last paragraph and any questions which follow the selection.
5) Study the author's style, especially his manner of structuring sentences and paragraphs.
6) Look for topic sentences in the paragraphs and take note of any pattern followed by the author. Quite often the topic sentence will be first in the paragraph, although some writers choose a different position to add variety to their writing.

473 **Determining a purpose** before you begin to read is a necessary step in the reading process. With a specific purpose in mind, you can take full advantage of several other pre-reading techniques:

1) You should *ask questions* which you hope to find the answers to in your selection. Continue to raise these questions throughout your reading. It is also a good idea to write down your questions as you think of them. It becomes a natural thing, then, to fill in the answers as you find them.
2) You should *learn to anticipate* what is coming up in each of the various sections of your article. This will help you to concentrate and to maintain an interest in what you are reading.

474 **Adjusting your rate** to suit your purpose and the difficulty of the material is another of the common sense techniques which often goes unused. Many college instructors have recently noted that a student's inability to adjust his reading rate can be a major cause of his difficulty in college coursework. There are three basic reading rates which you can use—*skimming, studying,* and *enjoying.*

1) **Skimming** is the fastest reading rate and is actually a form of previewing. You can use it to get a quick overview of the material you are reading or to find the answers to specific questions. One form of skimming is called **pacing.** Pacing is a technique you can use to increase your reading and skimming speed. By moving a card or your hand quickly down a page, you can consume many pages of print in the time it takes to read a single page. The card or hand acts in the same way as a pace car at the race track. As it moves steadily and quickly down the page, it forces the eyes to speed up to the same pace.

2) **Studying** is the slowest, most deliberate rate. It requires that previewing, questioning, anticipating, note-taking, and summarizing all take place during reading. There are several study techniques which include all of these steps in one form or another. Probably the most popular of these study methods is the SQ3R: *Survey, Question, Read, Recite, Review.*

SQ3R

Survey is to look over the entire reading assignment, noting such things as the title, headnote (the short paragraph found just after the title), chapter titles and subheadings, illustrations, and bold-faced words. By getting this overview of what the article is about, you are in a much better frame of mind to do a meaningful job of reading.

Question is to ask questions as you survey in the hopes of further establishing a positive foundation for the actual reading. The more questions you ask yourself during the survey, the more likely you are to find what you are looking for in the article.

Read is to read the article carefully from start to finish looking for main ideas, major details, and additional answers to the questions you have raised. It is suggested that when you come across a major detail or an answer, you reread that portion and immediately write a summary or note in your own words. For long, complex assignments, an outline may be necessary to keep these summaries organized for later use.

Recite is to recall or remember what you have read by answering (aloud or to yourself) all the questions you sought answers to while you were reading. This should be done at the end of each major section and again when you have finished the entire reading assignment. Applying the *who, what, when, where, why,* and *how* questions could help this final reciting.

Review is to look over all your notes in preparation for a test, discussion, demonstration, or whatever else may be required of you for this assignment. Many people find that it is much easier and more productive to review with another person than alone. This is a good study technique—one you should use often. It should be noted, though, that because you alone will have to respond to the questions on the test or quiz, you should do at least some reviewing by yourself. For this purpose note cards or flash cards are extremely helpful. They can be carried nearly anywhere and used where books and notebooks cannot be.

3) **Enjoying** is whatever rate or speed is most comfortable for you. This rate may well vary from day to day depending upon your state of mind, your surroundings, and your reading material.

475 **Summarizing** what you have read is extremely valuable if you need to understand and remember what you have read for any length of time. There are three basic ways to summarize material:

1) *Mark the material* in the book itself by underlining, circling, starring, color coding, margin marking, etc.
2) *Take notes* on (or write briefly about) the main ideas and important details contained in the reading. A good note is one which is written legibly and is easy to understand when it is reread days or even weeks later. Notes which are poorly constructed and quickly scribbled are nearly worthless. (See 421.)
3) *Outline* your thoughts. If you have a difficult time taking and using notes, you should consider using an outline for your reading summaries. Titles and chapter headings will usually serve as major points in your outline; subheadings and bold-faced or italicized words will often be secondary points. The third, fourth, and additional divisions will depend upon the amount and complexity of the material being read and also on how detailed a summary you will need later. (See "The Outline," 357-359.)

476

Using Your Outline as a Note-taking Guide

Use your outline. Follow it during the classroom review of the reading material. As you do, you will be prepared to answer any questions your teacher may ask you about the assignment. Your completed outline can also be used in class as a note-taking guide. To accomplish this most efficiently, you must leave room on your outline page for taking notes. (Use the left two-thirds of your paper for the outline summary; use the right one-third for class notes.) Follow your outline throughout the review and jot down anything which helps to clarify or adds to your understanding of what you have read. By combining your reading and classroom summaries in this way, you should end up with a well-organized set of study notes.

Chapter 10: "The Disinherited"

Outlined Reading Assignment	Class Notes
I. The Clash of Cultures	Early settlers had
A. Pioneer attitude toward the Indian	few problems; as more trappers and
1. Inferior being	hunters moved in,
a. Lacked "civilization"	conflicts started.
b. Lacked "religion"	Indians labeled
2. Easily exploited	"pagans"; anti-
a. Swindled in trades	Indian sentiment
b. Set against other tribes	followed.
3. No property rights	
a. A "squatter on gov. land	Some argued that
b. False promises	because Indians did
c. Forced off land	not have the right
B. Indian reaction to treatment	to vote, they could
1. Bitterness surfaced	not own property.
a. Resulting action	
1) Move	Serious clashing
2) Defend	of the cultures
3) Attack	followed.

Remembering What You Have Read

477 In addition to the SQ3R study-memory technique discussed earlier in this section, there are several other methods which can be used to help you remember what you have read.

1) The **association method** is a technique in which each item being studied is associated with a memorable word. This linking or association word will be easier to recall at a later time because it is one you already know. If, for example, you are supposed to memorize the first ten amendments to the Constitution (Bill of Rights), you would begin by setting up an association for the first amendment. Since *Bill* has four letters and also begins with *b*, how about *four basic rights* as an association for the first amendment? What are the *four basic rights*? It is hoped that nearly everyone asking himself this question will come up with one or more of the following: freedom of religion, speech, press, and petition. Since even three of these is not enough, however, a second association will have to be set up to make sure all four are remembered. What might work best in this situation is an *acronym,* a word created by using the first letter(s) of each of the words in the group being studied. The words in this instance are *religion, speech, press,* and *petition,* which can be combined into several possible acronyms. Because this is the first amendment, the acronym *preps* might work. It can easily be associated with beginnings or *prep*arations. This particular word is a combination of the first letters of three of the words and the first and second letters of the fourth word, religion. Associations must now be worked out for the second through the tenth amendments.

2) **Acronyms** are words which are constructed from the first letter(s) of the words in a particular group or title: NATO—*North Atlantic Treaty Organization.* Some of the most commonly used acronyms are explained in the abbreviations section elsewhere in this handbook (117-118).

   To be useful as an aid to memory, the acronym must be composed of letters from all or nearly all the words in the group. The example constructed in the association method discussion above was *preps*. Do you remember what it stood for? If you recalled the first amendment or the four basic rights (press, religion, petition, and speech), you may understand why some people use acronyms regularly to help them remember.

   A slightly different version of the acronym technique is to treat a word which is difficult to spell as if it were an acronym. You must then work the acronym process in reverse. Instead of making up a word from the first letter(s) of a group of words, make up the group of words for which this word could be an acronym:

   geography . . . Giraffes eat old, greasy rugs and paint houses yellow.
   hastily   . . . Has anyone seen Tom's irreplaceable little yo-yo?
   fatigue   . . . Four angry truckers irately granted us exit.

3) **Rhyming words, phrases, or songs** can also be used as a way to supplement your natural memory:

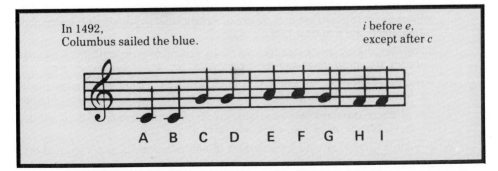

In 1492,
Columbus sailed the blue.

i before *e*,
except after *c*

A B C D E F G H I

Note-Taking Skills

478 Isn't it easier to remember something you have actually done than something you have only heard about? Taking notes is doing something. It changes information you have only heard about into information you have worked with. The information becomes more a part of you. You not only hear the information, you also process it in your mind, organizing it as you write it down. The information becomes much easier to remember and use.

Memory experts will tell you that the average person forgets at least half of what he learns within 24 hours of learning it. Taking notes helps to focus your attention on the most important information, information which you do not want to forget one day after learning it. Taking good notes can help you remember this information for weeks and even months afterward.

Students who have not studied the techniques of note-taking very often end up with one of the following kinds of notes:

1. notes which are so disorganized or so poorly written they are almost impossible to read;
2. notes which are so short and incomplete they are of little use when studying for a test; or
3. notes which are so full of details, illustrations, and examples they are impossible to use efficiently.

Luckily, note-taking skills can be learned. You can turn your notes into a valuable study aid for reviewing what your teacher taught you last week, last month, or even last semester. The most important thing to know about note-taking is that it's not simply hearing and writing: it's listening, thinking, reacting, questioning, summarizing, organizing, listing, labeling, illustrating—and writing.

Guidelines for Improving Note-Taking Skills

479 The guidelines below will help you understand better what you must do to improve your note-taking skills. Read and follow each suggestion carefully. (See also the "Guidelines for Improving Listening Skills," 411.)

1. Listen for and follow any special instructions, rules, or guidelines your classroom teacher may have regarding notebooks and note-taking.
2. Place the date and the topic of each lecture or discussion at the top of each page of notes.
3. Write your notes in ink, on one side of the paper, and as neatly as time will allow; leave space in the margin for revising or adding to your notes later.
4. Begin taking notes immediately. Don't wait for something new or earthshaking before you write your first note; instead, write a brief summary or a personal observation about the material being reviewed.
5. Remember, taking good notes does not mean writing down everything; it means summarizing the main ideas and listing only the important supporting details.
6. Write as concisely as you can. Leave out words that are not essential to the meaning; write your notes in phrases and thoughts rather than complete sentences.
7. Use as many standard abbreviations, acronyms, and symbols (U.S., avg., in., ea., lb., vs, @, #, $, %, &, +, −, <, ⅔, w/o, etc.) as you can.
8. In addition, develop your own system of abbreviations or a personal shorthand

method. Consider using abbreviations for words or phrases used frequently in a particular class. (Example: CW for Civil War in history class.)

9. Always copy down (or summarize) what the teacher puts on the board or on an overhead projector. Pay special attention to charts or diagrams.

10. Draw simple illustrations, charts, or diagrams in your notes whenever it would help make a point clearer.

11. Write a title or heading for each new topic covered in your notes.

12. Listen for transitions or signal words to help you organize your notes.

13. Use a special system of marking your notes to emphasize important information (underline, star, check, indent).

14. Number all related ideas, items in a list, and information presented in time sequence.

15. Label or indicate in some way information which is related by cause and effect, comparison or contrast, or some other special pattern or organization.

16. Circle those words or ideas which you will need to ask about or look up later.

17. Do not let your notes sit until it is time to review for a test. Read over the notes you have taken within 24 hours and recopy, highlight, or summarize them as needed. (Consider using a colored marker or pen to highlight those notes which you feel are especially important.)

18. Share your note-taking techniques, abbreviations, or special markings with others; you can then learn from what they share with you.

19. Consider switching to a new system of note-taking (outlining, mapping, 2-column) if you are unhappy with your present method.

Listening Skills

480 Listening is the easiest of all ways to learn. At the same time, listening is the most difficult of all the learning skills to master. Why?

First, listening requires that you think about what another person is saying. When you **read** or **write** or **think,** the process is happening within your own mind. But, when you **listen,** you must discipline yourself to think about what is going on in the mind of the speaker.

Second, listening requires you to follow the leader. When you **read,** you control the speed by telling your eyes how rapidly to move across a page. When you **write,** you are in control of what the pen produces on the paper. When you **think,** you are the one who decides what to think about. But when you **listen,** you are like a passenger in a car. The speaker is the driver who controls the speed, brakes, and direction; you are along only for the ride.

Most speakers drive too slowly. You can think four times as fast as the average teacher talks. As a result, your thoughts tend to wander into relaxing memories of the past or plans for the future. Only by demanding total attention on the **present** can you discipline yourself to be a good listener.

Instead of allowing your mind to wander, you must hold your attention on the speaker and what he is saying. First, you must **pay attention** to exactly what the speaker is saying. Second, you must **listen between the lines.** Your mind will stay on the subject if you spend free moments figuring out what discussion or test questions might come out of the material being presented, putting the teacher's statements into your own words, reviewing the main points made so far and anticipating the next major idea, separating facts from opinions, and challenging yourself to get the most out of what you are hearing.

Listening is not something we do automatically. Most of us were born with the ability to hear, but not with the ability to listen. We have to be taught this. But learning to listen demands total concentration and strong mental discipline. Listening is much more than sitting up straight, looking in the direction of the person speaking, and following what is being said with part of your mind. Training in what you should think about and do during the listening process is essential if you hope to improve your ability to learn through listening.

Guidelines for Improving Listening Skills

481   The guidelines listed below will help you understand better all that is involved in the listening process. Read and think about each guideline. Then begin working to improve your listening skills by following these suggestions.

1. Have a positive attitude toward the listening situation; if you are motivated to listen well, you probably will.

2. Prepare to listen by reading or thinking beforehand about what you may hear; write down any questions you may have and be ready to ask them. Bring the rest of your notes with you as well.

3. Keep an open mind about the speaker and the topic; do not conclude beforehand that you are not going to like or benefit from what is about to be said.

4. Avoid poor listening habits such as day dreaming, pretending to listen, giving up when the material becomes difficult, being distracted, prejudging the speaker or the topic, and getting too emotionally involved.

5. Take time to decide why you are listening (to gather information for tests, to learn how to . . . , etc.).

6. Try to figure out why the speaker is telling you what he is (to motivate, to explain, to clarify, to inform, etc.).

7. Concentrate on the speaker and his use of voice intonation, facial expression, and other gestures. This may help you determine which points are most important as well as what the speaker is inferring (saying between the lines).

8. Listen for spoken directions and follow them carefully.

9. Listen for the speaker's plan of organization or sequence in presenting main points, important supporting details, and examples. This can help you anticipate what is going to be covered next.

10. Listen for the speaker's use of transitions or signal words and phrases like *as a result, next, secondly, more importantly,* etc. These signals can help you follow the speaker from one point to the next.

11. Think about what is being said. How does this material relate to me? What can I associate it with in my personal life to help me remember? How might I use this information in the future?

12. Listen with pen in hand. Take notes on any information you have to remember for tests or discussions; do not, however, take so many notes that you miss some of the important points or the overall idea of what is being said.

13. Summarize each main point as it is discussed and draw conclusions about the importance of each; it can also be helpful to distinguish between new and old ideas in your notes.

14. Write down questions you would like to ask; ask them as soon as it is appropriate to do so.

15. Listen for bias or prejudice on the part of the speaker. Is the speaker using emotional appeals or propaganda techniques to sway his listeners? (See "Fallacies of Thinking.") Is the speaker making clear what is fact and what is opinion?

16. Try to conclude the listening experience on a positive note. Clarify any questions you may still have, ask for additional information, or find out how much of the information you will be expected to know in the future.

17. Summarize the entire talk in one or two sentences as a final test of whether or not you understood what was said.

Study Skills

1. Know exactly what the reading assignment is, when it is due, and what you must do to complete it successfully.

2. Gather any additional materials you may need to complete your assignment (notebook, handouts, reference books, etc.).

3. Decide how much time you will need to complete the assignment and plan accordingly.

4. Decide when and where (library, study hall, home) you will do your assignment; read in a quiet, comfortable place whenever possible.

5. If you have trouble doing your reading assignments as you should, try doing them at the same time each day. This will help you control the urge to wait until you are "in the mood" before starting.

6. Do not plan your study-reading when you are either especially hungry or tired.

7. Plan to take breaks only after completing each assignment and stick to that schedule.

8. Read and follow all directions carefully.

9. Know your textbooks and what they contain; use the index, glossary, and footnotes.

10. Use a specific approach to your study reading—the SQ3R approach, for example—and avoid the five most common poor reading habits: head movement, pointing, regressions, sub-vocalizing, and margin reading. (See "The Mechanics of Reading.")

11. Preview each chapter or assignment before you begin reading to get an overall picture of what the reading selection is about; if there are questions, read them over before you begin reading.

12. Use the titles, headings, and subheadings before and while you are reading to ask yourself questions about the material.

13. Try to identify the main idea of each paragraph as well as the important supporting details; notice words or phrases which are in italics or boldface.

14. Attempt to figure out the author's pattern of organization or development as you read.

15. Look closely at maps, charts, graphs and other illustrations to help you understand and remember important information.

16. Take good notes of everything you read—summarize, outline, star, underline, highlight, or whatever else works best for you.

17. Use all of your senses when you read. Try to imagine what something looks, feels, and tastes like and draw illustrations in your notes.

18. Realize that some reading material is much more difficult than other material; vary your reading speed and concentration accordingly.

19. Use sound, structure, and context clues to figure out the meaning of unfamiliar words; look up any words which you cannot figure out and write them in your notebook.

20. Practice summarizing out loud what you have read whenever possible.

21. Try hard to reason out difficult material by re-reading first; then ask someone for an explanation or find a simpler explanation in another book.

22. Make out note cards or flashcards of difficult material to study later.

23. Keep a list of things you want to check on or ask your teacher about.

24. Keep a separate list of things you feel may appear on tests.

25. Remember that reading is thinking and often requires a good deal of effort and concentration. Have a specific purpose and positive attitude each time you read.

Guidelines for Writing Assignments

Planning Your Work Session

1. First of all, know exactly what the writing assignment is, when it is due, and what you must do to complete it successfully.

2. Gather any materials you may need to complete your assignment (journal, notebook, handouts, dictionary, handbook, etc.)

3. Decide how much time you will need to complete the assignment and plan accordingly.

4. Decide when and where (library, study hall, home) you will do your assignment; write in a quiet, comfortable place whenever possible.

5. If you have trouble doing your writing assignments as you should, try doing them at the same time and place each day. This will help you control the urge to wait until you are "in the mood" before starting.

6. Do not plan to do your writing when you are either hungry or tired.

7. Plan to take breaks only after completing a certain amount of each assignment and stick to that schedule. If necessary, ask your family not to disturb you and hold any phone calls you may get.

Preparing to Write

8. Remember that writing is thinking and often requires a good deal of effort and concentration. Have a specific purpose and positive attitude each time you sit down to write.

9. Remember, too, that some writing assignments are more difficult than others; vary your pace and concentration accordingly.

10. Begin the actual writing by reviewing carefully all the directions and guidelines your teacher may have given you for this assignment. Look up any words you are unsure of and write down the meaning of each.

11. Keep a list of things you need to check on or ask your teacher about. (Remember, all writing is basically an attempt to solve a problem. You must clearly understand a problem before you can solve it.)

Selecting and Supporting Your Topic

12. If you have not been given a specific topic to write about, begin listing possibilities. Try first to think of topics you are interested in or know something about. Consider the suggestions given by your teacher; look in newspapers or magazines for ideas; if necessary, consult any lists of topics you may have available.

13. When you have a topic you feel will work for this assignment, place a clear, concise statement of that topic and how you plan to handle it at the top of your paper. This statement can serve as the controlling idea (thesis statement) for your assignment.

14. Next list all your initial thoughts and ideas about the topic, including details you may want to include later in your writing.

15. Continue to gather information (from as many sources as necessary) until you have enough to support your topic sentence or thesis statement. (It is always a good idea to collect more information than you think you actually need.)

Arranging Your Information

16. Look carefully at your information and begin arranging it into the best possible order: order of importance, chronological (time) order, order of location, etc. Even though you may later add details or change their order, it is always a good idea to start with a specific plan or design.

17. Put your main points into a working outline. This will help you spot any gaps which may exist and make clear where you must add more details.

Writing Your Assignment

18. Continue writing. Listen to your ideas as you are putting them on paper. Good writing sounds natural and honest. Here are some pointers which may help you keep your writing sincere and clear:

    a. Don't go hunting for a big word when a small one will do — a big word is one you probably wouldn't use in a classroom conversation.

    Do, however, use your thesaurus when you need a word which is more specific or more exact than the word you first used.

    b. Don't use slang — not all your readers will understand it — or qualifiers like *kind of, sort of, quite,* or *a bit* which add nothing to what you have already said.

    Do, however, use contractions if they sound more natural.

    c. Don't use cliches or euphemisms — they tend to make your writing sound phony.

    Do, however, use words and phrases which "sound" good and make your writing more appealing. To be appealing, your writing should have a certain bounce or rhythm to it.

    d. Don't use filler or padding — when you have said all that needs to be said, stop writing.

    Do, however, include enough details (examples, reasons, comparisons, etc.) to prove your point or paint a complete picture.

    e. Don't use adverbs or adjectives when they are unnecessary: return *back, complete* monopoly, *more* perfect, screamed *loudly, muffled* silence, *individual* person, *final* result.

    Do use verbs which are vivid and nouns which are concrete; by doing so, you eliminate the need for additional modifiers:

    > *sprinted, dashed, scampered, bolted* — not *ran fast*
    >
    > *engineer, conductor, porter, fireman* — not *railroad worker*

19. Work for an ending which leaves the reader with a good feeling about what he has just read. A good ending will give the reader something to take with him and share with others.

Revising and Proofreading

20. Check your writing for fragments and run-ons. (Reading each paragraph backwards one sentence at a time can help you locate these errors.)

21. Revise and proofread your writing carefully. (Use a checklist if necessary.) Always check for spelling, usage, and punctuation errors. Most of these errors are avoidable and should never find their way into a final copy.

Writing Your Final Copy

22. Follow the directions of your teacher when it comes to writing or typing your final copy. Keep your final copy in a safe, clean, dry place. Don't let your paper get wrinkled or dirty; also, don't fold your paper.

23. Turn your writing assignment in on time and be open to any suggestions your teacher may give you for future improvement. The only way to improve your writing is to write, rewrite, and write again. There are no substitutes or shortcuts, so welcome the advice you are given as an opportunity to improve your writing and to better yourself.

Test-Taking Skills

Organizing and Preparing Test Material

1. Ask the teacher to be as specific as possible about what·will be on the test.
2. Ask how the material will be tested (true/false, multiple choice, essay).
3. Review your class notes and recopy those sections which are especially important. When you recopy your notes, use a different method of organizing. If, for instance, your history notes are arranged chronologically, copy them over by definition, by *good* and *bad*, by nation, etc.
4. Get any notes or materials you may have missed from the teacher or another student.
5. Set up a specific time(s) to study for an exam and schedule other activities around it.
6. Make a list of special terms important in each subject and study that list thoroughly.
7. Look over quizzes and exams you took earlier in that class.
8. Prepare an outline of everything to be tested to get an overview of the unit.
9. Prepare a detailed study sheet for each part of your outline.
10. Attempt to predict test questions and write practice answers for them.
11. Set aside a list of questions to ask the teacher or another student.

Reviewing and Remembering Test Material

1. Begin reviewing early. Don't wait until the night before the test.
2. Whenever possible, relate the test material to your personal life or to other subjects you are taking.
3. Look for patterns of organization in the material you study (cause/effect, comparison, chronological, etc.).
4. Use association techniques by relating the unfamiliar to the familiar.
5. Use maps, lists, diagrams, acronyms, rhymes, or any other special memory aids. For example, *random* means "no definite order." The *n, d, o* can help you remember this. Share especially good memory aids with your classmates; they'll then share theirs with you.
6. Use flash cards or note cards and review with them whenever time becomes available.
7. Recite material out loud whenever possible as you review.
8. Skim the material in your textbooks, noting key words and ideas; practice for the test by summarizing the importance of these ideas.
9. Study with others only after you have studied well by yourself.
10. Test your knowledge of a subject by teaching or explaining it to someone else.
11. Review especially difficult material just before going to bed the night before the exam.
12. Go over your material as often as possible on exam day.

Taking the Test

1. Make sure you are ready for the test both mentally and physically.
2. Check to see that you have all the materials you need for a particular test.
3. Report to the room as quickly as possible on the day of the exam.
4. Review especially difficult material right up to the time the test starts.
5. Listen carefully to the final instructions of the teacher. How much time do you have to complete the test? Do all the questions count equally? Can you use any

aids such as a dictionary or handbook? Are there any corrections, changes, or additions to the test?

6. Begin the test immediately and watch the time carefully.

7. Read the directions carefully, underlining or marking special instructions.

8. Follow all special instructions like showing your work on math tests.

9. Read all questions carefully, paying attention to words like *always, only, all,* and *never.*

10. Answer the questions you are sure of first.

11. Use context clues to help you with unfamiliar words.

12. Use material on the test itself to help you answer more difficult questions.

13. When being tested on long passages, read the questions before you read the passage.

14. Move on to the next question when you get stuck on a particular question. You might *code* each question you skip. You can do this by writing a *3* next to very difficult questions, a *2* next to difficult ones, and a *1* next to those you think you know the answers to. After you've gone through all the questions, go back to the *1's* first.

485 Taking the Objective Test

486 True/False Test

1. Read the entire question before answering. Often the first half of a statement will be true or false, while the second half is just the opposite. For an answer to be true, the entire statement must be true.

2. Read each word and number carefully. Pay special attention to names and dates which are similar and could easily be confused. Also, watch for numbers which contain the same numerals but in a different order. (*Example:* 1619 . . . 1691)

3. Be especially careful of true/false statements which contain words like *all, every, always, never,* etc. Very often these statements will be false simply because there is an exception to nearly every rule.

4. Watch for statements which contain more than one negative word. *Remember:* Two negatives make a positive. (*Example:* It is *unlikely* ice will *not* melt when the temperature rises above 32 degrees F.)

5. Remember that if one part of the statement is false, the whole statement is false.

487 Matching Test

1. Read through both lists quickly before you begin answering. Note any descriptions which are similar and pay particular attention to the details that make them different.

2. When matching word to phrase, read the phrase first and look for the word it describes.

3. Cross out each answer as you find it — *unless* you are told that the answers can be used more than once.

4. If you get stuck when matching word to word, determine the part of speech of each word. If the word is a verb, for example, match it with another verb.

5. Fill in the blanks with capital letters rather than lower-case letters since they are less likely to be misread by the person correcting the test.

488 Multiple Choice Test

1. Read the directions very carefully to determine whether you are looking for the *correct* answer or the *best* answer. Also check to see if some questions can have two (or more) correct answers.

2. Read the first part of the question very carefully, looking for negative words like *not, never, except, unless,* etc.

3. Try to answer the question in your mind before looking at the choices.

4. Read all the choices before selecting your answer. This is especially important in tests where you are to select the best answer or on tests where one of your choices is a combination of two or more answers. (*Example:* c. Both a and b, d. All of the above, e. None of the above).

5. As you read through the choices, eliminate those which are obviously incorrect; then go back and reconsider the remaining choices carefully.

6. Use words and context clues in the question to help you figure out difficult answers. Guess at an answer only as a last resort.

489 Fill in the Blanks

1. If the word before the blank is *a,* the word you need probably begins with a consonant; if the word before the blank is *an,* your answer should begin with a vowel.

2. If the missing word is the subject of the sentence, the verb will tell you whether your answer should be singular or plural.

3. The length of the blank will often tell you how long your answer should be.

4. If there are several blanks in a row, it could well indicate the number of words which are needed in your answer.

5. If you don't know the answer immediately, read the statement again and look closely for clues which might help you determine the probable answer.

Vocabulary Skills

490 **Vocabulary development** is probably the most important of the reading improvement areas. Unless you have a good vocabulary, there is little hope for improving your reading speed or comprehension. Almost always, if your vocabulary is poorly developed, your comprehension and speed will also be poorly developed. There are a number of methods which you can use for improving vocabulary. If you are serious about improving your reading skills, you will make one of these methods work for you.

491 **Dictionary.** The standard procedure for finding out the meaning of a word has long been to "look it up in the dictionary." This is still true and probably always will be. A dictionary contains much information which will help the student improve his reading skills by improving his vocabulary. There are several things you can do to make using a dictionary a profitable, vocabulary-building exercise. One of these is to read all of the definitions given for a word, not just the first one. By understanding the full meaning of a word, you are much more likely to remember that word. Always check the pronunciation of every word you look up. It is nearly impossible to remember what a word means if you do not know how to pronounce it. (See 443-453.)

492 **Thesaurus.** A thesaurus is a dictionary of synonyms and antonyms. It can be a great help to you as you work on your vocabulary improvement. The most efficient time to use a thesaurus is when you are writing a paper which calls for creativity as well as accuracy. Rather than settle for a common, overused word to describe something, use your thesaurus to find a synonym for that word. A word such as *angry,* for instance, might call to mind three or four synonyms: *mad, upset, sore,* etc. A quick check in the thesaurus under *angry* would expand that list considerably: *irate, wrathful, bitter, acrimonious, indignant, fuming, raging, furious, rabid, cross, peeved, huffy, inflamed, enraged, infuriated, exasperated, fiery,* and so on. Each of these words means *angry,* yet each has a slightly different shade of meaning. Depending upon the situation being described, any of these words could be used in place of *angry* to add color to the writing. Just as important, you will add new words to your working vocabulary. (See 442.)

493 **Vocabulary from context.** The context of a word is its environment or the words which surround it. By looking closely at these surrounding words, you can pick up hints or clues which will help you with the meaning of a difficult word. Research has shown that most good readers use context clues regularly. It has also been shown that these readers are generally aware of the different types of context clues. Knowing something about these different types can help sharpen your word attack skills and improve your overall reading ability. In the next chart, you will find seven different types of context clues.

Types of Context Clues
1) Clues supplied through **synonyms:** Carol is fond of using *trite,* worn-out expressions in her writing. Her favorite is "You can lead a horse to water, but you can't make him drink."
2) Clues contained in **comparisons and contrasts:** As the trial continued, the defendant's guilt became more and more obvious. With even the slightest bit of new evidence against him, there would be no chance of *acquittal.*
3) Clues contained in a **definition or description:** Peggy is a *transcriptionist,* a person who makes a written copy of a recorded message.
4) Clues through **association** with other words in the sentence: Jim is considered the most troublesome student ever to have walked the halls of Central High. He has not passed a single class in his four years there and seldom makes it through an entire hour of class without falling asleep or getting sent to the office. His teachers consider him completely *incorrigible.*
5) Clues which appear in a **series:** The *dulcimer,* fiddle, and banjo are all popular among the Appalachian Mountain people.
6) Clues provided by the **tone and setting:** The streets filled instantly with *bellicose* protesters, who pushed and shoved their way through the frantic bystanders. The scene was no longer peaceful and calm as the marchers had promised it would be.
7) Clues derived from **cause and effect:** Since nobody came to the first voluntary work session, attendance for the second one is *mandatory* for all the members.

494 As you can see, context clues are made up of synonyms, definitions, descriptions, and other kinds of specific information about the word you are trying to understand. In addition, clues can help explain how something works, where or when an event takes place, what the purpose or significance of an action is, and so on. Some context clues are not so direct as those listed above. They might be simply examples, results, or general statements; still, these indirect clues can be very helpful. Finally, you should realize that context clues do not always show up immediately. In a lengthy piece of writing, for example, the clues might not appear until several paragraphs later. Alert readers will be aware of this and continue to look for clues as they read. The more clues you can find as a reader, the closer you can get to the specific meaning of the word and, in turn, the overall meaning of the passage.

Look carefully at the italicized words in the sample passage taken from Jack London's *Call of the Wild.* Then look for direct and indirect context clues which might help the reader understand the meaning of these words. In addition to the clues available in this single paragraph, the reader would also have the advantage of having read the first 46 pages of the novel. Taken together, there is a good chance the reader could figure out the meaning of the italicized words. Using context clues intelligently can be a reader's most valuable vocabulary tool. See how well you can use context clues now that you understand a little better how they work.

They made Sixty Miles, which is a fifty-mile run, on the first day; and the second day saw them booming up the Yukon well on their way to Pelly. But such splendid running was achieved not without great trouble and *vexation* on the part of Francois. The *insidious* revolt led by Buck had destroyed the *solidarity* of the team. It no longer was as one dog leaping in the traces. The encouragement Buck gave the rebels led them into all kinds of petty *misdemeanors.* No more was Spitz a leader greatly to be feared. The old awe departed, and they grew equal to challenging his authority. Pike robbed him of half a fish one night and gulped it down under the protection of Buck. Another night Dub and Joe fought Spitz and made him forego the punishment they deserved. And even Billee, the good-natured, was less good-natured, and whined not half so *placatingly* as in former days. Buck never came near Spitz without snarling and bristling *menacingly.* In fact, his conduct approached that of a bully, and he was given to swaggering up and down before Spitz's very nose.

495   **Special study.** New words which are introduced in a science or social studies class are often learned in a cram session for a major exam and then forgotten. If you are a good reader, however, you will not let this happen. As long as these words have to be remembered for even a single day, why not remember at least some of them permanently?

496   One of the most popular special study units is one in **mythology.** You will often have a unit on Greek or Roman mythology somewhere between the sixth and tenth grades. This unit will contain many short stories or myths covering a variety of topics from the adventures of Hercules to the origin of the weeping willow tree. In addition, there are several myths which deal solely with the origin of certain Greek and Latin words. Nearly all of these words (along with hundreds of other Greek and Latin words) have been handed down to us. Below are two examples of the kinds of words found in mythology.

497   *Herculean* means "having great strength or size." It comes from Hercules, the godlike hero remembered for his completion of the twelve great labors. Each of the twelve tasks was thought to be impossible to complete. Because Hercules was able to accomplish all of them, he became the symbol of strength. Herculean still means "great strength" today.

Tantalize means "to tempt or tease by keeping something in view but just out of reach." The word comes from the mythological character, Tantalus, who was punished for an evil deed he had done. He was placed in water up to his chin—above him hung fruit-laden branches. But Tantalus was unable to enjoy either the water or the fruit. Every time he bent over to drink the water or reached up to pick the fruit, each receded. So it was that Tantalus was punished by being able to see the food and drink, but not being able to have either. Today, the word *tantalize* is used to describe any situation in which someone is put in a position similar to that of Tantalus: able to see, but not have.

498   **Prefix, Suffix, Root Study.** By studying the structure of a word (the prefix, suffix, and root combinations making up a word), it is possible to understand the meaning of that word. This requires you, however, to take an important step first: you must become familiar with the meanings of the most widely used prefixes, suffixes, and roots in our language. This could be as few as 50 or as many as 500, depending upon the amount of time and effort you have to put into this project. What makes this form of vocabulary study especially efficient is that the number of words added to your vocabulary will be much greater than the number of word parts you learn. For instance, the root *aster* is found in the word *asterisk,* where it means *star;* it is also found in the words *astrology, astronaut, asteroid, asterism, astrodome, astrolabe, astronomer,* and *asteriated* where, in each case, it also means *star.* Not all roots are found in as many as nine different words. Many are, however, and some are found in as many as thirty or forty different words. At the end of this section (499), you will find a list of those prefixes, suffixes, and roots which are used regularly in the English language. Look them over and see if you recognize any. Then learn as many as you can.

Just as you once learned to combine familiar words into new ones . . .   you can now learn a whole new set of word parts to combine.

154

499

A Dictionary of
Prefixes

a, an [*not, without*] amoral (without a sense of moral responsibility), atheism, anemia, atypical, atom (not cutable), apathy (without feeling)

ab, abs, a [*from, away*] abnormal, avert (turn away)

acro [*high*] acropolis (high city), acrobat, acrogen (of the highest class), acronym, acrophobia (fear of height)

ad (ac, af, ag, al, an, ap, ar, as, at) [*to, towards*] admire (look at with wonder), attract, admit, advance, allege, announce, assert, aggressive, accept

ambi, amb [*both, around*] ambidextrous (skilled with both hands), ambiguous, amble

amphi [*both*] amphibious (living on both land and water), amphitheater

ana [*on, up, backward*] analysis (loosening up or taking apart for study), anatomy, anachronism

ante [*before*] antedate, anteroom, antebellum, antecedent

anti, ant [*against*] anticommunist, antidote, anticlimax, antacid, antarctic

apo [*from, off*] apostasy (standing from, abandoning a professed belief), apology, apothecary, apostle

be [*on, away*] bedeck, belabor, bequest, bestow, beloved

bene, bon [*well*] benefit, benefactor, benevolent, benediction, bonus, bona fide, bonanza

bi, bis, bin [*both, double, twice*] bicycle, biweekly, binoculars, bilateral, biscuit

by [*side, close, near*] bypass, bystander, by-product, bylaw, byline

cata [*down, against*] catalogue, catapult, catastrophe, cataclysm

circum, circ [*around*] circumference, circumnavigate, circumspect

co (con, col, cor, com) [*together, with*] compose, copilot, conspire, collect, concord

coni [*dust*] coniosis (disease which comes from inhaling dust)

contra, counter [*against*] controversy, contradict, counterpart

de [*from, down*] demote, depress, degrade, deject, deprive

di [*two, twice*] dilemma, diatom, dissect, diploma

dia [*through, between*] diameter, diagonal, diagram, diagnosis, dialogue

dis, dif [*apart, away, reverse*] dismiss, distort, distinguish, diffuse

dys [*badly, ill*] dyspepsia (digesting badly, indigestion), dystrophy

em, en [*in, into*] embrace, enslave

epi [*upon*] epidermis (upon the skin, outer layer of skin), epitaph, epithet, epigram, epitome

eu, ev [*well*] eulogize (speak well of, praise), eupepsia, euphony, eugenics

ex, e, ec, ef [*out*] expel (drive out), ex-mayor, exit, exorcism, eccentric (out of the center position), eject, emit

extra, extro [*beyond, outside*] extraordinary (beyond the ordinary), extracurricular, extrovert, extraneous

for [*away or off*] forswear (to renounce an oath)

fore [*before in time*] foretell (to tell beforehand), forecast, foreshadow, foregone, forefather

hemi, demi, semi [*half*] hemisphere, hemicycle, semicircle, demitasse

homo [*man*] Homo sapiens, homicide, homunculus, hominid

hyper [*over, above*] hypercritical, hyperemia, hypersensitive, hypertensive, hyperactive

hypo [*under*] hypodermic, hypothesis, hypotension

idio [*private, personal*] idiom, idiosyncrasy, idiomatic

il (ir, in, im) [*not*] incorrect, illegal, immoral, irregular

in (il, im) [*into*] inject, inside, illuminate, impose, illustrate, implant, imprison

infra [*beneath*] infrared

inter [*between*] intercollegiate, interfere, intervene, interrupt (break between)

intra [*within*] intramural, intravenous (within the veins)

intro [*into, inward*] introduce, introvert (turn inward)

macro [*large, excessive*] macrodent (having large teeth), macrocosm

mal [*badly, poor*] maladjusted, malnutrition, malfunction, malady

meta [*beyond, after, with*] metabolism (thrown beyond, literally; hence, chemical and physical change), metaphor, metamorphosis, metaphysical

mis [*incorrect, bad*] misuse, misprint

miso [*hating, wrong*] misanthropist, misogamist, miser

mono [*one*] monoplane, monotone, monogamy, monochrome, monocle

multi [*many*] multiply, multiform, multilateral

neo [*new*] neopaganism, neoclassic, neologism, neophyte

non [*not*] nontaxable (not taxed), nontoxic, nonexistent, nonsense

ob (of, op, oc) [*towards, against*] obstruct, offend, oppose, occur

para [*beside, almost*] parasite (one who eats beside or at the table of another), paraphrase, parody, parachute, paramedic, parallel

penta [*five*] pentagon (figure or building having five angles or sides), Pentateuch, pentameter, pentathlon

per [*throughout, completely*] pervert (completely turn wrong, corrupt), perfect, perceive, permanent, persuade, pervade

peri [*around*] perimeter (measurement around an area), periphery, periscope, pericardium, period

poly [*many*] polygon (figure having many angles or sides), polygamy, polyglot, polychrome

post [*after*] postpone, postwar, postscript, postseason

pre [*before*] prewar, preview, precede, prevent, premonition

pro [*forward, in favor of*] project (throw forward), progress, pro-abortion, promote, prohibition

pseudo [*false*] pseudonym (false or assumed name), pseudo, pseudopodia

re [*back, again*] reclaim, revive, revoke, rejuvenate, retard, reject, return

retro [*backwards*] retrospective (looking backwards), retroactive, retrorocket, retrogression

se [*aside*] seduce (lead aside), secede, secrete, segregate

self [*by oneself*] self-determination, self-employed, self-service, selfish

sesqui [*one and a half*] sesquicentennial (one and one-half centuries)

sub [*under*] submerge (put under), submarine, subhuman, subject, substitute, subsoil, suburb

suf (sug, sup, sus) [*from under*] suffer, suggest, support, suspect, sufficient, suspend

super, supr, sur [*above, over, more*] supervise, superman, survivor, supreme, supernatural, superior

syn (sym, sys, syl) [*with, together*] sympathy, system, synthesis, symphony, syllable, synchronize (time together), synonym

trans, tra [*across, beyond*] transoceanic, transmit, traverse (lying across as a bridge over a stream), transfusion

tri [*three*] tricycle, triangle, tripod, tristate

un [*not, release*] unfair, unnatural, unbutton, unfasten

under [*beneath*] underground, underling

uni [*one, below*] unicycle, uniform, unify, universe, unique

ultra [*beyond, exceedingly*] ultramodern, ultraviolet, ultraconservative

vice [*in place of*] vice-president, vice-admiral, viceroy

500

Suffixes

able, ible [*able, can do*] capable, agreeable, edible, visible (can be seen)

ad, ade [*result of action*] monad (a unit, an individual), blockade (the result of a blocking action), lemonade

age [*act of, state of, collection of*] salvage (act of saving), storage, forage

al [*relating to*] sensual, gradual, manual, natural (relating to nature)

algia [*pain*] neuralgia (nerve pain)

an, ian [*native of, relating to*] Czechoslovakian (native of Czechoslovakia), African

ance, ancy [*action, process, state*] assistance, allowance, defiance, resistance

ant [*performing, agent*] assistant, servant, defiant

ar, er, or [*one who, that which*] doctor, baker, miller, teacher, racer, amplifier

ard, art [*one who*] drunkard, dullard, braggart

ary, ery, ory [*relating to, quality, place where*] dictionary, dietary, bravery, dormitory (a place where people sleep)

asis, esis, osis [*action, process, condition*] genesis, hypnosis, neurosis

ate [*cause, make*] enumerate, liquidate, segregate (causing a group to be set aside)

cian [*having a certain skill or art*] logician, musician, beautician, magician, physician

cide [*kill*] homicide, pesticide, genocide (killing a race of people)

cule, ling [*very small*] molecule, ridicule, duckling (very small duck), sapling

cy [*action, function*] hesitancy, prophecy, normalcy

dom [*quality, realm, office*] boredom, freedom, kingdom, stardom, wisdom (quality of being wise)

ee [*one who receives the action*] employee, devotee, nominee (one who is nominated), refugee, trustee

en [*made of, make*] silken, frozen, oaken (made of oak), wooden, lighten

ence, ency [*action, state of, quality*] difference, conference, proficiency (quality of being proficient), urgency

er (see *ar*)

ery (see *ary*)

esce [*to become*] acquiesce (become restful, peaceful), coalesce

escent [*in the process of*] convalescent, obsolescent

esis (see *asis*)

Roots

ese [*a native of, the language*] Japanese, Vietnamese

esque [*in the style of*] burlesque, arabesque

ess [*female*] actress, goddess, lioness

et, ette [*a small one, group*] midget, octet, baronet, bassinet

fic [*making, causing*] scientific, specific

ful [*full of*] frightful, careful, helpful (full of help)

fy [*make*] fortify (make strong), simplify, terrify, amplify

hood [*order, condition, quality*] manhood, womanhood, brotherhood

ible (see *able*)

ic [*nature of, like*] acidic, metalic (of the nature of metal), heroic, poetic

ice [*condition, state, quality*] justice, malice

id, ide [*a thing connected with or belonging to*] fluid, fluoride

ile [*relating to, suited for, capable of*] domicile, agile, juvenile, senile (related to being old), missile

ine [*nature of*] feminine, masculine, genuine, medicine

ion, sion, tion [*act of, state of, result of*] action, injection, infection, suspension (state of suspending)

ish [*origin, nature, resembling*] foolish, Irish, clownish (resembling a clown)

ism [*doctrine, system, manner, condition, characteristic*] alcoholism, exorcism, heroism (characteristic of a hero), Communism, realism

ist [*one who, that which*] artist, dentist, violinist, racist

ite [*nature of, quality of, mineral product*] expedite, Israelite, graphite, sulfite, dynamite (quality of being powerful)

ity, ty [*state of, quality*] captivity, chastity, fraternity, clarity

ive [*causing, making*] assertive, abusive (causing abuse), affirmative, exhaustive

ize [*make*] emphasize, liberalize (make liberal), idolize, penalize, publicize

less [*without*] baseless, careless (without care), artless, fearless, helpless

ling (see *cule*)

ly [*like, manner of*] carelessly, fearlessly, hopelessly, shamelessly

ment [*act of, state of, result*] contentment, alignment, amendment (state of amending), achievement

mony [*a resulting thing*] patrimony, alimony, acrimony

ness [*state of*] carelessness, restlessness, lifelessness

oid [*like, resembling*] asteroid, spheroid, tabloid, anthropoid

ology [*study, science, theory*] biology, anthropology, geology, neurology

or (see *ar*)

ory (see *ary*)

osis (see *asis*)

ous [*full of, having*] gracious, nervous, vivacious (full of life), spacious

rhea [*flowing, discharge*] pyorrhea, diarrhea, gonorrhea (discharge from the reproductive organs)

ship [*office, state, quality, skill, profession*] friendship, authorship, scholarship, dictatorship

some [*like, apt, tending to*] lonesome, threesome, gruesome

tude [*state of, condition of*] gratitude, multitude (condition of being many), aptitude, solitude

ure [*state of, act, process, rank*] culture, literature, pressure, rupture (state of being broken)

ward [*in the direction of*] eastward, forward, backward

y [*inclined to, tend to*] cheery, crafty, faulty, dirty, itchy

acer, acid, acri [*bitter, sour, sharp*] acerbic (bitter, harsh), acerbate (embitter), acidity (sourness), acrid, acrimony

acu [*sharp*] acute, acuity, acupuncture

ag, agi, ig, act [*do, move, go*] agent (doer), agenda (things to do), agile, navigate (move by sea), pedagogue (childmover, teacher), ambiguous (going both ways, not clear), retroactive, agitate

ali, allo, alter [*other*] alias (a person's other name), alternative, alibi, alien (from another country), alter (change to another form), allotment, allocate

altus [*high, deep*] altimeter, exalt, altitude, alto

am, amor [*love, liking*] amiable, amorous, enamored

anim [*mind, will*] unanimous, animosity, equanimity, magnanimous, animal

anni, annu, enni [*year*] anniversary, annually (yearly), centennial (occurring once in 100 years), per annum, annuity

anthrop [*man*] anthropoid (man-like, e.g., an ape), anthropology (study of mankind), misanthrope (hater of mankind), philanthropic (love of mankind)

antico [*old*] antique, antiquated, antiquity

arch [*chief, first, rule*] archangel (chief angel), architect (chief worker), archaic (first; very early), archives, monarchy (rule by one person), matriarchy (rule by the mother), patriarchy (rule by the father), archeology

aster, astr [*star*] aster (star flower), asterisk, asteroid, disaster (originally a bad happening from a contrary influence by a star), astrology (lit., star-speaking; pseudoscience of influence by stars and planets), astronomy (star law), astronaut (lit., star traveler; space traveler)

aud, aus [*hear, listen*] audible (can be heard), auditorium, audio, audition, audience, auditory, auscultate

aug, auc [*increase*] augment, auction, augur

auto, aut [*self*] automobile (self-moving vehicle), autograph (self-writing; signature), automatic (self-acting), autonomy (lit., self-laws; self-government), autobiography (lit., self-life writing)

belli [*war*] rebellion, belligerent (warlike or hostile), bellicose

bibl [*book*] Bible, bibliography (writing, list of books), bibliomania (craze for books), bibliophile (book lover)

bio [*life*] biology (study of live things), amphibious, biography, biopsy (cutting living tissue for examination), microbe (small, microscopic living thing), biogenesis

breve [*short*] breve, brevity, abbreviate, brief

bursa [*purse, payment*] reimburse, disbursements (money paid out)

cad, cas [*to fall*] cadaver, cadence, caducous (falling off), cascade

calor [*heat*] calorie (a unit of heat), calorify (to make hot), caloric, nonchalant

cande [*shine*] candor, candelabra, candid

cap, cip, cept [*take*] capable, capacity, capture, anticipate, participate, principal, accept, except, conception, deceptive, perception, conceive, receive, forceps

capit, capt [*head*] decapitate (to remove the head from), capital, captain, caption, recapitulate

carn [*flesh*] carnal, carnage, carnivorous (flesh eating), incarnate, reincarnation

caus, caut [*burn, heat*] cauterize, cauldron, caustic

cause, cuse, cus [*cause, motive*] because, excuse (to attempt to remove the blame or cause; exonerate), accusation

ced, ceed, cede, cess [*move, yield, go, surrender*] cede (yield), antecedent (moving, occurring before), accede, concede, intercede, precede, recede, secede (move aside from), proceed (move forward), success

chrom [*color*] chrome (color purity), chromatic, chromosome (color body in genetics), Kodachrome (one color), polychrome (many colored)

chron [*time*] chronological (in order of time), chronometer (time-measured), chronicle (record of events in time), synchronize (make time with, set time together), anachronism (lit., back in time; anything backwards in historical time)

cide [*kill*] suicide (self-killer or self-killing), homicide (man, human killer or killing), genocide (race killing), tyrannicide (tyrant killer or tyrant killing), pesticide (pest killer), germicide (germ killer), insecticide (insect killer)

cise [*cut*] decide (cut off uncertainty), precise (cut exactly right), concise, incision, scissors, criticize

cit [*to call, start*] incite, citation, cite

civ [*citizen*] civic (relating to a citizen), civil, civilian, civvies (citizen clothing), civilization

clam, claim [*cry out*] exclamation, clamor, proclamation, reclamation, acclamation, declamation, claim

clemen [*merciful*] inclement (not merciful), clemency, clement

clud, clus, claus [*shut*] include (to take in), recluse (one who shuts himself away from others), claustrophobia (abnormal fear of being shut up, confined), conclude, include, preclude, seclude, close, closet

cognosc, gnosi [*know*] prognosis (forward knowing), diagnosis (thorough knowledge), recognize (to know again), incognito (not known), agnostic (not knowing about God)

cosm [*universe, world*] cosmos (the universe), cosmic, cosmology, cosmopolitan (world citizen), cosmonaut, microcosm, macrocosm

cord, cor, card [*heart*] cordial (hearty, heartfelt), accord, concord, discord, record, courage, encourage (put heart into), discourage (take heart out of), core, coronary, cardiac

corp [*body*] corporation (a legal body), corpse, corps, corporal, corpulent

crat [*rule, strength*] autocracy, democratic

crea [*create*] creature (anything created), recreation, creation, creator

cred [*believe*] creed (statement of beliefs), credo (a creed), credence (belief), credit (belief, trust), credulous (believing too readily, easily deceived), credentials (statements that promote belief, trust), incredible

cresc, cret, crease, cru [*rise, grow*] crescendo (growing in loudness or intensity), crescent (growing, like the moon in first quarter), acretion, concrete (grown together, solidified), increment (amount of growth), increase, decrease, accrue (to grow, as interest in money)

crit [*separate, choose*] critical, criterion (that which is used in choosing), diacritical, hypocrisy

cub, cumb [*lie down, lean back*] incubate (to hatch by keeping), encumber (to place a burden upon), cumbersome, succumb, incumbent

cur, curs [*run*] current (running or flowing), concurrent, concur (run together, agree), curriculum (lit., a running, a course), cursory (done hastily, "on the run"), incur (run into), precursor (forerunner), recur, occur, courier

cura [*care*] manicure (caring for the hands), curator, curative

cus, cuse (see *cause*)

cycl, cyclo [*wheel, circular*] Cyclops (a mythical giant with one eye in the middle of his forehead), cyclone (a wind blowing circularly; a tornado), unicycle, bicycle

deca [*ten*] decade, decalogue, decapod (ten feet), Decapolis, decathlon

dem [*people*] democracy (people-rule), demagogue (people-leader, one who stirs up people for selfish ends), demography (vital statistics of the people: deaths, births, etc.), epidemic (on or among the people; general), pandemonium

dent, dont [*tooth*] dental (relating to teeth), orthodontist (a dentist who practices orthodontia), denture, dentifrice

derm [*skin*] hypodermic (under skin; injected under the skin), dermatology (skin study), epidermis (on skin; outer layer), taxidermy (arranging skin; mounting animals)

dic, dict [*say, speak*] diction (how one speaks, what one says), dictionary, dictate, dictator, dictum (a saying), dictaphone, dictagraph, dictatorial, edict, predict, verdict, contradict, adjudicate (to speak the law, to judge), benediction

domin [*master*] dominate, dominion, domain, predominant, Anno Domini (in the year of our Lord, abbreviated A.D.)

don [*give*] donate (make a gift), condone

dorm [*sleep*] dormant, dormitory

dox [*opinion, praise*] doxy (belief, creed, or ism), orthodox (having the correct, commonly accepted opinion), heterodox (differing opinion; contrary, self-contradictory), doxology (statement or song of praise), paradox

drome [*to run, step*] syndrome (run together; symptoms) hippodrome (a place where horses run)

duc, duct [*lead*] duke (leader), induce (lead into, persuade), seduce (lead aside), traduce (lead across in public disgrace, vilify), aquaduct (water leader, artificial channel), subdue, ductile (easily drawn out or hammered thin), viaduct, conduct, conduit, produce, reduce, educate

dura [*hard, lasting*] durable, duration, duramen, endurance

dynam [*power*] dynamo (power producer), dynamic, dynamite, hydrodynamics (lit., water power), dyne (unit of power, force), dynamometer, dynasty (power, rule by successive members of a family)

end, endo [*within*] endoral (within the mouth), endocardial (within the heart), endoskeletal, endoplasm

erg [*work*] energy, erg (unit of work), allergy, ergophobia (morbid fear of work), ergometer, ergograph

equi [*equal*] equinox, equilibrium

fac, fact, fic, fect [*do, make*] factory (the place where workmen are employed in making goods of various kinds), fact (a thing done, a deed), facsimile, facility, manufacture, faculty, amplification, affect

fall, fals [*deceive*] fallacious, falsify, fallacy

fer [*bear, carry*] ferry (carry by water), odoriferous (bearing an odor), coniferous (bearing cones, as a pine tree), pestiferous (bearing disease), fertile (bearing richly), defer, infer, refer, suffer (bear under, as under yoke), referee, referendum, circumference, deference, Lucifer (light bearer)

fic, fect (see *fac*)

fid, fide, feder [*faith, trust*] fidelity, confident, confidante, infidelity, infidel, fiduciary (held in trust, confidential), perfidy (breaking faith), bona fide (in good faith), federal, confederacy, Fido

fila, fili [*thread*] filament (a threadlike conductor heated by electrical current), filiform (having the shape of a thread), filter, filet

fin [*end, ended, finished*] final, finite, infinite, finish, confine, fine, refine, define, finale

fix [*fix*] fix (a difficult position), transfix (to hold motionless), fixation (the state of being attached), fixture, affix, prefix, suffix

flex, flect [*bend*] flex (bend), reflex (bending back), flexible, flexor (muscle for bending), inflexibility, reflect, deflect, genuflect (bend the knee)

flu, fluc, fluv [*flowing*] influence (to flow in), fluctuate (to wave in an unsteady motion), fluviograph (instrument for measuring the flow of rivers), fluid, flue, flush, fluently, affluent

form [*form, shape*] form, uniform, conform, deform, reform, perform, formative, formation, formal, formula

fort, forc [*strong*] fort, fortress (a strong point, fortified), fortify (make strong), forte (one's strong point), forte (strong, loud in music), fortitude (strength for endurance), force, effort, comfort, pianoforte, force (power)

fract, frag [*break*] fracture (a break), infraction, fragile (easy to break), fraction (result of breaking a whole into equal parts), refract (to break or bend, as a light ray), refractive, fragment

fum [*smoke*] fume (smoke; odor), fumigate (destroy germs by smoking them out), perfume

gam [*marriage*] bigamy (two marriages), monogamy, polygamy (lit., many marriages), exogamy, endogamy, gamete, gambit

gastro [*stomach*] gastric, gastronomic, gastritis (inflammation of the stomach)

gen [*birth, race, produce*] genesis (birth, beginning), Genesis, genus, genetics (study of heredity), eugenics (lit., well-born), genealogy (lineage by race, stock), generate, progeny (offspring), genitals (the reproductive organs), congenital (existing as such at birth), indigenous (born, growing or produced naturally in a region or country), genetic, hydrogen (lit., water-borne element)

geo [*earth*] geometry (earth measurement), geography (lit., earth-writing), geocentric (earth centered), geology, geochemistry, geophysics

germ [*vital part*] germination (to grow), germ (seed; living substance, as the germ of an idea), germane

gest [*carry, bear*] congest (bear together, clog), suggestion (mental process by which one thought leads to another), congestive (causing congestion), gestation, suggestion, gesture

gloss, glot [*tongue*] polyglot (many tongues), epiglottis, glossary, glottic

glu, glo [*lump, bond, glue*] conglomerate (bond together), agglutinate (make to hold in a bond)

grad, gress [*step, go*] grade (step, degree), gradual (step by step), graduate (make all the steps, finish a course), graduated (in steps or degrees), aggressive (stepping toward, pushing), transgress (step across limits, break a law), congress (a going together, assembly), degradation

graph, gram [*write, written*] graph, graphic (written; vivid), autograph (self-writing, signature), photography (light-writing) graphite (carbon used for

writing), phonograph (sound-writing), bibliography, monograph (writing on one subject), telegram (far writing), epigram, diagram, cablegram, monogram, seismography, cartography

grat [*pleasing*] congratulate (express pleasure over success), gratis (as a favor, free), gratuitous (gratis), gratuity (mark of favor, a tip), grateful, gracious, ingrate (not thankful; hence, unpleasant), ingratiate

grav [*heavy, weighty*] grave, gravity, aggravate, gravitate

greg [*herd, group, crowd*] gregarian (belonging to a herd), congregation (a group functioning together), segregative (tending to group aside or apart), aggregation

hab, habit [*have, live*] habitat (the place in which one lives), inhabit (to live in; to establish as residence), rehabilitate, habitual

helio [*sun*] heliograph (as instrument for using the sun's rays), heliotrope (a plant which turns to the sun)

hema, hemo [*blood*] hematid (red blood corpuscle), hemotoxic (causing blood poisoning), hemorrhage, hemoglobin, hemophilia, hematose

here, hes [*stick*] adhere, cohere, inherent

hetero [*different*] heterogeneous (different in birth; miscellaneous), heterodox, heterochromatic (of different colors), heteromorphic (of different forms), superheterodyne, heterosexual (with interest in opposite sex)

homo [*same*] homogeneous (of same birth or kind), homonym (word with same name or pronunciation as another), homosexual (with sex desire for those of the same sex), homologous (same-minded, agreeing), homogenize

hum, human [*earth, ground, man*] humility (quality of lowliness), humane (marked by sympathy, compassion for other human beings and animals), humus, exhume, humanity

hypn [*sleep*] hypnoidal (relating to hypnosis or sleep), hypnosis, Hypnos (god of sleep), hypnotherapy (treatment of disease by hypnosis)

hydr, hydro, hydra [*water*] dehydrate (take water out of; dry), hydrant (water faucet), hydraulic (pertaining to water or to liquids), hydraulics, hydrogen, hydrophobia (fear of water), hydrodynamics, hydroelectric

ignis [*fire*] ignite, igneous, ignition

ject [*throw*] deject, inject, project (throw forward), eject, object, ejaculate

join, junct [*join*] junction (act of joining), enjoin (to lay an order upon; to command), juncture, conjunction, joint, adjoining, injunction

jud, judi, judic [*judge, lawyer*] judge (a public officer who has the authority to give a judgment), abjure (reject the case), judicial (relating to administration of justice), judicious, prejudice

jur, jus [*law*] justice (a just judgment; as justice must be served), conjure (to swear together; to imagine; to entreat; as, conjure the king to be merciful), juror, jurisdiction

juven [*young*] juvenile, juvenescent (becoming young), rejuvenate (to make young again)

later [*side, broad*] lateral, latitude

laut, lav, lot, lut [*wash*] lavish (flowing like water), dilute (to make a liquid thinner and weaker), ablution (a washing away), launder (to wash and iron clothes), lavatory, laundry, lotion, deluge

leg [*law*] legal (lawful; according to law), legislate (to enact a law), legislature (a body of persons who can make laws), legitimize (make legal), legacy

letter, lit, liter, litera [*letters*] litany (prayer consisting of invocations and responses), literary (concerned with books and writing), literature (the best works written during the century), literal, alliteration, obliterate

levis [*light*] alleviate (lighten a load), levitate, levity

lic, licit [*permit*] license (freedom to act), licit (permitted; lawful; conceded), illicit (not permitted), licentious (taking liberties; disregarding rules, especially in morals)

lith [*stone*] monolith (one stone, a single mass), lithography (stone writing, printing from a flat stone or metal plate), neolithic (new stone, of the layer stone age), paleolithic (ancient stone)

liver, liber [*free*] liberal (relating to liberty), delivery (freedom; liberation), liberalize (to make more free: as, to liberalize the mind from prejudice), deliverance

loc, loco [*place*] locomotion (act of moving from place to place), locality (locale; neighborhood), allocate (to assign; to place; apportion), relocate (to put back into their homes)

log, logo, ology [*word, study, speech*] Logo (the word, Jesus), logic (orig., speech; then reasoning), prologue, epilogue, dialogue, catalogue, logorrhea (a flux of words; excessively wordy), zoology (animal study), psychology (mind study), theology (god study)

loqu, locut [*talk, speak*] eloquent (speaking out well and forcefully), loquacious (talkative), colloquial (talking together; conversational or informal), obloquy (a speaking against, a reproach), circumlocution (talking around a subject), soliloquy

luc, lum, lus, lun [*light*] Luna (the moon goddess), lumen (a unit of light), luminary (a heavenly body; someone who shines in his profession), translucent (letting light come through), luster (sparkle; gloss; glaze), illuminate

lude [*play*] ludicrous, prelude (before play), interlude

magn [*great*] magnify (make great, enlarge), magnificent, magnanimous (great of mind or spirit), magnate, magnitude, magnum

man [*hand*] manual, manage, manufacture, manacle, manicure, manifest, maneuver, emancipate

mand [*command*] mandatory (commanded), remand (order back), writ of mandamus (written order from a court), countermand (order against, cancelling a previous order), mandate

mania [*madness*] mania (insanity; craze; excessive craving), monomania (mania on one idea), kleptomania (thief mania; abnormal tendency to steal), pyromania (insane tendency to set fires), dipsomania (uncontrollable craving for alcoholic drink), manic, maniac

mar, mari, mer [*sea, pool*] mermaid (fabled marine creature, half fish), marine (a sailor serving on shipboard), marsh (wetland, swamp), maritime (relating to the sea and navigation)

matri, matro, matric [*mother*] matrimony (state of wedlock), maternal (relating to the mother), matriarchate (rulership of a woman), matris (mother goddess of the Hindu deities), matron, metropolic (the mother city)

medi [*half, middle, between, halfway*] mediate (come between, intervene), medieval (pertaining to the middle ages), mediterranean (lying between lands), medium (a person having the faculty to make contact with the supernatural), mediocre

mega [*great*] megaphone (great sound), megacephalic (great-headed), megalith,

megalopolis (great city; an extensive urban area including a number of cities), megacycle (a million cycles), megaton (force of a million tons of TNT), omega (great)

mem [*remember*] memorandum (a note; a reminder), commemoration (the act of observing by a memorial or ceremony), memento, memoir, memo, memorable

meter [*measure*] meter (a measure), gravimeter (instrument for measuring weight and density), voltameter (instrument to measure volts in an electric circuit), barometer, thermometer

micro [*small*] microscope, microfilm, microcard, microwave, micrometer (device for measuring very small distance), micron (a millionth of a meter), microbe (small living thing), microorganism, omicron (small)

migra [*wander*] migrate (to wander), emigrant (one who leaves a country), immigrate (to come into the land to settle), migrator (one who roves; a wanderer)

mit, miss [*send*] emit (send out, give off), remit (send back, as money due), submit, admit, commit, permit, transmit (send across), omit, intermittent (sending between, at intervals), mission, missile

mob, mot, mov [*move*] mobile (capable of moving), motionless (without motion), motor (that which imparts motion; source of mechanical power), emotional (moved strongly by feelings), motivate, promotion, demote

mon [*warn, remind*] admonish (warn), admonition, monitor, premonition (forewarning), monument (a reminder or memorial of a person or event), reminisce

monstr, mist [*show*] demonstrate (to display; show) muster (to gather together; collect; put on display) demonstration, monstrosity

morph [*form*] amorphous (with no form, shapeless), anthropomorphic (man form), Morpheus (the shaper, god of dreams), morphine (drug making sleep and dreams), metamorphosis (a change of form, as a caterpillar into a butterfly), morphidite

mori, mort, mors [*mortal, death*] mortal (causing death or destined for death), immortal (not subject to death), mortality (rate of death), immortality, mortician (one who buries the dead), mortification (lit., made dead; shame; chagrin), mortuary (place for the dead, a morgue), remorse

multi, multus [*many, much*] multifold (folded many times), multilinguist (one who speaks many languages), multiped (an organism with many feet), multiply (to increase a number quickly by multiplication)

nasc, nat [*to be born, to spring forth*] nature (the essence of a person or a thing), innate (inborn, inherent in), international (between or among nations), renascence (a rebirth; a revival), natal, native, nativity

neur [*nerve*] neuritis (inflammation of a nerve), neuropathic (having a nerve disease), neurologist (one who practices neurology), neural, neurosis, neurotic

nom [*law, order*] autonomy (self-law, self-government), astronomy, Deuteronomy (lit., second law, as given by Moses), gastronomy (lit., stomach law; art of good eating), agronomy (lit., field law; crop production), economy (household law, management)

nomen, nomin [*name*] nomenclature, nominate, nominal

nounce, nunci [*warn, declare*] announcer (one who makes announcements publicly), enunciate (to pronounce carefully),

pronounce (declare; articulate), renounce (retract; revoke), denounce

nov [*new*] novel (new; strange; not formerly known), renovate (to make like new again), novice, nova, innovate

nox, noc [*night*] nocturnal, equinox (equal nights), noctiluca (something which shines by night)

null [*none*] null, nullification, nullify, nullifidian (one who has no faith), nulliparous

number, numer [*number*] numeral (a figure expressing a number), numeration (act of counting), numberable (can be numbered), enumerate (count out, one by one), innumerable

omni [*all, every*] omnipotent (all powerful), omniscient (all knowing), omnipresent (present everywhere), omnivorous (all eating), omnibus (covering all things)

onus [*burden*] onerous (burdensome), onus, exonerate (to take out or take away a burden)

onym [*name*] anonymous (without a name), pseudonym (false name), antonym (against name; word of opposite meaning), synonym

oper [*work*] opera (a work which has been set to music and is sung instead of spoken), operate (to labor; function), opus (a musical composition or work), cooperate (work together)

ortho [*straight, correct*] orthodox (of the correct or accepted opinion), orthodontist (tooth straightener), orthopedic (originally pertaining to straightening a child), orthography (correct writing, spelling), unorthodox

oss, osteo [*bone*] ossicle (a small bone), ossification (the process of making into bone), osteopath (one who practices osteopathy), osteoporosis (a condition in old age when bones become porous and fragile)

pac [*peace*] pacifist (one for peace only; opposed to war), pacify (make peace, quiet), Pacific Ocean (peaceful ocean)

pan [*all*] Pan American, panacea (cureall), pandemonium (place of all the demons; wild disorder), pandemic, panchromatic (sensitive to all colors), pantheism (all-god belief; belief that God is all and all is God), pantheon (temple of all gods)

pater, patr [*father*] patriarch (the head of the tribe, family), patron (a wealthy person who supports as would a father), paternity (fatherhood, responsibility, etc.), patriot

path, pathy [*feeling, suffering*] pathos (feeling of pity, sorrow), pathetic, sympathy, antipathy (against feeling), apathy (without feeling), empathy (feeling or identifying with another), telepathy (far feeling; through transference), pathogenic (disease being born; causing suffering or disease)

ped, pod [*foot*] pedal (lever for a foot), impede (get the feet in a trap, hinder), impediment, pedestal (foot or base of a statue), pedestrian (foot traveler), centipede, tripod (three-footed support), podiatry (care of the feet), antipodes (opposite feet; parts of the earth diametrically opposed), podium (platform for a performer)

pedo [*child*] orthopedic, pedagogue (child leader, teacher), pedant (narrow-minded teacher), pediatrics (medical care of children)

pel, puls [*drive, urge*] compel, dispel, expel, repel, impel, propel, pulse, impulse, pulsate, compulsory, expulsion, repulsive

pend, pens, pond [*hang, weigh*] pendant (a hanging object), appendix, pendulum, depend, impend, suspend, perpendicular, pending, dispense, pensive (weighing thought), appendage, ponderous (weighty)

phan, phen [*show, appear*] phantom, phenomenal, fantasy

phemi [*speak*] euphemism (speak well of), prophet

phil [*love*] philosophy (love of wisdom), philanthropy, philharmonic, bibliophile, Philip, Philadelphia (city of brotherly love)

phobia [*fear*] phobia (abnormal fear), claustrophobia (fear of closed places), acrophobia (fear of high places), photophobia (fear of light), aquaphobia (fear of water), pyrophobia (fear of fire)

phon [*sound*] phonograph, phonetic (pertaining to sound), phonology, symphony (sounds with or together), polyphonic (having many sounds or tunes), dictaphone, euphony (pleasing sound)

photo [*light*] photograph (light-writing), photoelectric, photoflash, photogenic (artistically suitable for being photographed), photometer (light meter), photon (a quantum of light energy), photosynthesis (action of light on chlorophyll to make carbohydrates)

pict [*paint*] pictograph (writing with pictures or symbols), picture (make a mental image), depiction (the act of depicting or representing), picturesque, pictorial

plac, plais [*please*] placid (calm, unruffled), placatory (appeasing, soothing), placebo, placate, complacent (self-satisfied)

plenus [*full*] plenary, replenish, plentiful, plenteous

plic, pli, ply [*fold*] inexplicable, pliable, implicate

plu, plur, plus [*more*] plus (indicating that something is to be added), plural (more than one), pluralist (one who holds two or more jobs), plurisyllabic (having more than one syllable)

pneuma, pneumon [*breath*] pneumatic (pertaining to air, wind or other gases), pneumonia (disease of the lungs), pneumatogram (tracing of respiratory movements)

pod (see *ped*)

poli [*city*] metropolis (mother city; main city), police, politics, Indianapolis, megalopolis, Acropolis (high city, fortified upper part of Athens), cosmopolite (world citizen)

pon, pos, pound [*place, put*] postpone (put afterward), component, opponent (one put against), proponent, depose, expose, impose, purpose, propose deposit, deposition, expound, compound, posture (how one places himself), position, post

pop [*people*] population (the number of people in an area), Populist (a member of the Populist party), populous (full of inhabitants), popular

port [*carry*] porter (one who carries), portable, transport (carry across), report, export, import, support, comport, deportment (how one carries himself, behaves), portage, transportation, port, disport

portion [*part, share*] portion (a part; a share, as a portion of pie), proportion (the relation of one share to others), portionless (without portion; without dowry)

posse, potent [*power*] posse (an armed band; a force with legal authority), possible, potent, potentate, omnipotent, impotent

prehend [*seize*] apprehend (seize a criminal, seize an ideal), comprehend (seize with the mind), comprehensible,

comprehensive (seizing much, extensive), reprehensible (needing to be seized back, rebuked)

prim, prime [*first*] primacy (state of being first in rank), prima donna (the first lady of opera), primitive (from the earliest or first time), primary, primal

proto [*first*] prototype, protocol, protagonist, protozoan

psych [*mind, soul*] psyche (soul, mind), psychic (sensitive to forces beyond the physical), psychiatry (healing of the mind), psychology, psychopath (mind feeling; one with mental disease), psychosis (serious mental disorder), psychotherapy (mind treatment), psychogenic (of psychic birth, origin)

punct [*point, dot*] punctual (being exactly on time), punctum (a dot; a point), compunction (remorse; points of guilt), punctuation, puncture, acupuncture

put [*think*] computer (a computing or thinking machine), deputy, reputable (honorable; estimable; a thinker), dispute, repute

quies [*be at rest*] acquiesce, quiescent, quiet

reg, recti [*straighten*] regular, rectify (make straight), regiment, rectangle, correct, direct, erect, incorrigible

ri, ridi, risi [*laughter*] ridicule (laughter at the expense of another; mockery), deride (make mock of; jeer at), risible (likely to laugh), ridiculous

rog, roga [*ask*] prerogative (privilege; asking before), interrogation (questioning; the act of questioning), surrogate, derogatory

rupt [*break*] rupture (break), interrupt (break into), abrupt (broken off), disrupt (break apart), erupt (break out), incorruptible (unable to be broken down)

salv, salu [*safe, healthy*] salvation (act of being saved), salvage (that which is saved after appearing to be lost), salvable, salubrious (healthy), salutary (promoting health), salute (wish health to)

sat, satis [*enough*] sate (to satisfy, sate with food), satisfy (to give pleasure to; to give as much as is needed), satient (giving pleasure, satisfying), satiate, saturate

sci [*know*] science (knowledge), conscious (knowing, aware), omniscient (knowing everything), prescient (knowing beforehand)

scope [*see, watch*] scope (extent one can see), telescope, microscope, kaleidoscope (instrument for seeing beautiful forms), periscope, horoscope (hour watcher), episcopal (overseeing; pertaining to a bishop), stethoscope

scrib, script [*write*] scribe (a writer), scribble, inscribe, describe, subscribe, prescribe, ascribe, scrivener, manuscript (written by hand), scripture (the Bible)

sed, sess, sid [*sit*] sedentary (characterized by sitting), sedate (sitting, settled, dignified), preside (sit before), president, reside, subside, sediment (that which sits or settles out of a liquid), session (a sitting), obsession (an idea that sits stubbornly in the mind), possess

sent, sens [*feel*] sentiment (feeling), presentiment (feeling beforehand), assent, consent, resent, dissent, sentimental (having strong feeling or emotion), sense, sensation, sensitive, sensory, dissension

sen [*old*] senior, senator, senescent (growing old), senile (old; showing the weakness of old age)

sequ, secu, sue [*follow*] sequence (following of one thing after another), sequel, consequence, subsequent, obsequious (blindly following), prosecute, execute, consecutive (following in order), ensue, pursue, second (following first)

serv [*save, serve*] servant, service, subservient, servitude, servile, reservation, preserve, conserve, deserve, observe, conservation

sign, signi [*sign, mark, seal*] signal (a gesture or sign to call attention), signature (the mark of a person written in his own handwriting), design, insignia (distinguishing marks), signify

silic [*flint*] silicon (a nonmetallic element found in the earth's crust), silicosis (a disease prevalent among miners and stone cutters who breathe much dust)

simil, simul [*like, resembling*] similar (resembling in many respects), simulate (pretend; put on an act to make a certain impression), simulation (pretense; counterfeit display), assimilate (to make similar to), simile

sist, sta, stit, stet [*stand*] assist (to stand by with help), circumstance, stamina (power to withstand, to endure), persist (stand firmly; unyielding; continue), stanchion (a standing brace or support), substitute (to stand in for another), status (standing), state, static, stable, stationary

solus [*alone*] solo, soliloquy, solitaire, solitude

solv, solu [*loosen*] solvent (a loosener, a dissolver), solve, solvency, insolvency, absolve (loosen from, free from), resolve, soluble, solution, resolution, resolute, dissolute (loosened morally)

somnus [*sleep*] somnific, insomnia (not being able to sleep), somnambulant (a sleepwalker)

soph [*wise*] sophomore (wise fool), philosophy (love of wisdom), sophisticated (worldly wise), sophistry, sophist, theosophy (wise about God)

sphere [*ball, sphere*] sphere (a planet; a ball), stratosphere (the upper portion of the atmosphere), hemisphere (half of the earth), biosphere, spheroid

spec, spect, spic [*look*] specimen (an example to look at, study), specific, spectator (one who looks), spectacle, speculate, aspect, expect, inspect, respect, prospect, retrospective (looking backwards), suspect (look under), perspective, circumspect, introspective, conspicuous, despicable

spir [*breathe*] spirit (lit., breath), conspire (breathe together; plot), inspire (breathe into), aspire (breathe toward), expire (breathe out, die), spirant, perspire, respiration

spond, spons [*pledge, answer*] sponsor (one who pledges responsibility to a project), correspond (to communicate by letter; sending and receiving answers), irresponsible, respond

stereo [*solid*] stereotype (to fix in lasting form), stereome (strengthening tissue in plants), stereograph

string, strict [*draw, tight*] stringent (draw tight, rigid), astringent (drawing tightly, as skin tissue), strict, restrict, constrict (draw tightly together), boa constrictor (snake that constricts its prey)

stru, struct [*build*] structure, construct, instruct, obstruct, construe (build in the mind, interpret), destroy, destruction, instrument (originally, a tool for building)

sume, sump [*take, use, waste*] assume (to take; to use), consume (to use up), presume (to take upon oneself before knowing for sure), presumption, sump pump (a pump which takes up water)

tact, tang, tag, tig, ting [*touch*] contagious (transmission of disease by touching), contact (touch), tact (sense of touch for the appropriate), intact (untouched, uninjured), intangible (not able to be touched), tangible, contingent (touching together, depending on something), tactile

techni [*skill, art*] technician (one who is skilled in the mechanical arts), pyrotechnics (display of fireworks), technique, technology

tele [*far*] telephone (far sound), telegraph (far writing), telegram, telescope (far look), television (far seeing), telephoto (far photograph), telecast, telepathy (far feeling), teletype, teleprompter

tempo [*time*] tempo (rate of speed), pro tem (for the time being), extemporaneously, contemporary (those who live at the same time), temporary, temporal

ten, tin, tain [*hold*] tenacious (holding fast), tenant, tenure, untenable, detention, retentive, content, pertinent, continent, obstinent, abstain, contain, pertain, detain, obtain, maintain

tend, tent, tens [*stretch, strain*] tendency (a stretching; leaning), extend, intend, contend, pretend, superintend, tender, tent, tension (a stretching, strain), tense, tensile, attention

terra [*earth*] territory, terrestrial, terrain, terrarium

test [*to bear witness*] testament (a will; bearing witness to someone's wishes), detest, attest (certify; affirm; bear witness to), testimony, contest, intestate

the, theo [*God, a god*] monotheism (belief in one god), polytheism (belief in many gods), atheism (belief there is no god), pantheism (belief that God is all things), theogony (birth, origin of the gods), theology

therm [*heat*] therm (heat unit), thermic, thermal, thermometer, thermos bottle, thermostat (heat plus stationary; a device for keeping heat constant), hypothermia (subnormal body temperature), thermonuclear

thesis, thet [*place, put*] antithesis (place against), hypothesis (place under), synthesis (put together), epithet

tom [*cut*] atom (not cutable; smallest particle of matter), appendectomy (cutting out an appendix), tonsillec-

tomy, epitome (cut on; a summary), dichotomy (cutting in two; a division), anatomy (cutting, dissecting to study structure)

tort, tors [*twist*] torsion (act of twisting, as a torsion bar), torture (twisting to inflict pain), retort (twist back, reply sharply), extort (twist out), distort (twist out of shape), contort, tortuous (full of twists, as a mountain road)

tox [*poison*] toxic, intoxicate, antitoxin

tract, tra [*draw, pull*] tractable (can be handled), abstract (to draw away), tractor, attract, subtract, subtrahend (the number to be drawn away from another)

trib [*pay, bestow*] tribute (a fine paid to a conquering power), distribute (to divide among many), redistribute, contribute (to give money to a cause), attribute, retribution, tributary

trophy [*nourishment, development*] dystrophy (badly nourished), atrophy

tui, tuit, tut [*guard, teach*] tutor (one who teaches a pupil), tuition (payment for instruction or teaching fees), intuent (knowing by intuition)

turbo [*disturb*] turbulent, turmoil, disturb, turbid

typ [*print*] type, prototype (first print, model), typical, typography, typewriter, typology (study of types, symbols), typify

ultima [*last*] ultima (last; final; most remote), ultimate (man's last destiny), ultimatum (the final or last offer that can be made)

unda [*wave, flow*] abundant, inundate, undulation, redundant

uni [*one*] unicorn (a legendary creature with one horn), uniface (a design that appears only on one side), unify (make into one), university, unanimous, universal

vac [*empty*] vacate (to make empty), vacuum (a space entirely devoid of matter), evacuate (to remove troops or people), vacation, evacuee, vacant

vale, vali, valu [*strength, worth, valor*] valor (value; worth), validity (truth; legal strength), equivalent (of equal worth), evaluate (find out the value; appraise actual worth), valedictorian, valiant, value

ven, vent [*come*] convene (come together, assemble), intervene (come between), circumvent (coming around), adventure, invent, subvention, venturesome, convent, inventory, venture, venue, event, eventually, souvenir, contravene (come against), avenue, advent, convenient, prevent

ver, veri [*true*] verity (truth), very, verify (show to be true), verisimilitude, aver (say to be true, affirm), verdict

vert, vers [*turn*] avert (turn away), divert (turn aside, amuse), invert (turn over), introvert (turn inward, one interested in his own reactions), extrovert (turn outward, one interested in what is happening outside himself), controversy (a turning against; a dispute), reverse, versatile (turning easily from one skill to another), convertible, adversary, adverse

vest [*clothe, to dress*] vest (an article of clothing; vestment), investor (one who has laid out money for profit), travesty, vestry, vestment

vic, vicis [*change, substitute*] vicarious, vicar, vicissitude

vict, vinc [*conquer*] victor (conqueror, winner), evict (conquer out, expel), convict (prove guilty), convince (conquer mentally, persuade), invincible (not able to be conquered), evince, eviction

vid, vis [*see*] video (television), vision, evident, provide, providence, visible, revise, supervise (oversee), vista, visit, visage

viv, vita, vivi [*alive, life*] revive (make live again), survive (live beyond, outlive), vivid (full of life), vivify (enliven), convivial (fond of "living it up" with friends), vivisection (surgery on a living animal), vitality, vivacious (full of life)

voc [*call*] vocation (a calling), avocation (occupation not one's calling), convocation (a calling together), invocation (calling in), evoke, provoke, revoke, advocate, provocative, vocal, vocation, vocabulary

vol [*will*] malevolent, benevolent (one of good will), volunteer, volition

vola [*to fly*] volatile (able to fly off or vaporize), volley, volery, volitant

volcan, vulcan [*fire*] Vulcan (Roman god of fire), volcano (a mountain erupting fiery lava), volcanize (to undergo volcanic heat), vulcanist

volvo [*turn about, roll*] voluble (easily turned about or around), voluminous, volution, revolt

vor [*eat greedily*] voracious, carnivorous (flesh-eating), herbivorous (plant-eating), omnivorous (eating everything), devour (eat greedily)

zo [*animal*] zoo (short for zoological garden), zoology (study of animal life), zoomorphism (attributing animal form to God), zodiac (circle of animal constellations), protozoa (first animals; one-celled animals)

502

Numerical Prefixes

Prefix	Symbol	Multiples and Submultiples	Equivalent	Prefix	Symbol	Multiples and Submultiples	Equivalent
tera	T	10^{12}	trillionfold	centi	c	10^{-2}	hundredth part
giga	G	10^{9}	billionfold	milli	m	10^{-3}	thousandth part
mega	M	10^{6}	millionfold	micro	u	10^{-6}	millionth part
kilo	k	10^{3}	thousandfold	nano	n	10^{-9}	billionth part
hecto	h	10^{2}	hundredfold	pico	p	10^{-12}	trillionth part
deka	da	10	tenfold	femto	f	10^{-15}	quadrillionth part
deci	d	10^{-1}	tenth part	atto	a	10^{-18}	quintillionth part

LITERARY TERMS

503 An **abstract** word or phrase has as a referent (something referred to) an idea rather than a concrete object or thing. *Liberty, prejudice, love,* and *freedom* are examples of abstract words.

504 **Action** is what happens in a story: the events or conflicts. If the action is well organized, it will develop into a pattern or plot.

505 **Allegory** is a story in which the characters and the action represent an idea or generalization about life; allegories often have a strong moral or lesson.

506 **Allusion** is a reference in literature to a familiar person, place, thing, or event.

507 **Analogy** is the comparing of two or more similar objects so as to suggest that if they are alike in certain respects, they will probably be alike in other ways as well. (655)

508 **Anecdote** is a short summary of a funny or humorous event. Abe Lincoln was famous for his anecdotes, especially this one:

> Two fellows, after a hot dispute over how long a man's legs should be in proportion to his body, stormed into Lincoln's office one day and confronted him with their problem. Lincoln listened intently to the arguments given by each of the men and after some reflection rendered his verdict: "This question has been a source of controversy for untold ages," he said, slowly and deliberately, "and it is about time it should be definitely decided. It has led to bloodshed in the past, and there is no reason to suppose it will not lead to the same in the future.
>
> "After much thought and consideration, not to mention mental worry and anxiety, it is my opinion, all side issues being swept aside, that a man's lower limbs, in order to preserve harmony of proportion, should be at least long enough to reach from his body to the ground."

509 **Antagonist** is the person or thing opposing the protagonist or hero of the work. When this is a person, he is usually called the *villain.*

510 **Autobiography** is an author's account or story of his own life.

511 **Ballad** is a poem which tells a story and usually rhymes every other line.

512 **Biography** is the story of a person's life written by another person.

513 **Caricature** is a representation or imitation of a person's features so exaggerated or inferior as to be comic or absurd. (See illustration.)

514 **Character** is a person in a story or poem.

515 **Characterization** is the method an author uses to reveal his characters and their various personalities.

516 **Cliche** is a word or phrase which is so overused that it is no longer effective in most writing situations, as in "as busy as a bee" and "I slept like a log."

517 **Climax** is the high point or turning point in a work, usually the most intense point.

518 **Comedy** is literature which is concerned with man's inability to deal with reality. In comedy, human errors or problems appear funny.

519 A **concrete** word has as a referent (something referred to) a material object which can be heard, seen, felt, tasted, or smelled. *Wall, desk, car,* and *cow* are examples of concrete words.

520 **Conflict** is the colliding or clashing of thoughts, feelings, actions, or persons: in other words, the problems or complications in the story. There are five basic types of conflict:

Man vs. Man: One character in a story has a problem with one or more of the other characters.

Man vs. Society: A character has a conflict or problem with some element of society — the school, the law, the accepted way of doing things, and so on.

Man vs. Himself: A character has trouble deciding what to do in a particular situation.

Man vs. Nature: A character has a problem with some natural happening: a snowstorm, an avalanche, the bitter cold, or any of the other elements common to nature.

Man vs. Fate (God): A character has to battle what seems to be an uncontrollable problem. Whenever the problem seems to be a strange or unbelievable coincidence, fate can be considered as the cause of the conflict.

521 **Connotation** is all the emotions or feelings a word can arouse, such as the negative or bad feeling associated with the word *pig* or the positive or good feeling associated with the word *love.*

522 **Context** is the environment of a word; that is, the words which surround a particular word and help to determine or deepen its meaning. (See 490-494.)

523 **Denotation** is the literal or dictionary meaning of a word. (See *Connotation.*)

524 **Denouement** is the resolution or outcome of a play or story. (See 587 and 622.)

525 **Description** is a type of writing which sets forth the characteristics or qualities of the thing being written about. It creates a clear picture of the person, place, or thing being described.

526 **Dialogue** is the conversation carried on by the characters in a literary work.

527 **Diction** is an author's choice of words based on their correctness, clearness, or effectiveness.

Diction

528 **Archaic** words are those which are old-fashioned and no longer sound natural when used, as *"I believe thee not"* for *"I don't believe you."*

529 **Colloquialism** is an expression which is usually accepted in informal writing or speaking but not in a formal situation, as in *"Hey, man, what's happenin'?"*

530 **Profanity** is language used to degrade someone or something which is regarded as holy or sacred.

531 **Slang** is the language used by a particular group of people among themselves; it is also language which is used conversationally or informally to lend color and feeling: *dynamite, super,* and *far out.*

532 **Trite** expressions are those which have been overused to the point of losing their effectiveness: *twinkling stars, right on,* and *rainin' cats and dogs.*

533 **Vulgarity** is a type of language which is generally considered common, earthy, crude, gross, and, at times, offensive. It can, however, enhance the realism of a work if handled properly.

534 A **didactic** literary work has as its main purpose to present a moral or religious statement. It can also be, as in the case of Dante's *Divine Comedy* and Milton's *Paradise Lost,* a work which stands on its own as valuable literature.

535 **Drama** is the form of literature known as *plays;* but drama also refers to the type of serious play that is often concerned with the leading character's relationship to society rather than with some tragic flaw within his personality.

536 **Dramatic monologue** is a poem in which the character speaks either to himself or to another character in a way which reveals much about that character.

537 **Elegy** is a formal poem mourning the death of a certain individual.

538 **Empathy** is putting yourself in someone else's place and imagining how that person must feel. The phrase *"What would you do if you were in my shoes?"* is a request for one person to empathize with another.

539   **Epic** is a long narrative poem which tells of the deeds and adventures of a hero.

540   **Epigram** is a brief, witty poem or saying often dealing with its subject in a satirical manner: "There never was a good war or a bad peace" (Ben Franklin).

541   **Epitaph** is a short poem or verse in memory of someone.

542   **Epithet** is a word or phrase used in place of a person's name; it is characteristic of that person: *Alexander the Great, Hammerin' Hank,* and *Mr. Nice Guy.*

543   **Essay** is a piece of prose which expresses an individual's point of view; usually, it is a series of closely related paragraphs which combine to make a complete piece of writing.

544   **Exaggeration** (*hyperbole*) is overstating or stretching the truth for literary effect: "My shoes are killing me."

My shoes are
killing me.

545   **Exposition** is writing which is intended to make clear or explain something which might otherwise be difficult to understand; in a play or novel, it would be that portion which helps the reader to understand the background or situation in which the work is set.

546   **Falling action** is the action of a play or story which works out the decision arrived at during the climax. It ends with the resolution. (587)

547   **Farce** is literature which has one purpose: to make the audience laugh.

548   **Figurative language** is language which cannot be taken literally since it was written to create a special effect or feeling.

549   **Figure of speech** is a literary device used to create a special meaning through emotional and connotative use of words. The most common types are *antithesis, apostrophe, hyperbole, litotes, metaphor, metonymy, personification, simile, symbol, synecdoche,* and *understatement* (644).

Figures of Speech

550   **Antithesis** is an opposing or contrast of ideas: "Ask not what your country can do for you. Ask what you can do for your country" (John F. Kennedy).

551   **Apostrophe** is a poetic device in which the poet talks to an absent person, place, or thing as if it were present: "O Captain! My Captain! Our fearful trip is done" (Walt Whitman).

552   **Hyperbole** (hi-pur´ba-li) is an exaggeration or overstatement: "I was so embarrassed, I could have died." (544)

553   **Litotes** (li´ta-tez) is a form of understatement in which something is expressed by a negation of the contrary: "He was a man *of no small means*" (meaning *of considerable means*).

554   **Metaphor** is a comparing of two unlike things in which no words of comparison (*like* or *as*) are used: "That new kid in our class is really a squirrel."

555   **Metonymy** (ma-ton´a-mi) is the substituting of one word for another which is closely related to it: The *White House* has decided to provide a million more public service jobs. (*White House* is substituting for *President.*)

556 Personification is a literary device in which the author elevates an animal, object, or idea to the level of a human such that it takes on the characteristics of a human personality: "The rock stubbornly refused to move."

The rock stubbornly refused to move.

557 Simile is a comparison of two unlike things in which a word of comparison (*like* or *as*) is used: She eats like a bird.

558 Symbol is a concrete object used to represent an idea: A black object usually symbolizes death or sorrow.

559 Synecdoche (si-nek'da-ki) is using part of something to represent the whole: *All hands* on deck. (*Hands* is being used to represent the whole person.)

560 Flashback is returning to an earlier time in a story for the purpose of making something in the present more clear.

561 Foreshadowing is a suggestion of what is to come later in the work by giving hints and clues.

562 Form is the way a work is organized or designed; it is the structure or frame into which the story is written.

563 Genre is a French word often used as a synonym for *form* or *type* when referring to literature. The novel, essay, and poem are three of the many genres or forms of literature.

564 Gothic novel is a type of fiction which is usually characterized by gloomy castles, ghosts, and supernatural or sensational happenings — all of which is supposed to create a mysterious, chilling, and sometimes frightening story. Mary Shelley's *Frankenstein* as well as several works by Edgar Allan Poe are probably the best known gothic works still popular today.

565 Imagery is used to describe the words or phrases which bring forth a certain picture or image in the mind of the reader.

566 Impressionism is the recording of events or situations as they have been impressed upon the mind. Impressionism deals with vague thoughts and remembrances; realism, with objective facts. In "A Child's Christmas in Wales," Dylan Thomas remembers his winters in Wales as they impressed him as a boy:

> "... we waited to snowball the cats. Sleek and long as jaguars and horrible-whiskered, spitting and snarling, they would slink and sidle over the white back-garden walls, and the lynx-eyed hunters, Jim and I, fur-capped and moccasined trappers from Hudson Bay, off Mumbles Road, would hurl our deadly snowballs at the green of their eyes. The wise cats never appeared."

567 **Irony** is using a word or phrase to mean the exact opposite of its literal or normal meaning. There are three kinds of irony:

> **dramatic irony**, wherein the reader or the audience sees a character's mistakes or misunderstandings which the character is unable to see himself.
>
> **verbal irony**, in which the writer says one thing and means another.
>
> **irony of situation**, in which there is a great difference between the purpose of a particular action and the result.

568 **Limerick** is a light, humorous verse of five lines with an *aabba* rhyme scheme:

> There was a young lady from Maine,
> Who was as thin as a cane;
> When her bathing was done
> And the water did run,
> She slid through the hole in the drain.

569 **Local color** is the use of details which are common in a certain region or section of the country.

570 **Malapropism** is the type of pun or play on words which results when two words become jumbled in the speaker's mind. The term comes from a character in Sheridan's comedy, *The Rivals*. The character, Mrs. Malaprop, is constantly mixing up her words, as when she says "as headstrong as an *allegory* (she means *alligator*) on the banks of the Nile." Both words fit in the sentence, which is precisely what makes a malapropism a pun rather than a simple mistake.

571 **Melodrama** is an exaggerated, sensational form of drama which is intended to appeal to the emotions of the audience, as with many of the television soap operas.

572 **Mood** is the feeling a piece of literature arouses in the reader: happy, sad, peaceful, etc.

573 **Moral** is the particular value or lesson the author is trying to get across to the reader. The "moral of the story" is an especially popular phrase in Aesop's fables and other children's literature.

574 **Motif** is a term for an often-repeated character, incident, or idea in literature. The hero's saving a damsel in distress is a common *motif* of American melodrama.

575 **Myth** is a traditional story which attempts to explain or justify a certain belief, especially a religious belief, as with Atlas and Hercules in Greek mythology.

576 **Narrator** is the person who is telling the story. (616)

577 **Narration** is the type of writing which relates an event or series of events: a story.

578 **Naturalism** is an extreme form of realism in which the author tries to show the relation of man to his environment. Often, the author finds it necessary to show the base or ugly side of that relationship.

579 **Novel** is a term which covers a wide range of prose materials which have two common characteristics: they are fictional and lengthy.

580 **Parable** is a short, descriptive story whose purpose is to illustrate a particular belief or moral.

581 **Paradox** is a statement that is seemingly contrary to common sense yet is, in fact, true; a self-contradictory statement: "The coach considered this a good loss."

582 **Parallelism** is the repeating of phrases or sentences that are similar (parallel) in meaning and structure, as with "of the people, by the people, and for the people."

583 **Parody** is a literary form which is intended to mock a particular literary work or its style; a *burlesque* or comic effect is created.

584 **Pathos** is a Greek root meaning *suffering* or *passion*. It is usually applied to the part in a play or story which is intended to bring out pity or sorrow from the audience or reader.

585 **Plagiarism** is using someone else's writing or ideas and trying to pass them off as your own.

586 **Plot** is the action in a story. It is usually a series of related incidents which builds and grows as the story develops. There are five basic parts or elements in a plot which make up a *plot line*.

587 **Plot line** is the graphic representation of the action or events in a story: *exposition, rising action, climax, falling action, resolution.*

588 **Poetic justice** is a term which describes a character "getting what he deserves" in the end, especially if what he deserves is punishment. The purest form of poetic justice is when one character plots against another but ends up being caught in his own evil trap.

589 **Poetry** is language which reflects imagination, emotion, and thinking in verse form. There are many elements used in writing effective poetry:

Poetry Terms

590 **Alliteration** is the repetition of initial consonant sounds in neighboring words as in "rough and ready." Many poetic examples of alliteration can be found in today's songs: " . . . though the *tangled trails* of *time* have led us far astray, the memory seems to stay" (from "Lonely People," Harry Chapin).

Rough and Ready

591 **Assonance** is the repetition of vowel sounds without the repetition of consonants as in " . . . my words like silent raindrops fell . . ." (from "Sounds of Silence," Paul Simon).

592 **Blank verse** is an unrhymed form of poetry which normally consists of ten syllables in which every other syllable, beginning with the second, is stressed. Since blank verse is often used in very long poems, such as Frost's *Death of the Hired Man*, it may depart from the strict pattern from time to time to avoid monotony.

593 **Canto** is a division of a long poem.

594 **Caesura** is a pause or sudden break in a line of poetry.

595 **Closed couplet** (See 601).

596 **Consonance** is the repetition of consonant sounds, especially in poetry. Consonance is similar to alliteration except that it is not limited to the first letter of each word as is alliteration: " . . . and high school girls with clear skin smiles . . ." (from "At Seventeen," Janis Ian).

597 **End rhyme** is the rhyming of words which appear at the ends of two or more lines of poetry.

598 **Foot** is a unit of meter which denotes the combination of stressed and unstressed syllables. (615)

    Iambic: an unstressed followed by a stressed syllable (repeát)
    Anapestic: two unstressed followed by a stressed syllable (interrupt)
    Trochaic: a stressed followed by an unstressed syllable (older)
    Dactylic: a stressed followed by two unstressed syllables (openly)
    Spondaic: two stressed syllables (heartbreak)
    Pyrrhic: two unstressed syllables (Pyrrhic is very rare and seldom appears by itself.)

599   **Free verse** is poetry that does not have a regular meter or rhyme scheme: Edgar Lee Master's *Silence* is written in free verse.

600   **Haiku** is a form of Japanese poetry which has three lines; the first line has five syllables, the second has seven syllables, and the third has five syllables. The subject of the haiku has traditionally been nature as in:

> Behind me the moon
> Brushes shadows of pine trees
> Lightly on the floor.

601   **Heroic couplet** (*closed couplet*) consists of two successive rhyming lines which contain a complete thought. It is usually written in iambic pentameter.

602   **Internal rhyme** occurs when the rhyming words appear in the same line of poetry: "We'll drink a *toast* to those who *most* believe in what they've won" (from "Tea and Sympathy," Janis Ian).

603   **Lyric** is a short verse which is intended to express the emotions of the author; quite often these lyrics are set to music.

604   **Meter** is the repetition of stressed and unstressed syllables in a line of poetry. (See *Foot.*)

605   **Ode** is a lyric poem written to someone or something. It is serious and elevated in tone. Allen Tate's "Ode to the Confederate Dead" is a eulogy (words of high praise) written for the Southern soldiers after the Civil War.

606   **Onomatopoeia** is the use of a word whose sound suggests its meaning, as in *clang, buzz,* and *twang.*

607   **Paradox** is a statement which at first seems contradictory but which turns out to have a profound meaning as in Bob Dylan's lyric: "I was so much older then; I'm younger than that now."

608   **Pastoral** is a poem or dramatic work which was originally characterized by an ideal look at **shepherd and rustic** life. The term has since been extended to include any work which deals with the subject of rural life.

609   **Psalm** is a sacred or religious song or lyric.

610   **Refrain** is the repetition of a line or phrase of a poem at regular intervals, especially at the end of each stanza. The refrain in a song is called the *chorus.*

611   **Repetition** is the repeating of a word or phrase within a poem or prose piece to create a sense of rhythm: "But I sometimes think the difference is just in how I think and feel, and that the only changes *going on* are *going on* in me" (from "Changes," Harry Chapin).

612   **Rhyme** is the similarity or likeness of sound existing between two words. *Sat* and *cat* are perfect rhymes because the vowel and final consonant sounds are exactly the same.

613   **Rhymed verse** is verse with end rhyme; it usually has regular meter.

614   **Stanza** is a division of poetry named for the number of lines it contains:

Couplet:	two-line stanza	**Sestet:**	six-line stanza
Triplet:	three-line stanza	**Septet:**	seven-line stanza
Quatrain:	four-line stanza	**Octave:**	eight-line stanza
Quintet:	five-line stanza		

(*Note:* All others are called nine-, ten-, eleven-, and so on, line stanzas.)

615   **Verse** is a metric line of poetry. It is named according to the kind and number of feet composing it: *iambic pentameter, anapestic tetrameter* . . . . (See 598.)

Monometer:	one foot	**Pentameter:**	five feet
Dimeter:	two feet	**Hexameter:**	six feet
Trimeter:	three feet	**Heptameter:**	seven feet
Tetrameter:	four feet	**Octometer:**	eight feet

Verse is usually found in one of three forms: *rhymed, blank,* or *free verse.*

616 **Point of view** is the vantage point from which the story is told. In the **first-person** point of view, the story is told by one of the characters: *"I'm not reading that stupid book."* In the **third-person** point of view, the story is told by someone outside the story: *"He felt justified in refusing to read. After all, he couldn't read that book— it was too hard."*

There are three basic **third-person points of view:**

Omniscient is a viewpoint which allows the narrator to relate the thoughts and feelings of all the characters; a *god-like* intuition.

Limited omniscient allows the narrator to relate the thoughts and feelings of only one character.

Camera view (Objective view) is seeing and recording the action from a neutral or unemotional point of view.

617 **Protagonist** is the main character or hero of the story.

618 **Pseudonym** means *false name* and is usually applied to the name writers use in place of their natural name. Mark Twain, which is probably the most famous pseudonym in literature, was assumed by the Hannibal, Missouri writer, Samuel Langhorne Clemens.

619 **Pun** is a word or phrase which is used in such a way as to suggest more than one possible meaning. Words used in the pun are words that sound the same (or nearly the same) but have different meanings: "I really don't mind going to school; it's the *principle (principal)* of the thing."

620 **Realism** is literature which attempts to represent life as it really is by paying close attention to what otherwise might be considered insignificant details.

621 **Renaissance**, which means *rebirth*, is the period of history following the Middle Ages. This period began late in the fourteenth century and continued through the fifteenth and sixteenth centuries. Milton (1608-1674) is often regarded as the last of the great Renaissance poets. The term now applies to any period of time in which intellectual and artistic interest is revived or reborn.

622 **Resolution** is the portion of the play or story where the problem is solved. It comes after the climax and falling action and is intended to bring the story to a satisfactory end; *denouement*. (524, 587)

623 **Rising action** is the series of conflicts which build a play toward a climax. (587)

624 **Romance** is a form of literature which presents life as we would like it to be rather than as it actually is. Usually, it has a great deal of adventure, love, and excitement.

625 **Sarcasm** is the use of praise to mock someone or something, as in "He's a real *he-man*," or "She's a real *winner*."

626 **Satire** is a literary tone used to ridicule or make fun of human vice or weakness.

627 **Setting** is the time and place in which the action of a literary work occurs.

628 **Slapstick** is a form of low comedy which makes its appeal through the use of violent and exaggerated action. The "pie in the face" routine is a classic piece of *slapstick* as are the Charlie Chaplin and Mack Sennett films.

629 **Slice of life** is a term which describes the type of realistic or naturalistic writing which accurately reflects what life is really like. This is done by giving the reader a sample or *slice* of life.

630 **Soliloquy** is a speech delivered by a character when he is alone on stage.

631 **Sonnet** is a poem which consists of fourteen lines of iambic pentameter. There are two popular forms of the sonnet, the Italian (or Petrarchan) and the Shakespearean (or English).

632 **Italian (Petrarchan)** sonnet has two parts: an octave of eight lines and a sestet of six lines, and usually rhyming *abbaabba, cdecde*. Often a question is raised in the octave and answered in the sestet.

633 **Shakespearean (English or Elizabethan)** sonnet consists of three quatrains and a final rhyming couplet. The rhyme scheme is *abab, cdcd, efef, gg*. Usually, the question or theme is set forth in the quatrains while the answer or resolution appears in the final couplet.

634 **Stereotype** is a pattern or form which does not change. A character is "stereotyped" if he has no individuality and fits the mold of that particular kind of person. For many years, Blacks were stereotyped in literature as maids, butlers, shoeshine boys, and other servant-type characters.

635 **Stream of consciousness** is a style of writing in which the thoughts and feelings of the writer are recorded as they occur.

636 **Structure** is the form or organization a writer uses for his literary work. There are a great number of possible forms or structures used regularly in literature: *parable, fable, romance, satire, farce, slapstick*, and so on.

637 **Style** is *how* the author writes (form) rather than *what* he writes (content).

638 **Theme** is the statement about life a particular work is trying to get across to the reader. In stories written for children, the theme is often spelled out clearly at the end when the author says, "... and so, the moral of the story is: Never tell your mother or father something that isn't true or they may not believe you when you tell the truth." In more complex literature, the theme may not be so moralistic in tone, or at least not so clearly spelled out.

639 **Tone** is the attitude of the author toward his audience and characters. This attitude may be *serious, mock-serious, humorous, satiric,* and so on.

640 **Total effect** is the final, overall impression left with the reader by a literary work.

641 **Tragedy** is a literary work in which the hero is destroyed by some flaw within his character and by forces which he cannot control.

642 **Tragic hero** is a character who experiences an inner struggle because of some flaw within his character. That struggle ends in the defeat of the hero.

643 **Transcendentalism** is a philosophy which requires that man go beyond (transcend) reason in his search for truth. Man can arrive at the basic truths of life through spiritual intuition or instinct if he takes the time to meditate or think seriously about it.

644 **Understatement** is the stating of an idea with considerable restraint or holding back so as to emphasize what is being talked about. Mark Twain once described Tom Sawyer's Aunt Polly as being "prejudiced against snakes." Since she could not stand snakes, this way of saying so is called *understatement.*

Tom Sawyer's Aunt Polly was "prejudiced against snakes."

SPEECH SKILLS

Determining the Purpose

645 The purpose behind all speaking—whether it be the nonsense syllables of a small child or the meaningful insights of an aged philosopher — is the same. It is to pass on ideas or feelings and get a favorable response in return. When you are faced with the reality of having to ''give a speech,'' you must remember that the purpose remains the same. There is one important difference, however. When you know beforehand that you have to speak, there is immediately a certain uneasiness about what to say and how to say it. This at first seems to complicate the otherwise clear purpose of speaking: passing on ideas or feelings. What it actually does, however, is force you to think carefully about what is to come and plan accordingly. This pressure is good and necessary for anyone preparing a speech.

>''Half the world is composed of people who have something to say and can't, and the other half who have nothing to say and keep on saying it.''
>
> - Robert Frost

646 There are a number of questions which you can ask yourself as part of this preparation:
  1) Why am I giving the speech? to inform my audience? to persuade them? to amuse? to stimulate?
  2) Who will be in my audience? my teacher and classmates? my boss and co-workers? my family and friends?
  3) Does my speech have to be about a particular topic or am I able to select a topic I like and one which I think my audience might like as well?
  4) Is there any time limit or other important restriction?
  5) Will the occasion be formal or informal?
  6) Will the place, occasion, and topic be suited to the use of visual aids?

Once these and other questions have been considered, you are ready to begin your search for an appropriate topic.

Selecting and Narrowing the Topic

647 There are several worthwhile things to keep in mind as you begin to look for a specific topic:
  1) Nearly any subject can be made to work as a topic for a speech. Only those which are clearly wrong for the occasion or the audience should be ruled out. Keep an open mind as you search and try to fashion each new subject into a speech topic.
  2) If there is a subject which interests you — one which you may have done some work on before — consider that subject first. Using a familiar topic allows you to talk of things you care about or have experienced firsthand.

You can then communicate your ideas and feelings on a more personal level. This acquaintance with the subject will help you to feel more self-confident and enthusiastic.

3) If you are not able to use a familiar topic and have no other workable ideas, you will need to find help from some other source. Possibly one of your teachers or a close friend will have some suggestions for you. If not, the next logical place for you to look is in the library. There you will find numerous sources for ideas which can stimulate your thinking:

   a) The *vertical file*, which is a file of newspaper clippings, brochures, pamphlets, etc., can provide you with hundreds of ideas on current topics. It can also serve as a source of current material for the later writing of the speech.

   b) The *Reader's Guide to Periodical Literature*, which is an ongoing publication listing magazine articles by author and subject, will keep you thinking for hours about possible topics. It will also give you an indication of how much information is available on each subject you are considering.

   c) A *newspaper* or *magazine* will update you on the major issues of the day. With this information, you can decide whether it would be worthwhile to look more closely at a particular topic or issue.

   d) A *special* display set up in the library to feature new or popular books might provide you with an idea. These displays usually feature high-interest or current material which is what makes displays good sources for a speech topic.

   e) Even though they are often frowned upon by teachers as the source of any writing assignment, *encyclopedias* can be very helpful tools when it comes to finding a speech topic. You would do well, however, to check out other books, magazines, newspapers, etc., and not rely too heavily on the encyclopedia for information.

4) Once you have found a possible topic, skim through several (not just one) articles on the topic. Try to determine just how much information there is on the subject, especially how much new or interesting information there is.

5) If you are satisfied that this topic will work, focus in on the particular area which seems best suited for the time limit, the audience, and the occasion. This narrowed-down version becomes your specific topic.

6) You should then be able to state your topic and purpose in one declarative sentence, often referred to as your **thesis statement.** You can begin the wording of your thesis statement with "My purpose is . . ." and follow that with one of the four main goals of public speaking: to inform, to convince, to stimulate, to interest. Lastly, add your specific, narrowed-down topic to complete your thesis statement.

   Example: "My purpose is to convince my audience that high school study halls are inefficient and, therefore, should be done away with."

Researching and Analyzing the Topic

648 Once you have determined your topic and purpose, you are then ready to gather material for support. Set aside a portion of your notebook and begin writing down personal remembrances, experiences, thoughts, etc., related to the topic. Continue to jot down ideas which come to you from radio, television, classroom discussion, magazines, and so on. This continued attention will provide you with many good details which you can use when you are writing your speech. (These notes can also be arranged into your **working outline.** See 357.)

Next, go to your library and take full advantage of the material which is available there. (Refer to the "Library Skills" section of this handbook for a detailed description of the card catalog, *Reader's Guide,* and other helpful materials.)

(*Note:* If your speech assignment calls for extensive research with note cards, footnotes, or some other form of documentation, turn to "The Research Paper" for additional steps to follow.)

Writing the Speech

649   Writing a speech is much the same as writing a paragraph or an essay. You must write in a clear, concise manner and use a logical pattern of organization which has a beginning, a middle, and an end. Your writing should move smoothly from one point to the next.

But it cannot be said that a speech is entirely the same as other forms of writing. It is not. A speech is written to be heard rather than read. It must, therefore, *sound* good as well as look good on paper. It must be written in such a way that your audience can transcribe what it hears into a clear, colorful picture—a picture which they can take with them and talk about later.

Using the Senses

650   Your audience needs vivid, descriptive details to help them visualize your ideas. They need to see, hear, feel, smell, and taste them. They must experience with you "the sticky stillness of a tenement house on a flyswatter summer night" and "the sour-milk smell of an unwashed baby." Through the use of vivid sensory details, you can paint a picture your audience will remember long after they have forgotten the "startling statements" and "documented data" often used in public speaking.

Creating an Effective Style

651   After you have jotted down several appropriate sensory details, you must next arrange them into effective phrases and sentences. This process of choosing the right words and putting them in the right order is called **style.** As with any piece of writing, the style of a speech has to be sharp and appealing. A bland or flat speech has little chance of either getting your ideas across or of getting a favorable response from your audience. There are certain **stylistic devices** which can help you create a speech which has a style appealing in sound and structure.

Establishing an Appropriate Tone

652   Closely related to the style of your speech is the **tone.** Tone is the attitude or feeling which you bring to each of the words, phrases, or sentences in your speech. Tone is especially important in writing which is intended to be spoken because your attitude or feeling is sure to be reflected in your voice. This "tone of voice" is nearly as important as the words themselves in determining the success or failure of a speech. As you work with your speech, be aware of the tone it is taking on. Select words, phrases, and stylistic devices which help to create the appropriate tone.

Stylistic Devices and Appeals

653   Below you will find excerpts from the speeches of John F. Kennedy. More than any other president of recent times, he is remembered for his appealing blend of stylistic devices and appropriate tone in his speeches. (The tone of each sample is listed above the excerpt and labeled as an **appeal**—a word which reflects both the writer's personal feelings and attitudes and the feelings he hopes his audience will also experience.)

654   **Parallel structuring** is the repeating of phrases or sentences which are similar (parallel) in meaning and structure; **repetition** is the repeating of the same word or phrase to create a sense of rhythm and emphasis.

Appeal for Commitment

Let every nation know, whether it wishes us well or ill, that we shall *pay any price, bear any burden, meet any hardship, support any friend, oppose any foe,* in order to assure the survival and the success of liberty (Inaugural Address, 1961).

(Note: In this sample, the three-word phrases in italics are parallel because each begins with the same kind of word—a verb—and each ends with the same kind of word—a noun. These parallel phrases also contain repetition in the form of the word *any.)*

655 **Analogy** is a comparison of an unfamiliar idea to a simple, familiar one. The comparison is usually quite lengthy, suggesting several points of similarity. An analogy is especially useful when attempting to explain a difficult or complex idea.

Appeal to Common Sense

In our opinion the German people wish to have one united country. If the Soviet Union had lost the war, the Soviet people themselves would object to a line being drawn through Moscow and the entire country. If we had been defeated in war, we wouldn't like to have a line drawn down the Mississippi River. . . (Interview, November 25, 1961).

656 **Alliteration** is the repetition of initial consonant sounds in neighboring words as in *wet, wild,* and *wooly.*

Appeal to the Democratic Principle

I ask you to look into your hearts—not in search of charity, for the Negro neither wants nor needs condescension—but for the one *plain, proud,* and *priceless* quality that unites us all as Americans: a sense of justice (Message to Congress, 1963).

657 **Allusion** is a reference in a speech to a familiar person, place, or thing.

Appeal to the Democratic Principle

One hundred years of delay have passed since *President Lincoln* freed the slaves, yet their heirs, their grandsons, are not fully free (Radio and television address, 1963).

658 **Metaphor** is comparing two things without using words of comparison *(like* or *as).*

Appeal for Involvement, Commitment

Let the word go forth from this time and place, to friend and foe alike, that the *torch* has been passed to a new generation of Americans. . . (Inaugural Address, 1961).

(Note: In this instance, the word *torch* is used metaphorically. The changing of the Presidents is being compared to the passing of the torch, a traditional symbol of ongoing causes.)

659 **Simile** is comparing two unlike things using *like* or *as.*

Appeal to the Democratic Principle

Only an educated and informed people will be a free people; . . . the ignorance of one voter in a democracy impairs the security of all, and . . . if we can, as Jefferson put it, "enlighten the people generally . . . tyranny and the oppressions of mind and body will vanish, *like the evil spirits at the dawn of the day."*

660 **Irony** is using a word or phrase to mean the exact opposite of its literal meaning or to show a result which is the opposite of what would be expected or appropriate.

Appeal to Common Sense

They see no harm in paying those to whom they entrust the minds of their children a smaller wage than is paid to those to whom they entrust the care of their plumbing (Vanderbilt University, 1961).

661 **Antithesis** is balancing or contrasting one word or idea against another, usually in the same sentence.

Appeal to Common Sense, Commitment

Let us never negotiate out of fear. But let us never fear to negotiate (Inaugural Address, 1961).

Mankind must put an end to war or war will put an end to mankind (Address to the U.N., 1961).

662 **Anecdote** is a short story told to illustrate a point.

Appeal to Pride, Commitment

Frank O'Connor, the Irish writer, tells in one of his books how as a boy, he and his friends would make their way across the countryside and when they came to an orchard wall that seemed too high and too doubtful to try and too difficult to permit their voyage to continue, they took off their hats and tossed them over the wall—and then they had no choice but to follow them.

This Nation has tossed its cap over the wall of space, and we have no choice but to follow it. Whatever the difficulties, they will be overcome. (San Antonio Address, November 21, 1963)

663 **Negative definition** is describing something by telling what it is *not* rather than or in addition to what it is.

Appeal for Commitment

. . . members of this organization are committed by the Charter to promote and respect human rights. Those rights are not respected when a Buddhist priest is driven from his pagoda, when a synagogue is shut down, when a Protestant church cannot open a mission, when a cardinal is forced into hiding, or when a crowded church service is bombed (United Nations, September 20, 1963).

664 **Extended definition** is defining a concept through the use of several different devices or approaches.

Appeal to Common Sense

World peace, like community peace, does not require that each man love his neighbor—it requires only that they live together in mutual tolerance, submitting their disputes to a just and peaceful settlement.

Genuine peace must be the product of many nations, the sum of many acts. It must be dynamic, not static, changing to meet the challenge of each new generation. For peace is a process—a way of solving problems.

Peace is a daily, a weekly, a monthly process, gradually changing opinions, slowly eroding old barriers, quietly building new structures. And however undramatic the pursuit of peace, the pursuit must go on. (From two addresses, 1963)

665 **Quotations,** especially of well-known individuals, can be effective in nearly any speech.

Appeal for Emulation or Affiliation

At the inauguration, Robert Frost read a poem which began "the land was ours before we were the land's"—meaning, in part, that this new land of ours sustained us before we were a nation. And although we are now the land's—a nation of people matched to a continent—we still draw our strength and sustenance . . . from the earth (Dedication speech, 1961).

666 **Rhetorical question** is a question posed for emphasis of a point, not for the purpose of getting an answer.

Appeal to Common Sense, Democratic Principle

"When a man's ways please the Lord," the Scriptures tell us, "he maketh even his enemies to be at peace with him." And is not peace, in the last analysis, basically a matter of human rights—the right to live out our lives without fear of devastation—the right to breathe air as nature provided it—the right of future generations to a healthy existence? (Commencement Address, 1963)

667 **Pun** is a play on words which is either humorous or witty. In either case, it involves using words in a way or in a situation different from their normal use.

Appeal to a Sense of Humor

What more can be said today, regarding all the dark and tangled problems we face, than: Let there be light (University of Washington, 1961).

Appeal to Hope

For every apparent blessing contains the seeds of danger—every area of trouble gives out a ray of hope—and the one unchangeable certainty is that nothing is certain or unchangeable (State of the Union, 1962).

668 Below you will find a sample speech labeled for stylistic devices.

Student Commentary	
I grew up in a decade when youth became very important. In those days—the sixties—you could be one of two things: young or wrong. As time passed, it wasn't incredible anymore to see a forty-year-old woman trying to look eighteen, or a sixty-year-old man trying to act thirty.	**Parallelism**
At first, those who clung to their youth were part of a fad. Those who tried to act youthful were the exception—now they're the norm. I remember older people who were embarrassed to reminisce about days gone by. They're not embarrassed anymore. They just refuse to admit there ever was a past.	**Repetition**
This holding onto our youth has not gone unencouraged. Madison Avenue and the businesses they represent have been there all the way. You've probably noticed that there aren't many senior citizens in the "Pepsi generation" or "living the gusto life." It has become an accepted maxim: If you don't act and look young, you don't really live at all.	**Allusion (Metonymy)** **Irony** **Antithesis**
It is difficult to pass judgment on whether the path we've followed is the right one. To some, I'm sure it is; to others, I doubt it ever could be. Our holding onto youth is a fact, though. Maybe Bob Dylan put it best when he sang: "I was so much older then, I'm younger than that now."	**Quotation (Paradox)**

Using Evidence and Logic

669 As you work on the style of your speech, you must make sure your reasons, evidence, and overall logic are also sound. This is especially important in speeches which are written to prove or argue a point.

An argument is a chain of reasons which a person uses to support a conclusion. To use argument well, you need to know both how to draw logical conclusions from sound evidence and how to recognize and avoid false arguments. **Logical fallacies** are sometimes described in the complicated terms of formal logic, but more often they are cataloged according to informal types.

The informal fallacies described in this section are the bits of fuzzy or dishonest thinking that crop up often in our own speaking and writing, as well as in the advertisements, political appeals, editorials, and so on that we daily consume.

Logical fallacies are fairly harmless (though not excusable) when they are used to support an argument which is true anyway on other grounds. But they are dishonest and dangerous when a person uses them deliberately to satisfy some greedy, prejudiced, or spiteful desire. After all, an argument may be completely false and yet *effective* in swaying an audience which is not equipped to resist its emotional appeal. In fact, it is mainly *because* fallacies are effective that they are so often used as improper shortcuts to persuasion.

Fallacies of Thinking

670 A logical way of grouping the many types of logical fallacies is according to the part of the argument that they chiefly falsify. Some distort the original question; some are used to sabotage the whole argument; others make use of improper evidence or language; and still others draw faulty conclusions from the evidence available. In the list below, traditional Latin names are provided in italics if they are still in common use.

Distorting the Question

1. The Bare Assertion   ("That's just how it is.") The most basic way to distort a question is to deny that there is one. Refusing to back up a disputed claim with proper reasons is an irresponsible argument-stopper.

2. Begging the Question   This fallacy consists of *assuming* in a definition or in the premises of your argument the very point you are trying to prove. Note how circular this sort of reasoning is:

> Phil: I hate Mr. Baldwin's class because I'm never happy in there.
> (But what's wrong with the *class*?)

3. Oversimplification   Beware of phrases like, "It all boils down to. . . ." or "It's a simple question of. . . ." Almost no dispute among reasonably intelligent people is "a simple question of. . . ." Anyone who feels, for example, that capital punishment "all boils down" to a matter of protecting society ought to question, in succession, a doctor, an inmate on death row, his wife, a sociologist, a minister, and a political philosopher.

4. Black and White Thinking   ("Either . . . or . . . .") This familiar fallacy consists of reducing all possible options to two extremes: "America: Love It or Leave It." "Put up or shut up." "If you can't stand the heat, get out of the kitchen." Usually when a person eliminates all "greys" from consideration like this, that person leaves little doubt about which option he or she considers white and which black. Thus, the black/white fallacy usually appears in the argument of someone who is not listening for a reply.

5. Complex Question   Sometimes by phrasing a question a certain way, you may ignore or cover up an even larger, more urgent question. For example, Roger asks the high school principal, "Why can't I get academic credit for monitoring the bathroom?"; he ignores the larger question whether *anyone* should get credit for monitoring a bathroom.

Sabotaging the Argument

6. Red Herring   *Red herring* refers to a stinky smoked fish dragged across a trail to throw a tracking dog off the scent. Certain issues are like that: so volatile and controversial that, once introduced into a discussion, they tend to sidetrack everyone involved. Let's say you are discussing the need for tobacco subsidies in the federal budget and somebody asserts, beside the point, that all restaurants should have no-smoking sections — off you go, chasing that tasty fish.

7. Misuse of Humor   Jokes have a healthy way of lightening the mood, but when humor is used the way an octopus squirts ink — to blind and befuddle, and possibly to injure — it qualifies as a subversive activity (a kind of logical guerrilla warfare) and is a confession of weakness in the saboteur's position.

8. Appeal to Force   ("Might Makes Right.") One simple way of sabotaging an argument is to break the opponent's leg. On a more subtle level, someone may imply that your argument cannot be true because his own is in the majority. Needless to say, one needs a degree of courage to resist such "logic."

Misusing Evidence

9. Impressing With Large Numbers   ("Hop on the Bandwagon.") This fallacy can take at least two forms. One person can try to "snow" another by slinging impressive figures. ("I paid $6,958.36 for this bomb — isn't she a beaut?") Just as commonly, one person will try to make his claim sound reasonable by saying that "everybody"

177

agrees. ("The pain reliever used by one out of three Americans . . . . ") This uncritical use of numbers can easily lead to absurdity: "Eat garbage — 7 billion flies can't be wrong!"

10. **Irrelevant Appeals to Authority**   You can take Dr. Carl Sagan's word on the composition of Saturn's rings, but the moment he, like the famous quarterback Joe Namath a few years ago, tries to peddle pantyhose on TV, watch out!

11. **Appeal to Popular Sentiment**   *(Argumentum ad populum)* Associating your cause with all the popular virtues — flag-waving patriotism, baseball, apple pie, fluoride in drinking water — may seduce your listeners into smiling agreement, but it bases your argument on unfulfillable promises. If the other guy is unscrupulous, he may use the same tactic.

12. **Appeal to Personal Factors**   *(Argumentum ad hominem,* or, argument directed "at the man.") By focusing on a person's lifestyle or other personal qualities, one may evade the true issue at hand. *Ad hominem* arguments can have either a positive or a negative thrust. For example, while campaigning for Senator Buzof, you might say, "Senator Buzof is a family man and a former Eagle Scout." You might turn that same fact against him: "Would you trust this Buzof fellow in your Congress? He has a mind like a Boy Scout!"

When personal factors are cited in an argument to undercut an opponent's credibility or to assassinate his character, the fallacy is called "Poisoning the Well." Supposedly, if the "well" is polluted, no good argument could ever come of it.

Another type of *ad hominem* argument goes by the name *tu quoque* (or, "you're another"). If someone charges you with some shortcoming or wrongdoing, you "defend" yourself, fallaciously, by asserting that the other person is equally guilty. Children are experts in this fallacy: "Suzy did it, too!" But the most famous user of this fallacy was Adam in the Garden of Eden who, with his cheeks still fat with apple, pointed the accusing finger at Eve.

13. **Appeal to Pity**   *(Argumentum ad misericordium)* This fallacy may be heard in courts of law when an attorney begs for leniency because his client's mother is ill, his brother is out of work, his cat has a hairball, and blah, blah, blah. The strong tug on the heartstrings has a classic variant in the classroom when the student says to the teacher, "May I have an extension on this paper? I worked till my eyeballs fell out, but it's still not done."

14. **Appeal to Ignorance**   *(Argumentum ad ignorantiam)* One commits this fallacy by claiming that since no one has ever proved a claim it must therefore be false. ("Show me one study that proves marijuana leads to harder drugs.") Or, vice versa, one may claim that some belief must be true since no one can disprove it. ("Sure I believe in flying saucers — half of all sightings have never been explained.") This fallacy unfairly shifts the burden of proof onto someone else.

15. **Hypothesis Contrary to Fact**   ("If only . . . . ") This false argument bases its claim on what one supposes would have happened if one thing or another had not happened instead. Such claims, being pure speculation, cannot be tested by logic.

16. **False Analogy**   Sometimes you may argue that X is good (or bad, or promising, etc.) because it is like Y (which, in its own turn, is good, bad, or promising, etc.). Such an analogy may be helpful if it illuminates the subject. But the analogy weakens an argument if it is *improper,* if the grounds for comparison are too *vague,* or if the analogy is *stretched too far.*

Misusing Language

All of the fallacies listed in this section could be termed "misuses of language," but the following three fallacies are all based specifically on a misleading selection of words.

17. **Obfuscation**   ("Fuzzy Language") Technical buzzwords (*interface, inverse efficiency ratio, streamlined target refractory system, community sanitary output,* etc.), sometimes combined with twisted language, may obscure behind their brilliant facade the fact that the passage of speech or prose in which they occur means practically nothing.

18. **Ambiguity**   Sometimes a word or sentence structure will allow for two or more opposite interpretations, as in the following: "We were introduced to the head hunter; the next day he had us for lunch." When ambiguity appears in argument, it is sometimes an unintended result of careless thinking, a kind of joke that recoils on the teller. At other times, however, a speaker or writer may deliberately be ambiguous to avoid being pinned down.

19. **Slanted Language**   By choosing words with strongly positive or negative connotations, a person can add a persuasive emotional charge to an argument. Such words may be used to express genuine and appropriate feeling, or they may be the vehicle for mindless prejudice. The philosopher Bertrand Russell once illustrated the bias involved in slanted language when he compared three synonyms for the word "stubborn": "I am *firm*. You are *obstinate*. He is *pigheaded*."

Drawing Faulty Conclusions

20. **Hasty Generalization**   A reasonable conclusion must be backed by sufficient evidence. Basing conclusions on inadequate evidence, on the other hand, is always a fallacy, even if the conclusion could be justified by a different set of proofs. ("I saw the principal drive away at noon. He must have another job somewhere on the side.")

21. **Composition and Division**   The twin fallacies of composition and division are based, respectively, on the belief that the whole of something will have the same quality as each of its parts and the converse belief that each part will have the quality of the whole. The fallacy of composition is clear when a choir director says after an audition, "All of the singers were excellent. What an excellent choir we shall have." The result? Forty-six excellent altos, one excellent baritone, and one less-than-excellent choir!

22. **False Cause**   (*Post hoc, ergo propter hoc*, or "after this, therefore because of this.") If *A* precedes *B*, it need not therefore be the cause of *B*, even though we may lazily assume that it is. *A* may have been the only sufficient cause of *B*; it may also have been one of several necessary causes; or, finally, *A* and *B* may be entirely coincidental. Notice the fallacy of "false cause" at work in the following: "Since that new school was built, drug use among our young people has skyrocketed. Better that it would never have been built."

The Introduction, Body, and Conclusion

671   **The Introduction:** After you have finished wording your speech, you must arrange your details into an introduction, body, and conclusion. You should, for example, use an especially interesting detail in your opening or **introduction.** It should be combined with other thoughts so as to accomplish the following:

- Gain the attention of your audience.
- Motivate your audience to want to listen to you.
- State clearly the purpose and central idea of your talk (thesis statement).
- Serve as a transition or bridge into the main part of your speech.

You can structure your opening remarks using any of the stylistic devices discussed earlier in this section or by selecting one of the following techniques:

1. an appropriate quotation
2. a startling statement
3. a challenging question or series of questions
4. a humorous story
5. a short demonstration
6. an attention-capturing incident or illustration
7. an immediate issue or challenge
8. a personal reference or greeting
9. a reference to something related to the occasion
10. a brief reference to your subject or problem

The Body: The **body** of the speech should be arranged so that it builds to a climax. This can be a growing, dramatic build *(crescendo)* which reaches an intense, emotional peak at the conclusion. In this instance, the voice works with the written copy to heighten and amplify the climax. The climax can also be a slow, diminishing fade which captivates your audience much like a whisper in a dramatic scene. It pinpoints a specific idea or emotion and draws your speech to a thoughtful, quiet close much the same as a eulogy or memorial reading.

The Conclusion: The **conclusion** you choose will depend a great deal on which of the two styles of climax you choose. It must, in either case, draw your important thoughts into a final, meaningful focus. It should leave your audience with a picture which is clear and vivid—one which they will remember whenever this subject is mentioned in the future.

Preparing the Speech for Delivery

672   Once you are satisfied that the written portion of your speech is in its final form, you can write or type your final copy. Follow the suggestions listed below when you type:

1) Always double-space your copy and leave an extra-wide margin at the bottom.
2) Never run a sentence from one page to another.
3) Keep your copy neat and clean.
4) Never abbreviate unless you intend the material to be delivered as an abbreviation. Example: FCC, YMCA, and FBI may be abbreviated because they will be delivered as abbreviations. "The press questioned him this a.m." is not acceptable because you are not going to say *a.m.,* you are going to say *morning.*
5) Number the pages (beginning with page one) in the upper right-hand corner.

Practicing the Delivery

673   You must next turn your attention to the delivery of the speech. The best way to assure a smooth, effective presentation is to practice out loud as often as you can. Try to get an audience of family or friends to listen to you. They can offer a more realistic setting than an empty room and can also offer suggestions for improvement. If you cannot find an audience, a reasonable substitute would be a recorder. By listening to your playback (or listening and watching if you have access to video tape equipment), you will be in a better position to make improvements in your written copy as well as in your delivery technique.

Marking for Interpretation

674   As you decide what changes you want to make, note them on your speech copy. This applies to changes in delivery technique as well. Noting delivery techniques on your paper is called "marking your copy" and involves using a set of symbols to represent voice patterns. These special symbols will remind you to pause in certain key places during your presentation, to emphasize a certain word or phrase, or to add color to a word which might otherwise be misunderstood, and so on. Below is a sample list of copy-marking symbols:

675

Copy-Marking Symbols
Inflection *(arrows)* . . . . for a rise in pitch, for a drop in pitch.
Emphasis *(underlining)* . . . . for additional <u>drive</u> or <u>force</u>.
Color *(curved line)* . . . . for additional feeling or intonation.
Pause *(dash, diagonal, ellipsis)* . . . . for a pause—or / break . . . in the flow.
Rate *(hyphen)* . . . . for a rapid-or-connected-rate.

Marking for Pronunciation

676   Whenever you are unsure of the correct pronunciation of a word, look it up in the dictionary. There is no quicker or surer way to lose credibility as a speaker than to mispronounce a key word. Each word in a dictionary is labeled with special marks (called *diacritical markings)* which show you the correct way to say a word. Copy this diacritically marked word immediately following the difficult word on your speech copy. You can refer to these markings when you get to that word during your presentation. You should practice saying the word enough so that it sounds natural when you pronounce it.

If you need to know the pronunciation of a word which is not in the dictionary—perhaps a current world figure—ask a teacher or librarian to help you with the pronunciation. If he pronounces it for you but does not have the diacritical markings, copy the word phonetically (spelled as it sounds). To do this, you will need a standard set of phonetic symbols which you can use whenever this particular situation arises. The guide below is one which is used by broadcasters who face this very problem nearly every day. This guide may also work well for you. *Note:* For sounds not listed here, use the standard alphabet.

Phonetic Guide

AH as in father	*E* as in red	*OO* as in school
A as in animal	*EE* as in kneel	*UH* as in stuff
EH as in fair	*I* as in fin	*ZH* as in rouge
AY as in bake	*Y* as in dime	*J* as in giraffe
	OH as in toe	

677 Below is an actual student speech marked for interpretation and pronunciation:

Student Editorial: Pet Peeve

As far as I'm concerned, it's already too late to talk about Union High School students and their study halls. I believe changes should have been made long ago. Unluckily, we're still talking.

A relatively large portion of this school's student population / have gone through the process of receiving a pass, going to the principal's office, and being confronted with evidence proving they have skipped study hall. It's obvious to me that a great deal of effort is being exerted by students and the administration / to avoid being caught and attempting to catch, respectively. (REE SPEK TIV LEE)

With all the time and trouble both sides are going to, you'd expect someone to suggest a solution to the problem. But no one seems to care that much about why students skip study hall. The big concern is in rounding them up and getting them back in. I suspect that if you were to take the time to ask students why they skip, you would hear a great many tell you it's because the study halls are useless and boring. I feel they'd be right.

It's time we stop "dealing with skippers"; it's time we stop complaining about the people who skip; and, above all else, it's time we stop avoiding the real problem and start looking at why skipping occurs in the first place.

The administration, school board, and students have spent too much time worrying about the insignificant aspects of the skipping issue / and too little time on the problem itself. Continued neglect won't make skipping go away; reasonable solutions will.

Evaluating Your Speech

678 As you continue to prepare the delivery portion of your speech, remember to review the voice characteristics necessary for effective speaking. The **Speech Evaluation Form** which follows (679) can serve as a reminder of the things you should or should not do when delivering a speech. Following the evaluation form is a list of **Speech Terms** which you can refer to when reviewing the aspects of voice which are important in a speech.

Speech Evaluation Form

Speaker _____ Date_____

Title/Subject of Presentation_____

	Rating	Comments
Subject Significant topic? Clear purpose? Appropriate to the audience?		
Research/Analysis Full investigation? Clear and logical analysis? Sources documented?		
Organization Introduction as an attention-getter? Introduction states purpose/links? Body logically arranged? Appropriate conclusion?		
Language Suited to the audience? Clear and direct? Original and appealing? Vivid word picture? Appropriate tone?		
Stylistic Technique Use of effective repetition/parallelism? Appeal to emotion/logic? Call for involvement? Anecdotes/Analogies? Figurative language?		
Delivery Appropriate action and gestures? Eye contact? Loudness and quality of voice? Pronunciation/Enunciation? Drive/Pause/Rate/Color?		
Overall Effectiveness Attention maintained? Enthusiasm and concern shown throughout? Purpose met?		
FINAL RATING		

Evaluated by_____

Speech Terms

ACOUSTICS: The science of sound or the way the walls, floor, ceiling, and other parts of a room react to sound. The quality of speech sounds depends in part on the acoustics of the room in which they are produced.

AD LIB: Making up or composing the words to a speech as you deliver it.

ARTICULATION: The uttering of speech sounds in a clear, distinct manner. The tongue, lips, teeth, cheeks, palate, and uvula all partake in the articulation process.

CADENCE: The rhythm or flow of a speech. A smooth, even flow is described as being *legato;* a bouncy, jerky flow is called *staccato.*

CLIMAX: The high point or peak in a speech.

COLOR: The emotional treatment given certain key words in a speech to convey the special meanings or connotations of those words. The voice is greatly inflected and the force usually increased to accomplish this distinct vocal appeal.

COMMENTARY: An organized group of remarks or observations on a particular subject; an interpretation, usually of a complex social issue.

CONTINUITY: The state or quality of being continuous or unbroken. A speech with continuity will move smoothly from the introduction through the conclusion by way of effective linking or transitional devices.

EDITORIAL: A carefully organized piece of writing in which an opinion is expressed.

EMPHASIS: Giving more attention to a particular word or phrase than to the others. This can be done by varying the force, pace, pitch, or color of the voice.

ENUNCIATION: The clearness or crispness of a person's voice. If a speaker's enunciation is good, it will be easy to understand each sound or word he creates.

EYE CONTACT: The communicating a speaker does with his eyes during a speech. It is very important that a speaker establish early, sincere eye contact with his audience so that full communication can take place.

FORCE (Drive): The amount of pressure or punch behind the speaker's voice; *loudness.*

GESTURE: The motion a speaker uses to emphasize a point. Hand and facial gestures are usually effective additions to a speech, although they can also be visual distractions and take away from the speaker's effectiveness. The important thing to remember is to keep gestures as natural as possible and not to overuse them.

INFLECTION: The rising and falling in the pitch of the voice.

MONOTONE: A voice which is unchanging in inflection or color; *dullness.*

ORATORY: The art of public speaking.

PACE: The rate of movement of a speech. It is often a combination of rates, selected for their appropriateness to the message and the audience.

PAUSE: The momentary stopping in a speech to give additional emphasis to a particular word, phrase, or idea.

PITCH: The highness or lowness of a voice. By properly varying the pitch of the voice, the speaker can emphasize or color the words in his script.

PRESENCE: The sense of closeness of the speaker to his audience. If a speaker is sincere and open with his audience, his degree of presence or believability will be high.

PROJECTION: Directing or throwing the voice so it can be heard at a distance.

RATE: The speed (fastness or slowness) of the speech pattern.

READ-Y (reed e): The term used to describe a speech which sounds so much like it is being read it becomes distracting.

REPETITION: The repeating of words or phrases to add a sense of balance and rhythm to a piece of writing, as in Lincoln's *Gettysburg Address* " . . . of the people, by the people, and for the people."

RESONANCE: The prolonging of a sound through vibration. In the speech process, the resonance is intensified by the chest, throat, and nose. The quality of the resulting sound will be determined by whichever of these three cavities acts as the primary resonator.

SCRIPT (Manuscript): The written copy of the speech used during a presentation.

SPEECH: The process of communicating with the voice through a combination of breathing, resonating, and articulating.

STAGE FRIGHT: The tension or nervousness a speaker feels when he is preparing to deliver or is actually delivering a speech.

Journalism Terms

Print Terms

ANGLE: A particular point of view or way of looking at a subject.

BANNER: One-line head extending all the way across the top of the page.

BEAT: A specified territory regularly covered by a reporter.

BLEED: Illustration that extends beyond usual margins, generally to the edge of the page.

BOLDFACE: Heavier version of a type style (abbreviated *bf*): **boldface.**

BY-LINE: Credit line at the beginning of a story telling who wrote it.

CAPTION: Description or comment that goes with an illustration. Also called a *cutline.*

COPYREADER (COPY EDITOR): Person who corrects or improves stories to get them ready for typesetting.

CROPPING: Marking or cutting a photo to eliminate parts of it that do not suit the purpose for which it is being used.

CUTLINE: See *Caption.*

DISPLAY TYPE: Any type larger than body type—used mostly for headlines and ads.

DOWNSTYLE: In headlines, using normal sentence capitalization rather than capitalizing the first letter of all important words as is done in book titles.

DUMMY: Diagram of a particular page layout or of general appearance of a publication.

EDITOR: Person who prepares copy for publication. Also, a person with a defined area of staff leadership which may not include working with copy.

EDITORIAL: An article which reflects the opinion of the writer or the management of the news organization.

EDITORIALIZING: The fault of injecting personal opinion into a news story.

EVERGREEN STORIES: Items which can be held back when space is unavailable and used when they are needed.

FEATURE: A story which appeals to an audience because of the human interest of its contents rather than the importance of its content.

FLAG: The *nameplate* or printed inscription containing the name of the newspaper.

FLUSH-LEFT or FLUSH-RIGHT: Copy or headlines aligned with the margin, left or right.

FOLIO: Page number.

FOLIO LINE: Information run with the page number, usually including the publication's name, the date of publication, and sometimes information about the contents of the page.

FONT: An assortment of one style or size of type.

GRABBER: An attention-getting lead.

GUTTER: Space between columns; more often, the wider space where adjoining pages meet.

HALFTONE: A negative of a photo or art which converts the image into dots suitable for printing. On the final page, large black dots will appear black, medium sized ones appear as shades of gray, and small ones look white.

INVERTED-PYRAMID STRUCTURE: A method of organizing a news story such that the most important information is in the lead; the remaining information is presented in order of decreasing importance.

ITALIC: Type which slants to the right: *italic.*

JUMP: To continue a story on another page.

JUMP HEAD: Headline over a jumped part of a story.

JUMP LINE: Brief information telling where to find the rest of a continued story.

JUSTIFIED: Type with lines adjusted to be flush with both left and right margins. Unjustified type, with only the left margin flush, is called *ragged right.*

KICKER: A smaller emphasis headline appearing above a larger head.

LEAD (Pronounced *leed*): Opening of a story, usually a summary of its most significant information.

LIBEL: Written or printed material that defames a person's character or exposes him to ridicule.

MASTHEAD: The identification statement usually placed on the editorial page. It includes the *nameplate*, policy statement, key personnel, and so on.

MUG SHOT: A photo showing someone's face or sometimes head and shoulders.

PASTEUP: A layout sheet with copy and heads pasted down and positions for illustrations indicated.

PICA: Unit of measure used by printer and page designers. Six picas roughly equal an inch.

POINT: A printer's unit used to designate the height of a line of copy or headline or the thickness of a ruling line; 12 points equals one pica and 72 points equals one inch.

PROOFREADING: Carefully checking printed copy for errors before the publication goes to press.

SERIF: Small finishing stroke at the ends of many letters in some type styles. Styles that do not have such strokes or lines are called *sans-serif* (serif . . . sans-serif).

TOMBSTONING: Placing similar headlines side-by-side (which may cause readers to confuse them).

TYPO: Common abbreviation for typographical error.

X-HEIGHT: The height of a lower-case *x* and thus all letters without vertical strokes extending above or below such letter.

Broadcast Terms

Radio

AMPLIFIER: A device for increasing the power of a radio or television signal.

AUDIO: The sound portion of radio and television (music, voice, sound effects).

BIT: A small part in a show.

BLOOPER: An obvious error in performance by cast or production crew.

BRING IT UP: An expression meaning to increase the volume of the sound.

CALL LETTERS: Initials assigned by the FCC to identify stations (WISN, WLS, WOKY).

CART (Cartridge): A continuous-loop, audio tape recorder with instant cueing.

CHANNEL: Bank of frequencies given by the FCC to each radio and television station for broadcasting. (The number on the dial indicates the frequency.)

CONTEMPORARY: Modern; the "Top 40" format.

CONTINUITY: The script prepared by an author, an advertising agency, or the radio station which ensures the smooth running of the show; the smooth, even flow of a spot or program.

CONTROL BOARD: The panel before which the control engineer sits and which includes the volume indicator and various faders. Also called control panel or mixing panel.

CROSS-FADE: To fade in one sound from one source while sound from another is faded out.

CUE: A signal, verbal or visual, to proceed with action as rehearsed or indicated in the script.

CUE SHEET: An orderly list of program material containing all cues.

CUSHION: The "fill-in" used at the end of a show which runs short of the rehearsal time on the air. Often, the musical theme or mood music is used for this purpose.

CUT: To stop transmission of any part of the program abruptly. Also, the deletion of program material to fit the time schedule.

DEAD AIR: Any place in the program where there is no sound due to slow pickup, fluff, or poor transmission.

DRAMATIC PAUSE: A hesitancy or break in the reading to suggest an emotional reaction or to emphasize a point.

DRESS: A program rehearsed exactly as it is to be broadcast.

DUB: To add sound to a recording. ("Dub it off" is to record all or part of a program.)

EDIT: To revise or alter the content of a program.

EDITORIAL: The expression of an opinion in a carefully organized presentation.

FADE OUT: Slowly decreasing the volume to zero.

FEEDBACK: Howling in a speaker caused by a kickback of sound waves.

FIDELITY: The degree to which a recording sounds like the original.

FORMAT: The type or style of a program.

FREQUENCY: The number of cycles of electromagnetic waves per second. A station is located on the radio dial according to its frequency.

GENERATION: The duplication stage of an audio or video tape. (First generation is the first copy made from the original; the second generation is a copy made from this "first generation" copy, etc.)

I.D.: Station identification.

LEAD-IN: The introduction to each piece of program material.

LEVEL: A voice check to determine the lowest and highest volume of a song, voice, or other sound.

LOG: A record kept by stations and networks of every minute of broadcasting.

MIX: To manipulate the faders on the control board so as to blend two or more program elements together.

OFF MIKE: Speech directed away from the microphone so as to create a "distant" sound.

ON THE NOSE: The signal which indicates the program is running right on schedule or on time.

OPEN COLD: To open a show without one or more of the following: theme, musical introduction, or rehearsal.

PRODUCTION: Building, organizing, and presenting a program.

PSA: Public Service Announcement.

SOUND EFFECTS: Various devices or recordings used to produce lifelike sound imitations.

S.P.: Station promotion.

SPOT: A short announcement usually under one minute.

STAND BY: The signal for all personnel to get ready to go on the air.

STATION BREAK: The pause in regular programming to give local identification of a station, usually on the hour, half-hour, or quarter-hour.

STRETCH: A direction to actors or performers to slow up the pace or to fill time.

TALENT: The collective name for all performers.

TIE-IN: The announcement that connects the program with a commercial or PSA.

Television

ASPECT RATIO: The proportion of picture dimensions in TV; the relation of height (three units of height measurement) to width (four units).

BACKGROUND PROJECTION: Projection of a scene on a translucent screen used as a background for a studio set. Also called a *rear screen projection*.

BLOCKING: Sometimes called a *breakdown*, this is the preliminary working out of the basic pattern of movement and/or camera shots in show or scene.

BOOM: The mechanical structure for moving a suspended microphone overhead. Also, the action of moving a camera crane up or down.

BUSY PICTURE: A picture with so much background detail that it is confusing. It usually spoils the actor's scene since there is a tendency for the viewer to watch the scenery or props instead of the action.

CABLE TV: A system which delivers the television picture directly by wire (cable); CATV.

CLOSED CIRCUIT: A live television program not telecast but shown on monitors or viewing screens for the benefit of a selected audience. Used also for auditions or private showings to a restricted audience.

DOWNSTAGE: "Bring it closer" or move closer to the camera.

DRY RUN: A rehearsal without the use of cameras.

FLATS: Units of scenery for stage use.

FLIP BOARD: Device for manual changing of visuals by dropping or pulling.

HEADROOM: Free space on the TV screen between the top of any figure or a performer's head and the upper boundary of the screen.

LAPEL MIKE: A mike clipped to the lapel or clothing of a performer.

LEADER: Film in advance of a picture used for threading through a projector before the picture or sound starts. Also used on audio-tape.

LIMBO: A subject with a black background.

LOGO: Identifying symbol.

MASK: Used to block out part of the lens for a special effect.

MATTE: Cutout for use in front of lens—foreground scenery.

MONITOR: Equivalent to television receiver (usually in studio).

MONTAGE: Combining several pictures to make one.

MURAL: Scenic backdrops.

PREEMPT: To remove a local program from regular air time to accommodate a network program desiring the same time slot.

PRIME TIME: The most popular air time: Radio, 6:00-9:00 a.m. and 3:00-6:00 p.m.; TV, 8:00-11:00 p.m. E.S.T.

STRIKE: To remove furniture, sets, or props from a scene at a designated cue or time.

SUPER: A superimposition of one picture over another by electronic means.

SWITCH: To switch from one camera to another, from one studio to another, or from one source to another. Often called *take*.

SYNC: Synchronization of action and lip movement with voice and sound. Also the pulses which lock the scanning beam in the camera pickup tube with that in the receiver.

TALK BACK: The loudspeaker circuit from the director to the studio.

TALLY LIGHT: The red light on front of camera to indicate whether that camera is on the air.

TRAFFIC: The scheduling of programs and commercials.

TREATMENT: How a topic, theme, or television show should be handled.

VCR: Video cassette recorder.

VOICE OVER: When the announcer's voice is broadcast but he is not shown. Most often refers to commercials with film clips or slides as video.

VTR: Video tape recording.

TABLES, MAPS, LISTS

Using the World Maps

The following index alphabetically lists the countries that can be located on the handbook maps. Because some of the countries are small and difficult to find, the latitude and longitude specifications for each are also listed. Latitude and longitude refer to imaginary lines that mapmakers use. When used together, these lines will be helpful in locating any point on Earth.

The imaginary lines that go from east to west around the Earth are called lines of **latitude.** Latitude is measured in degrees with the equator being 0 degrees (0º). From the equator, latitude is measured from 0º to 90º North (the North Pole) and from 0º to 90º South (the South Pole). On a map, latitude numbers are printed along the left- and right-hand sides.

Imaginary lines that run from the North Pole to the South Pole are lines of **longitude.** Longitude is also measured in degrees. The prime meridian, which passes through Greenwich, England, is 0º longitude. Lines east of the prime meridian are called *east longitude.* Lines west of the prime meridian are called *west longitude,* and the two meet exactly opposite the prime meridian at 180º longitude. On a map, longitude numbers are printed at the top and bottom.

The latitude and longitude numbers of a place are sometimes called its *coordinates*. In each set of coordinates, latitude is given first, then longitude. To locate a spot on a map using its coordinates, find the spot where the given lines cross. The place will be at or near this point. Take, for example, the country of Australia, which has coordinates 25º S, 135º E. After finding the equator (0º), locate the line 25º south of that. Next, find the line of prime meridian (0º), and then the line 135º to its east. The point at which these two imaginary lines intersect pinpoints Australia.

Index to World Maps

Country	Latitude	Longitude	Country	Latitude	Longitude
Afghanistan	33º N	65º E	Cambodia	13º N	105º E
Albania	41º N	20º E	Cameroon	6º N	12º E
Algeria	28º N	3º E	Canada	60º N	95º W
Andorra	42º N	1º E	Cape Verde	16º N	24º W
Angola	12º S	18º E	Central African Rep.	7º N	21º E
Antigua and Barbuda	17º N	61º W	Chad	15º N	19º E
Argentina	34º S	64º W	Chile	30º S	71º W
Australia	25º S	135º E	China	35º N	105º E
Austria	47º N	13º E	Colombia	4º N	72º W
Bahamas	24º N	76º W	Comoros	12º S	44º E
Bahrain	26º N	50º E	Congo	1º S	15º E
Bangladesh	24º N	90º E	Costa Rica	10º N	84º W
Barbados	13º N	59º W	Cuba	21º N	80º W
Belgium	50º N	4º E	Cyprus	35º N	33º E
Belize	17º N	88º W	Czechoslovakia	49º N	17º E
Benin	9º N	2º E	Denmark	56º N	10º E
Bhutan	27º N	90º E	Djibouti	11º N	43º E
Bolivia	17º S	65º W	Dominica	15º N	61º W
Botswana	22º S	24º E	Dominican Republic	19º N	70º W
Brazil	10º S	55º W	Ecuador	2º S	77º W
Brunei	4º N	114º E	Egypt	27º N	30º E
Bulgaria	43º N	25º E	El Salvador	14º N	89º W
Burkina Faso/U.Volta	13º N	2º W	Equatorial Guinea	2º N	9º E
Burma	22º N	98º E	Ethiopia	8º N	38º E
Burundi	3º S	30º E	Fiji	19º S	174º E

Country	Latitude	Longitude	Country	Latitude	Longitude
Finland	64° N	26° E	Norway	62° N	10° E
France	46° N	2° E	Oman	22° N	58° E
Gabon	1° S	11° E	Pakistan	30° N	70° E
The Gambia	13° N	16° W	Panama	9° N	80° W
East Germany	52° N	12° E	Papua New Guinea	6° S	147° E
West Germany	51° N	9° E	Paraguay	23° S	58° W
Ghana	8° N	2° W	Peru	10° S	76° W
Greece	39° N	22° E	Philippines	13° N	122° E
Greenland	70° N	40° W	Poland	52° N	19° E
Grenada	12° N	61° W	Portugal	39° N	8° W
Guatemala	15° N	90° W	Qatar	25° N	51° E
Guinea	11° N	10° W	Romania	46° N	25° E
Guinea-Bissau	12° N	15° W	Rwanda	2° S	30° E
Guyana	5° N	59° W	St. Christopher & Nevis	17° N	62° W
Haiti	19° N	72° W	Saint Lucia	14° N	61° W
Honduras	15° N	86° W	Saint Vincent		
Hungary	47° N	20° E	and the Grenadines	13° N	61° W
Iceland	65° N	18° W	San Marino	44° N	12° E
India	20° N	77° E	Sao Tome and Principe	1° N	7° E
Indonesia	5° S	120° E	Saudi Arabia	25° N	45° E
Iran	32° N	53° E	Scotland	57° N	5° W
Iraq	33° N	44° E	Senegal	14° N	14° W
Ireland	53° N	8° W	Seychelles	5° S	55° E
Israel	31° N	35° E	Sierre Leone	8° N	11° W
Italy	42° N	12° E	Singapore	1° N	103° E
Ivory Coast	8° N	5° W	Solomon Islands	8° S	159° E
Jamaica	18° N	77° W	Somalia	10° N	49° E
Japan	36° N	138° E	South Africa	30° S	26° E
Jordan	31° N	36° E	Spain	40° N	4° W
Kenya	1° N	38° E	Sri Lanka	7° N	81° E
Kiribati	0° N	175° E	Sudan	15° N	30° E
North Korea	40° N	127° E	Suriname	4° N	56° W
South Korea	36° N	128° E	Swaziland	26° S	31° E
Kuwait	29° N	47° E	Sweden	62° N	15° E
Laos	18° N	105° E	Switzerland	47° N	8° E
Lebanon	34° N	36° E	Syria	35° N	38° E
Lesotho	29° S	28° E	Taiwan	23° N	121° E
Liberia	6° N	10° W	Tanzania	6° S	35° E
Libya	27° N	17° E	Thailand	15° N	100° E
Liechtenstein	47° N	9° E	Togo	8° N	1° E
Luxembourg	49° N	6° E	Tonga	20° S	173° W
Madagascar	19° S	46° E	Trinidad/Tobago	11° N	61° W
Malawi	13° S	34° E	Tunisia	34° N	9° E
Malaysia	2° N	112° E	Turkey	39° N	35° E
Maldives	2° N	70° E	Tuvala	8° S	179° E
Mali	17° N	4° W	Uganda	1° N	32° E
Malta	36° N	14° E	USSR	60° N	80° E
Mauritania	20° N	12° W	United Arab Emirates	24° N	54° E
Mauritius	20° S	57° E	United Kingdom	54° N	2° W
Mexico	23° N	102° W	United States	38° N	97° W
Monaco	43° N	7° E	Uruguay	33° S	56° W
Mongolia	46° N	105° E	Vanuatu	17° S	170° E
Morocco	32° N	5° W	Venezuela	8° N	66° W
Mozambique	18° S	35° E	Vietnam	17° N	106° E
Namibia	22° S	17° E	Wales	53° N	3° W
Nauru	1° S	166° E	Western Samoa	10° S	173° W
Nepal	28° N	84° E	North Yemen	15° N	44° E
Netherlands	52° N	5° E	South Yemen	15° N	48° E
New Zealand	41° S	174° E	Yugoslavia	44° N	19° E
Nicaragua	13° N	85° W	Zaire	4° S	25° E
Niger	16° N	8° E	Zambia	15° S	30° E
Nigeria	10° N	8° E	Zimbabwe	20° S	30° E
Northern Ireland	55° N	7° W			

THE WORLD
MERCATOR PROJECTION
Capitals of Countries..............●

Copyright by C.S. HAMMOND & Co., N.Y.

NORTH AMERICA

LAMBERT AZIMUTHAL EQUAL-AREA
PROJECTION

SCALE OF MILES

SCALE OF KILOMETERS

Capitals of Countries
International Boundaries
Canals

© Copyright HAMMOND INCORPORATED, Maplewood, N.J.

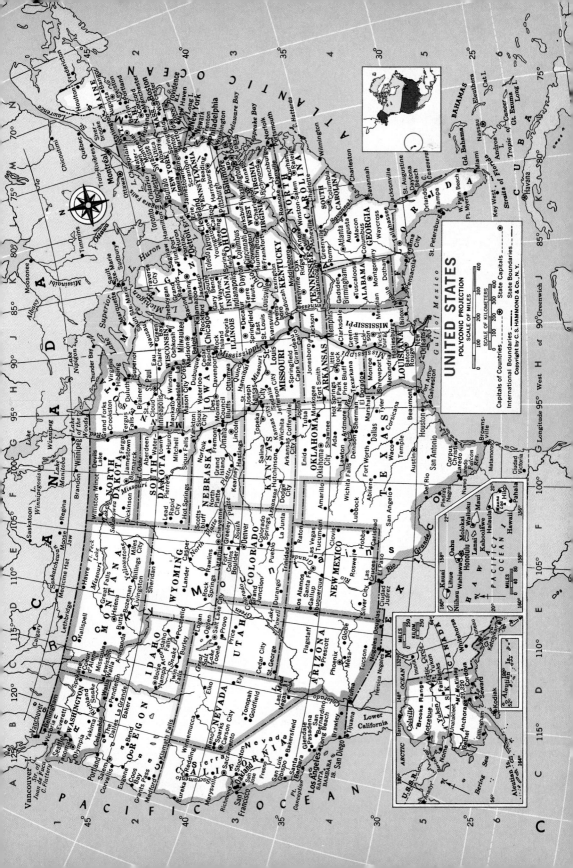

SOUTH AMERICA

LAMBERT AZIMUTHAL
EQUAL-AREA PROJECTION

MILES
0   200   400   600

KILOMETERS
0 200 400 600

Capitals of Countries .... ⊚
International Boundaries .... —·—·—

© Copyright by HAMMOND INCORPORATED, Maplewood, N.J.

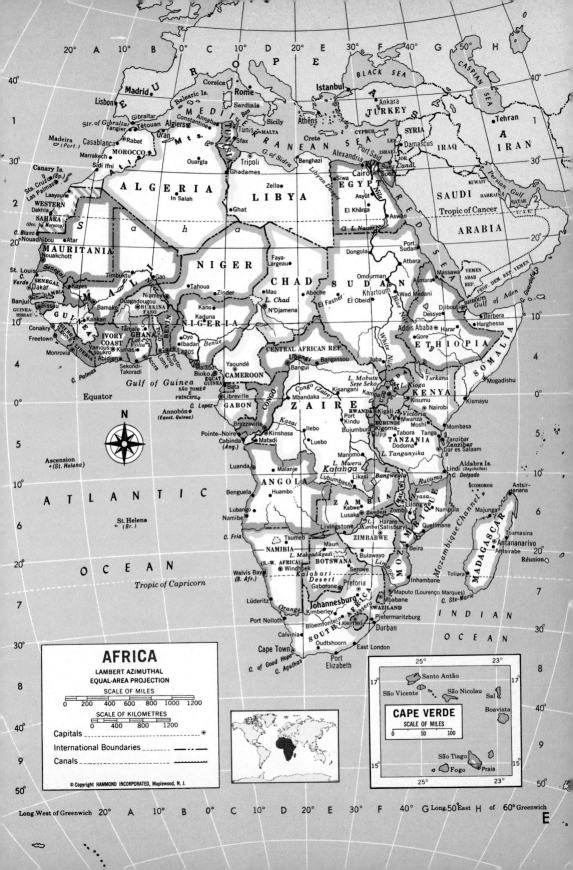

AFRICA

LAMBERT AZIMUTHAL
EQUAL-AREA PROJECTION

SCALE OF MILES

0   200 400 600 800   1200

SCALE OF KILOMETRES

0   400   800   1200

Capitals _____ ⦿

International Boundaries _____ ▬▬

Canals _____

© Copyright HAMMOND INCORPORATED, Maplewood, N.J.

CAPE VERDE

SCALE OF MILES

0   50   100

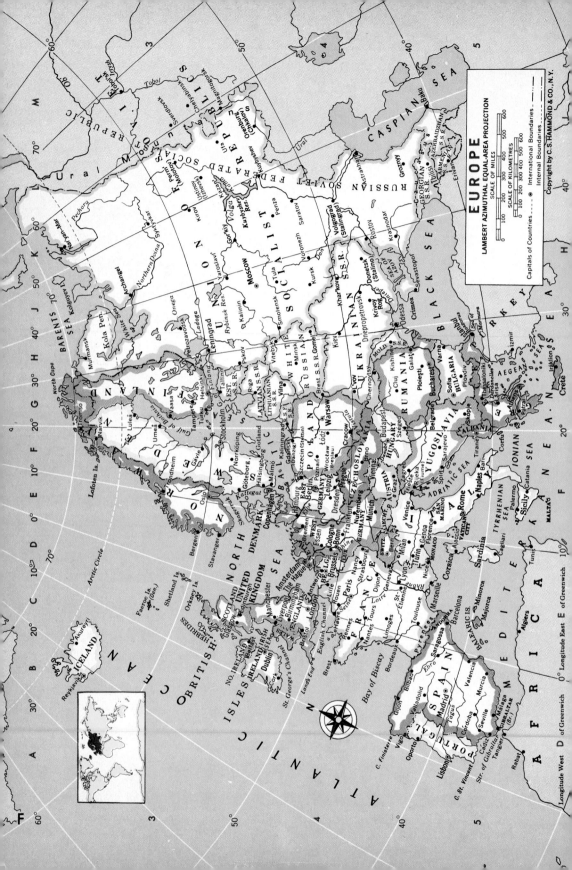

EUROPE
LAMBERT AZIMUTHAL EQUAL-AREA PROJECTION

SCALE OF MILES

100   200   300   400   500   600

SCALE OF KILOMETRES

100   200   300   400   500   600

Capitals of Countries ----- ⊛   International Boundaries -·-·-·-

Internal Boundaries ---------

Copyright by C.S. HAMMOND & CO., N.Y.

ATLANTIC OCEAN

GREENLAND

North Pole

A B C D E F G H I J K L M
20 40 60 80 100 120 140 160 180

ARCTIC OCEAN

UNITED STATES
ALASKA

BERING SEA

ALEUTIAN IS.

Iceland

Svalbard

Komandorskiye Is.

BRITISH ISLES

NORTH SEA

BALTIC SEA

London
Paris
Berlin
Vienna
Warsaw
Kiev
Moscow
Leningrad

NOVAYA ZEMLYA

BARENTS SEA

SEVERNAYA ZEMLYA

KARA SEA

LAPTEV SEA

NEW SIBERIAN IS.

EAST SIBERIAN SEA

Anadyr'

Kolyma

Petropavlovsk-Kamchatskiy

Koryaksk

OKHOTSK

Magadan

KURIL IS. (U.S.S.R.)

Sakhalin I.

3

60°

2

80°

2

60°

3

EUROPE

UNION OF SOVIET SOCIALIST REPUBLICS

Nordvik

Arctic Circle

Lena

Dudinka

Salekhard

Tura

Yakutsk

Srednekolymsk

SEA

Hokkaido

40°

BLACK SEA

TURKEY
Istanbul
Ankara
Izmir Adana
Erzurum

CYPRUS
SYRIA
Aleppo
Mosul

Beirut
Damascus
Jerusalem
JORDAN
Cairo

AFRICA

RED SEA

Mecca
Jidda
Medina
SAUDI ARABIA
Riyadh
Hofuf
KUWAIT
BAHRAIN
QATAR
U. ARAB EMIR.

YEMEN ARAB REP.
San'a
PEOP. DEM. REP. YEMEN
Hodeida
Ta'izz
Aden G. of Aden
Mukalla
Djibouti
Socotra (P.D.R. Yemen)

ARABIAN SEA

Khanty-Mansiysk
Perm'
Sverdlovsk
Chelyabinsk
Magnitogorsk
Ural'sk
Gur'yev
Ob'

Omsk
Tomsk
Novosibirsk
Novokuznetsk
Barnaul
Semipalatinsk
Karaganda

L. Balkhash
Aral Sea
Kzyl-Orda
Alma-Ata
Frunze
Tashkent
Bukhara
Samarkand
Kokand
Krasnovodsk
Ashkhabad
Meshed

CASPIAN SEA

Baku
Tbilisi
Tabriz
Tehran
IRAN
Isfahan
Kerman
Shiraz
Bandar Abbas
Sharjah
G. of Oman
Muscat
Gwadar

IRAQ
Baghdad
Basra

Irtysh
Yenisey

Krasnoyarsk
Kirensk

L. Baykal
Ulan-Ude
Irkutsk
Chita

Skovorodino

Amur
Blagoveshchensk
Komsomol'sk
Khabarovsk

Nikolayevsk

SEA OF JAPAN

Vladivostok

Harbin
Changchun
Qiqihar

MANCHURIA

Shenyang
Dalian
Dandong

KOREA
P'yongyang
Seoul
Pusan

YELLOW SEA

JAPAN
Sapporo
Honshu
Sendai
Niigata
Tokyo
Yokohama
Nagoya
Kyoto
Osaka
Kobe
Hiroshima
Nagasaki
Kyushu
Shikoku

Tropic of Cancer

40°

MONGOLIA
Uliastay
Hovd
Ulaanbaatar

INNER MONGOLIA

Gobi

GREAT WALL

Peking (Beijing)
Tianjin
Jinan
Qingdao

Nanjing
Shanghai
Hangzhou

EAST CHINA SEA

RYUKYU IS. (Jap.)

4

AFGHANISTAN
Herat
Kabul
Kandahar
Quetta
Kalat
PAKISTAN
Islamabad
Lahore

Srinagar

SINKIANG
Aksu
Ürümqi
Shache
Hotan
Lop Nur

Garyarsa
Lhasa
TIBET

CHINA

Yumen
Jiuquan
Lanzhou
Xi'an
Kaifeng

Huang (Hwang)
Chang (Yangtze)

Chongqing
Wuhan
Changsha
Guiyang
Kunming
Mengzi
Guilin
Xiamen
Fuzhou
Canton

Taipei
Taiwan (Formosa)

GRAND CANAL

20°

New Delhi
Delhi
Jaipur
Kanpur
Lucknow
Varanasi
Patna

Kathmandu
NEPAL
BHUTAN

Brahmaputra
Ganges

Himalaya

Dhaka
BANGLA DESH

Mandalay
Myitkyina

BURMA
Hainan

G. of Tonkin

SOUTH CHINA SEA

INDIA
Ahmadabad
Indore
Nagpur
Bombay
Daman
Poona
Hyderabad
Panjim
Bangalore
Madras
Pondicherry
Karikal
Madurai
Cannanore (Laccadive) Is. (India)
Mahe

Calcutta
Chandernagore
Sittwe

Rangoon
Moulmein

Yanam

Chittagong

Vientiane
THAIL'D
Bangkok
CAMBODIA
Phnom Penh
VIETNAM
Hanoi
Haiphong
Hue
Ho Chi Minh City (Saigon)

Palawan

Manila
Luzon
PHILIPPINES
Mindoro
Samar
Leyte

Davao
Mindanao

5

SRI LANKA (CEYLON)
Colombo
Kandy
Nicobar Is. (India)
Andaman Is. (India)
G. of Thailand

BAY OF BENGAL

George Town
Str. of Malacca
MALAYA
Kuala Lumpur
SINGAPORE
Medan
Kuching
SARAWAK
SABAH
Kota Kinabalu
BRUNEI
Borneo
Manado
CELEBES SEA

MALDIVES
Male

Equator

INDIAN OCEAN

SEYCHELLES

Diego Garcia
BRIT. IND. OC. TERR.

Padang
Sumatra
Palembang
Banjarmasin
Jakarta
JAVA SEA
Surabaya
Java
Sumbawa
FLORES
Celebes
Ujung Pandang
FLORES SEA
Timor
INDONESIA
SUNDA IS.

6

MADAGASCAR

Cocos Is. (Austr.)

Christmas I. (Austr.)

Tropic of Capricorn

Broome

AUSTRALIA

20°

20°

Perth

7

N

SE

S

N

MALDIVES

ASIA
LAMBERT AZIMUTHAL
EQUAL-AREA PROJECTION
SCALE OF MILES
0 300 600 900 1200
SCALE OF KILOMETERS
0 300 600 900 1200
Capitals of Countries .... ⊛
International Boundaries .... _ _ _
Canals ....

© Copyright HAMMOND INCORPORATED, Maplewood, N.J.

40°

E

60°

F

Longitude 80° East of G Greenwich 100°

H

120°

J G

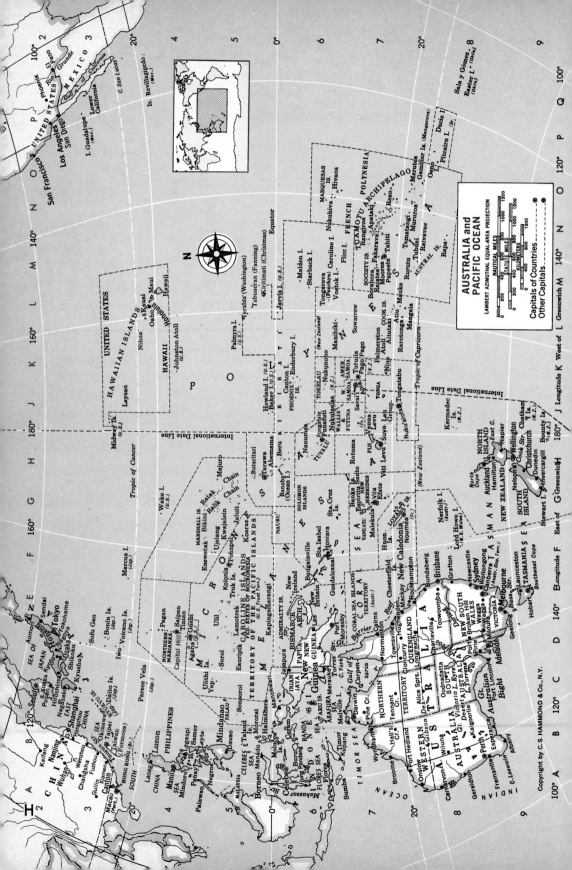

AUSTRALIA and
PACIFIC OCEAN

LAMBERT AZIMUTHAL EQUAL-AREA PROJECTION

NAUTICAL MILES

STATUTE MILES

KILOMETERS

Capitals of Countries .... ⊛
Other Capitals .... •

Copyright by C.S. HAMMOND & Co., N.Y.

Symbols, Signs, Shapes

● rain
* snow
⊠ snow on ground
▲ hail
△ sleet
∨ frostwork

≡ fog
∞ haze; dust haze
⊤ thunder
< sheet lightning
⌐ thunderstorm
\ direction
☉ or ☼ sun
● or ⬤ new moon
☽ first quarter
○ or ☯ full moon
☾ last quarter

MATH

+ plus
− minus
± plus or minus
∓ minus or plus
× multiplied by
÷ divided by
= equal to
≠ or ≄ not equal to
≈ or ≒ nearly equal to
≡ identical with
≢ not identical with
⇌ equivalent
∼ difference
≅ congruent to
> greater than
≯ not greater than
< less than

≮ not less than
≧ or ≥ greater than
   or equal to
≦ or ≤ less than
   or equal to
√ radical; square root
∛ cube root
∜ fourth root
Σ sum
∞ infinity
∫ integral
ƒ function
: is to; ratio
∷ as; proportion
π pi
∴ therefore
∵ because

MISC

© copyright
% per cent
‰ care of
a/c account of
@ at
# number
& or & and
Ω ohm
℞ take (from Latin *Recipe*)
ĀĀ or Ā or āā of each
   (doctor's prescription)
♂ or ♂ male
♀ female
lb pound
℥ ounce
ʒ dram
f℥ fluid ounce
fʒ fluid dram
° degree
′ minute
″ second

SHAPES

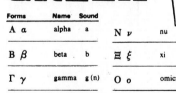

□ rectangle
▱ parallelogram
○ circle
⌒ arc of circle
⊥ equilateral
≙ equiangular

‖ parallel
⊥ perpendicular
∠ angle
∟ right angle
△ triangle
□ square

GREEK

Forms	Name	Sound
A α	alpha	a
B β	beta	b
Γ γ	gamma	g (n)
Δ δ	delta	d
E ε	epsilon	e
Z ζ	zēta	z
H η	ēta	ē
Θ θ	thēta	th
I ι	iota	i
K κ	kappa	k
Λ λ	lambda	l
M μ	mu	m

Forms	Name	Sound
N ν	nu	n
Ξ ξ	xi	x
O o	omicron	o
Π π	pi	p
P ρ	rhō	r (rh)
Σ σ ς	sigma	s
T τ	tau	t
Υ υ	upsilon	u
Φ φ	phi	ph
X χ	khi	kh
Ψ ψ	psi	ps
Ω ω	ōmega	ō

HAND SIGNS

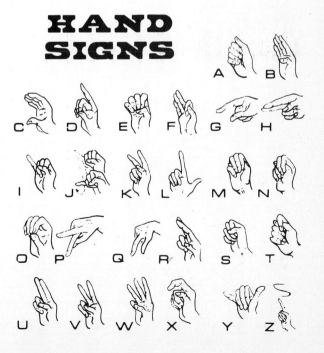

Multiplication and Division Table

A number in the top line (11) multiplied by a number in the extreme left-hand column (12) produces the number where the top line and side line meet (132).

A number in the table (208) divided by the number at the top of the same column (13) results in the number (16) in the extreme left-hand column. A number in the table (208) divided by the number at the extreme left (16) results in the number (13) at the top of the column.

1	2	3	4	5	6	7	8	9	10	11	12	13	14	15	16	17	18	19	20	21	22	23	24	25
2	4	6	8	10	12	14	16	18	20	22	24	26	28	30	32	34	36	38	40	42	44	46	48	50
3	6	9	12	15	18	21	24	27	30	33	36	39	42	45	48	51	54	57	60	63	66	69	72	75
4	8	12	16	20	24	28	32	36	40	44	48	52	56	60	64	68	72	76	80	84	88	92	96	100
5	10	15	20	25	30	35	40	45	50	55	60	65	70	75	80	85	90	95	100	105	115	115	120	125
6	12	18	24	30	36	42	48	54	60	66	72	78	84	90	96	102	108	114	120	126	132	138	144	150
7	14	21	28	35	42	48	56	63	70	77	84	91	98	105	112	119	126	133	130	147	154	161	168	175
8	16	24	32	40	48	56	64	72	80	88	96	104	112	120	128	136	144	152	160	168	176	184	192	200
9	18	27	36	45	54	63	72	81	90	99	108	117	126	135	144	153	162	171	180	189	198	207	216	225
10	20	30	40	50	60	70	80	90	100	110	120	130	140	150	160	170	180	190	200	210	220	230	240	250
11	22	33	44	55	66	77	88	99	110	121	132	143	154	165	176	187	198	209	220	231	242	253	264	275
12	24	36	48	60	72	84	96	108	120	132	144	156	168	180	192	204	216	228	240	252	264	276	288	300
13	26	39	52	65	78	91	104	117	130	143	156	169	182	195	208	221	234	247	260	273	286	299	312	325
14	28	42	56	70	84	98	112	126	140	154	168	182	196	210	224	238	252	266	280	294	308	322	336	350
15	30	45	60	75	90	105	120	135	150	165	180	195	210	225	240	255	270	185	300	315	330	345	360	375
16	32	48	64	80	96	112	128	144	160	176	192	208	224	240	256	272	288	304	320	336	352	368	384	400
17	34	51	68	85	102	119	136	153	170	187	204	221	238	255	272	289	306	323	340	357	374	391	408	425
18	36	54	72	90	108	126	144	162	180	198	216	234	252	270	288	306	324	342	360	378	396	414	432	450
19	38	57	76	95	114	133	152	171	190	209	228	247	266	285	304	323	342	361	380	399	418	437	456	475
20	40	60	80	100	120	140	160	180	200	220	240	260	280	300	320	340	360	380	400	420	440	460	480	500
21	42	63	84	105	126	147	168	189	210	231	252	273	294	315	336	357	378	399	420	441	462	483	504	525
22	44	66	88	110	132	154	176	198	220	242	264	286	308	330	352	374	396	418	440	462	484	506	528	550
23	46	69	92	115	138	161	184	207	230	253	276	299	322	345	368	391	414	437	460	483	506	529	552	575
24	48	72	96	120	144	168	192	216	240	264	288	312	336	360	384	408	432	456	480	504	528	552	576	600
25	50	75	100	125	150	175	200	225	250	275	300	325	350	375	400	425	450	475	500	525	550	575	600	625

Animal Crackers

Animal	Male	Female	Young	Collective	Gestation	Longevity	(Record)
Ass	Jack	Jenny	Foal	Herd	340-385	18-20	(63)
Bear	He-bear	She-bear	Cub	Sleuth	180-240	18-20	(34)
Cat	Tom	Queen	Kitten	Clutter/Clowder	52-65	10-12	(27)
Cattle	Bull	Cow	Calf	Drove/Herd	280	9-12	(25)
Chicken	Rooster	Hen	Chick	Brood/Clutch	21	7-8	(14)
Deer	Buck	Doe	Fawn	Herd	140-250	10-15	(26)
Dog	Dog	Bitch	Pup	Pack	55-70	10-12	(24)
Duck	Drake	Duck	Duckling	Brace/Herd	21-35	10	(15)
Elephant	Bull	Cow	Calf	Herd	515-760	30-40	(98)
Fox	Dog	Vixen	Cub/Kit	Skulk	51-60	8-10	(14)
Goat	Billy	Nanny	Kid	Tribe, Trip	135-163	12	(17)
Goose	Gander	Goose	Gosling	Flock/Gaggle	30		
Horse	Stallion	Mare	Filly/Colt	Herd	304-419	20-25	(50+)
Lion	Lion	Lioness	Cub	Pride	105-111	10	(29)
Monkey	Male	Female	Boy/Girl	Band/Troop	149-179	12-15	(29)
Rabbit	Buck	Doe	Bunny		27-36	6-8	(15)
Sheep	Ram	Ewe	Lamb	Flock/Drove	121-180	12	(16)
Swan	Cob	Pen	Cygnet	Bevy	30		
Swine	Boar	Sow	Piglet	Litter	101-130	10	(15)
Tiger	Tiger	Tigress	Cub		105	19	
Whale	Bull	Cow	Calf	Gam/Pod	276-365	37	
Wolf	Dog	Bitch	Pup	Pack	63	10-12	(16)

Commonly Used Parliamentary Motions

Motion	Purpose	Needs Second	Debatable	Amend-able	Vote	May Interrupt Speaker	Subsidiary Motion Applied
I. Original or Principal Motion							
1. Main Motion (general) Main Motions (specific)	To introduce business	Yes	Yes	Yes	Majority	No	Yes
a. To reconsider	To reconsider previous motion	Yes	When original motion is	No	Majority	Yes	No
b. To rescind	To nullify or wipe out previous action	Yes	Yes	Yes	Majority or two-thirds	No	No
c. To take from the table	To consider tabled motion	Yes	No	No	Majority	No	No
II. Subsidiary Motions							
2. To lay on the table	To defer action	Yes	No	No	Majority	No	No
3. To call for previous question	To close debate and force vote	Yes	No	No	Two-thirds	No	Yes
4. To limit or extend limits of debate	To control time of debate	Yes	No	Yes	Two-thirds	No	Yes
5. To postpone to a certain time	To defer action	Yes	Yes	Yes	Majority	No	Yes
6. To refer to a committee	To provide for special study	Yes	Yes	Yes	Majority	No	Yes
7. To amend	To modify a motion	Yes	When original motion is	Yes (once only)	Majority	No	Yes
8. To postpone indefinitely	To suppress action	Yes	Yes	No	Majority	No	Yes
III. Incidental Motions							
9. To rise to point of order	To correct error in procedure	No	No	No	Decision of chair	Yes	No
10. To appeal from decision of chair	To change decision on procedure	Yes	If motion does not relate to indecorum	No	Majority or tie	Yes	No
11. To suspend rules	To alter existing rules and order of business	Yes	No	No	Two-thirds	No	No
12. To object to consideration	To suppress action	No	No	No	Two-thirds	Yes	No
13. To call for division of house	To secure a countable vote	No	No	No	Majority if chair desires	Yes	Yes
14. To close nominations	To stop nomination of officers	Yes	No	Yes	Two-thirds	No	Yes
15. To reopen nominations	To permit additional nominations	Yes	No	Yes	Majority	No	Yes
16. To withdraw a motion	To remove a motion	No	No	No	Majority	No	No
17. To divide motion	To modify motion	No	No	Yes	Majority	No	Yes
IV. Privileged Motions							
18. To fix time of next meeting	To set time of next meeting	Yes	No, if made when another question is before the assembly	Yes	Majority	No	Yes
19. To adjourn	To dismiss meeting	Yes	No	Yes	Majority	No	No
20. To take a recess	To dismiss meeting for specific time	Yes	No, if made when another question is before the assembly	Yes	Majority	No	Yes
21. To raise question of privilege	To make a request concerning rights of the assembly	No	No	No	Decision of chair	Yes	No
22. To call for orders of the day	To keep assembly to order of business	No	No	No	None unless objection	Yes	No
23. To make a special order	To ensure consideration at specified time	Yes	Yes	Yes	Two-thirds	No	Yes

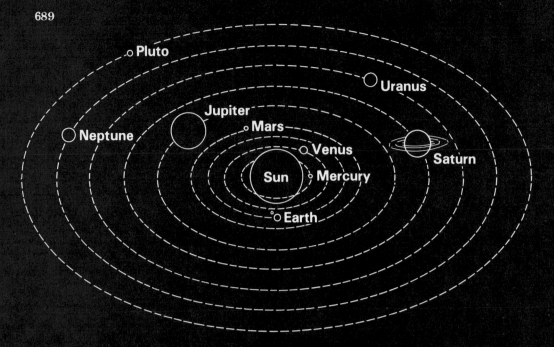

Our solar system is located in the Milky Way Galaxy. Even though this galaxy contains approximately 100 billion stars, our solar system contains only one star—the sun. The sun, which is the center of our solar system, has 9 planets and a myriad of asteroids, meteors, and comets orbiting it. The planets are large, nonluminous bodies which follow fixed elliptical orbits about the sun. (See the illustration above.) The planets are divided into two categories: the terrestrial planets—Mercury, Venus, Earth, Mars, and Pluto—which resemble the Earth in size, chemical composition, and density; and the Jovian planets—Jupiter, Saturn, Uranus, and Neptune—which are much larger in size and have thick, gaseous atmospheres and low densities. (See the table below.)

Planet Profusion

	Sun	Moon	Mercury	Venus	Earth	Mars	Jupiter	Saturn	Uranus	Neptune	Pluto
Orbital Speed (in miles per second)		.6	29.8	21.8	18.5	15.0	8.1	6.0	4.1	3.4	2.9
Rotation on Axis	24 days 16 hr. 48 min.	27 days 7 hr. 38 min.	59 days	243 days	23 hr. 56 min.	1 day 37 min.	9 hr. 50 min.	10 hr. 8 min.	10 hr. 46 min.	18 hr. 12 min.	6 days 9 hr.
Mean Surface Gravity (Earth = 1.00)		0.16	0.33	0.87	1.00	0.37	2.64	1.15	.99	1.27	0.5 (less than)
Density (times that of water)	100	3.3	5.4	5.3	5.5	3.9	1.3	0.7	1.2	1.6	1.0
Mass (times that of earth)	333,000	0.012	0.055	0.8	6×10^{21} metric tons	0.1	318	95	15	17	0.002
Approx. weight of a Human (in pounds)		25	49	130	150	55	396	172	148	190	75
Number of Satellites	9 planets	0	0	0	1	2	16	17	5	2	1
Mean Distance to Sun (in millions of miles)		93.0	36.0	67.22	93.0	141.6	483.5	886.5	1,785	2,793	3,664
Revolution around Sun		365.25 days	88.0 days	224.7 days	365.25 days	686.99 days	11.86 years	29.46 years	84.0 years	164.8 years	247.6 years
Approximate Surface Temperature (degrees Fahrenheit)	27,000,000°	lighted side 200° dark side -230°	lighted side 800° dark side -275°	900°	60°	-60°	-200°	-300°	-355°	-330°	-382°
Diameter (in miles)	867,000	2,155	3,031	7,680	7,921	4,218	88,700	74,940	32,190	30,760	3,600

MOVABLE HOLIDAYS

CHRISTIAN AND SECULAR

Ash Wednesday	Easter	Pentecost	Labor Day	Election Day	Thanksgiving	1st Sunday Advent	
Feb. 20	April 7	May 26	Sept. 2	Nov. 5	Nov. 28	Dec. 1	— 1985
Feb. 12	March 30	May 18	Sept. 1	Nov. 4	Nov. 27	Nov. 30	— 1986
March 4	April 19	June 7	Sept. 7	Nov. 3	Nov. 26	Nov. 29	— 1987
Feb. 17	April 3	May 22	Sept. 5	Nov. 8	Nov. 24	Nov. 27	— 1988
Feb. 8	March 26	May 14	Sept. 4	Nov. 7	Nov. 23	Dec. 3	— 1989
Feb. 28	April 15	June 3	Sept. 3	Nov. 6	Nov. 22	Dec. 2	— 1990
Feb. 13	March 31	May 19	Sept. 2	Nov. 5	Nov. 28	Dec. 1	— 1991
March 4	April 19	June 7	Sept. 7	Nov. 3	Nov. 26	Nov. 29	— 1992

JEWISH

Purim	1st day Passover	1st day Shavuot	1st day Rosh Hashana	Yom Kippur	1st day Sukkot	Simhat Torah	1st day Hanukkah	
March 7	April 6	May 26	Sept. 16	Sept. 25	Sept. 30	Oct. 8	Dec. 8	— 1985
March 25	April 24	June 13	Oct. 4	Oct. 13	Oct. 18	Oct. 26	Dec. 27	— 1986
March 15	April 14	June 3	Sept. 24	Oct. 3	Oct. 8	Oct. 16	Dec. 16	— 1987
March 3	April 2	May 22	Sept. 12	Sept. 21	Sept. 26	Oct. 4	Dec. 4	— 1988
March 21	April 20	June 9	Sept. 30	Oct. 9	Oct. 14	Oct. 22	Dec. 23	— 1989
March 11	April 10	May 30	Sept. 20	Sept. 29	Oct. 4	Oct. 12	Dec. 12	— 1990
Feb. 28	March 30	May 19	Sept. 9	Sept. 18	Sept. 23	Oct. 1	Dec. 2	— 1991
March 14	April 18	June 7	Sept. 28	Oct. 7	Oct. 12	Oct. 20	Dec. 20	— 1992

The Signs of the Zodiac

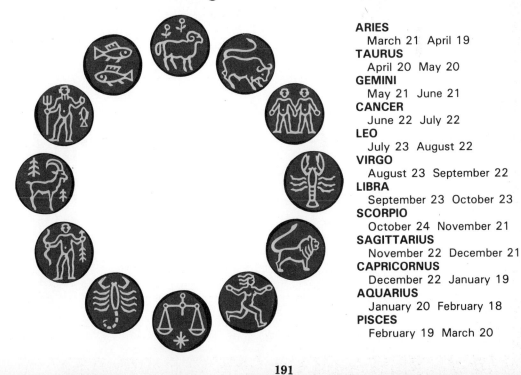

ARIES
March 21 April 19
TAURUS
April 20 May 20
GEMINI
May 21 June 21
CANCER
June 22 July 22
LEO
July 23 August 22
VIRGO
August 23 September 22
LIBRA
September 23 October 23
SCORPIO
October 24 November 21
SAGITTARIUS
November 22 December 21
CAPRICORNUS
December 22 January 19
AQUARIUS
January 20 February 18
PISCES
February 19 March 20

Table of Weights and Measures

Linear Measure

1 inch		= 2.54 centimeters
1 foot	= 12 inches	= 0.3048 meter
1 yard	= 3 feet	= 0.9144 meter
1 rod (or pole or perch)	= 5½ yards or 16½ feet	= 5.029 meters
1 furlong	= 40 rods	= 201.17 meters
1 (statute) mile	= 8 furlongs or 1,760 yards or 5,280 feet	= 1,609.3 meters
1 (land) league	= 3 miles	= 4.83 kilometers

Square Measure

1 square inch		= 6.452 square centimeters
1 square foot	= 144 square inches	= 929 square centimeters
1 square yard	= 9 square feet	= 0.8361 square meter
1 square rod	= 30¼ square yards	= 25.29 square meters
1 acre	= 160 square rods or 4,840 square yards or 43,560 square feet	= 0.4047 hectare
1 square mile	= 640 acres	= 259 hectares or 2.59 square kilometers

Cubic Measure

1 cubic inch		= 16.387 cubic centimeters
1 cubic foot	= 1,728 cubic inches	= 0.0283 cubic meter
1 cubic yard	= 27 cubic feet	= 0.7646 cubic meter
1 cord foot	= 16 cubic feet	
1 cord	= 8 cord feet	= 3.625 cubic meters

Chain Measure

(Gunter's or surveyor's chain)

1 link	= 7.92 inches	= 20.12 centimeters
1 chain	= 100 links or 66 feet	= 20.12 meters
1 furlong	= 10 chains	= 201.17 meters
1 mile	= 80 chains	= 1,609.3 meters

(Engineer's chain)

1 link	= 1 foot	= 0.3048 meter
1 chain	= 100 feet	= 30.48 meters
1 mile	= 52.8 chains	= 1,609.3 meters

Surveyor's (Square) Measure

1 square pole	= 625 square links	= 25.29 square meters
1 square chain	= 16 square poles	= 404.7 square meters
1 acre	= 10 square chains	= 0.4047 hectare
1 square mile or 1 section	= 640 acres	= 259 hectares or 2.59 square kilometers
1 township	= 36 square miles	= 9,324 hectares or 93.24 square kilometers

Nautical Measure

1 fathom	= 6 feet	= 1.829 meters
1 cable's length (ordinary)	= 100 fathoms	

(In the U.S. Navy 120 fathoms or 720 feet = 1 cable's length; in the British Navy 608 feet = 1 cable's length)

1 nautical mile (6,076.10333 feet, by international agreement in 1954) = 10 cables' lengths = 1 nautical mile = 1.852 kilometers
1.1508 statute miles (length of a minute of longitude at the equator) = 1 nautical mile
1 marine league (3.45 statute miles) = 3 nautical miles = 5.56 kilometers
1 degree of a great circle of the earth = 60 nautical miles

Dry Measure

1 pint		= 33.60 cubic inches	= 0.5505 liter
1 quart	= 2 pints	= 67.20 cubic inches	= 1.1012 liters
1 peck	= 8 quarts	= 537.61 cubic inches	= 8.8096 liters
1 bushel	= 4 pecks	= 2,150.42 cubic inches	= 35.2383 liters

Liquid Measure

1 gill		= 7.219 cubic inches	= 0.1183 liter
4 fluid ounces (see next table)			
1 pint	= 4 gills	= 28.875 cubic inches	= 0.4732 liter
1 quart	= 2 pints	= 57.75 cubic inches	= 0.9463 liter
1 gallon	= 4 quarts	= 231 cubic inches	= 3.7853 liters

Apothecaries' Fluid Measure

1 minim		= 0.0038 cubic inch	= 0.0616 milliliter
1 fluid dram	= 60 minims	= 0.2256 cubic inch	= 3.6966 milliliters
1 fluid ounce	= 8 fluid drams	= 1.8047 cubic inches	= 0.0296 liter
1 pint	= 16 fluid ounces	= 28.875 cubic inches	= 0.4732 liter

Circular (or Angular) Measure

60 seconds (″)	= 1 minute (′)
60 minutes	= 1 degree (°)
90 degrees	= 1 quadrant or 1 right angle
4 quadrants or 360 degrees	= 1 circle

Avoirdupois Weight

(The grain, equal to 0.0648 gram, is the same in all three tables of weight)

1 dram or 27.34 grains		= 1.772 grams
1 ounce	= 16 drams or 437.5 grains	= 28.3495 grams
1 pound	= 16 ounces or 7,000 grains	= 453.59 grams
1 hundredweight	= 100 pounds	= 45.36 kilograms
1 ton	= 2,000 pounds	= 907.18 kilograms

Troy Weight

(The grain, equal to 0.0648 gram, is the same in all three tables of weight)

1 carat	= 3.086 grains	= 200 milligrams
1 pennyweight	= 24 grains	= 1.5552 grams
1 ounce	= 20 pennyweights or 480 grains	= 31.1035 grams
1 pound	= 12 ounces or 5,760 grains	= 373.24 grams

Apothecaries' Weight

(The grain, equal to 0.0648 gram, is the same in all three tables of weight)

1 scruple	= 20 grains	= 1.296 grams
1 dram	= 3 scruples	= 3.888 grams
1 ounce	= 8 drams or 480 grains	= 31.1035 grams
1 pound	= 12 ounces or 5,760 grains	= 373.24 grams

Miscellaneous

3 inches	= 1 palm
4 inches	= 1 hand
6 inches	= 1 span
18 inches	= 1 cubit
21.8 inches	= 1 Bible cubit
2½ feet	= 1 military pace

The Metric System

Linear Measure

1 centimeter	= 10 millimeters	= 0.3937 inch
1 decimeter	= 10 centimeters	= 3.937 inches
1 meter	= 10 decimeters	= 39.37 inches or 3.28 feet
1 decameter	= 10 meters	= 393.7 inches
1 hectometer	= 10 decameters	= 328 feet 1 inch
1 kilometer	= 10 hectometers	= 0.621 mile
1 myriameter	= 10 kilometers	= 6.21 miles

Square Measure

1 square centimeter	= 100 square millimeters	= 0.15499 square inch
1 square decimeter	= 100 square centimeters	= 15.499 square inches
1 square meter	= 100 square decimeters	= 1,549.9 square inches or 1.196 square yards
1 square decameter	= 100 square meters	= 119.6 square yards
1 square hectometer	= 100 square decameters	= 2.471 acres
1 square kilometer	= 100 square hectometers	= 0.386 square mile

Capacity Measure

1 centiliter	= 10 milliliters	= .338 fluid ounce
1 deciliter	= 10 centiliters	= 3.38 fluid ounces
1 liter	= 10 deciliters	= 1.0567 liquid quarts or 0.9081 dry quart
1 decaliter	= 10 liters	= 2.64 gallons or 0.284 bushel
1 hectoliter	= 10 decaliters	= 26.418 gallons or 2.838 bushels
1 kiloliter	= 10 hectoliters	= 264.18 gallons or 35.315 cubic feet

Land Measure

1 centare	= 1 square meter	= 1,549.9 square inches
1 are	= 100 centares	= 119.6 square yards
1 hectare	= 100 ares	= 2.471 acres
1 square kilometer	= 100 hectares	= 0.386 square mile

Volume Measure

1 cubic centimeter	= 1,000 cubic millimeters	= .06102 cubic inch
1 cubic decimeter	= 1,000 cubic centimeters	= 61.02 cubic inches
1 cubic meter	= 1,000 cubic decimeters	= 35.314 cubic feet

Weights

1 centigram	= 10 milligrams	= 0.1543 grain
1 decigram	= 10 centigrams	= 1.5432 grains
1 gram	= 10 decigrams	= 15.432 grains
1 decagram	= 10 grams	= 0.3527 ounce
1 hectogram	= 10 decagrams	= 3.5274 ounces
1 kilogram	= 10 hectograms	= 2.2046 pounds
1 myriagram	= 10 kilograms	= 22.046 pounds
1 quintal	= 10 myriagrams	= 220.46 pounds
1 metric ton	= 10 quintals	= 2,204.6 pounds

Roman Numerals

I	1	VIII	8	LX	60	
II	2	IX	9	LXX	70	
III	3	X	10	LXXX	80	
IV	4	XX	20	XC	90	
V	5	XXX	30	C	100	
VI	6	XL	40	D	500	
VII	7	L	50	M	1,000	

V̄	5,000
X̄	10,000
L̄	50,000
C̄	100,000
D̄	500,000
M̄	1,000,000

Handy Conversion Factors

To change	to	multiply by
acres	hectares	.4047
acres	square feet	43,560
acres	square miles	.001562
Celsius	Fahrenheit	*9/5
	* (then add 32)	
centimeters	inches	.3937
centimeters	feet	.03281
cubic meters	cubic feet	35.3145
cubic meters	cubic yards	1.3079
cubic yards	cubic meters	.7646
degrees	radians	.01745
Fahrenheit	Celsius	*5/9
	* (after subtracting 32)	
feet	meters	.3048
feet	miles (nautical)	.0001645
feet	miles (statute)	.0001894
feet/sec.	miles/hr.	.6818
furlongs	feet	660.0
furlongs	miles	.125
gallons (U. S.)	liters	3.7853
grains	grams	.0648
grams	grains	15.4324
grams	ounces avdp.	.0353
grams	pounds	.002205
hectares	acres	2.4710
horsepower	watts	745.7
hours	days	.04167
inches	millimeters	25.4000
inches	centimeters	2.5400
kilograms	pounds avdp or t	2.2046
kilometers	miles	.6214
kilowatts	horsepower	1.341
knots	nautical miles/hr.	1.0
knots	statute miles/hr.	1.151
liters	gallons (U. S.)	.2642
liters	pecks	.1135
liters	pints (dry)	1.8162
liters	pints (liquid)	2.1134
liters	quarts (dry)	.9081
liters	quarts (liquid)	1.0567
meters	feet	3.2808
meters	miles	.0006214
meters	yards	1.0936
metric tons	tons (long)	.9842
metric tons	tons (short)	1.1023
miles	kilometers	1.6093
miles	feet	5,280
miles (nautical)	miles (statute)	1.1516
miles (statute)	miles (nautical)	.8684
miles/hr.	feet/min.	88
millimeters	inches	.0394
ounces avdp.	grams	28.3495
ounces	pounds	.0625
ounces (troy)	ounces (avdp.)	1.09714
pecks	liters	8.8096
pints (dry)	liters	.5506
pints (liquid)	liters	.4732
pounds ap or t	kilograms	.3782
pounds avdp.	kilograms	.4536
pounds	ounces	.1012
quarts (dry)	liters	1.1012
quarts (liquid)	liters	.9463
rods	meters	5.029
rods	feet	16.5
square feet	square meters	.0929
square kilometers	square miles	.3861
square meters	square feet	10.7639
square meters	square yards	1.1960
square miles	square kilometers	2.5900
square yards	square meters	.8361
tons (long)	metric tons	1.1060
tons (short)	metric tons	.9072
tons (long)	pounds	2240
tons (short)	pounds	2000
watts	BTU/hr.	3.4129
watts	horsepower	.001341
yards	meters	.9144
yards	miles	.0005682

Decimal Equivalents of Common Fractions

1/2	.5000	1/32	.0313	3/11	.2727	6/11	.5455
1/3	.3333	1/64	.0156	4/5	.8000	7/8	.8750
1/4	.2500	2/3	.6667	4/7	.5714	7/9	.7778
1/5	.2000	2/5	.4000	4/9	.4444	7/10	.7000
1/6	.1667	2/7	.2857	4/11	.3636	7/11	.6364
1/7	.1429	2/9	.2222	5/6	.8333	7/12	.5833
1/8	.1250	2/11	.1818	5/7	.7143	8/9	.8889
1/9	.1111	3/4	.7500	5/8	.6250	8/11	.7273
1/10	.1000	3/5	.6000	5/9	.5556	9/10	.9000
1/11	.0909	3/7	.4286	5/11	.4545	9/11	.8182
1/12	.0833	3/8	.3750	5/12	.4167	10/11	.9091
1/16	.0625	3/10	.3000	6/7	.8571	11/12	.9167

694

Traffic Signs

Construction area signs are orange. Those signs which do not appear in yellow are black and white, red and white, or a combination of the three.

NO TURN ON RED

YIELD

YIELD

DON'T WALK

WALK

DO NOT ENTER

ONLY

ONLY

NO PASSING ZONE

STOP

MERGE

SLOW MOVING VEHICLE
The SMV sign is triangular, reflective red-orange, and visible day or night.

SCHOOL ZONE
A five-sided sign shaped like an old school house indicates a school crossing or zone.

R R

DO NOT PASS

HILL

Service and Guide Signs

CAMPING

CAMPING

TRAIL

HOSPITAL

BIKE ROUTE

Trail and Bike Route signs are green in color. Other Service and Guide signs are in blue.

NO U TURN

NO LEFT TURN

NO RIGHT TURN

KEEP RIGHT

PED XING

CATTLE XING

SIGNAL AHEAD

DIVIDED HIGHWAY ENDS

DIVIDED HIGHWAY

TWO WAY TRAFFIC

SLIPPERY WHEN WET

BIKE XING

DEER XING

194

Constitution of the United States of America

Note: The original text of the Constitution has been edited to conform to contemporary American usage. The bracketed words have been added to help you locate information more quickly; they are not part of the Constitution.

The oldest federal constitution in existence was framed by a convention of delegates from twelve of the thirteen original states in Philadelphia in May, 1787, Rhode Island failing to send a delegate. George Washington presided over the session, which lasted until September 17, 1787. The draft (originally a preamble and seven Articles) was submitted to all thirteen states and was to become effective when ratified by nine states. It went into effect on the first Wednesday in March, 1789, having been ratified by New Hampshire, the ninth state to approve, on June 21, 1788. The states ratified the Constitution in the following order:

Delaware	December 7, 1787	South Carolina	May 23, 1788
Pennsylvania	December 12, 1787	New Hampshire	June 21, 1788
New Jersey	December 18, 1787	Virginia	June 25, 1788
Georgia	January 2, 1788	New York	July 26, 1788
Connecticut	January 9, 1788	North Carolina	November 21, 1789
Massachusetts	February 6, 1788	Rhode Island	May 29, 1790
Maryland	April 28, 1788		

[Preamble]

We the people of the United States, in order to form a more perfect Union, establish justice, insure domestic tranquility, provide for the common defense, promote the general welfare, and secure the blessings of liberty to ourselves and our posterity, do ordain and establish this Constitution for the United States of America.

Article I

Section 1

[Legislative powers vested in Congress] All legislative powers herein granted shall be vested in a Congress of the United States, which shall consist of a Senate and House of Representatives.

Section 2

1. **[Make-up of the House of Representatives]** The House of Representatives shall be composed of members chosen every second year by the people of the several States, and the electors in each State shall have the qualifications requisite for electors of the most numerous branch of the State Legislature.

2. **[Qualifications of Representatives]** No person shall be a Representative who shall not have attained to the age of twenty-five years, and been seven years a citizen of the United States, and who shall not, when elected, be an inhabitant of that State in which he shall be chosen.

3. **[Apportionment of Representatives and direct taxes—census]** (Representatives and direct taxes shall be apportioned among the several States which may be included within this Union, according to their respective numbers, which shall be determined by adding to the whole number of free persons, including those bound to service for a term of years, and excluding Indians not taxed, three-fifths of all other persons.—*Amended by the 14th Amendment, section 2.)* The actual enumeration shall be made within three years after the first meeting of the Congress of the United States, and within every subsequent term of ten years, in such manner as they shall by law direct. The number of Representatives shall not exceed one for every thirty thousand, but each State shall have at least one Representative; and until such enumeration shall be made, the State of New Hampshire shall be entitled to choose three; Massachusetts, eight; Rhode Island and Providence Plantations, one; Connecticut, five; New York, six; New Jersey, four; Pennsylvania, eight; Delaware, one; Maryland, six; Virginia, ten; North Carolina, five; South Carolina, five; and Georgia, three.

4. **[Filling of vacancies in representation]** When vacancies happen in the representation from any State, the Executive Authority thereof shall issue writs of election to fill such vacancies.

5. **[Selection of officers; power of impeachment]** The House of Representatives shall choose their Speaker and other officers; and shall have the sole power of impeachment.

Section 3

1. **[The Senate]** (The Senate of the United States shall be composed of two Senators from each State, chosen by the Legislature thereof, for six years; and each Senator shall have one vote.—*Amended by the 17th Amendment, section 1.)*

2. **[Classification of Senators; filling of vacancies]** Immediately after they shall be assembled in consequence of the first election, they shall be divided as equally as may be into three classes. The seats of the Senators of the first class shall be vacated at the expiration of the second year, of the second class at the expiration of the fourth year, and of the third class at the expiration of the sixth year, so that one-third may be chosen every second year; and if vacancies happen by resignation, or otherwise, (during the recess of the Legislature of any State,) the Executive thereof may make temporary appointments (until the next meeting of the Legislature, which shall then fill such vacancies.—*Amended by the 17th Amendment.)*

3. **[Qualification of Senators]** No person shall be a Senator who shall not have attained to the age of thirty years, and been nine years a citizen of the United States, and who shall not, when elected, be an inhabitant of that State for which he shall be chosen.

4. **[Vice President to be President of Senate]** The Vice President of the United States shall be President of the Senate, but shall have no vote, unless they be equally divided.

5. **[Selection of Senate officers; President pro tempore)** The Senate shall choose their other officers, and also a President pro tempore, in the absence of the Vice President, or when he shall exercise the office of President of the United States.

6. **[Senate to try impeachments]** The Senate shall have the sole power to try all impeachments. When sitting for that purpose, they shall be on oath or affirmation. When the President of the United States is tried, the Chief Justice shall preside: and no person shall be convicted without the concurrence of two-thirds of the members present.

7. **[Judgment in cases of impeachment]** Judgment in cases of impeachment shall not extend further than to removal from office, and disqualification to hold and enjoy any office of honor, trust, or profit under the United States; but the party convicted shall nevertheless be liable and subject to indictment, trial, judgment, and punishment, according to Law.

Section 4

1. **[Control of congressional elections]** The times, places, and manner of holding elections for Senators and Representatives shall be prescribed in each State by the Legislature thereof; but the Congress may at any time by law make or alter such regulations, except as to the places of choosing Senators.

2. **[Time for assembling of Congress]** The Congress shall assemble at least once in every year, (and such meeting shall be on the first Monday in December, unless they shall by law appoint a different day.—*Amended by the 20th Amendment, section 2.)*

Section 5

1. **[Each House to be the judge of the election and qualifications of its members; regulations as to quorum]** Each House shall be the judge of the elections, returns, and qualifications of its own members, and a majority of each shall constitute a quorum to do business; but a smaller number may adjourn from day to day, and may be authorized to compel the attendance of absent members, in such manner, and under such penalties as each House may provide.

2. **[Each House to determine its own rules]** Each House may determine the rules of its proceedings, punish its members for disorderly behavior, and, with the concurrence of two-thirds, expel a member.

3. **[Journals and yeas and nays]** Each House shall keep a journal of its proceedings, and from time to time publish the same, excepting such parts as may in their judgment require secrecy; and the yeas and nays of the members of either House on any question shall, at the desire of one-fifth of those present, be entered on the journal.

4. **[Adjournment]** Neither House, during the session of Congress, shall, without the consent of the other, adjourn for more than three days, nor to any other place than that in which the two Houses shall be sitting.

Section 6

1. **[Compensation and privileges of members of Congress]** The Senators and Representatives shall receive a compensation for their services, to be ascertained by law, and paid out of the Treasury of the United States. They shall in all cases, except treason, felony, and breach of the peace, be privileged from arrest during their attendance at the session of their respective Houses, and in going to and returning from the same; and for any speech or debate in either House, they shall not be questioned in any other place.

2. **[Incompatible offices; exclusions]** No Senator or Representative shall, during the time for which he was elected, be appointed to any civil office under the authority of the United States, which shall have been created, or the emoluments whereof shall have been increased during such time; and no person holding any office under the United States shall be a member of either House during his continuance in office.

Section 7

1. **[Revenue bills to originate in House]** All bills for raising revenue shall originate in the House of Representatives; but the Senate may propose or concur with amendments as on other bills.

2. **[Manner of passing bills; veto power of President]** Every bill which shall have passed the House of Representatives and the Senate, shall, before it becomes a law, be presented to the President of the United States; if he approve, he shall sign it, but if not he shall return it, with his objections to that House in which it shall have originated, who shall enter the objections at large on their journal, and proceed to reconsider it. If after such reconsideration two-thirds of that House shall agree to pass the bill, it shall be sent, together with the objections, to the other House, by which it shall likewise be reconsidered, and if approved by two-thirds of that House, it shall become a law. But in all such cases the votes of both Houses shall be determined by yeas and nays, and the names of the persons voting for and against the bill shall be entered on the journal of each House, respectively. If any bill shall not be returned by the President within ten days (Sundays excepted) after it shall have been presented to him, the same shall be a law, in like manner as if he had signed it, unless the Congress by their adjournment prevent its return, in which case it shall not be a law.

3. **[Concurrent orders or resolutions to be passed by President]** Every order, resolution, or vote to which the concurrence of the Senate and House of Representatives may be necessary (except on a question of adjournment) shall be presented to the President of the United States; and before the same shall take effect, shall be approved by him, or being disapproved by him, shall be repassed by two-thirds of the Senate and House of Representatives, according to the rules and limitations prescribed in the case of a bill.

Section 8

[General powers of Congress] The Congress shall have the power:

1. **[Taxes, duties, imposts, and excises]** To lay and collect taxes, duties, imposts, and excises, to pay the debts and provide for the common defense and general welfare of the United States; but all duties, imposts, and excises shall be uniform throughout the United States; *(See the 16th Amendment.)*

2. **[Borrowing of money]** To borrow money on the credit of the United States;

3. **[Regulation of commerce]** To regulate commerce with foreign nations, and among the several States, and with the Indian tribes;

4. **[Naturalization and bankruptcy]** To establish a uniform rule of naturalization, and uniform laws on the subject of bankruptcies throughout the United States;

5. **[Money, weights, and measures]** To coin money, regulate the value thereof, and of foreign coin, and fix the standard of weights and measures;

6. **[Counterfeiting]** To provide for the punishment of counterfeiting the securities and current coin of the United States;

7. **[Post offices]** To establish post offices and post roads;

8. **[Patents and copyrights]** To promote the progress of science and useful arts, by securing for limited times to authors and inventors the exclusive right to their respective writings and discoveries;

9. **[Inferior courts]** To constitute tribunals inferior to the Supreme Court;

10. **[Piracies and felonies]** To define and punish piracies and felonies committed on the high seas, and offenses against the law of nations.

11. **[War; marque and reprisal]** To declare war, grant letters of marque and reprisal, and make rules concerning captures on land and water;

12. **[Armies]** To raise and support armies, but no appropriation of money to that use shall be for a longer term than two years;

13. **[Navy]** To provide and maintain a navy;

14. **[Land and naval forces]** To make rules for the government and regulation of the land and naval forces;

15. **[Calling out militia]** To provide for calling forth the militia to execute the laws of the Union, suppress insurrections, and repel invasions.

16. **[Organizing, arming, and disciplining militia]** To provide for organizing, arming, and disciplining the militia, and for governing such part of them as may be employed in the service of the United States, reserving to the States, respectively, the appointment of the officers, and the authority of training the militia according to the discipline prescribed by Congress;

17. **[Exclusive legislation over District of Columbia]** To exercise exclusive legislation in all cases whatsoever, over such district (not exceeding ten miles square) as may, by cession of particular States, and the acceptance of Congress, become the seat of the Government of the United States, and to exercise like authority over all places purchased by the consent of the Legislature of the State in which the same shall be, for the erection of forts, magazines, arsenals, dock-yards, and other needful buildings;—And

18. **[To enact laws necessary to enforce Constitution]** To make all laws which shall be necessary and proper for carrying into execution the foregoing powers, and all other powers vested by this Constitution in the Government of the United States, or in any department or officer thereof.

Section 9

1. **[Migration or importation of certain persons not to be prohibited before 1808]** The migration or importation of such persons as any of the States now existing shall think proper to admit, shall not be prohibited by the Congress prior to the year one thousand eight hundred and eight, but a tax or duty may be imposed on such importation, not exceeding ten dollars for each person.

2. **[Writ of habeas corpus not to be suspended; exception]** The privilege of the writ of habeas corpus shall not be suspended, unless when in cases of rebellion or invasion the public safety may require it.

3. **[Bills of attainder and ex post facto laws prohibited]** No bill of attainder or ex post facto law shall be passed.

4. **[Capitation and other direct taxes]** No capitation, or other direct, tax shall be laid, unless in proportion to the census or enumeration herein before directed to be taken. *(See the 16th Amendment.)*

5. **[Exports not to be taxed]** No tax or duty shall be laid on articles exported from any State.

6. **[No preference to be given to ports of any State; interstate shipping]** No preference shall be given by any regulation of commerce or revenue to the ports of one State over those of another: nor shall vessels bound to, or from, one State, be obliged to enter, clear, or pay duties in another.

7. **[Money, how drawn from treasury; financial statements to be published]** No money shall be drawn from the Treasury, but in consequence of appropriations made by law; and a regular statement and account of the receipts and expenditures of all public money shall be published from time to time.

8. **[Titles of nobility not to be granted; acceptance by government officers of favors from foreign powers]** No title of nobility shall be granted by the United States: and no person holding any office of profit or trust under them, shall, without the consent of the Congress, accept of any present, emolument, office, or title, of any kind whatever, from any king, prince, or foreign state.

Section 10

1. **[Limitations of the powers of the several States]** No state shall enter into any treaty, alliance, or confederation; grant letters of marque and reprisal; coin money; emit bills of credit; make anything but gold and silver coin a tender in payment of debts; pass any bill of attainder, ex post facto law, or law impairing the obligation of contracts, or grant any title of nobility.

2. **[State imposts and duties]** No State shall, without the consent of the Congress, lay any imposts or duties on imports or exports, except what may be absolutely necessary for executing its inspection laws: and the net produce of all duties and imposts, laid by any State on imports or exports, shall be for the use of the Treasury of the United States; and all such laws shall be subject to the revision and control of the Congress.

3. **[Further restrictions on powers of States]** No State shall, without the consent of Congress, lay any duty of tonnage, keep troops, or ships of war in time of peace, enter into any agreement or compact with another state, or with a foreign power, or engage in war, unless actually invaded, or in such imminent danger as will not admit of delay.

Article II

Section 1

1. **[The President; the executive power]** The executive power shall be vested in a President of the United States of America. He shall hold his office during the term of four years, and together with the Vice President, chosen for the same term, be elected, as follows:

2. **[Appointment and qualifications of presidential electors]** Each State shall appoint, in such manner as the Legislature thereof may direct, a number of electors, equal to the whole number of Senators and Representatives to which the State may be entitled in the Congress: but no Senator or Representative, or person holding an office of trust or profit under the United States, shall be appointed an elector.

3. **[Original method of electing the President and Vice President]** (The electors shall meet in their respective States, and vote by ballot for two persons, of whom one at least shall not be an inhabitant of the same State with themselves. And they shall make a list of all the persons voted for, and of the number of votes for each; which list they shall sign and certify, and transmit sealed to the seat of the Government of the United States, directed to the President of the Senate. The President of the Senate shall, in the presence of the Senate and House of Representatives, open all the certificates, and the votes shall then be counted. The person having the greatest number of votes shall be the President, if such number be a majority of the whole number of electors appointed; and if there be more than one who have such majority, and have an equal number of votes, then the House of Representatives shall immediately choose by ballot one of them for President; and if no person have a majority, then from the five highest on the list the said House shall in like manner choose the President. But in choosing the President, the votes shall be taken by States, the representation from each State having one vote; a quorum for this purpose shall consist of a member or members from two-thirds of the States, and a majority of all the states shall be necessary to a choice. In every case, after the choice of the President, the person having the greatest number of votes of the electors shall be

the Vice President. But if there should remain two or more who have equal votes, the Senate should· choose from them by ballot the Vice President.—*Replaced by the 12th Amendment.)*

4. **[Congress may determine time of choosing electors and day for casting their votes]** The Congress may determine the time of choosing the electors, and the day on which they shall give their votes; which day shall be the same throughout the United States.

5. **[Qualifications for the office of President]** No person except a natural born citizen, or a citizen of the United States, at the time of the adoption of this Constitution, shall be eligible to the office of President; neither shall any person be eligible to that office who shall not have attained to the age of thirty-five years, and been fourteen years a resident within the United States. *(For qualifications of the Vice President, see the 12th Amendment.)*

6. **[Filling vacancy in the office of President]** (In case of the removal of the President from office, or of his death, resignation, or inability to discharge the powers and duties of the said office, the same shall devolve on the Vice President, and the Congress may by law provide for the case of removal, death, resignation or inability, both of the President and Vice President, declaring what officer shall then act as President, and such officer shall act accordingly, until the disability be removed, or a President shall be elected.—*Amended by the 20th and 25th Amendments.)*

7. **[Compensation of the President]** The President shall, at stated times, receive for his services, a compensation, which shall neither be increased nor diminished during the period for which he shall have been elected, and he shall not receive within that period any other emolument from the United States, or any of them.

8. **[Oath to be taken by the President]** Before he enter on the execution of his office, he shall take the following oath or affirmation:—"I do solemnly swear (or affirm) that I will faithfully execute the office of President of the United States, and will to the best of my ability, preserve, protect, and defend the Constitution of the United States."

Section 2

1. **[The President to be Commander-in-Chief of army and navy and head of executive departments; may grant reprieves and pardons]** The President shall be Commander-in-Chief of the Army and Navy of the United States, and of the militia of the several States, when called into the actual service of the United States; he may require the opinion, in writing, of the principal officer in each of the executive departments, upon any subject relating to the duties of their respective offices, and he shall have power to grant reprieves and pardons for offenses against the United States, except in cases of impeachment.

2. **[President may, with concurrence of Senate, make treaties, appoint ambassadors, etc.; appointment of inferior officers, authority of Congress over]** He shall have power, by and with the advice and consent of the Senate, to make treaties, provided two-thirds of the Senators present concur; and he shall nominate, and by and with the advice and consent of the Senate, shall appoint ambassadors, other public ministers and consuls, judges of the Supreme Court, and all other officers of the United States, whose appointments are not herein otherwise provided for, and which shall be established by law: but the Congress may by law vest the appointment of such inferior officers, as they think proper, in the President alone, in the courts of law, or in the heads of departments.

3. **[President may fill vacancies in office during recess of Senate]** The President shall have power to fill up all vacancies that may happen during the recess of the Senate, by granting commissions which shall expire at the end of their session.

Section 3

[President to give advice to Congress; may convene or adjourn it on certain occasions; to receive ambassadors, etc.; have laws executed and commission all officers] He shall from time to time give to the Congress information of the state of the Union, and recommend to their consideration such measures as he shall judge necessary and expedient; he may, on extraordinary occasions, convene both Houses, or either of them, and in case of disagreement between them, with respect to the time of adjournment, he may adjourn them to such time as he shall think proper; he shall receive ambassadors and other public ministers: he shall take care that the laws be faithfully executed, and shall commission all the officers of the United States.

Section 4

[All civil officers removable by impeachment] The President, Vice President, and all civil officers of the United States shall be removed from office on impeachment for, and conviction of, treason, bribery, or other high crimes and misdemeanors.

Article III

Section 1

[Judicial powers; how vested; term of office and compensation of judges] The judicial power of the United States, shall be vested in one Supreme Court, and in such inferior courts as the Congress may from time to time ordain and establish. The judges, both of the supreme and inferior courts, shall hold their offices during good behavior, and shall, at stated times, receive for their services, a compensation, which shall not be diminished during their continuance in office.

Section 2

1. **[Jurisdiction of Federal courts]** (The judicial power shall extend to all cases, in law and equity, arising under this Constitution, the laws of the United States, and treaties made, or which shall be made, under their authority; to all cases affecting ambassadors, other public ministers and consuls; to all cases of admiralty and maritime jurisdiction; to controversies to which the United States, shall be a party; to controversies between two or more States; between a State and citizens of another State; between citizens of different States, between citizens of the same State claiming lands under grants of different states, and between a State, or the citizens thereof, and foreign states, citizens, or subjects.—*Amended by the 11th Amendment.)*

2. **[Original and appellate jurisdiction of Supreme Court]** In all cases affecting ambassadors, other public ministers and consuls, and those in which a State shall be party, the Supreme Court shall have original jurisdiction. In all the other cases before mentioned, the Supreme Court shall have appellate jurisdiction, both as to law and fact, with such exceptions, and under such regulations, as the Congress shall make.

3. **[Trial of all crimes, except impeachment, to be by jury]** The trial of all crimes, except in cases of impeachment, shall be by jury; and such trial shall be held in the State where the said crimes shall have been committed; but when not committed within any State, the trial shall be at such place or places as the Congress may by law have directed.

Section 3

1. **[Treason defined; conviction of]** Treason against the United States, shall consist only in levying war against them, or, in adhering to their enemies, giving them aid and comfort. No person shall be convicted of treason unless on the testimony of two witnesses to the same overt act, or on confession in open court.

2. **[Congress to declare punishment for treason; proviso]** The Congress shall have power to declare the punishment of treason, but no attainder of treason shall work corruption of blood, or forfeiture except during the life of the person attainted.

Article IV

Section 1

[Each State to give full faith and credit to the public acts and records of other States] Full faith and credit shall be given in each State to the public acts, records, and judicial proceedings of every other State. And the Congress may by general laws prescribe the manner in which such acts, records, and proceedings shall be proved, and the effect thereof.

Section 2

1. **[Privileges of citizens]** The citizens of each State shall be entitled to all privileges and immunities of citizens in the several States.

2. **[Extradition between the several States]** A person charged in any State with treason, felony, or other crime, who shall flee from justice, and be found in another State, shall on demand of the Executive authority of the State from which he fled, be delivered up, to be removed to the State having jurisdiction of the crime.

3. **[Persons held to labor or service in one State, fleeing to another, to be returned]** (No person held to service or labor in one State, under the laws thereof, escaping into another, shall, in consequence of any law or regulation therein, be discharged from such service or labor, but shall be delivered up on claim of the party to whom such service or labor may be due.—*Eliminated by the 13th Amendment.*)

Section 3

1. **[New States]** New States may be admitted by the Congress into this Union; but no new State shall be formed or erected within the jurisdiction of any other State; nor any State be formed by the junction of two or more States, or parts of States, without the consent of the Legislatures of the States concerned as well as of the Congress.

2. **[Regulations concerning territory]** The Congress shall have power to dispose of and make all needful rules and regulations respecting the territory or other property belonging to the United States; and nothing in this Constitution shall be so construed as to prejudice any claims of the United States, or of any particular State.

Section 4

[Republican form of government and protection guaranteed the several States] The United States shall guarantee to every State in this Union a Republican form of government, and shall protect each of them against invasion; and on application of the Legislature, or of the Executive (when the Legislature cannot be convened) against domestic violence.

Article V

[Ways in which the Constitution can be amended] The Congress, whenever two-thirds of both Houses shall deem it necessary, shall propose amendments to this Constitution, or, on the application of the Legislatures of two-thirds of the several States shall call a convention for proposing amendments, which, in either case, shall be valid to all intents and purposes, as part of this Constitution, when ratified by the Legislatures of three-fourths of the several States, or by conventions in three-fourths thereof, as the one or the other mode of ratification may be proposed by the Congress; provided that no amendment which may be made prior to the year one thousand eight hundred and eight shall in any manner affect the first and fourth clauses in the ninth Section of the first Article; and that no State, without its consent, shall be deprived of its equal suffrage in the Senate.

Article VI

1. **[Debts contracted under the confederation secured]** All debts contracted and engagements entered into, before the adoption of this Constitution, shall be as valid against the United States under this Constitution, as under the Confederation.

2. **[Constitution, laws, and treaties of the United States to be supreme]** This Constitution, and the laws of the United States which shall be made in pursuance thereof; and all treaties made, or which shall be made, under the authority of the United States, shall be the supreme law of the land; and the judges in every State shall be bound thereby, anything in the Constitution or laws of any State to the contrary notwithstanding.

3. **[Who shall take constitutional oath; no religious test as to official qualification]** The Senators and Representatives before mentioned, and the members of the several State Legislatures, and all executive and judicial officers, both of the United States and of the several States, shall be bound by oath or affirmation, to support this Constitution; but no religious test shall ever be required as a qualification to any office or public trust under the United States.

Article VII

[Constitution to be considered adopted when ratified by nine States] The ratification of the conventions of nine States shall be sufficient for the establishment of this Constitution between the States so ratifying the same.

Amendments to the Constitution of the United States

Note: Amendments I to X, popularly known as the Bill of Rights, were proposed and sent to the states by the first session of the First Congress. They were ratified Dec. 15, 1791.

Amendment 1

[Freedom of religion, speech, of the press, and right of petition] Congress shall make no law respecting an establishment of religion, or prohibiting the free exercise thereof; or abridging the freedom of speech, or of the press; or the right of the people peaceably to assemble, and to petition the Government for a redress of grievances.

Amendment 2

[Right of people to bear arms not to be infringed] A well-regulated militia, being necessary to the security of a free State, the right of the people to keep and bear arms, shall not be infringed.

Amendment 3

[Quartering of troops] No soldier shall, in time of peace be quartered in any house, without the consent of the owner, nor in time of war, but in a manner to be prescribed by law.

Amendment 4

[Persons and houses to be secure from unreasonable searches and seizures] The right of the people to be secure in their persons, houses, papers, and effects, against unreasonable searches and seizures, shall not be violated, and no warrants shall issue, but upon probable cause, supported by oath or affirmation, and particularly describing the place to be searched, and the persons or things to be seized.

Amendment 5

[Trials for crimes; just compensation for private property taken for public use] No person shall be held to answer for a capital, or otherwise infamous crime, unless on a presentment or indictment of a Grand Jury, except in cases arising in the land or naval forces, or in the militia, when in actual service in time of war or public danger; nor shall any person be subject for the same offense to be twice put in jeopardy of life or limb; nor shall be compelled in any criminal case to be a witness, against himself, nor be deprived of life, liberty, or property, without due process of law; nor shall private property be taken for public use, without just compensation.

Amendment 6

[Right to speedy trial, witnesses, counsel] In all criminal prosecutions, the accused shall enjoy the right to a speedy and public trial, by an impartial jury of the State and district wherein the crime shall have been committed, which district shall have been previously ascertained by law, and to be informed of the nature and cause of the accusation; to be confronted with the witnesses against him; to have compulsory process for obtaining witnesses in his favor, and to have the assistance of counsel for his defense.

Amendment 7

[Right of trial by jury] In suits at common law, where the value in controversy shall exceed twenty dollars, the right of trial by jury shall be preserved, and no fact tried by a jury, shall be otherwise re-examined in any court of the United States, than according to the rules of the common law.

Amendment 8

[Excessive bail, fines, and punishments prohibited] Excessive bail shall not be required, nor excessive fines imposed, nor cruel and unusual punishments inflicted.

Amendment 9

[Reserved rights of people] The enumeration in the Constitution, of certain rights, shall not be construed to deny or disparage others retained by the people.

Amendment 10

[Rights of States under Constitution] The powers not delegated to the United States by the Constitution, nor prohibited by it to the States, are reserved to the States, respectively, or to the people.

Amendment 11

(The proposed amendment was sent to the states March 5, 1794, by the Third Congress. It was ratified Feb. 7, 1795. It changes Article III, Sect. 2, Para. 1.)

[Judicial power of United States not to extend to suits against a State] The judicial power of the United States shall not be construed to extend to any suit in law or equity, commenced or prosecuted against one of the United States by citizens of another State, or by citizens or subjects of any foreign state.

Amendment 12

(The proposed amendment was sent to the states Dec. 12, 1803, by the Eighth Congress. It was ratified July 27, 1804. It replaces Article II, Sect. 1, Para. 3.)

[Manner of electing President and Vice President by electors] (The electors shall meet in their respective states, and vote by ballot for President and Vice President, one of whom, at least, shall not be an inhabitant of the same state with themselves; they shall name in their ballots the person voted for as President, and in distinct ballots the person voted for as Vice President, and they shall make distinct lists of all persons voted for as President, and of all persons voted for as Vice President, and of the number of votes for each, which lists they shall sign and certify, and transmit sealed to the seat of the government of the United States, directed to the President of the Senate; the President of the Senate shall, in the presence of the Senate and House of Representatives, open all the certificates and the votes shall then be counted; the person having the greatest number of votes for President, shall be the President, if such number be a majority of the whole number of electors appointed; and if no person have such majority, then from the persons having the highest numbers not exceeding three on the list of those voted for as President, the House of Representatives shall choose immediately, by ballot, the President. But in choosing the President, the votes shall be taken by states, the representation from each State having one vote; a quorum for this purpose shall consist of a member or members from two-thirds of the states, and a majority of all the states shall be necessary to a choice. And if the House of Representatives shall not choose a President whenever the right of choice shall devolve upon them, before the fourth day of March next following, then the Vice President shall act as President, as in the case of the death or other constitutional disability of the President. The person having the greatest number of votes as Vice President, shall be the Vice President, if such number be a majority of the whole number of electors appointed, and if no person have a majority, then from the two highest numbers on the list, the Senate shall choose the Vice President; a quorum for the purpose shall consist of two-thirds of the whole number of Senators, and a majority of the whole number shall be necessary to a choice. But no person constitutionally ineligible to the office of President shall be eligible to that of Vice President of the United States.—*Amended by the 20th Amendment, sections 3 and 4.)*

Amendment 13

(The proposed amendment was sent to the states Feb. 1, 1865, by the Thirty-eighth Congress. It was ratified Dec. 6, 1865. It eliminates Article IV, Sect. 2, Para. 3.)

Section 1

[Slavery prohibited] Neither slavery nor involuntary servitude, except as a punishment for crime whereof the party shall have been duly convicted, shall exist within the United States, or any place subject to their jurisdiction.

Section 2

[Congress given power to enforce this article] Congress shall have power to enforce this article by appropriate legislation.

Amendment 14

(The proposed amendment was sent to the states June 16, 1866, by the Thirty-ninth Congress. It was ratified July 9, 1868. It changes Article 1, Sec. 2, Para. 3.)

Section 1

[Citizenship defined; privileges of citizens] All persons born or naturalized in the United States, and subject to the jurisdiction thereof, are citizens of the United States and of the State wherein they reside. No State shall make or enforce any law which shall abridge the privileges or immunities of citizens of the United States; nor shall any State deprive any person of life, liberty, or property, without due process of law; nor deny to any person within its jurisdiction the equal protection of the laws.

Section 2

[Apportionment of Representatives] Representatives shall be apportioned among the several States according to their respective numbers, counting the whole number of persons in each State, excluding Indians not taxed. But when the right to vote at any election for the choice of electors for President and Vice President of the United States, Representatives in Congress, the executive and judicial officers of a State, or the members of the Legislature thereof, is denied to any of the male inhabitants of such State, being twenty-one years of age, and citizens of the United States, or in any way abridged, except for participation in rebellion, or other crime, the basis of representation therein shall be reduced in the proportion which the number of such male citizens shall bear to the whole number of male citizens twenty-one years of age in such State.

Section 3

[Disqualification for office; removal of disability] No person shall be a Senator or Representative in Congress, or elector of President and Vice President, or hold any office, civil or military, under the United States, or under any State, who, having previously taken an oath, as a member of Congress, or as an officer of the United States, or as a member of any State Legislature, or as an executive or judicial officer of any State, to support the Constitution of the United States, shall have engaged in insurrection or rebellion against the same, or given aid or comfort to the enemies thereof. But Congress may by a vote of two-thirds of each House, remove such disability.

Section 4

[Public debt not to be questioned; payment of debts and claims incurred in aid of rebellion forbidden] The validity of the public debt of the United States, authorized by law, including debts incurred for payment of pensions and bounties for services in suppressing insurrection or rebellion, shall not be questioned. But neither the United States nor any State shall assume or pay any debt or obligation incurred in aid of insurrection or rebellion against the United States, or any claim for the loss or emancipation of any slave; but all such debts, obligations, and claims shall be held illegal and void.

Section 5

[Congress given power to enforce this article] The Congress shall have power to enforce, by appropriate legislation, the provisions of this article.

Amendment 15

(The proposed amendment was sent to the states Feb. 27, 1869, by the Fortieth Congress. It was ratified Feb. 3, 1870.)

Section 1

[Right of certain citizens to vote established] The right of citizens of the United States to vote shall not be denied or abridged by the United States or by any State on account of race, color, or previous condition of servitude.

Section 2

[Congress given power to enforce this article] The Congress shall have power to enforce this article by appropriate legislation.

Amendment 16

(The proposed amendment was sent to the states July 12, 1909, by the Sixty-first Congress. It was ratified Feb. 3, 1913.)

[Income taxes authorized] The Congress shall have power to lay and collect taxes on incomes, from whatever source derived,without apportionment among the several States, and without regard to any census or enumeration.

Amendment 17

(The proposed amendment was sent to the states May 16, 1912, by the Sixty-second Congress. It was ratified April 8, 1913. It changes Article 1, Sect. 3, Para. 1 and 2.)

[Election of United States Senators; filling of vacancies; qualifications of electors] The Senate of the United States shall be composed of two Senators from each State, elected by the people thereof, for six years; and each Senator shall have one vote. The electors in each State shall have the qualifications requisite for electors of the most numerous branch of the State Legislatures.

When vacancies happen in the representation of any State in the Senate, the executive authority of such State shall issue writs of election to fill such vacancies: Provided, that the legislature of any State may empower the executive thereof to make temporary appointment until the people fill the vacancies by election as the legislature may direct.

This amendment shall not be so construed as to affect the election or term of any Senator chosen before it becomes valid as part of the Constitution.

Amendment 18

(The proposed amendment was sent to the states Dec. 18, 1917, by the Sixty-fifth Congress. It was ratified by three-quarters of the states by Jan. 16, 1919, and became effective Jan. 16, 1920. It was

repeated by the 21st Amendment.)

Section 1
[Manufacture, sale, or transportation of intoxicating liquors, for beverage purposes, prohibited] After one year from the ratification of this article the manufacture, sale, or transportation of intoxicating liquors within, the importation thereof into, or the exportation thereof from the United States and all territory subject to the jurisdiction thereof for beverage purposes is hereby prohibited.

Section 2
[Congress and the several States given concurrent power to pass appropriate legislation to enforce this article] The Congress and the several States shall have concurrent power to enforce this article by appropriate legislation.

Section 3
[Provisions of article to become operative, when adopted by three-fourths of the States] This article shall be inoperative unless it shall have been ratified as an amendment to the Constitution by the legislatures of the several States, as provided in the Constitution, within seven years from the date of the submission hereof to the States by Congress.

Amendment 19
(The proposed amendment was sent to the states June 4, 1919, by the Sixty-sixth Congress. It was ratified Aug. 18, 1920.)

[The right of citizens to vote shall not be denied because of sex] The right of citizens of the United States to vote shall not be denied or abridged by the United States or by any State on account of sex.

[Congress given power to enforce this article] Congress shall have power to enforce this article by appropriate legislation.

Amendment 20
(The proposed amendment, sometimes called the "Lame Duck Amendment," was sent to the states March 3, 1932, by the Seventy-second Congress. It was ratified Jan. 23, 1933; but, in accordance with Section 5, Sections 1 and 2 did not go into effect until Oct. 15, 1933. It changes Article 1, Sect. 4, Para. 2 and the 12th Amendment.)

Section 1
[Terms of President, Vice President, Senators, and Representatives] The terms of the President and Vice President shall end at noon on the twentieth day of January, and the terms of Senators and Representatives at noon on the third day of January, of the years in which such terms would have ended if this article had not been ratified; and the terms of their successors shall then begin.

Section 2
[Time of assembling Congress] The Congress shall assemble at least once in every year, and such meeting shall begin at noon on the third day of January, unless they shall by law appoint a different day.

Section 3
[Filling vacancy in office of President] If, at the time fixed for the beginning of the term of the President, the President-elect shall have died, the Vice President-elect shall become President. If a President shall not have been chosen before the time fixed for the beginning of his term, or if the President-elect shall have failed to qualify, then the Vice President shall have qualified; and the Congress may by law provide for the case wherein neither a President-elect nor a Vice President-elect shall have qualified, declaring who shall then act as President, or the manner in which one who is to act shall be selected,

and such person shall act accordingly until a President or Vice President shall have qualified.

Section 4
[Power of Congress in Presidential succession] The Congress may by law provide for the case of the death of any of the persons from whom the House of Representatives may choose a President whenever the right of choice shall have devolved upon them, and for the case of the death of any of the persons from whom the Senate may choose a Vice President whenever the right of choice shall have devolved upon them.

Section 5
[Time of taking effect] Sections 1 and 2 shall take effect on the 15th day of October following the ratification of this article.

Section 6
[Ratification] This article shall be inoperative unless it shall have been ratified as an amendment to the Constitution by the legislatures of three-fourths of the several States within seven years from the date of its submission.

Amendment 21
(The proposed amendment was sent to the states Feb. 20, 1933, by the Seventy-second Congress. It was ratified Dec. 5, 1933. It repeals the 18th Amendment.)

Section 1
[Repeal of Prohibition Amendment] The eighteenth article of amendment to the Constitution of the United States is hereby repealed.

Section 2
[Transportation of intoxicating liquors] The transportation or importation into any State, territory, or possession of the United States for delivery or use therein of intoxicating liquors, in violation of the laws thereof, is hereby prohibited.

Section 3
[Ratification] This article shall be inoperative unless it shall have been ratified as an amendment to the Constitution by convention in the several States, as provided in the Constitution, within seven years from the date of the submission thereof to the States by the Congress.

Amendment 22
(The proposed amendment was sent to the states March 21, 1947, by the Eightieth Congress. It was ratified Feb. 27, 1951.)

Section 1
[Limit to number of terms a President may serve] No person shall be elected to the office of the President more than twice, and no person who has held the office of President, or acted as President for more than two years of a term to which some other person was elected President shall be elected to the office of the President more than once. But this article shall not apply to any person holding the office of President when this article was proposed by the Congress, and shall not prevent any person who may be holding the office of President, or acting as President, during the term within which this article becomes operative from holding the office of President or acting as President during the remainder of such term.

Section 2
[Ratification] This article shall be inoperative unless it shall have been ratified as an amendment to the Constitution by the legislatures of three-fourths of the several States within seven years from the date of its submission to the States by the Congress.

Amendment 23

(The proposed amendment was sent to the states June 16, 1960, by the Eighty-sixth Congress. It was ratified March 29, 1961.)

Section 1

[Electors for the District of Columbia] The District constituting the seat of Government of the United States shall appoint in such manner as the Congress may direct:

A number of electors of President and Vice President equal to the whole number of Senators and Representatives in Congress to which the District would be entitled if it were a State, but in no event more than the least populous State; they shall be in addition to those appointed by the States, but they shall be considered, for the purposes of the election of President and Vice President, to be electors appointed by a State; and they shall meet in the District and perform such duties as provided by the twelfth article of amendment.

Section 2

[Congress given power to enforce this article] The Congress shall have the power to enforce this article by appropriate legislation.

Amendment 24

(The proposed amendment was sent to the states Aug. 27, 1962, by the Eighty-seventh Congress. It was ratified Jan. 23, 1964.)

Section 1

[Payment of poll tax or other taxes barred in federal elections] The right of citizens of the United States to vote in any primáry or other election for President or Vice President, for electors for President or Vice President, or for Senator or Representative in Congress, shall not be denied or abridged by the United States or any State by reasons of failure to pay any poll tax or other tax.

Section 2

[Congress given power to enforce this article] The Congress shall have the power to enforce this article by appropriate legislation.

Amendment 25

(The proposed amendment was sent to the states July 6, 1965, by the Eighty-ninth Congress. It was ratified Feb. 10, 1967.)

Section 1

[Succession of Vice President to Presidency] In case of the removal of the President from office or of his death or resignation, the Vice President shall become President.

Section 2

[Vacancy in office of Vice President] Whenever there is a vacancy in the office of the Vice President, the President shall nominate a Vice President who shall take office upon confirmation by a majority vote of both Houses of Congress.

Section 3

[Vice President as Acting President] Whenever the President transmits to the President pro tempore of the Senate and the Speaker of the House of Representatives his written declaration that he is unable to discharge the powers and duties of his office, and until he transmits to them a written declaration to the contrary, such powers and duties shall be discharged by the Vice President as Acting President.

Section 4

[Vice President as Acting President] Whenever the Vice President and a majority of either the principal officers of the executive departments or of such other body as Congress may by law provide, transmit to the President pro tempore of the Senate and the Speaker of the House of Representatives their written declaration that the President is unable to discharge the powers and duties of his office, the Vice President shall immediately assume the powers and duties of the office as Acting President.

Thereafter, when the President transmits to the President pro tempore of the Senate and the Speaker of the House of Representatives his written declaration that no inability exists, he shall resume the powers and duties of his office unless the Vice President and a majority of either the principal officers of the executive department or of such other body as Congress may by law provide, transmit within four days to the President pro tempore of the Senate and the Speaker of the House of Representatives their written declaration that the President is unable to discharge the powers and duties of his office. Thereupon Congress shall decide the issue, assembling within forty-eight hours for that purpose if not in session. If the Congress, within twenty-one days after receipt of the latter written declaration, or, if Congress is not in session, within twenty-one days after Congress is required to assemble, determines by two-thirds vote of both Houses that the President is unable to discharge the powers and duties of his office, the Vice President shall continue to discharge the same as Acting President; otherwise, the President shall resume the powers and duties of his office.

Amendment 26

(The proposed amendment was sent to the states March 23, 1971, by the Ninety-second Congress. It was ratified July 1, 1971.)

Section 1

[Voting for 18-year-olds] The right of citizens of the United States, who are 18 years of age or older, to vote shall not be denied or abridged by the United States or by any state on account of age.

Section 2

[Congress given power to enforce this article] The Congress shall have power to enforce this article by appropriate legislation.

How a Bill Becomes a Law

When a Senator or a Representative introduces a bill, he sends it to the clerk of his house, who gives it a number and title. This is the *first reading,* and the bill is referred to the proper committee.

The committee may decide the bill is unwise or unnecessary and *table* it, thus killing it at once. Or it may decide the bill is worthwhile and hold hearings to listen to facts and opinions presented by experts and other interested persons. After members of the committee have debated the bill and perhaps offered amendments, a vote is taken; and if the vote is favorable, the bill is sent back to the floor of the house.

The clerk reads the bill sentence by sentence to the house; this is known as the *second reading.* Members may then debate the bill and offer amendments. In the House of Representatives, the time for debate is limited by a *cloture rule,* but there is no such restriction in the Senate for cloture. Instead, 60 votes are required to limit debate. This makes possible a *filibuster,* in which one or more opponents hold the floor in an attempt to defeat the bill.

The *third reading* is by title only, and the bill is put to a vote, which may be by voice or roll call, depending on the circumstances and parliamentary rules. Members who must be absent at the time but who wish to record their vote may be paired if each negative vote has a balancing affirmative one.

The bill then goes to the other house of Congress, where it may be defeated or passed with or without amendments. If the bill is defeated, it dies. If it is passed with amendments, a joint Congressional committee must be appointed by both houses to iron out the differences.

After its final passage by both houses, the bill is sent to the President. If he approves, he signs it, and the bill becomes a law. However, if he disapproves, he *vetoes* the bill by refusing to sign it. He then sends the bill back to the house of origin with his reasons for the veto. The objections are read and debated, and a roll-call vote is taken. If the bill receives less than a two-thirds vote, it is defeated and goes no farther. But if it receives a two-thirds vote or greater, it is sent to the other house for a vote. If that house also passes it by a two-thirds vote, the President's veto is *overridden,* and the bill becomes a law.

Should the President desire neither to sign nor to veto the bill, he may retain it for ten days, Sundays excepted, after which time it automatically becomes a law without signature. However, if Congress has adjourned within those ten days, the bill is automatically killed, that process of indirect rejection being known as a *pocket veto.*

Emancipation Proclamation

696

January 1, 1863

By the President of the United
States of America:

A Proclamation

Whereas on the 22d day of September, A.D. 1862, a proclamation was issued by the President of the United States, containing, among other things, the following, to wit:

"That on the 1st day of January, A.D. 1863, all persons held as slaves within any State or designated part of a State the people whereof shall then be in rebellion against the Union States shall be then, thenceforward, and forever free; and the executive government of the United States, including the military and naval authority thereof, will recognize and maintain the freedom of such persons and will do no act or acts to repress such persons, or any of them, in any efforts they may make for their actual freedom.

"That the executive will on the 1st day of January aforesaid, by proclamation, designate the States and parts of States, if any, in which the people thereof, respectively, shall then be in rebellion against the United States; and the fact that any State or the people thereof shall on that day be in good faith represented in the Congress of the United States by members chosen thereto at elections wherein a majority of the qualified voters of such States shall have participated shall, in the absence of strong countervailing testimony, be deemed conclusive evidence that such State and the people thereof are not then in rebellion against the United States."

Now therefore, I, Abraham Lincoln, President of the United States, by virtue of the power in me vested as Commander-in-Chief of the Army and Navy of the United States in time of actual armed rebellion against the authority and government of the United States, and as a fit and necessary war measure for suppressing said rebellion, do, on this 1st day of January, A.D. 1863, and in accordance with my pur-

pose so to do, publicly proclaimed for the full period of one hundred days from the first day above mentioned, order and designate as the States and parts of States wherein the people thereof, respectively, are this day in rebellion against the United States the following, to wit:

Arkansas, Texas, Louisiana (except the parishes of St. Bernard, Plaquemines, Jefferson, St. John, St. Charles, St. James, Ascension, Assumption, Terrebonne, Lafourche, St. Mary, St. Martin, and Orleans, including the city of New Orleans), Mississippi, Alabama, Florida, Georgia, South Carolina, North Carolina, and Virginia (except the forty-eight counties designated as West Virginia, and also the counties of Berkeley, Accomac, Northhampton, Elizabeth City, York, Princess Anne, and Norfolk, including the cities of Norfolk and Portsmouth), and which excepted parts are for the present left precisely as if this proclamation were not issued.

And by virtue of the power and for the purpose aforesaid, I do order and declare that all persons held as slaves within said designated States and parts of States are, and henceforward shall be, free; and that the Executive Government of the United States, including the military and naval authorities thereof, will recognize and maintain the freedom of said persons.

And I hereby enjoin upon the people so declared to be free to abstain from all violence, unless in necessary self-defense; and I recommend to them that, in all cases when allowed, they labor faithfully for reasonable wages.

And I further declare and make known that such persons of suitable condition will be received into the armed service of the United States to garrison forts, positions, stations, and other places, and to man vessels of all sorts in said service.

And upon this act, sincerely believed to be an act of justice, warranted by the Constitution upon military necessity, I invoke the considerate judgment of mankind and the gracious favor of Almighty God.

U.S. Presidents

(* Did not finish term)

#	President	Term	Vice President	#
1	George Washington	April 30, 1789 - March 3, 1797	John Adams	1
2	John Adams	March 4, 1797 - March 3, 1801	Thomas Jefferson	2
3	Thomas Jefferson	March 4, 1801 - March 3, 1805	Aaron Burr	3
	Thomas Jefferson	March 4, 1805 - March 3, 1809	George Clinton	4
4	James Madison	March 4, 1809 - March 3, 1813	George Clinton	
	James Madison	March 4, 1813 - March 3, 1817	Elbridge Gerry	5
5	James Monroe	March 4, 1817 - March 3, 1825	Daniel D. Tompkins	6
6	John Quincy Adams	March 4, 1825 - March 3, 1829	John C. Calhoun	7
7	Andrew Jackson	March 4, 1829 - March 3, 1833	John C. Calhoun	
	Andrew Jackson	March 4, 1833 - March 3, 1837	Martin Van Buren	8
8	Martin Van Buren	March 4, 1837 - March 3, 1841	Richard M. Johnson	9
9	William Henry Harrison*	March 4, 1841 - April 4, 1841	John Tyler	10
10	John Tyler	April 6, 1841 - March 3, 1845		
11	James K. Polk	March 4, 1845 - March 3, 1849	George M. Dallas	11
12	Zachary Taylor*	March 5, 1849 - July 9, 1850	Millard Fillmore	12
13	Millard Fillmore	July 10, 1850 - March 3, 1853		
14	Franklin Pierce	March 4, 1853 - March 3, 1857	William R. King	13
15	James Buchanan	March 4, 1857 - March 3, 1861	John C. Breckinridge	14
16	Abraham Lincoln	March 4, 1861 - March 3, 1865	Hannibal Hamlin	15
	Abraham Lincoln*	March 4, 1865 - April 15, 1865	Andrew Johnson	16
17	Andrew Johnson	April 15, 1865 - March 3, 1869		
18	Ulysses S. Grant	March 4, 1869 - March 3, 1873	Schuyler Colfax	17
	Ulysses S. Grant	March 4, 1873 - March 3, 1877	Henry Wilson	18
19	Rutherford B. Hayes	March 4, 1877 - March 3, 1881	William A. Wheeler	19
20	James A. Garfield*	March 4, 1881 - Sept. 19, 1881	Chester A. Arthur	20
21	Chester A. Arthur	Sept. 20, 1881 - March 3, 1885		
22	Grover Cleveland	March 4, 1885 - March 3, 1889	Thomas A. Hendricks	21
23	Benjamin Harrison	March 4, 1889 - March 3, 1893	Levi P. Morton	22
24	Grover Cleveland	March 4, 1893 - March 3, 1897	Adlai E. Stevenson	23
25	William McKinley	March 4, 1897 - March 3, 1901	Garret A. Hobart	24
	William McKinley*	March 4, 1901 - Sept. 14, 1901	Theodore Roosevelt	25
26	Theodore Roosevelt	Sept. 14, 1901 - March 3, 1905		
	Theodore Roosevelt	March 4, 1905 - March 3, 1909	Charles W. Fairbanks	26
27	William H. Taft	March 4, 1909 - March 3, 1913	James S. Sherman	27
28	Woodrow Wilson	March 4, 1913 - March 3, 1921	Thomas R. Marshall	28
29	Warren G. Harding*	March 4, 1921 - Aug. 2, 1923	Calvin Coolidge	29
30	Calvin Coolidge	Aug. 3, 1923 - March 3, 1925		
	Calvin Coolidge	March 4, 1925 - March 3, 1929	Charles G. Dawes	30
31	Herbert C. Hoover	March 4, 1929 - March 3, 1933	Charles Curtis	31
32	Franklin D. Roosevelt	March 4, 1933 - Jan. 20, 1941	John N. Garner	32
	Franklin D. Roosevelt	Jan. 20, 1941 - Jan. 20, 1945	Henry A. Wallace	33
	Franklin D. Roosevelt	Jan. 20, 1945 - April 12, 1945	Harry S. Truman	34
33	Harry S. Truman	April 12, 1945 - Jan. 20, 1949		
	Harry S. Truman	Jan. 20, 1949 - Jan. 20, 1953	Alben W. Barkley	35
34	Dwight D. Eisenhower	Jan. 20, 1953 - Jan. 20, 1961	Richard M. Nixon	36
35	John F. Kennedy*	Jan. 20, 1961 - Nov. 22, 1963	Lyndon B. Johnson	37
36	Lyndon B. Johnson	Nov. 22, 1963 - Jan. 20, 1965		
	Lyndon B. Johnson	Jan. 20, 1965 - Jan. 20, 1969	Hubert H. Humphrey	38
37	Richard M. Nixon	Jan. 20, 1969 - Jan. 20, 1973	Sprio T. Agnew	39
	Richard M. Nixon*	Jan. 20, 1973 - Aug. 9, 1974	Gerald R. Ford	40
38	Gerald R. Ford	Aug. 9, 1974 - Jan. 20, 1977	Nelson A. Rockefeller	41
39	James E. Carter	Jan. 20, 1977 - Jan. 20, 1981	Walter Mondale	42
40	Ronald Reagan	Jan. 20, 1981 - Jan. 20, 1985	George Bush	43
	Ronald Reagan	Jan. 20, 1985 -	George Bush	

Order of Presidential Succession

1. The Vice President
2. Speaker of the House
3. President pro tempore of the Senate
4. Secretary of State
5. Secretary of the Treasury
6. Secretary of Defense
7. Attorney General
8. Secretary of the Interior
9. Secretary of Agriculture
10. Secretary of Commerce
11. Secretary of Labor
12. **Secretary of Health, Education, & Welfare**
13. Secretary of Housing and Urban Development
14. Secretary of Transportation

Emergency First Aid

If a person is injured in a serious accident, do the following:

A) Restore breathing.
B) Stop severe bleeding.
C) Give first aid for poisons.
D) Keep the person lying down and comfortable.
E) Check all injuries.
F) Plan your action.
G) Complete the first aid procedures described below:

1) Sprains:
   a) Keep the sprained part of the body quiet.
   b) Treat the injury as a dislocation or fracture.
   c) Place a cold application on the area for the first half hour.
   d) Administer treatment for shock.
   e) Instruct the person to see a doctor for x-rays.

2) Fainting
   a) If an individual feels he will faint, instruct him to lower his head between his knees.
   b) If he does faint, lay him down and raise his feet. He should stay in this position until recovery is complete.
   c) Administer treatment for shock.

3) Exhaustion from Heat
   Symptoms of severe cases: much perspiration; extreme weakness; pale, clammy skin; normal temperature; possible vomiting. (Seldom is the person unconscious.)
   a) Have the victim rest in bed.
   b) Have him drink the following solution at least four times at 15-minute intervals: ½ teaspoonful of salt mixed in a glass of water.
   c) For severe cases, get help from a doctor.

4) Stroke from Heat
   Symptoms of severe cases: hot dry skin, high temperature.
   a) Get medical help immediately.
   b) If you have time before help arrives, attempt to cool the victim's body by sponging it with alcohol or water.

5) Shock
   a) Lay the person flat.
   b) Maintain his body heat by placing a covering beneath him and on top of him. (It is better if he is slightly cool than warm.)
   c) Get medical help immediately.
   d) Stay by him and watch him.

6) Dislocation or Fractures
   a) The ends of the broken bone and adjacent joints must be kept quiet.
   b) If the individual is wounded, apply a sterile dressing and control the bleeding by carefully administering direct pressure.
   c) Administer first aid for shock.
   d) Call a doctor.

7) Poisoning
   a) Read the instructions on the container and do what they say.
   b) Then dilute the poison by having the victim drink several glasses of milk or water.
   c) Induce vomiting unless the poison was 1) acid, 2) alkali, or 3) a petroleum product. Note the following instructions:
   Acid poisoning — Neutralize with baking soda, milk or magnesia. Do not give enough to cause vomiting.
   Alkali poisoning — Neutralize with vinegar or lemon juice. Do not give enough to cause vomiting.
   Petroleum product poisoning — If mineral oil is available, have the person consume 4 ounces. If mineral oil is not available, substitute milk or water: one glass for a child; two glasses for an adult.
   d) Have the person drink milk, egg white or olive oil to coat the stomach.
   e) Administer shock treatment.
   f) Get help from the police, fire department, rescue squad, hospital, or doctor.

8) Burns
   a) Examine the skin. If the skin becomes red or if blisters appear, place the burned area in cool water or wrap it in a cool wet pack.
   b) If tissues below the surface tissue are also destroyed, apply a dry sterile dressing and get medical help immediately.
   c) Administer treatment for shock.

9) Wounds
   a) The first objective must be to control the bleeding. If the bleeding is severe, apply direct pressure on the wound. If the bleeding does not stop, apply pressure to the supplying blood vessel, i.e., pressure point. Get medical help quickly.
   b) Minor injuries must be cleaned carefully and completely. Soap and water can be used for this purpose.
   c) A dry sterile dressing should be applied. The dressing must be bandaged firmly so it will not move.
   d) If you notice any infection in the wound, get help from a doctor immediately.
   e) Administer treatment for shock.

10) Foreign Particle

--If a foreign particle is in the throat or air passage:

a) Allow the person to try to cough it up. Don't distract him.

b) Do not use your finger or any other object to probe in the throat or air passage.

c) If the victim is a child, turn him upside-down and smack him on the back.

--If a foreign particle is in the food passage:

a) Take the person to a doctor.

b) Although you may not be able to detect it, the foreign particle may be lodged in the passage.

c) Do not give the victim bulky foods or cathartics.

--If a foreign particle is in the eye:

a) Be careful not to rub the eye.

b) Attempt to cause the foreign particle to adhere to the inside of the eyelid.

c) Carefully roll back the eyelid and remove the particle with the corner of a tissue or handkerchief.

d) If the particle is imbedded, close the eye, bandage it shut, and get medical help.

11) Heart Attack

The following symptoms will indicate a heart attack: chest pain, chronic cough, bluish color of the fingernails and lips, swelling of the ankles, and breathing difficulty.

a) Have the person lie in a flat position or in any position which he finds comfortable.

b) Raise the victim's head and chest if he has difficulty breathing.

c) Administer mouth-to-mouth respiration if he has stopped breathing. (See the following section for details.)

d) Get medical help immediately.

e) If the person is conscious, help him take medicine which a doctor has previously advised him to take.

f) Administer treatment for shock.

Mouth-To-Mouth Artificial Respiration

A) Lay the person on his back.

B) Check his mouth for foreign matter. If you find something, remove it.

C) Place one hand under the person's neck and lift the neck. Place the other hand on his forehead and tilt the head back until the chin is pointed upward. (Please notice picture #1.)

D) You are now ready to blow air into the lungs. However, to prevent air from escaping through the nose, pinch the nose shut. Use your thumb and index finger on the hand which is placed on the victim's forehead. (Please notice picture #2.)

E) Remember: a) the head must be tilted back b) the neck must be tilted c) the chin must point upward and d) the nostrils must be pinched shut.

Then make a complete seal by placing your mouth over the person's mouth. Exhale into his mouth. (Please notice picture #3.) Remove your mouth and listen for him to exhale.

If it is necessary, turn the victim's head to the side and allow secretions to flow out. Then immediately begin mouth-to-mouth once again.

Do step E 5-12 times each minute for an adult.

Do step E 20 times each minute for a child.

Do not stop mouth-to-mouth respiration until the victim begins to breathe by himself, or until a doctor declares him dead.

(Prepared in consultation with the Racine, Wisconsin chapter of the American Red Cross)

Periodic Table of the Elements

Key:

Atomic Number	2
Symbol	He
Atomic Weight (or Mass Number of most stable isotope if in parentheses)	Helium 4.0026

1a	2a	3b	4b	5b	6b	7b	8	8	8	1b	2b	3a	4a	5a	6a	7a	0
1 H Hydrogen 1.00797																	2 He Helium 4.0026
3 Li Lithium 6.939	4 Be Beryllium 9.0122											5 B Boron 10.811	6 C Carbon 12.01115	7 N Nitrogen 14.0067	8 O Oxygen 15.9994	9 F Fluorine 18.9984	10 Ne Neon 20.183
11 Na Sodium 22.9898	12 Mg Magnesium 24.312											13 Al Aluminum 26.9815	14 Si Silicon 28.086	15 P Phosphorus 30.9738	16 S Sulfur 32.064	17 Cl Chlorine 35.453	18 Ar Argon 39.948
19 K Potassium 39.102	20 Ca Calcium 40.08	21 Sc Scandium 44.956	22 Ti Titanium 47.90	23 V Vanadium 50.942	24 Cr Chromium 51.996	25 Mn Manganese 54.9380	26 Fe Iron 55.847	27 Co Cobalt 58.9332	28 Ni Nickel 58.71	29 Cu Copper 63.546	30 Zn Zinc 65.37	31 Ga Gallium 69.72	32 Ge Germanium 72.59	33 As Arsenic 74.9216	34 Se Selenium 78.96	35 Br Bromine 79.909	36 Kr Krypton 83.80
37 Rb Rubidium 85.47	38 Sr Strontium 87.62	39 Y Yttrium 88.905	40 Zr Zirconium 91.22	41 Nb Niobium 92.906	42 Mo Molybdenum 95.94	43 Tc Technetium (97)	44 Ru Ruthenium 101.07	45 Rh Rhodium 102.905	46 Pd Palladium 106.4	47 Ag Silver 107.868	48 Cd Cadmium 112.40	49 In Indium 114.82	50 Sn Tin 118.69	51 Sb Antimony 121.75	52 Te Tellurium 127.60	53 I Iodine 126.9044	54 Xe Xenon 131.30
55 Cs Cesium 132.905	56 Ba Barium 137.34	57-71* Lanthanides	72 Hf Hafnium 178.49	73 Ta Tantalum 180.948	74 W Tungsten 183.85	75 Re Rhenium 186.2	76 Os Osmium 190.2	77 Ir Iridium 192.2	78 Pt Platinum 195.09	79 Au Gold 196.967	80 Hg Mercury 200.59	81 Tl Thallium 204.37	82 Pb Lead 207.19	83 Bi Bismuth 208.980	84 Po Polonium 210.05	85 At Astatine (210)	86 Rn Radon 222.00
87 Fr Francium (223)	88 Ra Radium 226.00	89-103** Actinides (227)	104 Unq Unnilquadium (261)	105 Unp†† Unnilpentium (262)	106 Unh Unnilhexium (263)	107 Uns Unnilseptium (262)			109 Une Unnilennium (266)								

*Lanthanides

57 La Lanthanum 138.91	58 Ce Cerium 140.12	59 Pr Praseodymium 140.907	60 Nd Neodymium 144.24	61 Pm Promethium (145)	62 Sm Samarium 150.35	63 Eu Europium 151.96	64 Gd Gadolinium 157.25	65 Tb Terbium 158.924	66 Dy Dysprosium 162.50	67 Ho Holmium 164.930	68 Er Erbium 167.28	69 Tm Thulium 168.934	70 Yb Ytterbium 173.04	71 Lu Lutetium 174.97

**Actinides

89 Ac Actinium (227)	90 Th Thorium 232.038	91 Pa Protactinium 231.10	92 U Uranium 238.03	93 Np Neptunium 237.00	94 Pu Plutonium 239.05	95 Am Americium 243.13	96 Cm Curium (247)	97 Bk Berkelium (248)	98 Cf Californium (251)	99 Es Einsteinium (254)	100 Fm Fermium (257)	101 Md Mendelevium (258)	102 No Nobelium (259)	103 Lw Lawrencium (260)

† Other proposed names are kurchatovium (USSR) and hahnium (U.S.)
†† Other proposed names are nielsbohrium (USSR) and rutherfordium (U.S.)

Computer Terms

Address: A number used to identify the location of a piece of information in a computer's memory.

Algorithm: The plan of attack showing each sequential step used in the solution of a problem.

ALU: *(Arithmetic Logic Unit)* This is the device in the computer which performs all mathematical and some logical functions.

Analog: The term used to describe information going into or coming out of a computer system which is not in digital form. A device operating on continuous signals rather than the 1's and 0's of a digital or binary machine.

Array: A group of related variables called by the same name, but different from each other by being subscripted.

ASCII: *(American Standard Code for Information Interchange)* The universally accepted standard code for representing numbers, letters, and other characters in such a way that computers and computer devices can exchange information between themselves. Each character is represented by a unique combination of seven bits (ones and zeros).

Assembly language: A low-level language which allows computers to be programmed in machine language using symbolic rather than binary instructions.

Back-up: A copy of data or programs used as protection against the original copy being lost, stolen, or destroyed.

BASIC: *(Beginners All-purpose Symbolic Instruction Code)* A computer language specifically designed for ease of learning and use. It is commonly used with smaller computers.

Batch: A noninteracting operating system which processes programs individually and one at a time.

Baud: The rate at which information can be transmitted from one computer or device to another as measured in bits of information transmitted per second.

Binary: The number system commonly used by computers because the values 0 and 1 can easily be represented electronically in the computer.

Bit: *(BInary digiT)* The smallest piece of information understood by a computer consisting of either a 0 or a 1.

Boot: To start up a computer system by loading a program into the memory.

Buffer: An area outside the main memory used to temporarily store data and instructions. (Printers, for example, have buffers to temporarily store the data which is being printed.)

Bug: An error found in a computer program.

Byte: A string of eight bits commonly acting or being acted upon as a single piece of information.

Character: A letter, digit, or other written symbol used in displaying information.

Chip: A small piece of silicon containing thousands of electrical elements. Also referred to as an integrated circuit.

COBOL: *(COmmon Business Oriented Language)* A language used for data processing and business applications.

Command: An instruction to a computer to perform a specified task.

Compiler: A program which translates an instruction written in a high-level language into machine language so that the instruction can be understood by the computer.

Computer: An electronic device for performing programmed computations quickly and accurately. A computer is made up of five basic blocks: memory, control, the arithmetic logic unit (ALU), input, and output.

Computer program: A list of statements, commands, and instructions written in an appropriate computer language which, when executed, will perform a desired task or function.

Control character: A character that is entered by holding down the control key while depressing another key. The control character "controls" or modifies information which is printed or displayed.

CPU: *(Central Processing Unit)* The hardware portion of a computer which executes instructions in a manner such that the memory, ALU, I/O, and the CPU itself function properly. The "brain" of the computer which controls all other devices.

CRT: *(Cathode Ray Tube)* An electronic vacuum tube, such as that found in a TV, which is used to display information.

Cursor: A symbol on a computer screen which points out where the next character typed from the keyboard will appear.

Daisy wheel printer: A printing device which prints by striking a wheel containing raised letters, numbers, and characters. The impact forces an impression against an inked ribbon and onto a piece of paper.

Data: Information used or produced by a computer program.

Data base: A collection of information which is organized in such a way that a computer can process it efficiently.

Debug: The act of removing errors from a computer program.

Device: A hardware component of a computer system designed to perform a certain task. A CRT, printer, or disk drive are examples of computer devices.

Digit: A character used to express numbers in a number system. For instance, 0 and 1 are digits in base 2; 0 to 7 are digits in base 8; 0 to 9 are digits in base 10; and 0 to 9, A, B, C, D, E, and F are digits in base 16.

Digital: A class of computers which process information which is in binary form. It is also used to describe information which is in binary form.

Digital logic: A set of well-defined rules which govern the operation of a central processing unit. *And, Not,* and *Or* are the three basic logical functions which are used in a CPU.

Dimension: A statement in a program which tells a computer how large an array is and to set aside the proper amount of memory for that array.

Disk: A magnetic storage device used to record computer information. Each disk appears flat and square on the outside; inside, the disk is circular and rotates so that information can be stored on its many circular tracks.

Disk drive: The device that writes and reads information on the surface of a disk.

Documentation: A practice used by all good programmers in which comments are inserted into a computer program so that someone else can look at the program and understand what a program is supposed to do and how it does it.

DOS: *(Disk Operating System)* A software system that allows a computer to communicate with and control one or more disk drives.

Dot matrix printer: An output device (printer) which represents characters by selecting and printing the appropriate dots to duplicate the characters desired, much like a scoreboard uses many individual lights to form numbers and letters.

Dump: To copy the entire contents of a disk, main memory, or a storage device onto another storage device.

Edit: To change an original document or program by adding, deleting, or replacing parts of it, thus creating a new document or program.

Error: A programming mistake which will cause the program to run incorrectly or not run at all.

Error message: A message, displayed or printed, which signifies an error or problem within a program.

Execute: To run a computer program; to sequentially carry out the instructions in a computer program.

File: A collection of information stored on a computer device accessible under a given file name.

Firmware: Software stored permanently in ROM. This software can never be modified or erased.

Floppy disk: A storage device made of a thin, magnetically coated plastic.

Flowchart: A diagram which shows schematically the sequential steps in a computer program.

Format: To prepare a blank disk for use by a particular DOS by dividing it into sectors and tracks (also *initialize*).

FORTRAN: *(FORmula TRANslator)* A computer language designed specifically for applications requiring extensive numerical calculations.

Friction drive: The drive unit on typewriters and some printers which feeds paper or forms through the carriage by turning the platen. Friction between the platen, paper, and rollers forces the paper to follow the platen while it is being rotated, thus advancing the paper or form.

Graphics: Information processed by a computer which is displayed as pictures or images rather than characters.

Hardcopy: A printed copy of a program, data, or results.

Hardware: The actual electronic and mechanical components of a computer system. A floppy disk is *hardware*, while a program stored on it is *software*.

Hexadecimal: The base 16 number system, which uses the digits 0 to 9, A, B, C, D, E, and F to represent 0 through 15 respectively, in base 10. Also used to represent the 16 possible values of a string of four consecutive bits.

High-level language: A programming language in which instructions closely resemble English-language statements. One instruction written in a high-level language will consist of several machine-language instructions. BASIC, FORTRAN, PASCAL, and COBOL are examples of commonly used high-level languages.

IC: *(Integrated Circuit)* A computer chip made most commonly of silicon and consisting of a large number of electrical elements.

Input: Information taken from a disk drive, keyboard, or other device and transported into a computer.

Instruction: A machine-language command corresponding to an action to be taken by the CPU *(central processing unit)* of a computer.

Interactive: A computer system in which the operator and computer frequently exchange information.

Interface: The hardware, software, and firmware which is used to link one computer or computer device to another.

Interpreter: A program written in one language which translates instructions from another language and executes the translation.

I/O: *(Input/Output)* The passage of information in either direction between a computer and an external device.

K: Two to the 10th power or 1024. A term used when describing the capacity of a computer memory or storage device. For example, 16K equals 16x1024 or 16,384 memory addresses.

Keyboard: An input device used to enter information into a computer by striking keys which are laid out and labeled much like those on a standard typewriter.

Keystroke: The process of inputting a character into a computer by pressing one or more keys on the keyboard.

Letter-quality printer: A printer that produces type quality similar to that of an electric typewriter.

Library: A collection of programs which may be referred to often.

List: A display or printout of a computer program or file.

Load: To take information from an external storage device and *load* it into a computer's memory.

LOGO: A language which combines graphics and words to teach programming to children.

Loop: A series of instructions which is repeated, usually with different data or values on each pass.

Low-level language: Programming languages which will translate nearly directly into machine-language instructions. Low-level language programs written for one model or brand of computer generally cannot function properly on another model or brand of computer.

Machine language: The language used to directly instruct computer hardware. The computer uses this language to process data and instructions in binary form.

Mainframe computer: A large computer generally with many operators using it at one time.

Main memory: The memory that is built into a computer and can be directly accessed by the processor.

Megabyte: A term used in describing the memory capacity of a storage device equal to one million bytes.

Memory: The part of the computer which stores information and program instructions until they are needed. Types of memory include RAM, ROM, and PROM.

Memory location: A place in the main memory which contains a single item of information and which can be accessed by specifying the address of the memory location.

Menu: A detailed list of choices presented in a program from which a user can select.

Microcomputer: A small, inexpensive computer using a microprocessor as its processing unit.

Microprocessor: A computer processor contained on a single chip.

Minicomputer: A computer larger than a microcomputer whose CPU cannot be contained on a single chip; generally used in small business, scientific, and engineering applications.

Modem: *(MOdulator DEModulator)* A device which allows computers to communicate over telephone lines.

Monitor: A video screen on which information from a computer can be displayed. By viewing the displayed information, the user can supervise the operation of a program.

Network: A system of interconnected

computers, each individually controlled, and the hardware and software used to connect them.

Octal: The base 8 number system which uses the digits 0 to 7. Also used to represent the eight possible values of a string of three consecutive bits.

Operating system: A software system that coordinates and governs the operation of a computer and computer programs.

Output: Information transported from a computer to a disk drive, monitor, printer, or any other external device.

Parallel interface: An interface in which information is transmitted by sending many bits at the same time over multiple lines, one bit per transmission line.

PASCAL: A high-level language designed to teach the principles of structured programming. (Named after Blaise Pascal, a 17th century mathematician.)

Peripheral device: An external device such as a plotter, disk drive, or printer added to a computer system to increase the capabilities of the system.

PILOT: *(Programmed Inquiry, Learning, Or Teaching)* A high-level language used for computer aided instruction.

Pixel: *(PIcture ELement)* The smallest dot of light on a graphics screen that can be individually turned on and off in order to form graphics.

Plotter: A peripheral device used to output information which is in the form of a graph, chart, or other configuration which cannot be handled by a printer.

Printed circuit board: A flat, rigid board commonly made of fiberglass. It is used to hold and electronically connect computer chips and other electrical elements.

Printer: A peripheral device (similar to a typewriter) used to produce printed copies of computer data or programs.

Printout: A copy of computer output produced on paper by a printer.

Processor: The portion of computer hardware that executes machine-language instructions and controls all other components of the computer.

Program: A step-by-step list of instructions written in an appropriate computer language which a computer will follow in order to accomplish a specified task.

Programmer: A person involved in the writing, editing, and production of a computer program.

Programming language: A set of guidelines and rules for writing a program which will perform a predetermined task on a computer.

PROM: *(Programmable Read Only Memory)* A hardware device which can store data and programs for an indefinite length of time. The contents of PROM are loaded after the memory is manufactured, so that unlike ROM, the contents of two identical PROM devices manufactured at the same time can be totally different. The contents of PROM can be changed by a complicated process, but generally is left in the original form after being loaded into the device.

Prompt: A question asked by an interactive computer program which asks the user to input information to be processed or to tell the computer which part of a program to branch to.

RAM: *(Random Access Memory)* A portion of the computer hardware which stores software. The contents of RAM can easily be accessed, read, or changed. (See ROM.)

Register: A memory location not found in main memory which is used to store data or instructions for a short time.

Resolution: Describes the quality of a video image displayed on a computer monitor or graphics screen.

RF modulator: *(Radio Frequency modulator)* A device used to convert video signals from a computer into a form which a television set can process to display information.

ROM: *(Read Only Memory)* A portion of hardware which stores firmware. The contents of ROM can easily be accessed or read, but can never be changed or altered.

RPG: *(Report Program Generator)* A high-level language used to produce reports, memos, and letters. RPG is a word-processing language.

Save: To take a program or file from main memory and store it on a peripheral device (disk, cassette, etc.) for later use.

Sector: A fraction of the recording surface on a disk; a sector is a fraction of a *track*.

Serial interface: An interface in which information is transmitted one bit at a time over a single transmission line.

Software: Programs which instruct a computer how to perform a desired task.

Spreadsheet: A program used to organize numbers and figures into a worksheet format.

Statement: An instruction in a program which when executed will perform a desired operation.

Storage: Describes the main memory or external devices where information or programs can be stored.

String: A group of consecutive letters, numbers, and characters which are not used for computational purposes.

Subroutine: A group of statements which can be accessed and executed from several places in a main program.

System: The collection of hardware, software, and firmware that when combined form a functioning computer which interacts with external devices to perform specified tasks.

Telecommunications: Sending and receiving information from one computer to another over long distances via phone lines, satellites, or other forms of communication equipment.

Terminal: A peripheral device which contains a keyboard for transmitting information to a computer and a monitor to receive output from a computer.

Text: Information in the form of characters which can be read by an individual.

Thermal printer: A printer that forms characters by selectively applying heat to heat-sensitive paper.

Time sharing: An operating system which controls many terminals simultaneously and independently by allowing the computer to carry on a dialog with one terminal for a specified amount of time and switching to the next terminal in succession after the designated time elapses.

Track: A fraction of the recording surface on a disk. (A track can be compared to the space used by each song on an album.) The number of tracks on a disk varies with each disk-operating system.

Tractor drive: A drive unit on a printer which uses rotating spiked wheels to feed paper or forms through the carriage. The paper or forms must have holes on the far left and right edges which fit over the spikes on the wheel such that the paper or forms advance through the carriage when the wheel turns.

Transducer: A device which converts a measured quantity into a voltage which can be used as an analog input.

User: A person *using* a computer system.

Variable: A place in the computer's memory which can be assigned a value or have that value read, changed, or deleted from memory by the programmer.

Word: A string of bits treated as a single unit by a computer.

Word processor: A program designed to assist a user in creating letters, memos, and other kinds of text.

Write-enable notch: The small, rectangular cutout in the edge of a disk's jacket used to protect the contents of a disk. If the notch is not present, or is covered by a write-protect tab, information cannot be written on the disk.

Write-protect: To apply a write-protect tab to a disk, making it impossible for new information to be written on the disk. The information on the disk is now protected from being over-written.

Write-protect tab: A sticker used to cover the write-enable notch on a disk.

Command Statements

DATA: Allows data to be stored in a computer program. This data can be retrieved during the running of the program by the READ statement.

DIM: The *dimension* statement gives the size of an array so the computer can set aside adequate memory.

END: The last statement in a program which stops the program and returns control of the computer to the user.

FOR: Allows the programmer to set up a loop which is to be repeated a specified number of times.

GOSUB: Causes the program to temporarily branch to a subroutine. When a RETURN statement is made in the subroutine, the program returns to the line following the GOSUB statement.

GOTO: Causes the computer to go to a particular line in the program.

IF: A conditional statement which tells the computer to go directly to the next line in the program if the argument following the IF statement is false or to go to a given line number if the argument is true.

INPUT: Allows the user to input information from the keyboard for use in a program.

LET: An optional instruction which can be used when a variable in a program is assigned a value. (*Example:* Let A=25.)

LIST: Displays or prints a copy of the program presently in the computer.

NEXT: Used with the FOR statement. When a NEXT statement is used in a program, the computer branches back to the FOR statement until the loop has been repeated the specified number of times.

PRINT: Instructs the computer to type or display information from a program.

READ: Instructs the computer to read the information in a DATA statement; takes information from a DATA statement and assigns the information to the variable(s) immediately following the READ statement.

REM: Allows the programmer to insert remarks and comments into a program which are used to make the program easier to understand.

RETURN: This command will instruct the computer to go back to the main part of the program. When encountered in a subroutine, this statement will cause the computer to branch to the first statement after the GOSUB command which sent the computer to the subroutine.

RUN: Causes the computer to "run" the program in memory.

THEN: Used with the IF statement. When the argument between the IF and THEN is true, the statements following the THEN statement are executed.

Common Abbreviations

abr. abridge; abridgment

ac, AC alternating current

ack. acknowledge; acknowledgment

acv actual cash value

A.D. anno Domini (usually small capitals A.D.)

a.m. Also **A.M.** ante meridiem (usually small capitals A.M.)

ASAP as soon as possible

avg., av. average

BBB Better Business Bureau

B.C. 1. before Christ (usually small capitals B.C.) 2. British Columbia

bibliog. bibliographer; bibliography

biog. biographer; biographical; biography

C 1. Celsius 2. centigrade 3. coulomb

c. circa (about)

cc cubic centimeter

cc. chapters

CDT, C.D.T. Central Daylight Time

cm. centimeter

c.o. Also **c/o** care of

COD, C.O.D. 1. cash on delivery 2. collect on delivery

co-op. cooperative

CST, C.S.T. Central Standard Time

cu. Also **c** cubic

D.A. district attorney

d.b.a. doing business as

dc, DC direct current

dec. deceased

dept. department

disc. discount

DST, D.S.T. Daylight-Saving Time

dup. duplicate

ea. each

ed. edition; editor

EDT, E.D.T. Eastern Daylight Time

e.g. for example (Latin *exempli gratia*)

EST, E.S.T. Eastern Standard Time

etc. and so forth (Latin *et cetera*)

ex. example

F Fahrenheit

FM, fm frequency modulation

F.O.B., f.o.b. free on board

ft foot

g 1. gravity 2. gram

gal. gallon

gds. goods

gloss. glossary

GNP gross national product

hdqrs. headquarters

hgt. height

Hon. Honorable (title)

hp horsepower

Hz hertz

id. the same (Latin *idem*)

i.e. that is (Latin *id est*)

illus. illustration

inc. incorporated

IQ, I.Q. intelligence quotient

IRS Internal Revenue Service

ISBN International Standard Book Number

JP, J.P. justice of the peace

jr., Jr. junior

K 1. kelvin (temperature unit) 2. Kelvin (temperature scale)

kc kilocycle

kg kilogram

km kilometer

kn. knot

kt. karat

kw kilowatt

l liter

lat. latitude

lb pound (Latin *libra*)

l.c. lower-case

lit. literary; literature

log logarithm

long. longitude

ltd., Ltd. limited

m meter

M.A. Master of Arts (Latin *Magister Artium*)

man. manual

Mc megacycle

M.C., m.c. master of ceremonies

M.D. Doctor of Medicine (Latin *Medicinae Doctor*)

mdse. merchandise

mfg. manufacture; manufactured

mg milligram

mi. 1. mile 2. mill (monetary unit)

misc. miscellaneous

ml milliliter

mm millimeter

mpg, m.p.g. miles per gallon

mph, m.p.h. miles per hour

MS 1. manuscript 2. Mississippi (with ZIP code) 3. multiple sclerosis

Ms., Ms Title of courtesy for a woman

MST, M.S.T. Mountain Standard Time

neg. negative

n.s.f., N.S.F. not sufficient funds

O.D. Doctor of Optometry

oz, oz. ounce

PA 1. Pennsylvania (with ZIP code) 2. public-address system

pct. percent

pd. paid

Pfc, Pfc. private first class

pg. page (also **p.**)

p.m. Also **P.M.** post meridiem (usually small capitals P.M.)

P.O. 1. Personnel Officer 2. Also **p.o.** petty officer; post office 3. postal order

pop. population

POW, P.O.W. prisoner of war

pp. pages

ppd. 1. postpaid 2. prepaid

PR 1. Also **P.R.** public relations 2. Puerto Rico (with ZIP code)

psi, p.s.i. pounds per square inch

PST, P.S.T. Pacific Standard Time

PTA, P.T.A. Parent-Teachers Association

qt. quart

RD rural delivery

RF radio frequency

rpm, R.P.M. revolutions per minute

r.s.v.p., R.S.V.P. please reply

SOS 1. international distress signal 2. Any call or signal for help

Sr. 1. senior (after surname) 2. sister (religious)

SRO, S.R.O. standing room only

ST standard time

St. 1. saint 2. strait 3. street

std. standard

syn. synonymous; synonym

tbs., tbsp. tablespoon

TM trademark

uhf, UHF ultra high frequency

USSR Union of Soviet Socialist Republics

V 1. *Physics:* velocity 2. *Electricity:* volt 3. volume

VA 1. Also **V.A.** Veterans Administration 2. Virginia (with ZIP code)

vhf, VHF very high frequency

VIP *Informal* very important person

vol. 1. volume 2. volunteer

vs. versus

W 1. *Electricity:* watt 2. *Physics:* (Also **w**) work 3. West

whse., whs. warehouse

whsle. wholesale

wkly. weekly

w/o without

wt. weight

yd yard (measurement)

zool. zoological; zoology

INDEX